Need to learn an application fast?
Want to learn it on your own computer?

Now you can with e-Course!

e-Course is a revolutionary new series of software products that will get you up and running fast on just about any microcomputer application. The e-Course software sits right on top of the live application, directing you as you go. But e-Course is not just software. e-Course also includes a WorkText – filled with study plans, self tests, and more.

How can e-Course help you?

- **You're never left on your own.** Step boxes guide you in learning the application through step-by-step instruction, online practice, pop-up reminders, tips, animations, and more. Make a mistake? The Back-on-Track feature points you in the right direction.

- **It's more than software.** Each e-Course module comes with an accompanying WorkText that provides an overview of the application, a Study Plan, Tech Talk, 40-50 review questions with answers, and 25 projects per tutorial for additional practice and reinforcement.

- **You can check your progress.** Online Practice and CheckPoints within each tutorial help you assess how you're doing.

- **You can work at your own pace.** e-Course is extremely flexible, easy-to-use, and self-paced. Once you've installed the e-Course CD to your hard drive, you can use e-Course where you need it, when you need it.

Limited Time Offer! Order Now and Receive a 10% Discount!

To order, call: 1-800-347-7707 and press 4 or fill out and send in the card below.

Please cut along dotted line

Yes, I need to get up and running fast on the following Microsoft® and/or Netscape application(s):

Qty	Module	ISBN	Price
____	Access®7	(0-7600-5393-6)	$24.95
____	Access®97	(0-7600-5366-9)	$24.95
____	Excel®7	(0-7600-5391-X)	$24.95
____	Excel®97	(0-7600-5364-2)	$24.95
____	Internet Explorer	(0-7600-5374-X)	$19.95
____	Netscape Navigator™	(0-7600-5370-7)	$19.95
____	Office 95 Prof.®	(0-7600-5372-3)	$49.95
____	Office 97 Prof.®	(0-7600-5360-X)	$49.95
____	PowerPoint®7	(0-7600-5395-2)	$19.95
____	PowerPoint®97	(0-7600-5368-5)	$19.95
____	Windows®95	(0-7600-5358-8)	$19.95
____	Windows®NT	(0-7600-5401-0)	$19.95
____	Word 7	(0-7600-5389-8)	$24.95
____	Word 97	(0-7600-5362-6)	$24.95

_____ # of items ordered

_____ Subtotal

_____ 10% special discount

_____ Shipping/Handling(add $6.00 for first item, and $2.00 for each additional item)

_____ Applicable Sales Tax (for your state)

_____ Total Amount

fold and tape; please do not staple

Payment method

_____ Check   Amount enclosed: $_____

_____ Visa

_____ MasterCard

_____ American Express

Account #_____

Exp. Date_____

Signature_____

Shipping and Mailing Information (sorry, no P.O. Boxes)

Name _____

Address _____

_____

_____

City _____ State _____

Zip _____

E-mail address _____

Phone number _____

School _____

Course Name & Number _____

This limited time offer expires 5/31/98.

For more information visit our web site at:

www.course.com

e-Course™

T5-CVG-089

What do I need to run e-Course?

486 processor minimum, Pentium computer with 16 MB RAM recommended

Windows 95 or later

Runs over software, so application software is required (e.g. need Excel 7 to use e-Course Excel 7 module)

Sound card optional

CD-ROM needed for installation only

For more information visit our web site at

www.course.com

An Introduction to
INFORMATION SYSTEMS

An Introduction to
INFORMATION SYSTEMS

Ralph M. Stair
Florida State University

COURSE
TECHNOLOGY

ONE MAIN STREET, CAMBRIDGE, MA 02142

an International Thomson Publishing company I(T)P®

Cambridge • Albany • Bonn • Boston • Cincinnati • London • Madrid • Melbourne • Mexico City
New York • Paris • San Francisco • Singapore • Tokyo • Toronto • Washington

Managing Editor:	Kristen Duerr
Product Manager:	Jennifer Normandin
Project Management:	Elm Street Publishing Services, Inc.
Composition House:	GEX Publishing Services
Text and Cover Design:	Elm Street Publishing Services, Inc.
Marketing Manager:	Suzanne Walker
Editorial Assistant:	Lisa Ayers

© 1997 by Course Technology
A Division of International Thomson Publishing, Inc.

For more information contact:

Course Technology
One Main Street
Cambridge, MA 02142

International Thomson Publishing Europe
Berkshire House 168-173
High Holborn
London WCIV 7AA
England

Thomas Nelson Australia
102 Dodds Street
South Melbourne, 3205
Victoria, Australia

Nelson Canada
1120 Birchmount Road
Scarborough, Ontario
Canada M1K 5G4

International Thomson Editores
Campos Eliseos 383, Piso 7
Col. Polanco
11560 Mexico D.F. Mexico

International Thomson Publishing GmbH
Königswinterer Strasse 418
53227 Bonn
Germany

International Thomson Publishing Asia
211 Henderson Road
#05-10 Henderson Building
Singapore 0315

International Thomson Publishing Japan
Hirakawacho Kyowa Building, 3F
2-2-1 Hirakawacho
Chiyoda-ku, Tokyo 102
Japan

Trademarks
Course Technology and the open book logo are registered trademarks of Course Technology.
I⊤P® The ITP logo is a registered trademark of International Thomson Publishing.
Microsoft and Windows 95 are registered trademarks of Microsoft Corporation.
Some of the product names and company names used in this book have been used for identification purposes only and may be trademarks or registered trademarks of their manufacturers and sellers.

Disclaimer
Course Technology reserves the right to revise this publication and make changes from time to time in its content without notice.

ISBN: 0-7600-4158-X

Printed in the United States of America
10 9 8 7 6 5 4 3 2 1

To Lila and Leslie

Ralph Stair

PREFACE

An Introduction to Information Systems continues the tradition started with *Principles of Information Systems.* This new book is a shorter version of the successful *Principles of Information Systems* text. It embraces the fundamental principles of information systems (IS) and is intended for the first introductory IS concepts course. As such, it presumes little or no previous knowledge or experience of business organizations or information systems.

This book stands proudly at the beginning of the IS curriculum and offers basic information systems ideas, concepts, and principles that every student should know. In the past, instructors of the introductory course faced a dilemma. On one hand, a wide knowledge of, or experience in, businesses and nonprofit organizations allows students to grasp the complexities underlying important IS concepts. For this reason, many delayed presenting these concepts until students completed a large portion of the core course requirements. Yet, delaying the presentation of these concepts until students have matured within the curriculum often forces the one or two required introductory IS courses to focus only on personal computer application software tools and, at best, merely to introduce computer concepts. With the pervasive influence of computers in business and personal life, this old approach forces an unnatural barrier between the disciplines. Segregating business principles from IS principles can rob students of important real-life experience and problem-solving skills. This text treats the appropriate computer and information systems concepts together with a strong business emphasis.

APPROACH OF THE TEXT

This text continues the approach established with *Principles of Information Systems*, offering a number of benefits to students. Exposing students to the fundamental IS concepts provides a service to those students who do not later return to the discipline for advanced courses in these topics. Furthermore, presenting IS concepts at the introductory level may create interest among students who will later choose IS as a field of concentration. This text:

- utilizes a problem-solving framework throughout and expands the scope of IS problem identification to include all activities
- includes appropriate coverage of computer concepts, stressing characteristics of information systems relevant to all students, whether they will use them for personal or business purposes
- presents the fundamental tenets, rules, guidelines — the principles — of IS about which every student must be knowledgeable
- emphasizes the promise of integrated information systems in providing vastly superior organizational efficiencies
- positions telecommunications technologies as enablers of change
- offers a broad survey of the IS discipline and shows the value of the discipline as an attractive field of specialization
- stresses a single, all-encompassing concept: the right information, if it is delivered to the right person, in the right fashion, and at the right time, can improve and ensure organizational effectiveness and efficiency

THE GOALS OF THIS TEXT

This book has three main goals:

1. To present a core of fundamental principles with which every student should be familiar.
2. To offer a survey of the IS discipline that will enable all students to understand the relationship of advanced courses to the curriculum as a whole.
3. To show the value of the discipline as an attractive field of specialization.

A Core of Fundamental Principles

The introduction of new information systems technology has often outpaced academic guidelines directing how information technology should best be employed. Because of these swift innovations, the driving force of the technology has captured the attention of most authors of introductory IS textbooks. Though the first course in information systems has historically concentrated on discussing the components of an information system (primarily the technological components), and perhaps to some degree how information systems are developed, it has often neglected the important aspects of why and how information systems should be used to meet organizational goals. As a result, graduates have been thrust into work environments in which information systems were critical to their success, but they were unprepared to interact with these systems. Even those with some understanding of IS technology have floundered; an understanding of the technology alone does not enable one to apply it successfully.

Information systems are critical to the success of every business. Books and courses dealing with important IS concepts have traditionally fallen late in the curriculum. Introductory texts have tended to focus on the descriptive (What have business managers been doing with IS?) rather than on the prescriptive (What should business managers do with IS to succeed?). This text offers the traditional coverage of computer concepts material but places it within a highly structured framework of overall IS functionality. These fundamental ideas are not buried within historical detail or technical jargon.

This introductory book, however, does not pretend to cover every aspect of the IS discipline. Some technical concepts introduced but never fully explained in other introductory texts are purposely avoided in this text. We believe that these concepts are best suited for advanced courses for students intending to become IS professionals. Instead, this text offers an essential core of computer concepts and IS principles for students to use as they face the career challenges ahead. We also feel that it is proper to include the more exciting aspects of the IS discipline relating to broad organizational impacts rather than putting off these topics until later in the curriculum. Including the real-life characteristics of IS in the introductory text will help to dispel the idea that IS is a specialized discipline, with IS professionals limited to their own specialty. Instead, the book paints a truer picture: one that shows the IS professional charged with maintaining the broadest enterprisewide outlook. This text serves both general students and those who will become IS professionals.

A Survey of the IS Discipline

The material in this book offers an overview of the entire IS discipline as well as solid preparation for further study in advanced IS courses. It serves as an introduction to database systems, systems development, decision support systems, and expert systems.

This book also introduces students to the expanding role of the IS professional. Once considered a dedicated specialist, the IS professional now is often called upon to be an internal consultant to all functional areas, knowledgeable about their needs and competent in bringing the power of IS to bear throughout the organization. The IS professional must exercise a broad perspective, encompassing the entire organization — and often going beyond it.

The scope of responsibilities of an IS professional today ranges not only throughout the organization but also throughout the entire interconnected network of suppliers, customers, competitors, and other entities, no matter where they may be located. This broad scope offers IS professionals a new challenge: how to help the organization survive in a highly interconnected, highly competitive, international environment. In accepting that challenge, the IS professional plays a pivotal role in shaping the business itself and ensuring its success. To survive, businesses must now strive for ultimate customer satisfaction and loyalty through ever-improving product and service quality. The IS professional assumes critical responsibility in determining the organization's approach to quality performance and, therefore, plays an important role in the ongoing survival of the organization. This new duality in the role of the IS employee — a professional called upon to exercise specialist's skills with a generalist's perspectives — is reflected throughout the book.

The Value of the Discipline as an Attractive Field for Further Study

It is important to show the value of the IS discipline as an attractive field of study for the average student. It is part of our ongoing responsibility to draw bright and interested students into the IS discipline. The information systems field is exciting, challenging, and rewarding. The IS major is no longer a technical recluse. Increasingly, we are seeing the brightest and most talented students attracted to the IS field. Throughout this text, the many exciting challenges and opportunities available to IS professionals are highlighted and emphasized. "Who's Who" boxes strengthen this theme by showing how IS professionals have helped organizations achieve their goals using information systems and technology. Students are shown that the IS discipline is not only rewarding but fun!

PEDAGOGICAL FEATURES AND THE COMPLETE PACKAGE

This book and its complete package offer many benefits to students and instructors, including front-of-chapter material, supplemental interest boxes, end-of-chapter material, and an array of supplements that accompany the text.

Front-of-Chapter Material

◆ **Chapter Outlines**. Each chapter starts with a chapter outline to show students and instructors the content of the chapter at a glance.
◆ **Opening Photo and Extended Caption**. An opening photo with an extended caption follows the chapter outline for each chapter. This caption describes a real company or situation. The material in the caption is related to the concepts discussed in the chapter, and the photo is revisited in the Discussion Questions at the end of the chapter.
◆ **Learning Objectives**. Carefully crafted learning objectives are included with every chapter. The learning objectives reflect what students should be able to accomplish after completing a chapter. They are also integrated with the chapter summaries. Each item in the chapter summary starts with a learning objective from the beginning of the chapter.

Supplemental Interest Boxes

Three different types of supplemental interest boxes are interspersed throughout the text. These boxes were designed to support the goals and themes of this text. Two of the boxes, "Business Bits" and "Eye on the Web," include discussion questions. Some questions tie the material to the text by asking students to relate chapter concepts to the topics in the supplemental boxes. Other questions challenge students to think "outside the box" to apply concepts to new situations in critical and creative ways.

Eye on the Web. These supplemental interest boxes show students how individuals and companies use the Internet and the World Wide Web. With the increased use of the Internet for commerce, these boxes are current and practical. Each box asks students to search the Web for answers to interesting questions. These boxes show students how they can benefit personally and professionally by using the Web.

Who's Who. These brief profiles of successful IS professionals can motivate students to consider IS as a major field of study. They show how IS professionals have made a meaningful contribution to the achievement of organizational goals. The subjects of these interviews were selected to provide balanced, realistic views of day-to-day life at all employee levels within the information systems field, from programmer to CIO.

Business Bits. By showing specific examples of how "real-world" organizations apply fundamental principles and benefit from them, students are able to see how information systems can make a difference. These boxes show students how businesses can increase efficiency, effectiveness, and competitiveness by their application. Some boxes also highlight cutting-edge products and technology or new developments in the IS field.

End-of-Chapter Material

To help students retain information systems principles and to expand their understanding of important IS concepts and relationships, IS basics, summaries, key terms, quizzes, questions, team activities, exercises, and cases have been incorporated at the end of every chapter. This end-of-chapter material will enhance student learning and improve student performance in the course.

- ◆ **IS Basics.** The end-of-chapter material begins with IS Basics, a brief review of important concepts and principles. Each review item is a one-sentence summary of a critical point made in the chapter.
- ◆ **Summary.** Every chapter includes a detailed summary. Each summary is tied to a learning objective to make sure students have mastered the material in the chapter.
- ◆ **Key Terms.** A listing of key terms with page numbers follows the summary for each chapter. Page numbers allow quick review of definitions.
- ◆ **Concept Quiz.** The concept quiz consists of true/false, multiple-choice, fill-in-the-blank, and short answer questions. Answers are conveniently placed at the end of the chapter, allowing students to test themselves and quickly check their answers.
- ◆ **Discussion Questions.** Very specifically linked to the text, these questions reinforce the key concepts and ideas within each chapter by asking students to apply what they have learned. These questions help instructors generate class discussion to move students beyond the concepts to explore the numerous aspects of information systems. The last discussion question revisits the opening photo scenario and relates chapter content to the scenario.
- ◆ **Team Activity.** These activities require students to work in small groups on a shared assignment. These problem-solving activities foster teamwork, communication, and mutual accountability. Students work to create a joint work product, such as a report, a database, or a group presentation. Some activities involve semistructured activities like visiting a local business, while others demand creative thinking, such as designing the "perfect PC" with a given set of system constraints and price parameters.
- ◆ **Applying IT.** These practical exercises ask students to apply what they have learned in the chapter to a realistic problem. The first activity places students in a situation and asks them to solve problems. The second activity requires students to do outside research — on the Internet, at the library, or in a real business.

◆ **Case**. Each chapter includes a comprehensive case of a real company using information systems to its benefit. Each case has several questions that ask students to go beyond what is presented in the case.

◆ **Answers to the Concept Quiz**. Each chapter concludes with answers to the Concept Quiz.

Supplements to Accompany This Text

There are many exciting supplements that will benefit students and help instructors deliver the best possible course. We are pleased to present these supplements to you for your use. Here are your options.

Instructor's Manual. Written by Mary Brabston of the University of Tennessee/ Chattanooga, the *Instructor's Manual* provides sample syllabi, learning objectives for each chapter, lecture outlines/lecture extensions, technical notes, review questions, extra case problems, and team/group problems.

Instructor's Manual in ASCII Format and in .pdf Format. The *Instructor's Manual* is available on the Instructor's Resource Kit CD-ROM in .pdf format and via the Internet. This feature gives you the flexibility to edit outlines and other materials specifically to match your individual course structure.

Course Test Manager 1.1 and Test Bank. *Course Test Manager* (CTM) is a cutting-edge Windows-based testing software program, developed exclusively for Course Technology, that helps instructors design and administer examinations and practice tests. This full-featured program allows students to randomly generate practice tests that provide immediate on-screen feedback and detailed study guides for questions incorrectly answered. Instructors can also use *Course Test Manager* to create printed and on-line tests. You can create, preview, and administer a test on any or all chapters of this textbook entirely over a local area network. *Course Test Manager* can automatically grade the tests students take at the computer and can generate statistical information on individual, as well as group, performance. The *Course Test Manager Test Bank* to accompany this text, prepared by Kevin Duffy of Florida State University, has been included on the Instructor's Resource Kit CD-ROM along with the engine. The *Test Bank* includes multiple-choice, true/false, short answer, and essay questions, many of which include graphics from the text.

Course Presenter. Prepared by Henry Zbyszynski of Northeastern University, this is a powerful presentation package developed using Microsoft PowerPoint. Presentations for each chapter have been enhanced with all of the text's graphics, sound, and video clips. This multimedia presentation tool will add a new dimension to your lectures.

OUR COMMITMENT

We are sincerely committed to serving the needs of our adopters and readers. Like the field of IS itself, the writing and publishing process is an evolutionary and participatory one. We encourage you to participate in our endeavor to bring you the freshest, most relevant information possible. We at Course Technology pride ourselves on listening to instructors and developing creative solutions to their problems and needs. We have listened to the comments of your colleagues and possibly yourself. Thank you for your time.

As always, we welcome your input and feedback. If you have any questions or comments regarding Ralph Stair's *An Introduction to Information Systems*, please contact us through your local ITP representative, via the Internet at mis@course.com or by mail. Address your comments, criticisms, suggestions, and ideas to:

Ralph M. Stair
c/o Course Technology
One Main Street
Cambridge, MA 02142

Acknowledgments

A book project of this size and complexity is always a team effort. I would like to thank every one of my fellow teammates at Course Technology for their dedication and hard work. Many thanks to my editor, Kristen Duerr. I would also like to thank Jennifer Normandin, product manager, and Samantha Smith, editorial assistant, for their help. Many thanks go to Abby Reip for her excellent photo research. For their hard work on the manuscript, I would like to acknowledge and thank the team at Elm Street Publishing Services. Karen Hill helped with all stages of this project. Barbara Campbell, Kelly Spiller, Melissa Morgan, and Abby Westapher ushered the book through production and attended to every detail. I would also like to thank DeVilla Williams for getting things started.

Many thanks to the sales force at Course Technology. You make this all possible. You helped to get important feedback from current and future adopters. As a Course Technology product user, I know how important you are. Viktor Frengut made teaching at Florida State University using Course Technology books a pleasure.

I would like to thank the Department of Information and Management Science, College of Business Administration at Florida State University for their support and encouragement. I would like to thank my family, Lila and Leslie, for their support.

I would also like to thank the reviewers of this book and *Principles of Information Systems*.

An Introduction to Information Systems:

John Anderson
*Virginia Polytechnic Institute
and State University*

Stanley J. Birkin
University of South Florida

Catherine J. Brotherton
Riverside Community College

Jan Carroll
Sam Houston State University

Gena C. Casas
*Florida Community College
at Jacksonville*

Mark Ciampa
Volunteer State Community College

Richard H. Davis
Cerritos College

Jan de Lassen
Brigham Young University

John Gessford
*California State University/
Long Beach*

Barbara A. Graham
University of North Dakota

John P. Grillo
Bentley College

Don Hammond
University of New Orleans

Jan Harris
Lewis & Clark College

Thomas M. Harris
Ball State University

Charlotte J. Hiatt
California State University/Fresno

Richard Kerns
East Carolina University

Rose M. Laird
Northern Virginia Community College

Joan B. Lumpkin
Wright State University

Gary Margot
Ashland University

Leah Pietron
University of Nebraska at Omaha

Kelly Rainer
Auburn University

Herbert F. Rebhun
University of Houston

Becky Reuber
University of Toronto

Chuck Riden
Arizona State University

Ali R. Salehnia
South Dakota State University

Vikram Sethi
Southwest Missouri State University

Anthony Wensley
University of Toronto

Ken Whitten
*Florida Community College
at Jacksonville*

Paula Worthington
Northern Virginia Community College

Principles of Information Systems, Second Edition:

Jan de Lassen
Brigham Young University

Kevin Gorman
*University of North Carolina
at Charlotte*

Jeff Hedrington
University of Wisconsin/Eau Claire

Ellen Monk
University of Delaware

Leah Pietron
University of Nebraska at Omaha

Michael E. Whitman
University of Nevada/Las Vegas

BRIEF CONTENTS

1   Introduction to Computer-based Information Systems 2

2   Hardware: Input, Processing, Output,
and Storage Devices 32

3   Software: Systems and Applications Packages 72

4   Telecommunications and Networks 106

5   Word Processing and Spreadsheet Applications 142

6   Database, Graphics, On-line Information,
and Other PC Applications 176

7   Business Information Systems 208

8   Security, Privacy, Environmental, and Ethical Issues 240

9   Issues and Trends: The Impact of Computers
at School, Home, and Work 276

Appendix A: Buying, Using, and
Upgrading a Personal Computer 304

Glossary 327

Notes 335

Index 337

Web Index 344

CONTENTS

1 Introduction to Computer-based
Information Systems 2

Essential Computer Concepts 4
    From Raw Data to Valuable Information 5
    Computers for Problem Solving 7

EYE ON THE WEB 8
Functions of an Information System 11
    Input 11
    Processing 12
    Output 12
    Feedback 12
    Manual versus Computerized Information Systems 13

BUSINESS BITS 14
    Maytag and IBM Team Up for Customer Service

Elements of a Computer-based Information System 15
    Evolution of Computer-based Information Systems 16
Computer-based Information Systems in Business 16
    Transaction Processing Systems 18
    Management Information Systems 18
    Decision Support Systems 19
    Expert Systems 20
Why Study Information Systems? 22
    Invaluable Benefits of Computers 22
    Benefits of Computing Literacy 24
    Benefits of Knowledge about Information Systems 24

WHO'S WHO 25
    Ellen Knapp / Coopers & Lybrand
    Resources for Literacy 25

CASE 29
    The City of Phoenix

2   Hardware: Input, Processing, Output, and Storage Devices 32

Computer Systems: Integrating the Power of Technology 34
Computer System Types 35
      Types of General-purpose Computer Systems 36

WHO'S WHO 37
      Michael Dell / Dell Computer

      Centralized, Distributed, and Decentralized Systems 39
Computer System Components 39
Processing Hardware 40
      The Form of Computer Data 40
      CPU Characteristics: Speed 41
      Additional Forms of Memory 43
      Multiprocessing 44
      System Unit: Housing for Processing and Memory Hardware 44
Secondary Storage Hardware 46
      Sequential and Direct Access 47
      Magnetic Tape Drives 47
      Magnetic Disks 48
      Optical Disks 52

BUSINESS BITS 53
      You Can Make Your Own CD

      Other Storage Alternatives 54
      Secondary Storage in the Information System 54
Input and Output Hardware: Gateways to a Computer System 55
      Speed and Functionality of Input and Output Hardware 55
      Input Hardware 56
      Output Hardware 60
Equipment Upgrades: Responding to Change 63
Hardware Buyer's Guide 64

EYE ON THE WEB 65
CASE 69
      IBM

3   Software: Systems and Applications Packages 72

Software Overview 74
Systems Software 75
      Operating Systems 75
      Current Operating Systems 79
      Initiating the Operating System: The Boot Process 82
      Utility Programs 83
Applications Software 84
      Proprietary Applications Software 85
      Off-the-Shelf Applications Software 86
      Support Provided by Applications Software 87
Programming Languages 89
      Generations of Programming Languages 90

WHO'S WHO 95
   Joe Liemandt / Trilogy Development Group

BUSINESS BITS 96
   Sun Microsystems' Java 1.0

   Classes of Programming Languages 97
   Language Translators 98
Software Buyer's Guide 99

EYE ON THE WEB 100
CASE 104
   TestDrive

4 Telecommunications and Networks 106

Overview of Communications Systems 108
Capabilities of Telecommunications Systems 109
   Types of Telecommunications Signals 110
   Transmission Capacity 112
Types of Communications Media 112
   Physical Cables 112
   Microwave and Satellite Transmissions 113

BUSINESS BITS 115
   Global Positioning Systems

   Other Transmission Options 117
Telecommunications Devices 118
   Modems 118
   Facsimile (Fax) Hardware 119
   Multiplexers 120
   Communications Processors 120
   Integrated Services Digital Network (ISDN) Technology 121
Communications Software and Protocols 122
   Functions of Communications Software 123
   Network Operating Systems 123
   Communications Protocols 124
Network Configurations and Classifications 125
   Local-area Networks 125
   Larger Networks 128
   The Internet 129

WHO'S WHO 131
   Jason and Matthew Olim: CDnow

   Intranets 132

EYE ON THE WEB 133

   Criteria for Successful Networking 133
Communications Buyer's Guide 135

CASE 140
   Reed Elsevier

5   Word Processing and Spreadsheet Applications 142

Word Processing Programs 145
    Basic Features of a Word Processor 145
    Supporting Features 150

BUSINESS BITS 153
    Lotus SmartSuite 96

    Integration with Other Applications 156
Suggestions for Using Word Processors 158

EYE ON THE WEB 159

Spreadsheet Programs 160
    Spreadsheet Basics 160

WHO'S WHO 161
    Dan Bricklin / VisiCalc

    Changing a Spreadsheet 164
    Supplemental Features 165
Dynamic Use of Spreadsheets 169

CASE 174
    Spreadsheets Come of Age

6   Database, Graphics, On-line Information, and Other PC Applications 176

Database Programs 178
    Basic Elements of a Database 179
    Manipulating a Relational Database 180
    Designing a Database Structure 183
    Building a Database 185
    Modifying an Existing Database Structure 186
    Reports, Documents, and Other Output 187
    Role of a Database in the Information System 189
    Integration with Other Applications 190
    Hints for Using a Database 191
Graphics Programs 192
    Paint and Draw Programs 193
    Presentation Graphics 194
    Hints for Using a Graphics Package 196

EYE ON THE WEB 197

On-line Information Services 197
    News and Features 198
    Business and Finance 198
    Travel 198
    Internet Shopping 199
Other Personal Computer Applications 199

Project Management 199

WHO'S WHO 200
Andrew D. Klein / Spring Street Brewing

Reference Software 201
Specialized Productivity Software 201

BUSINESS BITS 202
Cybershopping with Digital Cash

CASE 206
Corbis Corp.

7   **Business Information Systems 208**

Transaction Processing Systems 210
    Batch and On-line Transaction Processing 211
Management Information Systems 213
    Inputs to a Management Information System 214
    Outputs from a Management Information System 215
Decision Support Systems 217

BUSINESS BITS 218
The New DSS

    Components of a Decision Support System 219
    Support for Group Decisions 222
    Executive Decision Support 224
Artificial Intelligence 226
    Components of Artificial Intelligence 226

WHO'S WHO 229
    Katherine Hammer / Evolutionary Technologies International

EYE ON THE WEB 231

Systems Development 231
    Systems Development Life Cycle 232
    Computer-aided Software Engineering (CASE) 234
    Prototyping 235
    Object-oriented Systems Development 235

CASE 239
The SET Agreement

8   **Security, Privacy, Environmental, and Ethical Issues 240**

Computer Waste and Mistakes 242
    Computer Waste 242
    Computer Mistakes 243

Preventing Computer Waste and Mistakes 245
Computer Crime 247
    Computer Systems as Tools for Crime 249
    Computer Systems as Objects of Crime 249

EYE ON THE WEB 250

Preventing Computer-related Crime 255
Privacy 257
    Impact of Privacy Invasion 257
    Legal Protections for Privacy Rights 258

WHO'S WHO 259
    Chris Peterson / Times Direct Marketing

Business Policies about Privacy Rights 260
    Privacy and Fair Information Use: General Standards 263
Work Environment 264
    Work Force Composition 264
    Health Concerns 265
    Avoiding Health Problems 266
    Effects on the Natural Environment 267
Ethical Issues in Information Systems 267

BUSINESS BITS 268
    The Telecommunications Act

Four Ethical Issues in Information Systems 269
    Professional Associations and Ethical Codes of Conduct 271

CASE 275
    Raptor Systems

9   **Issues and Trends: The Impact of Computers at School, Home, and Work 276**

Issues and Trends at School and Home 279
    Computerized Schools: Computer-assisted Instruction 279
    Computerized Houses and Apartments 280

WHO'S WHO 281
    Douglas Lenat and Rodney Brooks

BUSINESS BITS 284
    Digital Video Disks

The Impact of Telecommunications 286
    Telecommunications at Home and School 286

EYE ON THE WEB 287

Telecommunications in Business 289
Business Trends and Information System Effects 293
Process Reengineering and Continuous Improvement 294
Emphasis on Quality 294
Emphasis on Speed 295
Embedded IS Technology 296
Global Business Environment 297
Effective Business Information Systems in Action 298

CASE 303
Smart Cars

A **Appendix: Buying, Using, and
Upgrading a Personal Computer 304**

Before Buying a Personal Computer System 306
Do You Need a Computer? 306
What Is Your Budget? 307
Study New Computer Developments and Prices 308
Buying a Personal Computer System 309
Buying Software 309
Finally, the Hardware 311

WHO'S WHO 313
Michael P. Krasny / CDW

Peripheral Components, Supplies, and Services 314
Using a Personal Computer System 315
Using Hardware 315
Using Software: General Principles 315
Using Software: User Interfaces 317
When Something Goes Wrong 318
General Strategy for Solving Problems 318

BUSINESS BITS 320
Getting Technical Support

Upgrading an Existing Computer System 321

Glossary 327
Notes 335
Index 337
Web Index 344

An Introduction to

INFORMATION SYSTEMS

CHAPTER 1

Introduction to Computer-based Information Systems

CHAPTER OUTLINE

Essential Computer Concepts
    From Raw Data to Valuable Information
    Computers for Problem Solving
Functions of an Information System
    Input
    Processing
    Output
    Feedback
    Manual versus Computerized Information Systems
Elements of a Computer-based Information System
    Evolution of Computer-based Information Systems
Computer-based Information Systems in Business
    Transaction Processing Systems
    Management Information Systems
    Decision Support Systems
    Expert Systems
Why Study Information Systems?
    Invaluable Benefits of Computers
    Benefits of Computing Literacy
    Benefits of Knowledge about Information Systems
Resources for Literacy

When you're ready to spend several thousand dollars on a car, why not use the latest technology to get the best deal? The days of driving all over town from one dealership to another and haggling with car salesmen are over. Instead, drive onto the information superhighway and use a service called Cars @ Cost (www.webcom.com/~carscost/). Cars @ Cost is the first Internet service that links its users to a nationwide network of auto dealers. Just decide on a car, e-mail an order form to Cars @ Cost, and let the service handle the details with the dealer. You can drive away without a hassle—often with a factory invoice price.

LEARNING OBJECTIVES

After completing Chapter 1, you will be able to:

1. Explain some basic concepts about computers and information systems.
2. Describe the functions of an information system.
3. List the elements of a computer-based information system.
4. Discuss the business applications of computer-based information systems.
5. Cite important reasons for studying information systems.

Computers are driving constant change in people's lives. More information is available—and it's easier to obtain. With the click of a mouse, you can take an on-screen tour of the White House for a homework assignment or visit a Web page to check the schedule for the Cubs' next home stand. You can pay your bills instantly simply by commanding your bookkeeping program to send information over the phone lines to your bank. Your parents can replenish your bank account just as quickly wherever they live using an electronic funds transfer system.

Computers have had especially powerful effects in business. They have made information one of the most important tools for workers in almost all companies. Information systems based on computers help companies to make effective decisions and to find the most efficient ways to implement them.

In fact, computers have transformed information from a business tool to a valuable product in itself. In the past, companies made their profits only by producing goods or providing services for customers. Computers have allowed a freer flow of information, so today's business transactions often involve exchanges of information rather than physical goods or services. In this way, the new technology has created an entirely new information economy.

An **Information system** can be defined as a set of related components used to collect, process, store, analyze, and disseminate information for a specific purpose. People and companies everywhere use systems based on computers to create, store, and transfer information.[1] Investors base multimillion-dollar decisions on output from these systems. Banks could not possibly handle cash transfers fast enough if someone had to carry sacks of cash around the world; instead, they electronically transfer funds instantly between information systems. A manufacturer places orders for new parts directly on suppliers' computers, so it can receive them faster than ever before; those suppliers can also contact the manufacturer's computers to gather information about future orders, so they can plan to produce needed goods on time. Electronic data interchange (EDI)—computer-to-computer communications for standard transactions—has revolutionized the way business is conducted.

Computers and information systems have forever changed our society, our businesses, and our lives. This chapter presents some basic ideas to help you understand how computers and information systems produce such critical effects. It also explains the importance of studying information systems. This general background will lead you toward exploration of more detailed concepts in later chapters as you learn how to unlock the potential of information systems.

ESSENTIAL COMPUTER CONCEPTS

information system

a set of related components used to collect, process, store, analyze, and disseminate information for a specific purpose

computer

an electronic device that can execute instructions or commands to accept data (input) and process them to produce and store useful information (output)

A **computer** is an electronic device that can execute instructions or commands to accept data (input) and process them to produce and store useful information (output). People routinely use familiar devices with input, processing, output, and storage abilities similar to those of a computer (see Figure 1.1). Your home entertainment center might include a TV with surround sound and a VCR. Through a cable hookup or antenna, the system receives signals for programs (input), such as news, sports, weather, and movies. The TV converts (processes) the signals into a picture on the screen (output). The surround sound feature transforms (processes) the audio input to generate multiple-channel stereo sound (output). The VCR can follow your predefined instructions (processing) to record (store) selected programs (input) so you can display the output later on the TV screen.

FIGURE 1.1

FIGURE 1.1

Input, Processing, Storage, and Output
A computer is an electronic device that can execute instructions or commands to accept data (input) and process it to produce and store useful information (output).

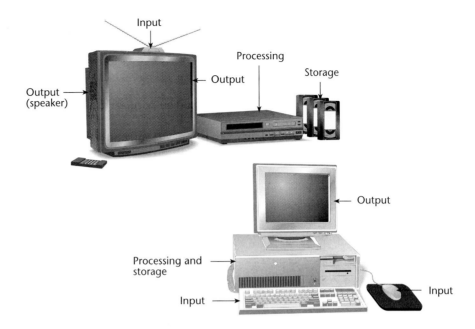

Of course, people transformed data into useful information before the invention of television. As far back as 10,000 B.C., humans made marks on clay tablets and stones to store useful information about the results of manual data processing. In the 1600s, the first mechanical adding machines were developed. In the 1940s, the first electronic computers filled large rooms. Today, people carry in briefcases and backpacks machines that offer more computing power than those rooms contained.

Humans have used manual methods to process data and store information for thousands of years. They have used mechanical devices for hundreds of years and electronic computers for only a few short decades. The accelerating progress in information technology means that during the time you take this class, someone will probably announce a major computer development that will have a profound impact on business and society for years to come.

Over a few decades, computers have gone from obscure curiosities to absolute daily necessities. Many people and almost all companies could not function without access to computers. Without computers, you could not get cash on the way to school before the bank opens or buy breakfast from a fast-food stand—the bank and the fast-food restaurant use computers to operate devices like ATMs and cash registers. Computers also help these businesses to gather valuable information and to solve problems.

From Raw Data to Valuable Information

Businesses and other organizations use computers to provide valuable information. Colleges analyze course registration from data collected by computers to determine whether student demand requires new sections. Grocery stores use computers to determine what food items they should stock to satisfy customers and maximize profits. This process starts with data.

data
raw facts

Data consist of raw facts, such as an employee's name and number of hours worked in a week, a part number in an inventory record, or a quantity desired in a sales order. Computers handle several types of data, listed in Table 1.1, to record and process facts like these.

TABLE 1.1

Types of Data	
Alphanumeric	Numbers, letters, and other characters
Image	Still pictures and other graphics
Audio	Music, speech, sound effects, error tones, and other sounds
Video	Moving pictures and images

files

where computers store and manipulate collections of related data

program file

a collection of instructions given to the computer to execute or run in order to perform some function for the user

document file

where data are stored by the user

information

a collection of facts organized in a way that gives them additional value beyond the value of the facts themselves

Data Types and Computer Files. Computers store and manipulate collections of related data in **files.** A unique name identifies each file. Different computer systems impose different rules for naming files.

A **program file** is a collection of instructions given to the computer to execute or run in order to perform some function for the user. Some programs, called *system software,* control the computer's operations; others, called *applications software,* help users to perform productive tasks like word processing, graphics creation, and spreadsheet calculations.

When you work with a computer program, you store the data you create in a **document file.** A document file created by a word processing program stores data in the form of letters and numbers (alphanumeric data). A document file for a spreadsheet program, which is used to collect, tabulate, and manipulate numbers, contains mostly numbers and formulas. Similarly, many computer programs help users to create, manipulate, and store graphic images and video segments; a document file for one of these programs stores data for a single image or segment. A program to support creation and manipulation of music or other sounds might store document files in a format called *Musical Instrument Digital Interface (MIDI).*

Processing Data: The Characteristics of Valuable Information. When people organize or arrange items of data in a meaningful way, either manually or via computer, they produce information. **Information** is a collection of facts organized in a way that gives them additional value beyond the value of the facts themselves. For example, a total monthly sales figure for all sales representatives might better suit a particular manager (it might be more valuable) than the separate sales totals for individual sales representatives.

Table 1.2 describes the characteristics that make information valuable to individuals and organizations. If decision makers lack accurate or complete information, they may make poor decisions that can cost their organizations large sums of money. Suppose that an inaccurate forecast of future demand leads a manager to expect very high sales when an accurate forecast would project weak sales; that manager might decide to invest millions of dollars to build a new plant and then wonder what became of the expected customers as the plant sits idle.

Along with accuracy and completeness, decision makers need a timely flow of information that is relevant to their decisions. They prefer simple statements over unnecessarily complex detail. Without the characteristics listed in Table 1.2, information may offer little value to the organization or its personnel.

This book cannot overemphasize the importance of valuable information. This discussion suggests a single, all-encompassing principle to guide an organization's use of information technology: *Effectiveness and efficiency depend on delivering the right information to the right person in the right form at the right time.* Effectiveness is doing the right things and efficiency is doing things right. These two principles will be discussed later in the chapter.

TABLE 1.2

Characteristics of Valuable Information

Accurate	*Accurate* information is free of errors. Inaccuracies in data often lead to inaccurate information. Remember an important information systems principle abbreviated *GIGO:* garbage in, garbage out.
Complete	*Complete* information includes all important facts. For example, an investment report would not give complete information if it were to omit costs.
Economical	*Economical* information does not cost more than necessary. Decision makers must always balance the value of information with the cost of producing it.
Flexible	*Flexible* information supports a variety of potential decisions. For example, information about the inventory level for a particular part can help a sales representative to set a customer delivery date, it can help a production manager decide whether to make more of the part, and it can help a financial manager to determine whether the company has invested the right amount of its funds in inventory.
Relevant	*Relevant* information is important to the decision maker. A computer chip maker probably would not need information about likely trends in lumber prices.
Simple	*Simple* information omits unneeded complexity. Decision makers should consider only the amount of detail that they need to make good choices. In fact, too much information can cause destructive information overload, in which excessive detail prevents decision makers from recognizing important conditions.
Timely	*Timely* information is delivered when decision makers need it. Information about last week's weather doesn't help you decide what coat to wear today.
Verifiable	*Verifiable* information allows decision makers to confirm questionable details. They can try to verify information by seeking the same facts from several sources.

Sources of Data and Information. In the past, computers generally produced information from data entered or stored only within their own systems. A company's computers might process payroll, sales, and inventory data stored in a single system to provide valuable information, such as total payroll costs, summaries of sales activity, and orders needed to restock inventory. Increasingly, however, computers obtain data and information from sources outside their own systems. Through phone lines and other communications links, computers can connect to vast networks of computers and other devices. The **Internet** is an example of an international network through which computers can gain access to a wealth of information. Using Internet browsers like Internet Explorer by Microsoft and Netscape, which are programs that allow access to the Internet, people and businesses can tap into vast pools of information on almost any topic. Each chapter of this text contains a boxed feature called "Eye on the Web" to help you become familiar with the Internet and explore its capabilities.

Internet

an example of an international network through which computers can gain access to a wealth of information

Computers for Problem Solving

By helping users to gather valuable information, computers aid people and businesses in the critical process of solving problems. To avoid the problem of spending too much money in September and October, you may need to project your expenses for the entire school year and compare them with your expected monthly income to develop a budget. A large fast-food chain may need to determine the least expensive way to ship fries, burgers, and other food items from warehouses while maintaining freshness, taste, and quality. In the **problem-solving process,** people identify threats or opportunities and formulate appropriate responses. By supporting good problem solving, computers can help you to achieve personal goals, and they can help businesses to reduce costs and increase profits.

problem-solving process

the process by which people identify threats or opportunities and formulate appropriate responses

EYE ON THE WEB

It's difficult to turn on the television or to read a magazine these days without hearing about the Information Superhighway, the World Wide Web, or the Internet. While this stream of jargon may seem intimidating at first, even beginning users can quickly develop the navigation skills to uncover a treasure of information readily available to the public.

The Internet was begun by the U.S. government as a means of sharing government research between organizations. It is a network of networks, allowing different agencies to communicate with each other via computer. Currently, the Internet is operating in over 30 countries throughout the world. In 1991, the Internet was opened to permit full commercial use; its growth since then has been phenomenal. Software giant Microsoft, for example, estimates that one million users per day browse one of its Web pages.

Although early Internet access was accomplished through text-driven menus, graphical user interfaces now provide a user-friendly means of searching through this storehouse of data. Netscape and Internet Explorer, for example, are browsers that provide such interfaces. These browsers give users access to the World Wide Web (WWW), a collection of documents known as Web sites. The documents—which contain text and sometimes graphics such as digital photographs—are housed on servers all over the country and the world. A user simply points a mouse and clicks on a menu item or object, and the screen responds with a dazzling array of colors and choices.

A URL is a document address (the location of the server computer where the document is housed); if you know the address of the document for which you are searching, click on the "Open" button, enter the address, and you're on your way.

Try to think of browsing as comparable to taking a different route to work or to school; you end up at the desired location, but you can discover new scenes or information along the way. Several search routines are available. For example, if you are accessing WWW through Netscape, click on the "Directory" item in the menu bar, and choose the option to begin an Internet Search. Alternately, if you click on the "Net Search" button and choose "Yahoo," this provides another search method. Enter a set of keywords (in plain English), and begin your search.

Conducting a search results in a listing of topics on the screen. Note that the topics are in different colors, and that your mouse pointer turns into a hand when you point at one of them. These are known as hypertext links, or *hotlinks*; clicking on a hypertext link instructs Netscape to open that particular document. (If at any time you believe that you may have strayed too far and are lost on the Internet, clicking on the "Home" button will instantly return you to the place where your session began. Likewise, clicking on the "Back" button will take you back to the most recently accessed site. If you believe that you've gone back farther than you had wanted to, clicking on the "Forward" button moves you forward one site.)

Students will discover that the Internet can guide them to up-to-date information on any topic imaginable. Perhaps you are deciding which employer fits your future plans. The Internet has many company sites, most of which contain job-related information. Trivia collectors may be searching for a cast list from a popular movie. Soap opera fans may desire a synopsis of a recent episode. These questions, and others, can be answered by the information housed on the Internet.

Now take a few minutes to search the Web. The only disappointment that you are likely to encounter is when you realize that it is time to stop.

WEB EXERCISES

1. Suppose you are planning a vacation. Select a destination, and search the Web for information about your destination. List at least three activities that you might plan for your vacation.
2. Assemble a cast list (the actors' names as well as the characters' names) for one of your favorite television programs.
3. The Internet has the potential to dramatically change the way we search for information. Suppose that you are searching for information on a company. Access at least two different sites. What different positions are listed by each company? Check to see how many involve knowledge of computers and information systems. (Confident users may wish to enter a request to receive information or even an application at a specific company.)

---

decision-making phase

the three stages of the problem-solving process that include intelligence, design, and choice

Effective problem solving depends on careful decision making. According to a well-known model developed by Herbert Simon, the **decision-making phase** encompasses three stages of the problem-solving process: intelligence, design, and choice.[2] George Huber later incorporated these steps into an expanded model of the entire problem-solving process to include implementation of the decision and monitoring to see whether it was effective or needs further improvement (see Figure 1.2).

The model implies a step-by-step process, but real-world problem solving seldom proceeds in such a smooth sequence. As decision makers analyze various alternatives over a period of time, they often recognize new possibilities during later stages of the process. They then repeat the intelligence and design stages to collect additional information on the new alternatives. This type of feedback and adjustment commonly alters the neat flow of the basic problem-solving model.

During the **intelligence stage,** decision makers identify and define potential problems and opportunities. They gather information about the cause and scope of the problem to investigate possible solutions and limitations. For example, a cooperative of Hawaiian pineapple farmers might gather intelligence about an opportunity to ship their fresh fruit to stores in Michigan. The perishability of the fruit and the price that consumers in Michigan are willing to pay create limitations for problem solving. Federal and state regulations for shipments of food products also affect the problem situation.

In the **design stage,** decision makers develop potential solutions to the problem at hand. They then evaluate the feasibility and implications of these alternatives. The Hawaiian farmers might invite proposals from several shipping and air freight companies and then study transportation times and costs for all the possibilities. This analysis might determine that they could not ship fruit by freighter to California and then by truck to Michigan because it would spoil before reaching stores.

In the last stage of decision making, the **choice stage,** someone with authority must select a course of action. The Hawaiian farmers might agree to select air freight as the best way to get their product to markets in Michigan. The choice stage would conclude with the selection of a specific air carrier.

The problem-solving process continues beyond the decision-making phase. In the **implementation stage,** the person or company puts the solution into effect. For example, the Hawaiian farmers might implement their decision to ship via a specific air freight company by informing the farm workers of the new arrangement, directing them to pack the fruit in appropriate shipping containers, and trucking the containers to the airport.

intelligence stage

the stage of the decision-making phase during which decision makers identify and define potential problems and opportunities

design stage

the stage of the decision-making phase during which decision makers develop potential solutions to the problem at hand

choice stage

the stage of the decision-making phase during which someone with authority must select a course of action

implementation stage

the stage of the problem-solving process during which a person or the company puts the solution into effect

FIGURE 1.2

Decision Making as Part of Problem Solving
The three stages of decision making—intelligence, design, and choice—are augmented by implementation and monitoring to complete the problem-solving process.

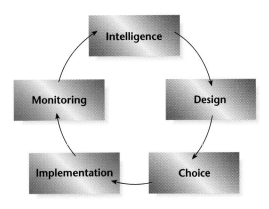

monitoring stage

the stage of the problem-solving process during which a person or the company evaluates the implementation of the solution to determine whether it has achieved the anticipated results

In the final stage of the problem-solving process, the **monitoring stage,** the person or company evaluates the implementation of the solution to determine whether it has achieved the anticipated results. This stage also includes changes to the solution in response to new information learned during the implementation stage. Monitoring continues and extends the cycle of feedback and adjustment, allowing the entire process to be fine-tuned. For example, after the first shipment of fruit, the Hawaiian farmers might learn that their chosen air carrier routes its flights through Portland, Oregon, where the plane sits exposed on the runway during a long stopover to load additional cargo. If the fruit deteriorates during this unexpected exposure to temperature and humidity, the farmers might have to adjust their solution to ship with a different air freight firm that flies directly to Michigan, or they may have to package the fruit in different containers to keep the fruit cool.

Computers make important contributions during all phases of decision making and problem solving. They can provide speed and flexibility to team with human imagination and creativity. Computer analysis of surveys and questionnaires can help in the intelligence stage to identify potential new products that a company or its competitors might offer. The computer can quickly identify many possibilities that could alert the company to more problems and opportunities for it to evaluate. During the design stage, decision makers can easily change data in computer-based models to explore and analyze probable effects of various alternatives. In this way, decision makers can evaluate many more scenarios and their results. They are not locked into one or two paths; instead, they have more flexibility. Finally, computers can help users to gather information to monitor the implementation of a chosen solution. Users can get more information readily, so it can help them spot problems sooner.

Computers can also support decision making and problem solving by individuals. Suppose that you are thinking about investing next semester's tuition in the stock market to make a return on your money before you pay your bills. Your problem is to select the best stock. During the intelligence stage of this decision-making process, you can use a computer connected to an information service such as CompuServe or Prodigy to gather information about return and risk for various stocks. During the design phase, you can use a computer to filter thousands of stocks to create a short list of those that meet your specified criteria. A computer can help you to access information so that you can select the best investment during the choice stage. You can then implement your decision by buying the chosen stock through one of the computer trading systems offered by many brokerage houses. Finally, you can use a computer to monitor your solution by checking daily on prices and news stories about your stock. If its price starts to drop, you might adjust your decision by entering a

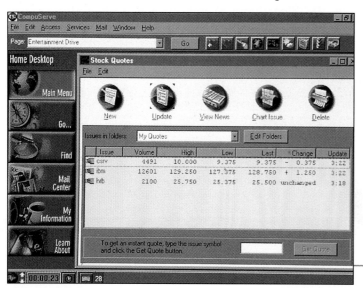

Information services can help you gather information and assist in decision making. (Source: Permission granted by CompuServe Incorporated.)

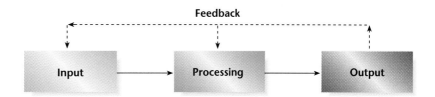

FIGURE 1.3

Components of an
Information System
Feedback provides critical
guidance for adjustments to
an information system.

hasty sell order through your broker's computer trading system. (You hope that the computer helps you to respond before you pay too high a price for an education in stock market risk.)

FUNCTIONS OF AN INFORMATION SYSTEM

Computers usually aid problem solving as part of organized information systems. For the purposes of this book, an information system (IS) is a set of interrelated components that collect data (input), manipulate and store this input (processing), and disseminate information (output). An IS must also provide a feedback mechanism that allows it to evaluate output and then adjust its methods for collecting and processing input to ensure that it produces the desired output (see Figure 1.3).

Input

input

the raw data that the system will manipulate and the activity of gathering that data

Input to an information system encompasses the raw data that the system will manipulate and the activity of gathering that data. For example, the payroll function of a company's information system must collect hours worked for every employee before it can calculate and print paychecks. A university's grading system requires input from instructors in each course about student grades before it can compile and send a summary of semester or quarter grades for each student.

Information systems capture input in many forms. The payroll system, for example, might gain input from employee time cards. A 911 emergency telephone system receives input from incoming calls for assistance. A marketing information system might receive interview responses as input. For any information system, the type of input depends on the desired output.

An information system can gather input through a manual process or an automated procedure. A payroll clerk might manually enter hours worked for each employee by typing on a computer keyboard. A grocery store's information system relies on automated input; a scanner reads a bar code, and the system then retrieves the name of the item and its price from stored records to ring up the sale correctly on the cash register. Regardless of its method of collecting input, an information system can produce the desired output only if it receives accurate input.

Scanners are automated input devices that we encounter on a regular basis. (Source: David Young Wolff / Tony Stone Images.)

Processing

processing

the action that an information system completes when it converts or transforms data to generate useful information

An information system completes **processing** when it converts or transforms data to generate useful information. Processing can include calculations such as simple addition to accumulate a running total. It can also include making comparisons and taking alternative actions based on the results. Finally, processing encompasses IS activities that store data for future use in a form different from that of the original input.

The processing function of a payroll system would multiply input about hours worked and wage rate for each employee to calculate gross pay. It would then calculate appropriate deductions for taxes or Social Security and subtract them to get each person's net pay. Net pay can also be stored for future use.

Output

output

the useful information usually in the form of documents, reports, and transaction data—that an information system produces

Output from an information system includes the useful information—usually in the form of documents, reports, and transaction data—that it produces. A payroll system would produce outputs like printed paychecks for employees, summaries of taxes withheld for government agencies, and detailed reports for managers; it would also contribute information for more general reports to stockholders, banks, government agencies, and other groups.

Output from one system or part of a system can become input for another. For example, output from one information system component that processes sales orders can provide input to a customer billing component. Sometimes, output from one system can provide input to control the operations of other systems or devices. For instance, output from a computerized design system in a car manufacturing shop can direct robots to make precise welds at exact locations.

Information systems produce output in a variety of ways. Computer-based systems commonly generate output through printers and display screens.

feedback

output that guides adjustments or changes to an information system's input or processing activities

Feedback

Every information system needs **feedback**—output that guides adjustments or changes to its input or processing activities. For example, errors or problems in output might indicate the need for changes in input data or processing steps. Perhaps a payroll clerk types the number of hours worked for an employee as 400 instead of 40. The payroll component of the company's information system needs a feedback function to verify that input data fall within certain predetermined ranges. For hours worked, the range might run from 0 to 100 hours, since it is unlikely that an employee would work more than 100 hours in any given week. The information system would provide feedback to indicate that the input of 400 hours exceeded the limit for hours worked, leading the payroll clerk to check and correct the input. The feedback routine would save the company from printing a paycheck for ten times more than it should pay. (It would also save the clerk from having to do some uncomfortable explaining.)

Output from a computerized design system in a car manufacturing facility can direct robots to make precise welds at exact locations. (Source: Courtesy of Toyota Motor Manufacturing, Kentucky, Inc.)

Feedback provides important guidance for decision makers, as well. For example, output from an information system might indicate low inventory levels for a few items. This feedback might lead the manager to order more supplies. The new orders then become input to the purchasing component of the company's inventory system.

Manual versus Computerized Information Systems

An information system can gather input, complete processing, and produce output either manually or with the assistance of computers. A payroll clerk could use a calculator or scratch pad to determine each employee's net pay and write everything in a ledger, but consider the work involved:

- The clerk would determine hours worked by an employee, perhaps from a time card, and look up that employee's hourly wage. Multiplying would give gross pay.
- If hours worked exceeded 40 for a single week, separate calculations would have to determine the worker's overtime wage, multiply it by hours in excess of 40, and then add the result to base pay.
- The clerk would have to scribble furiously to figure deductions and subtract them from gross pay to get net pay. The company must withhold the correct amounts for each employee's federal and state taxes. Different employees require different deductions for health and life insurance, savings plans, and other deductions. The clerk would have to consult company records to determine the charges that apply to each employee and then calculate them without mistakes.

A computer could simplify and streamline the payroll information system by quickly and automatically calculating the right amounts based on electronically stored information about individual employees. It could then store net pay and other important information in information system files.

Many information systems begin as manual systems and become computerized. For example, the U.S. Postal Service once sorted all mail by assigning employees to read each envelope and then manually place it in the bin for the correct ZIP code. Today, electronic systems scan the addresses on many letters passing through the postal system and route them to the appropriate bins automatically via conveyors. The computerized sorting system speeds mail handling. At the same time, it gathers information that helps postal service managers to control transportation planning.

The U.S. Postal Service uses a computerized sorting system to scan addresses and route letters to the appropriate bins. (Source: U.S. Postal Service.)

BUSINESS BITS

Maytag and IBM Team Up for Customer Service

In the TV commercial, the Maytag repairman is lonely and bored. No one calls him. He has nothing to do, because Maytag appliances are so trouble-free that customers never call him.

In the real world, Maytag fields around one million customer service phone calls per year. Granted, those calls aren't all related to repairs; some involve questions or orders, while others are compliments or complaints. Still, the calls must be answered, and each customer must receive a response. Several years ago, Maytag service team members still took notes on calls by hand, then keyed them into an old, mainframe-based customer system. Then a customer service rep would look up the answer to the question, thumbing through any of 50 volumes of product manuals, and call the customer back. With one million calls per year, this clearly was not the fastest, most reliable, or least expensive method for the $3 billion company to answer customer service calls. There had to be a better way.

"We wanted to take a different approach in dealing with our customers," recalls Ken Douglas, manager of customer assistance. "We knew we were already No. 1 in dependability, but we also wanted our customers to depend on us after the sale, whether it be to answer questions, provide product usage information, or to help with a problem."

Maytag turned to IBM for help. Although very good software packages for customer service are available, Maytag asked IBM to custom-build software. The new system, called CAIR (Customer Assistance Information Resource), integrates voice, data, and image technology; it also contains a database with 7.5 million customers on file. For speed, IBM installed Maytag's product image library on a separate image server, with the images on hard disks. Now Maytag's customer service consultants can just about work miracles. They can retrieve service data and product views in five seconds. When a customer on the other end of the line describes a problem with a product, a consultant can call up different views of the product to determine what the customer is describing. This is an important feature of the software because "one of the frustrating things about customer service is that people describe things differently," says Malcom Frank, vice president of marketing at Cambridge Technology Partners in Massachusetts.

The benefits of Maytag's new system are many. The company has added value to its products and services and enhanced customer service by being able to respond quickly and accurately to customer queries. It has also increased the chances of retaining repeat customers. "When customers experience a problem and you respond quickly, your retention repurchase rate will be higher than those who had no problems," explains James I. Cash, Jr., professor of business administration at Harvard Business School. In addition, errors are reduced, efficiency is increased, and communications are expanded. The Maytag repairman may finally have found something to do after all.

1. In addition to those mentioned above, what other benefits might Maytag gain through its new customer service system?
2. How might another industry use this approach?
3. What do you think is the most important component of Maytag's new customer service system? Why?
4. If you have Internet access, locate Maytag's home page. What information is available to assist customers? How could the company use it to enhance service?

Source: Doug Bartholomew, "Curtain Call," *Information Week*, June 17, 1996, pp. 54–62; http://www.informationweek.com. Maytag's home pages can be located at http://www.maytag.com and http://www.maytagcorp.com. Photo courtesy of Maytag Corporation.

Many organizations are abandoning paper-based information systems in favor of totally electronic systems. CREST, the London Stock Exchange's completely paperless electronic trading system, is replacing an earlier computer-based system that generated tons of paper trading records. Federal Express earns $10 billion per year moving other people's paper overnight from one location to another, but it is transforming its own information system to an entirely electronic system. It tracks aircraft maintenance records, schedules, and maintenance orders only through electronically stored files. Fred Hummel, manager of the maintenance department, summarizes the approach: "We won't have paper unless it's necessary for the end user."[3] Maytag has also computerized to streamline its customer service capabilities (see the "Business Bits" box).

ELEMENTS OF A COMPUTER-BASED INFORMATION SYSTEM

computer-based information system (CBIS)

hardware, software, databases, telecommunications, people, and procedures to collect and process data to produce and store information

hardware

computer equipment or devices that perform input, processing, and output functions

software

programmed sequences of instructions for the computer

A **computer-based information system (CBIS)** combines hardware, software, databases, telecommunications, people, and procedures to collect and process data to produce and store information. Figure 1.4 illustrates the elements of such a system.

Hardware consists of computer equipment or devices that perform input, processing, and output functions. Input devices include keyboards, pointing devices like the mouse, optical scanners, and many other kinds of equipment. Processing devices include the computer's central processing unit, memory, and storage units. Computers employ many output devices, including printers and video display screens.

Software consists of programmed sequences of instructions for the computer. Systems software controls the computer's internal operations, while applications software performs productive tasks at the user's direction. Application programs process payroll, store data, send bills to customers, and provide information to increase profits, reduce costs, and provide better customer service. A spreadsheet program is an example of application software.

FIGURE 1.4

Components of a Computer-based Information System

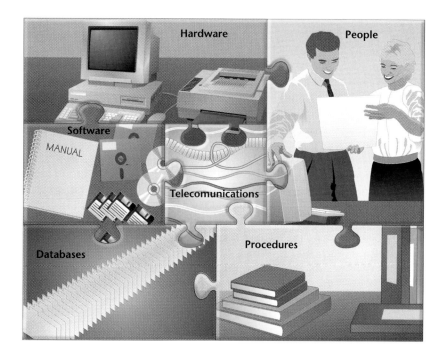

People comprise the most important element of a computer-based information system. (Source: Courtesy of AST Corporation.)

database

an organized collection of facts and information

telecommunications

components that allow organizations to link computer systems together into networks

procedures

the strategies, policies, methods, and rules that humans apply to operate a CBIS

first-generation computers

electronic computing devices that began with vacuum tube technology in the late 1940s and 1950s

second-generation computers

computers that processed data through circuits based on transistors

third-generation computers

computers that were devised after the development of microchips and integrated circuits in the 1960s

business

a formal collection of people and other resources established to accomplish a set of goals

A **database** is an organized collection of facts and information. A company's database can contain details about customers, employees, inventory, competitors' sales, and much more. Many managers consider a database to be one of the most valuable parts of a computer-based information system.

Telecommunications components allow organizations to link computer systems together into networks; in short, they let one computer "talk" to another. Networks of computers and related equipment allow users to share software and data throughout a building, across the country, or around the world.

People are the most important element in most computer-based information systems. Humans define the output they want from these systems and then organize components to generate that output. Information system personnel include all the people who manage, run, program, and maintain a computer system. Users are managers, decision makers, employees, and others who benefit from the work that computers do. Of course, IS personnel often qualify as computer users.

Procedures include the strategies, policies, methods, and rules that humans apply to operate a CBIS. For example, some procedures describe when to run particular programs. Other procedures determine who can have access to certain facts in the database. Still others describe appropriate reactions in case of disasters such as fires, earthquakes, or hurricanes.

Evolution of Computer-based Information Systems

Swift and numerous changes have continuously transformed computer-based information systems since their earliest days. Electronic computing devices began with vacuum tube technology in the late 1940s and 1950s **(first-generation computers). Second-generation computers** processed data through circuits based on transistors. The development of microchips and integrated circuits in the 1960s gave rise to **third-generation computers.**

Rapid, continuing changes in equipment and computing techniques since that time complicate attempts to classify later generations of computers. Some experts describe today's machines as fourth-generation computers; others argue for finer divisions that define the fifth or sixth generations of the Information Age (see Figure 1.5). Technical issues aside, each wave of changes in technology, reflected in each successive generation of computers, has extended the power of computer-based information systems to ever larger groups of individuals and, especially, businesses.

COMPUTER-BASED INFORMATION SYSTEMS IN BUSINESS

A **business** is a formal collection of people and other resources established to accomplish a set of goals, including generating profits or maximizing the value of the owners' investment. Individuals operate small businesses called *sole proprietorships.* Two or more individuals may operate a business as a partnership. Some businesses organize themselves as corporations, becoming legally recognized entities capable of operating independently of their owners. Large businesses often grow from small operations. Michael Dell began assembling personal computers in his dorm room while attending

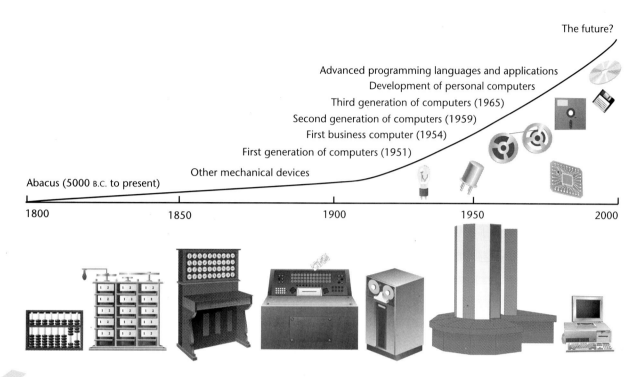

The future?

Advanced programming languages and applications
Development of personal computers
Third generation of computers (1965)
Second generation of computers (1959)
First business computer (1954)
First generation of computers (1951)
Other mechanical devices
Abacus (5000 B.C. to present)

1800   1850   1900   1950   2000

FIGURE 1.5

Progress in the Information Age
The Information Age began in the 1800s and continues today.

college as a pre-med student. Today, Dell Computers is one of the largest makers of PCs in the world.

Money, labor, materials, machines and equipment, data, information, and decisions constantly flow through any business. As Figure 1.6 shows, a business draws resources such as materials, people, and money from its environment. It transforms these resources to generate output, which it sends to the environment. Businesses usually produce information, products, and services as outputs. To survive, they must add value to the inputs and generate products or services that people will buy. For example, a sandwich shop combines a store,

FIGURE 1.6

General Model of a Business Organization
The information system supports and works within all parts of the business. Although this simple model omits some detail, remember that the information system can draw input from both internal and external sources. Before data enter the information system, they constitute an external business resource; once they enter the system, they become an internal resource. Likewise, the information system can output information products and services to either internal or external systems.

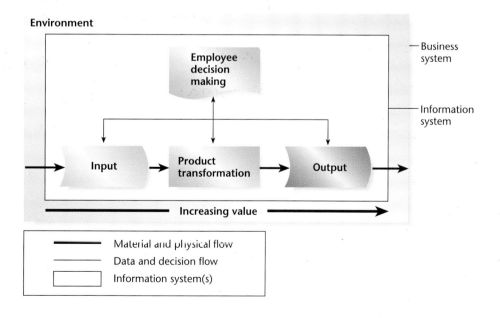

Environment

Business system

Information system

Employee decision making

Input → Product transformation → Output

Increasing value

——— Material and physical flow
——— Data and decision flow
▭ Information system(s)

employee labor, tools, ingredients like buns and meat, and other inputs to create sandwiches, which are worth more than the separate inputs. Businesses achieve their goals by providing value.

Computers have performed many kinds of tasks for businesses. The first computer-based information systems of the early 1950s completed routine business transactions like printing payroll checks and processing customer orders (thus the name *transaction processing systems*). Since that time, business computers have worked harder and done more complex tasks, providing valuable information (in *management information systems*, also sometimes referred to as *information reporting systems*) and supporting decision making (in *decision support systems*). Some companies even ask their computers for advice (in *expert systems*). The following sections introduce these fundamental business applications of computer technology.

Transaction Processing Systems

transaction processing system (TPS)

an organized collection of people, procedures, databases, and devices that records information about completed business transactions

Computers made their first contributions to businesses by helping to process transactions. A *transaction* is any business-related exchange such as a payment to employees, a sale to a customer, or a payment to a supplier. A **transaction processing system (TPS)** is an organized collection of people, procedures, databases, and devices that records information about completed business transactions (see Figure 1.7). A payroll TPS accepts inputs for employees' hours worked during the week and wage rates. Its primary output consists of printed paychecks.

Management Information Systems

management information system

an organized collection of people, procedures, databases, and devices that provides information about routine business operations to managers and decision makers

As businesses gained more understanding of the capabilities of computers, they created **management information systems.** These systems are organized collections of people, procedures, databases, and devices that provide information about routine business operations to managers and decision makers, primarily to enhance efficiency. They support functions like marketing, production, and finance, among others, by providing common databases of information about daily business activities. A management information system typically generates planned reports by processing data from the firm's transaction processing system (see Figure 1.8).

FIGURE 1.7

Payroll Transaction Processing System
The TPS transforms inputs (employees' hours worked and wage rates) to produce output (paychecks).

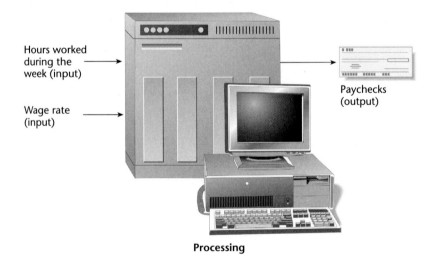

Hours worked during the week (input)

Wage rate (input)

Paychecks (output)

Processing

FIGURE 1.8

Components of a Management Information System
A management information system draws data from the organization's transaction processing system to generate information about routine operations.

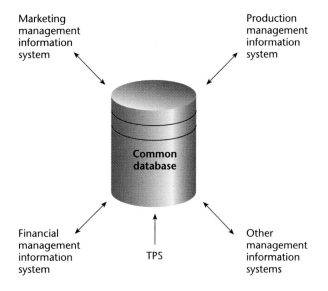

Many firms have begun to extend their transaction processing systems and management information systems to include suppliers and customers. Over telecommunications links, these organizations can share information that helps to improve efficiency for all of them. Customers can enter orders directly on suppliers' information systems, and suppliers can submit bills directly to customers' systems. These exchanges of information speed both delivery and payment and save the cost of personnel to enter data from paper records. Both firms can plan production from a single schedule, cutting waste and improving coordination.

Decision Support Systems

decision support system (DSS)

an organized collection of people, procedures, databases, and devices that helps managers to identify and study alternative solutions to specific problems and then choose between them

A **decision support system (DSS)** is an organized collection of people, procedures, databases, and devices that helps managers to identify and study alternative solutions to specific problems and then choose between them. A DSS focuses on promoting effectiveness in a business. While a management information system helps an organization do things right, a DSS helps it to do the right things.

Decision support systems address complex problems that require managers to find and interpret scarce information. A DSS supports careful managerial judgment, so managers often actively participate in its development and implementation. Many managers may use a DSS, so it must be flexible enough to accommodate different managerial styles and decision types. Remember that a DSS *supports* a manager's judgment; it does not *replace* it. DSSs can be used to decide where to locate a business, what type of staff and how many employees to hire for a proposed expansion, whether a new product line could be profitable, and so on.

As illustrated in Figure 1.9, the essential elements of a DSS include a collection of models that show a decision maker how changes in one area will likely affect conditions in another (model base). A DSS also needs procedures to simplify formulation of a problem (DSS generator), a collection of facts and information to assist in decision making (database), and systems and procedures that help decision makers and other users to interact with the DSS (user interface).

FIGURE 1.9

**Essential Elements of a
Decision Support System**

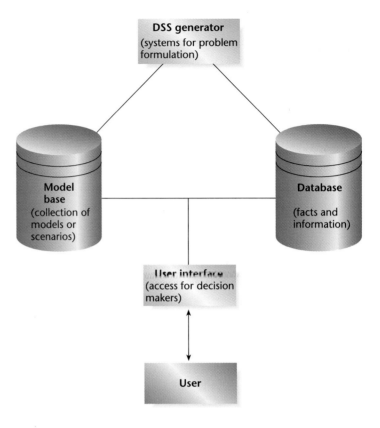

Expert Systems

expert system

an organized collection of people, procedures, databases, and devices that suggests decisions and acts like a human expert in a certain area or discipline

An **expert system** is an organized collection of people, procedures, databases, and devices that suggests decisions and acts like a human expert in a certain area or discipline. These computer systems are intended to react like human specialists with many years of experience in specific fields. In fact, part of the development of such a system requires extensive interviewing and observation of human experts. For example, expert systems have been developed to search for oil and gas, diagnose medical complaints, and pinpoint problems with electrical and mechanical devices. This description does not imply that expert systems can replace humans; they are programmed by human experts in particular fields to behave in predefined ways to display appropriate information.

An expert system is composed of four elements: a knowledge base, a rule base, an inference engine, and a user interface (see Figure 1.10). A knowledge base collects data, information, and statements of important

Medical Expert systems can help reduce prescription errors by employing a rules engineer or knowledge base that checks a prescription order against a patient's records and warns if a toxic overdose is reached. (Source: Pete Saloutos / The Stock Market.)

FIGURE 1.10

Components of an Expert System

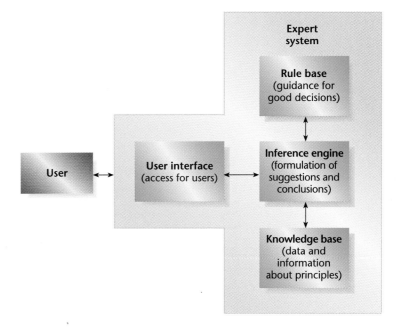

Expert system

Rule base
(guidance for good decisions)

Inference engine
(formulation of suggestions and conclusions)

User interface
(access for users)

User

Knowledge base
(data and information about principles)

principles about a field. For example, a knowledge base for a medical expert system would include information about symptoms and causes of a variety of diseases. The purpose of the knowledge base is to capture as much as possible of the experience of an expert. A rule base defines a series of rules or relationships that guide good decisions. A rule base for a medical expert system would include numerous conditions, such as "If a patient displays certain symptoms, make a specific diagnosis and prescribe a specified treatment." An inference engine interacts with the knowledge base and rule base to formulate conclusions, make appropriate suggestions, and provide expert advice in a particular situation, much as a human expert would. The user interface gives the decision maker or user access to the expert system.

Expert systems give business organizations a unique ability to capture and consult the wisdom of specialists. A firm can avoid completely losing years of experience and specific skills when a human expert dies, retires, or leaves for another job. In some cases, expert systems can fill a gap when an expert is unavailable or when it is not practical to obtain one-on-one advice. Businesses can apply expert systems to almost any field or discipline. Firms have used them to monitor complex systems like nuclear reactors, locate possible repair problems, design and configure information system components, and develop marketing plans for new products or new investment strategies.

Businesses seek to achieve a wide range of benefits through their computer-based information systems:

- Adding value to their goods and services by raising quality levels, reducing errors, enhancing customer service, expanding communications
- Improving safety, improving health care, giving access to more varied opportunities at work
- Establishing competitive advantage by increasing efficiency, enhancing productivity, reducing labor requirements, cutting costs
- Establishing more efficient administrative functions, enabling superior financial and management decision making, establishing stronger control over operations

WHY STUDY INFORMATION SYSTEMS?

Information systems play fundamental and ever-expanding roles in all business organizations. As part of your effort to develop a solid understanding of how business organizations operate, you need to understand the functions of information systems. Knowledge of information systems will help you to make a significant contribution on the job and to advance in your chosen career or field.

Business researchers have shown a major effect on organization success, including higher profits and lower costs, when managers and decision makers involve themselves in all aspects of their companies' information systems.[4] Moreover, trends leading up to the close of the century and beyond suggest there will be severe challenges for businesses to survive and prosper. For example, diminishing trade barriers, political and economic changes in former Eastern bloc countries, and global investment all point to an increasingly international business environment. In today's changing markets, businesses face increasingly complex issues and decisions. An understanding of information systems will help you to cope, adapt, and prosper in this competitive environment.

A weak understanding of computers and information systems can, however, threaten career success. Computers now do much of the work associated with accountants', financial planners', doctors', lawyers', and marketing researchers' jobs. For under $50, you can buy a program to write wills, sales contracts, and other legal documents for which a lawyer would charge hundreds or thousands of dollars.[5] Computerized expert systems now diagnose medical ailments, in the process supporting small rural health-care staffs, saving money, and reducing the need for doctors. Some believe that these expert systems propose more creative solutions and fresher ideas than human experts suggest.

Why should you study computers and information systems? The balance of this chapter suggests two basic reasons. First, computers have become invaluable tools for both businesses and individuals. Second, computer literacy and familiarity with information systems will help you to keep your job and advance in your career.

Invaluable Benefits of Computers

Most medium-sized to large businesses could operate for only a few days without their computers. Most companies could not easily pay their bills, order raw materials from suppliers, send products to customers, and pay their employees without access to their computer systems. Computers have become efficient and effective business tools by offering speed, reliability, large storage capacity, and low cost.

Speed. Computers work fast. The largest, most powerful computers execute commands or instructions so rapidly that if you could take a normal step for every command, you could walk around the earth at the equator about 30 times in one second. A computer can complete calculations more quickly than an office full of clerks, freeing people from tedious, routine tasks so they can accomplish more challenging and creative work.

CD-ROM encyclopedias can store full-motion video images and stereo sound and allow users to retrieve information in seconds. (Source: Courtesy of Microsoft Corporation.)

Reliability. Computers produce reliable results. They rarely make mistakes, and users can anticipate and prevent most causes of errors. A computer can make billions of calculations without a single mistake. How many people could match this performance?

Large Storage Capacity. Computers can store large amounts of data and information in small spaces. The computer files for the text of this book all fit on a single diskette no bigger than the palm of your hand. A single CD-ROM (the same size as a music compact disk) can store an encyclopedia that would fill 20 volumes. In addition to text and pictures like those in a book, the CD-ROM can store full-motion video images and stereo sound. Only computers can offer this type of information storage capacity.

Besides saving physical space and weight, storing large amounts of information in a single place permits fast search and retrieval. For a term paper, you could search through an entire encyclopedia or hundreds of business journals in a few seconds to find every mention of a chosen topic. How long would you have to spend at the library to search through hundreds of business journals?

Low Cost. Computers offer this amazing power at rapidly falling prices. One computer executive compared the development of computers since 1985 to the development of cars, saying that a 1985 Cadillac would have evolved to a weight of 42 pounds and a length of 4 feet, get 2,100 miles per gallon of gas, and cost $32 if it had followed the same development curve as computers in ten years.[6]

efficiency

a computer benefit that measures an amount of work produced (output) for a given amount of resources consumed (input)

effectiveness

a computer benefit that measures how well people or organizations realize their goals

Efficiency and Effectiveness. The speed, reliability, storage capacity, and low cost of computers make them important tools for improving efficiency and effectiveness. **Efficiency** measures an amount of work produced (output) for a given amount of resources consumed (input). A computer can help you to efficiently pay your bills, send out holiday cards, and prepare your income tax returns. It can enhance efficiency even more in a business, because companies need to perform more of these information-handling tasks than most individuals. A computer can process information in a fraction of the time that humans would take to do it by hand.

Effectiveness measures how well people or organizations realize their goals. You might set a goal of investing profitably in the stock market. As we discussed, a computer can help you to reach this goal by finding and monitoring information to select, buy, and sell the right stocks at the right times. Some advocates of computer-based investment systems claim that an ordinary person using an inexpensive computer can consistently outperform the market and make millions of dollars.

To summarize, efficiency is doing things right, while effectiveness is doing the right things. Throughout this book, each chapter will show you how computers can help people to improve and maintain efficiency and effectiveness. You can begin moving toward this goal by building your computing literacy.

Benefits of Computing Literacy

computer literacy

a basic knowledge of computer systems and equipment and how they function

As you come to understand more about information systems, you will develop computer literacy. **Computer literacy** is a basic knowledge of computer systems and equipment and how they function.[7] It stresses the operating routines of equipment and devices (hardware), programs and instructions (software), databases, and telecommunications.

Computer literacy gives you an understanding of various types of hardware and software, and you can apply your knowledge of how to use hardware and software later in your career to increase your firm's profits, cut costs, improve productivity, and increase customer satisfaction. Applying this knowledge also requires some understanding of how and why people (including managers, employees, stockholders, and others) use information technology. It also implies some understanding of organizational functions, decision-making methods, management activities, and information needs. This business background helps you to determine how your organization can use computers and information systems to achieve its goals.

Benefits of Knowledge about Information Systems

By studying information systems, you will gain both personal and professional benefits. These systems can help you to enrich your life by giving you access to new information, goods, and services: instant airplane ticket information, newspapers, and catalogs on line, computerized address books and schedule planners, to name a few. Through resources like the World Wide Web, they also bring you into contact with a rich stream of people and ideas that you would never experience in any other way.

Companies know that effective information systems can powerfully affect the strategies they pursue and the success they achieve.[8] The impact of these systems can benefit the organizations, users of their information systems, and any individual or group that interacts with them. Therefore, companies look for people with strong knowledge and skills in information systems when they want candidates for jobs and promotions.

Careers in Information Systems. Information systems also offer exciting career choices. Numerous colleges award degrees in information systems with various technical and business focuses through their computer science departments and business schools. Degrees in information systems have led many new graduates to find challenging positions with high salaries. Some schools and departments report that their information systems majors attain the highest starting salaries of all undergraduate business majors. For example, information systems majors in the College of Business at Florida State University averaged more than $31,000 annually in 1996, the highest average for all undergraduate business majors.

Aside from high starting salaries, these students can expect significant future job growth. IS occupations should grow rapidly as new computer technologies and information systems spread throughout government and business. In fact, one company has even instituted a new corporate position—chief knowledge officer (see "Who's Who: Ellen Knapp/Coopers & Lybrand).

WHO'S WHO

Ellen Knapp/Coopers & Lybrand

The idea of shaping a career around knowledge itself isn't new; scholars and researchers have done it for centuries. But the idea of shaping a career around the electronic manipulation of knowledge *is* new, and women like Ellen Knapp, a vice chairman of Coopers & Lybrand and their first chief knowledge officer, are seizing the opportunity. Knapp, whose previous position was vice chair, technology, has been appointed to "ensure that the firm has the processes, systems, and culture to facilitate effective knowledge sharing—both within Coopers & Lybrand and between the firm and its clients," she explains. The knowledge she talks about ranges from current industry practices to future trends. Her focus is somewhat different from that of an information officer, who deals with the management of data; instead, she must look at the bigger picture, identifying the knowledge that her company "needs to manage and leverage."

Companies are finding that they need a position like chief knowledge officer (or chief learning officer) and people like Knapp for a couple of reasons. First, pooling knowledge in such a way that everyone in the company can build upon it to solve new problems for clients means less wasted time and effort on each new project.

"Companies like professional services firms do not want to reinvent the wheel with every client," notes Russ Maney, an analyst at Forrester Research Inc. in Massachusetts. "The ability to tap and reuse this knowledge is what will differentiate competitors. A person who can help his company do this is very valuable." (In salary terms, this value can translate to $350,000 to $1 million a year.)

Second, people change jobs—and companies—much more frequently now than they used to. If knowledge isn't somehow stored within the company, it leaves the company when the person departs. "With increasingly large salaries luring many skilled information technology professionals to change jobs frequently, there is a need for companies to retain the knowledge that these people have accumulated," says Joel Koblentz, managing partner of the executive recruitment firm Egon Zehnder International. Companies have learned that knowledge is one of their most valuable resources—and hiring people like Ellen Knapp to find ways to retain and expand on that knowledge will most likely become an increasingly widespread strategy.

Source: Marianne Kolbasuk McGee (ed.), "The Person in the Know," *Information Week*, May 27, 1996, p. 94; http://techweb.cmp.com/iw. Photo courtesy of Coopers & Lybrand.

A company's information systems personnel typically work in an IS department as computer programmers, systems analysts, and computer operators and in a number of other positions. They may also fill supporting roles for the work of other functional departments. In addition to technical skills, information systems personnel also need skills in written and verbal communication, knowledge of organizations and how they operate, and the ability to work with people (users). Since they support activities throughout the organization, IS personnel must maintain the broadest possible companywide perspective.

Regardless of your chosen field or the organization for which you may work, you will almost certainly use information systems on the job. The potential to advance in your career, solve problems, realize opportunities, and meet personal goals gives you some compelling reasons to study computers and information systems. In addition to books like this one, many kinds of resources can help you maintain and expand your knowledge.

Resources for Literacy

The computer industry changes so quickly that keeping up with developments in information systems can be challenging. You can draw on many kinds of resources to keep current on new computer-related developments. Continuing education courses and seminars can provide knowledge of important trends, but these class-room sessions may not directly address specific issues that arise in your job.

Magazines and journals provide excellent coverage of computer developments and suggestions for ways that you can use them for your own benefit. These periodicals include personal computer magazines, computer industry journals, and business journals.

Personal Computer Magazines. Several excellent publications specialize in personal computer systems and applications. These magazines provide invaluable information about all aspects of buying, using, and maintaining personal computers. Their reviews of new personal computer systems, devices, and software provide especially helpful insights. Also, personal computer manufacturers and mail-order operations advertise their products in these periodicals. A short list would include:

- *PC Magazine*
- *PC World*
- *Internet World*
- *MAC World*

Computer Industry Journals. Various general computer journals report on news in the computer industry and profile companies that provide computer equipment, software, and services. These journals are required reading for people interested in careers in computers and information systems:

- *Computerworld*
- *Datamation*
- *InfoWorld*
- *Information Week*

Business Journals. General business journals cover all kinds of developments in business, including important information about applications of computers and information systems. Anyone who expects to work in a business setting should regularly read one or more of these journals:

- The *Wall Street Journal*
- *Business Week*
- *Forbes*
- *Fortune*

On-line Resources. The Internet can bring a wealth of information to your computer screen to help you keep up with current developments. Usenet newsgroups collect exchanges of information and opinions on a vast array of specific topics. You can read messages from people who deal daily with information systems to learn about their problems and solutions. Also, many companies maintain sites on the World Wide Web to offer all kinds of general and technical information about their products.

- Computers have become essential resources for many people and almost all businesses.
- The value of information varies, depending on its accuracy, completeness, timeliness, and other characteristics.
- The four major functions of an IS are input, processing, output, and feedback.
- Problem solving and supporting information systems quickly become cyclical processes of analysis and adjustment rather than simple, step-by-step progressions.
- Computers perform many tasks for businesses: transaction processing, information management, decision support, and expert advice.
- Computer literacy brings valuable personal and professional benefits for today's students.

SUMMARY

1. *Explain some basic concepts about computers and information systems.* A computer is an electronic device that can execute commands to accept and process input to produce and store useful output. Computers handle several kinds of data, or raw facts, to produce information, a collection of facts organized in a way that gives them additional value beyond the value of the facts themselves. Computers help people and businesses to complete the problem-solving process, composed of the decision-making phase (including the intelligence, design, and choice stages) supplemented by implementation and monitoring.

2. *Describe the functions of an information system.* An information system is a set of interrelated components that collect, process, and store input and disseminate information as an output. Feedback ensures that the system collects the right input and processes it in a way that produces the desired output.

3. *List the elements of a computer-based information system.* Within a computer-based information system, hardware includes physical equipment and devices. Software is programmed sequences of instructions for the computer. A database is an organized collection of facts and information that provides the data resource of IS activities. Telecommunications components link an information system to outside systems and resources. People define the output they want from an information system and organize IS resources to gather, process, and store the right input to generate that output. Procedures define how people operate an information system to collect and process data so that it produces and stores information as intended.

4. *Discuss the business applications of computer-based information systems.* Businesses use computer-based information systems to help them accomplish goals, including generating profits. Transaction processing systems track the results of business exchanges. Management information systems provide information to managers about routine operations. Decision support systems help business decision makers study and resolve specific problems. Expert systems attempt to capture and give access to the experience of specialists in many fields.

5. *Cite important reasons for studying information systems.* You should study information systems because they offer substantial personal and professional benefits. By offering speed, reliability, large storage capacity, and low cost, a computer-based information system can help users to improve both efficiency and effectiveness for themselves and their organizations. You should seek to develop computer literacy, which involves knowledge of and skills with computer hardware and software, so that you can use your knowledge later in your career to understand how and why individuals and organizations use data and information.

 ## Key Terms

information system 4
computer 4
data 5
file 6
program file 6
document file 6
Information 6
Internet 7
problem-solving process 7
decision-making phase 8
intelligence stage 9
design stage 9
choice stage 9

implementation stage 9
monitoring stage 10
input 11
processing 12
output 12
feedback 12
computer-based information system (CBIS) 15
hardware 15
software 15
database 16
telecommunications 16
procedures 16

first-generation computer 16
second-generation computer 16
third-generation computer 16
business 16
transaction processing system (TPS) 18
management information system 18
decision support system (DSS) 19
expert system 20
efficiency 23
effectiveness 23
computer literacy 24

 ## Concept Quiz

Mark "true" or "false" after each of the following statements.

1. Computers have actually been around for about 100 years. _____
2. Information is the same thing as data. _____
3. In general, effectiveness and efficiency of a business depend on people sending and receiving the right information to the right people at the right time. _____
4. The decision-making phase encompasses three stages of the problem-solving process (intelligence, design, and choice). _____
5. Computers are now capable of taking over the problem-solving process. _____

Fill in the blank left in each of the following statements.

6. _____ to an information system is the raw data that the system will manipulate.

7. _____ consists of programmed sequences of instructions for the computer and the user.
8. _____ are the most important element in most computer-based information systems.
9. Benefits of computers include _____, _____, _____, and _____.
10. Efficiency measures _____.
11. Effectiveness measures _____.

Answer each of the following questions.

12. What is computer literacy?
13. What types of careers are available in information systems?
14. What are the general types of resources available to help you develop computer literacy?

 ## Discussion Questions

1. In what ways might a computer help during the different stages of the problem-solving process if a domestic airline wanted to determine whether it would be feasible to expand its service overseas?

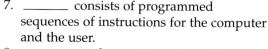

2. What might be some of the benefits of a computer-based information system to a restaurant chain that operates locations across the country?

3. Choose a professional field that interests you, such as financial services, health-care management, environmental science, manufacturing, any type of sales, or the like. Based on your reading in this chapter, in what ways do you think computer literacy could help you in your career in this field?

4. Making an automobile purchase has always been a complicated task. In what ways do you think Cars @ Cost (chapter opening photo) will change the way cars are bought and sold in the United States? What steps might auto sellers have to take to remain competitive? Would you buy a car this way? Why or why not?

Team Activity

The class divides into groups of three to five. In your group, choose one of the following tasks (or select one of your own): supermarket checkout; simple bank transaction; taking and filling catalog orders from customers. As a team, think of all the steps a clerk, bank teller, or mail-order employee would have to take manually to complete the task. Include problems or complications that might arise. Then brainstorm the ways a computerized information system would simplify, quicken, and make the process more accurate.

Applying IT

1. Imagine that you work for a small company that manufactures T-shirts and sweatshirts with school logos on them. The company is barely surviving, and so far management has resisted installing and using a management information system. Write a memo to the company president explaining the different ways you think the company could benefit—and ultimately profit—from the use of a management information system.

2. Investigate some of the resources available to you to develop your computer literacy. If possible, buy one or two of the computer magazines or computer industry journals and one of the business journals (or borrow them from the library) listed in the chapter. Compare the approach each takes to the use of computers. Then start your own informal bibliography on your computer, listing the titles and authors of major articles you think you might find helpful in the future, along with the name and date of the periodical. Add to your bibliography any time during this course.

CASE

The City of Phoenix

Information technology is blooming in the desert. A decade ago, the city of Phoenix began reengineering its management information systems (MIS) to a faster, more efficient, more current system designed to serve, not just city employees, but its citizens as well. As a result, the city now employs 200 workers in its Information Technology Department (ITD) and has trained others throughout city government to use the new information technology.

Here is what the new technology does for Phoenix and its citizens. The new $7.6 million geographic information system (GIS) combines census, geographic, infrastructure, and zoning data in a common database that allows Public Works Department managers to determine the best routes for trash collection. It allows fire and police department managers to determine quickly the best route for personnel to take to an emergency situation, based on population density of an area and the age of the buildings involved. With computer-aided dispatch, emergency workers can track important data through mobile data terminals (MDTs), and all data about an incident are compiled in a special database for future reference. Deputy Fire Chief Harry Beck believes that the system has significantly increased the speed with which emergency personnel can respond to a situation.

Citizens of Phoenix also now have easy, rapid access to their government as well as more convenient city services. The central library now has an electronic card catalog and a book-ordering system linked to other libraries through the Internet. City buses can allow passengers to pay with their Visas or MasterCards. The city also has a Web site (www.ci.phoenix.az.us) that offers guidelines for doing business with the city, city job listings, city-oriented entertainment schedules, and so forth. Citizens who don't have their own computers can still use the system by visiting one of 30 community centers scattered throughout the city that are equipped with PCs. Response from residents so far has been largely positive. "I'm very excited," says Ethel M. Griffin, a senior citizen. "We have a lot of young seniors in Phoenix, and they're interested in new things to help improve their quality of life."

City employees have had to make the adjustment in their careers to the new technology, but most seem willing. "We found people were more than happy to get rid of paper," notes Deputy City Clerk Jeannie Miller. City Manager Frank Fairbanks adds, "Very, very few people did not make the transition. They feel ownership. They're actively engaged in what's involved to improve the systems."

Fairbanks and other city officials believe that their government must keep pace with private business technologically if the city is to continue to offer competitive services (thus attracting business and residents). "As the private sector improves its product delivery and quality of service, we need to be every bit as fast, every bit as efficient and every bit as willing to break new ground."

But perhaps senior citizen Ethel Griffin says it best: "It's the way to go—the way of the future."

Questions

1. In addition to the benefits mentioned above, what other benefits might the city of Phoenix and its residents enjoy from its new use of information technology?
2. What might be some of the pitfalls that the city might encounter in its attempt to engage people in the use of information technology?
3. Other than those mentioned above, in what ways might the city be able to use decision support systems and expert systems?

Source: Tom Field, "Phoenix Rising," *CIO*, July 1996, pp. 87–102.

Answers to Concept Quiz

1. false **2.** false **3.** true **4.** true **5.** false **6.** Input
7. Software **8.** People **9.** speed, reliability, large storage
capacity, low cost **10.** an amount of work produced for a
given amount of resources consumed **11.** how well
people or organizations realize their goals **12.** Computer
literacy is a basic knowledge of computer systems and
equipment and how they function. **13.** Careers available
in information systems include computer programming,
systems analysis, and computer operation, as well as
supporting roles for the work of other departments.
14. Resources for literacy include personal computer
magazines, computer industry journals, business
journals, and on-line sites.

CHAPTER 2

Hardware: Input, Processing, Output, and Storage Devices

CHAPTER OUTLINE

Computer Systems: Integrating the Power of Technology
Computer System Types
    Types of General-purpose Computer Systems
    Centralized, Distributed, and Decentralized Systems
Computer System Components
Processing Hardware
    Physical Form of Computer Data
    CPU Characteristics: Speed
    Additional Forms of Memory
    Multiprocessing
    System Unit: Housing for Processing and Memory Hardware
Secondary Storage Hardware
    Sequential and Direct Access
    Magnetic Tape Drives
    Magnetic Disks
    Optical Disks
    Other Storage Alternatives
    Secondary Storage in the Information System
Input and Output Hardware: Gateways to a Computer System
    Speed and Functionality of Input and Output Hardware
    Input Hardware
    Output Hardware
Equipment Upgrades: Responding to Change
Hardware Buyer's Guide

Computer hardware has been freed from the desktop and two hands. Enter hands-free computing. Xybernaut Corporation has introduced the Mobile Assistant: a voice/activated, wearable PC. The Mobile Assistant is specially designed for active workers, such as technicians, mechanics, and inspectors, who alternately use their hands to access/enter data and perform their jobs. The head-mounted miniature VGA display is suspended in front of one eye, allowing the user to see both the computer image and the real world simultaneously. The processor unit, worn on a belt, is essentially a miniaturized desktop computer that weighs under 3 pounds! Hands-free mobile computing is now a reality. (Photo courtesy of Xybernaut Corporation.)

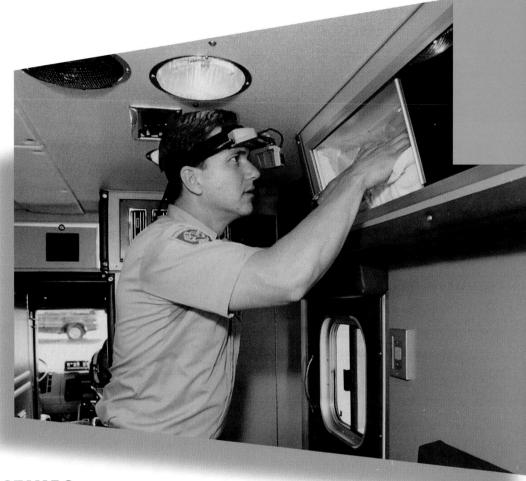

LEARNING OBJECTIVES

After completing Chapter 2, you will be able to:

1. Explain the contribution of technology to a business information system.
2. Describe the power, speed, and capacity characteristics of processing and memory devices.
3. List the access methods, capacity, and portability characteristics of secondary storage devices.
4. Demonstrate the functions and contributions of input and output devices.
5. Distinguish among types of computer systems.

To most people, *computer* means a metal or plastic box that does complicated things, apparently by some kind of magic. When they think of computers, they think of hardware. In fact, a computer-based information system includes much more than mysterious boxes. It combines hardware, software, databases, telecommunications components, people, and procedures to create an organized unit that inputs, processes, and outputs data and information.

This chapter explains the activities and characteristics of the equipment that performs the input, processing, and output functions of an information system. It tells what happens when you tap on the keys or click the mouse, how the processing circuitry transforms your input, and how the system shows the results of your work to you and others.

Professionals who are responsible for buying computers for business rely on information about the capabilities of various kinds of hardware to make difficult decisions about what equipment their organization needs. And if you are setting up your own system, you want to make a wise choice, too. One overriding consideration should govern this choice: how each piece of hardware supports the objectives of the information system and its goals. By carefully combining devices with the appropriate capabilities, you can create an effective system.

COMPUTER SYSTEMS: INTEGRATING THE POWER OF TECHNOLOGY

computer system

a collection of devices, centered on at least one electronic processing mechanism, that work together to input, process, store, and output data and information

A **computer system** is a collection of devices, centered on at least one electronic processing mechanism, that work together to input, process, store, and output data and information. The phrase "work together" implies more complicated arrangements than just connecting cables between boxes. To build a system, you must select and organize components to create the best possible tradeoff between a system's performance (measured by efficiency and effectiveness) and its cost, control, and complexity.

If you decide to restore a classic sports car, you don't want to waste the engine's horsepower by installing a transmission that cannot deliver full power to the wheels. Instead, you try to match components to the use of the vehicle. Your car requires a special type of engine, transmission, and tires. Someone with a Model T Ford would choose different hardware.

Also, you must consider more than just how much of the engine's power your transmission can deliver to the wheels (efficiency and effectiveness). Since you don't have an unlimited budget, you must balance performance against cost. You must also consider reliability (control) and ensure that you can work with the particular arrangement of gears (complexity).

If you are a member of the information systems staff for a business, you must assemble computer systems with the same attention to effectiveness, efficiency, and balance. Consider the Chicago Board of Trade (CBOT), an organization that oversees trades of contracts for exchanges of commodities like corn and soybeans. Buyers and sellers trade hundreds of contracts in each commodity every day by calling out bids in the CBOT's trading pits.

To build its business even more, however, the CBOT might establish an organizational goal of generating still more commodity trades. This decision would define an objective for its information system. To achieve the organization's goal, the transaction processing system might have to quickly display the price of the last contract traded to all potential traders so they do not have to wait for information to decide on their own trades. In turn, the TPS would need effective computer hardware to process information about each trade without delay.

To maximize speed, the CBOT's transaction processing system might provide voice-activated input devices so traders in the pit can instantly enter data about their trades. But this arrangement would sacrifice another major objective of the CBOT's transaction processing system: to record reliable and accurate information. Voice-activated input devices might not distinguish between the voices of several traders all shouting at once. In the noisy trading pit, the input devices might capture inaccurate data. For this reason, the CBOT places data-entry clerks near the pits to enter the latest trade data into the computer system. They may work more slowly than the voice input, but they help the CBOT to meet its need for reliable and accurate information.

Clearly, a computer system needs components that help it to satisfy the demands of the larger information system and the organization as a whole. The computer hardware actually forms a subsystem within the larger information system, but most people refer to it simply as a *computer system*. When you see this term, remember that the computer system serves objectives determined by those of the information system and the organization.

Each of these three systems—computer system, IS, and organization—uses interdependent components, such as input devices, people, procedures, and goals. Because the needs and performance of one system affect the others, you must evaluate all of them according to the same standards of effectiveness and efficiency, given the limitations of cost, control, and complexity.

The choice of computer hardware also must consider the current and future needs of all three systems. A particular computer system should always allow for adjustments to accommodate later improvements in the overall information system. Otherwise, it would be obsolete in no time. Whether you are planning to use a computer for personal or business use, you need to understand some hardware basics to be able to evaluate the components and their performance.

COMPUTER SYSTEM TYPES

Hardware components combine to form different types of computer systems with varying levels of power and complexity. The type of computer needed depends on its intended use. Some of the simplest computers serve special, limited purposes. Modern car designs incorporate processing hardware to control engine functions and adjust for changes in driving conditions. Systems like these are called **embedded computers**, because they act entirely within larger mechanical or electrical systems without direct control by operators. They receive input through engine sensors; as output, they activate mechanisms to control operating conditions like fuel–air mixture, spark timing, and ABS brakes. Other special-purpose, embedded computers control operations in a wide range of products from kitchen appliances to military weapons and spacecraft.

embedded computers

systems that act entirely within larger mechanical or electrical systems without direct control by operators

Some businesses rely on stand-alone, special-purpose computers. For example, Blockbuster Video and IBM tested an in-store, special-purpose computer system to help customers preview videos and identify available movie titles that meet specified criteria.[1] The system generated text, sound, and video output to assist a customer's search for a particular video based on input about the actors, title, or other partial information (e.g., "It had Tom Cruise in it, and I think the title had something to do with guns").

Still, general-purpose computers perform most of the input, processing, output, and storage functions in widely varied information systems. Companies complete the business processing tasks discussed throughout this book primarily using general-purpose computer systems. All of these systems incorporate hardware for processing, memory, storage, input, and output along with software and other components.

Auto mechanics rely on computers to diagnose problems or test emissions. (Source: William Taufic / The Stock Market.)

personal computers (PCs)

relatively small and inexpensive computers (also called microcomputers)

desktop computers

computers that place enough processing speed, memory, and storage capacity for complex business computing tasks on the surface of a desk

Types of General-purpose Computer Systems

General-purpose computers range in size, price, and complexity from an inexpensive personal computer that sits on the user's lap or a desktop to enormously expensive supercomputers housed in special large, climate-controlled facilities. These systems display an equally wide range of capabilities.

Personal Computers. Relatively small and inexpensive **personal computers (PCs)**, sometimes called *microcomputers*, have become familiar parts of daily life since their introduction in the late 1970s and early 1980s. While early personal computers functioned primarily as stand-alone systems for individual users, today's information systems often tie them into networks to share hardware, software, and data and to distribute the processing workload. These flexible and powerful networks have replaced larger, more expensive centralized systems for many applications.

Several types and sizes of systems fit into the category of personal computers. **Desktop computers**, the most common PC configuration, place enough processing speed, memory, and storage capacity for complex business computing tasks on the surface of a desk. Their blend of low cost and powerful functions has made them standard business tools; more than 30 million desktop PCs support information system needs in both large corporations and corner stores (see the "Who's Who" box on Michael S. Dell). Inexpensive network computers (NC), costing under $1000 for some models such as JavaStation by Sun Microsystems, are stripped down personal computers designed to work with network and the Internet.

Multimedia computers are PCs with hardware that allow users to input and output combinations of text, data, sound, and images. They incorporate input and output devices to form integrated systems for processing and displaying appealing, stimulating output. Today, many computers come equipped with multimedia capabilities, and upgrade kits allow users to add the required equipment to existing systems.

This kind of computer expands input capabilities by allowing the user to record sound through a microphone and capture images with a digital camera. A sound board fits in an expansion slot inside the system unit to process high-quality stereo sound, which the system outputs through speakers to produce stunning effects. A CD-ROM drive allows a multimedia PC to take advantage of many exciting programs, such as encyclopedias, reference materials, art guides, and more. While most multimedia PCs are desktop systems, some smaller computers also provide multimedia capabilities. The IBM Aptiva S Series can produce full stereo sound, respond to voice commands, and answer the phone. This personal computer has a sleek multimedia monitor with built-in speakers, and a pop-up media console that puts the disk and CD-ROM drive in easy reach.

IBM Aptiva S Series. (Source: Courtesy of IBM Corporation.)

WHO'S WHO

Michael Dell/Dell Computer

His name is Michael Dell, and he's the youngest-ever chief executive of a Fortune 500 company. He founded Dell Computer as a college student at the University of Texas, when he began to buy, rebuild, and resell computers. Now Dell Computer Corporation is the world's leading direct marketer of computer systems and one of the largest computer system manufacturers, with sales of $5.3 billion.

Dell's idea was to offer computers directly to the public (mostly business customers) without the cost of a middleman. The business community responded. In fact, Dell has surpassed IBM and HP in desktop sales to the American business market. It is now the second-largest PC manufacturer to corporate America. Most of Dell's customers are large corporate accounts, government agencies, and educational institutions.

Currently Dell Computer designs, develops, produces, markets, and services a complete range of computer systems that range from notebooks to networks.

All of these activities focus on the needs of the customer. "Dell provides continued resources beyond its products including dedicated account executives who work on-site with large business customers to provide direct, one-to-one support, and technical support via the phone and the Internet. Direct customer contact gives Dell first-hand knowledge of what customers want and need; this information is passed on to designers and service providers.

Dell has 9,000 employees in the United States and overseas subsidiaries. "I kind of saw the world a little differently than most people, even in high school. I look at everything as an opportunity," says Michael Dell. A good philosophy for an entrepreneur. Perhaps a good philosophy for everyone.

Sources: "The Story of Dell's Success," http://www.dell.com/corpinfo/success.html (October 4, 1996); press release, "Dell Overtakes IBM and HP in the U.S. Corporate PC Market," July 2, 1996; press release, "Dell #1 in Direct Sales to Federal Government," June 6, 1996. Photo courtesy of Dell Computer Corporation.

---

laptop computers

PCs that are small and lightweight enough to fit inside a briefcase

handheld personal computers

PCs that are smaller and more portable than laptops but are typically not as powerful

A **laptop computer** is a PC small and lightweight enough to fit inside a briefcase. The smallest and lightest laptops, called *notebook* and *subnotebook computers,* provide similar computing power. Some of them fit into docking stations that connect them with desktop computers to share data and enhance storage and processing capabilities. Small PCs continue to gain popularity because of their combination of portability and performance.

Handheld personal computers (HPC) are still smaller PCs, which increase portability still further, but they are typically not as powerful. These systems often include communications capabilities to allow contact with larger, stationary information systems. Apple Computer introduced its Newton personal digital assistant to offer note-taking, scheduling, and telecommunications functions in a unit the size of a pad of paper. Parking enforcement officers in Chicago record violations using more specialized handheld computers with telecommunications capabilities. These units transmit data to local police stations, where information systems instantly update drivers' traffic records. Revenue from ticket collection has doubled since the devices began increasing the efficiency of the enforcement officers' work,

Laptop computers are increasingly popular due to their performance and portability.
(Source: Courtesy of IBM Corporation.)

The Apple Newton Message Pad is a pen-based handheld computer that is designed to recognize handwriting as well as send and receive electronic messages via modem or wireless communications. (Source: Property of AT&T Archives. Reprinted with permission of AT&T.)

and traffic now flows more smoothly through the Loop (the local name for Chicago's downtown area).[2]

A pair of handheld computers by Hewlett-Packard have proved useful in medicine. The PalmVue wireless computer allows a doctor to monitor a patient's vital signs and prescribe treatments without having to sit continually at the bedside. The computer's built-in paging function helps other medical professionals to alert the doctor in case of important developments. The PalmVue ECGstat allows a cardiologist to receive and review the results of an electrocardiogram test to evaluate the electrical activity of a patient's heart.

workstations

advanced personal computers with more memory, processing capacity, and graphics capabilities than standard PCs.

minicomputers

larger systems that can accommodate several users at one time

Workstations and Minicomputers. **Workstations** are advanced personal computers with more memory, processing capacity, and graphics capabilities than standard PCs. Workstations support highly technical design work for new products and other extremely complex computing tasks. As ordinary personal computers become more powerful, an increasingly narrow division separates them from workstations.

Minicomputers are larger systems that can accommodate several users at one time. These systems often include additional storage devices with more capacity than those of personal computers. Increased computing power as compared with PCs allows minicomputers to support varied transaction processing activities, including payroll, inventory control, and invoicing. Their excellent processing and decision-support capabilities make them ideal tools for small to medium-sized organizations like manufacturers, real estate brokerages, and retail operations with multiple stores.

mainframe computers

large, powerful computers with impressive processing capabilities that meet the needs of medium-sized to large companies and universities

supercomputers

the largest computer systems with the fastest processing speeds

Mainframes and Supercomputers. **Mainframe computers** are large, powerful computers with impressive processing capabilities that meet the needs of medium-sized to large companies and universities. Links between mainframes and other computers can form powerful and flexible systems. An international hotel chain, for example, might use a large mainframe at headquarters to handle reservations, payroll, purchasing, and other central functions for the entire chain. Smaller computers at individual hotels could handle local processing like scheduling workers; in addition, they might receive information from the mainframe and return data on local operations. This same type of setup serves major airlines, national retail chains, grocery stores, and other organizations that have significant computing requirements.

For even larger processing tasks, researchers, the military, and other high-end users rely on **supercomputers,** the largest computer systems with the fastest processing speeds. Some large oil companies, for example, use supercomputers to perform sophisticated analyses of detailed data to help them explore for oil. IBM's

POWERparallel supercomputer is increasingly working in business environments with more than 400 systems shipped to customers worldwide per year. And IBM is developing an ultrasupercomputer for government use that is expected to do three trillion operations per second.

Centralized, Distributed, and Decentralized Systems

In addition to the type of computer used, computer systems may be categorized according to location and work performed by the components. An organization may divide its processing work between two or more computer systems. Such a system can be centralized, distributed, or decentralized. *Centralized systems* unify many diverse processing functions in a single location or facility to offer the highest degree of control. Centralized systems use large computers, usually mainframes.

A *distributed system* is a move away from centralized systems, allowing more independence. Computers are placed at different locations but are connected via telecommunications devices. Consider a manufacturing company head-quartered in New York with plants in Chicago and Atlanta, each with its own computer system. By connecting all the computer systems, a distributed system allows all the locations to share data and programs. At the same time, distributed processing also allows each plant to perform its own processing—say, for inventory—while the New York computer system coordinates and processes other applications, like payroll.

A *decentralized system* places processing devices at various locations, which operate independently. A drugstore chain, for example, may operate each location as a separate entity. Each outlet has its own computer system that works independently of the computers at other stores.

COMPUTER SYSTEM COMPONENTS

FIGURE 2.1

Hardware Components
Computer systems include input devices, processing devices, output devices, and storage devices comparable to those in a paper-based office.

Hardware components perform the input, processing, storage, and output functions in a computer system. To understand how these devices work together, consider an analogy from a paper-based office (see Figure 2.1).

Imagine a one-room office occupied by one person. This person performs processing functions in the office, including organizing and manipulating data; in a computer system, the central processing unit handles these tasks. The worker's memory holds data needed to complete extremely short-term processing; a collection of electronic circuits called *register storage* does this for the computer.

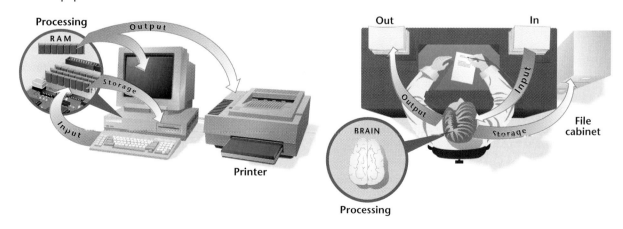

Processing — RAM — Output — Storage — Input — Printer

Out — In — Input — Output — Storage — File cabinet — BRAIN — Processing

The surface of the desk temporarily stores data for the current job, so the worker can quickly find it as needed; primary storage, also called random access memory (RAM), fulfills this role in the computer system. File cabinets provide more permanent storage for data that the worker does not need for the job at hand; a computer system includes secondary storage components like disk drives for this purpose. Trays for incoming and outgoing mail bring new data (input) into the office system and carry processed paperwork (output) outside the office; similarly, the computer might get input from its keyboard and generate output through a monitor and printer.

The following sections of the chapter explain the functions of these elements of the computer system. They also highlight the contributions of particular components to the larger information system.

PROCESSING HARDWARE

Hardware that organizes and manipulates (processes) data performs a critical function for a computer system. A computer accomplishes this processing through an interplay between one or more central processing units and primary storage. Each **central processing unit (CPU)** consists of electronic circuits that perform essential tasks to handle and manipulate data. At the heart of a personal computer's CPU, circuits densely etched onto a silicon wafer form a **microprocessor chip,** which completes basic processing functions. Surrounding circuitry completes the CPU and links it to the rest of the computer system.

Three associated elements make up a CPU: the arithmetic/logic unit, the control unit, and register areas. The **arithmetic/logic unit (ALU)** performs mathematical calculations and makes logical comparisons to execute program instructions. The **control unit** accesses program instructions sequentially and coordinates the flow of instructions and data into and out of the ALU, the registers, primary storage, and even secondary storage and output components. *Registers* are high-speed storage areas within the CPU that temporarily hold small units of program instructions and data immediately before, during, and after execution by the CPU.

Primary storage, also called **random access memory (RAM),** *main memory,* or just *memory,* is closely associated with the CPU. RAM holds program instructions and data for the CPU to process; it provides a temporary storage area—that is, an area that relies on a continuing flow of electrical current to store data. Data disappear if current no longer flows to RAM circuits, as when the user turns off the computer's power switch or disconnects its power cord from the electrical outlet. A computer can lose valuable data from RAM when electrical power fails or someone accidentally stumbles over its power cord.

The Form of Computer Data

Computers do not understand the significance of pieces of data or instructions they handle. Their memory and processing components actually store and process pulses of electricity called **bits** (short for *BInary digiTS*). Each tiny circuit in RAM and the CPU holds either electrical current (representing a 1 bit) or no current (representing a 0 bit). Groups of 1 and 0 bits form patterns that represent data and instructions with meaning to the user.

By convention, computers handle groups of eight bits called **bytes.** Each byte represents a unit of data such as the letter *A*. The capacity of both primary and secondary storage (RAM and disk drives, for example) is measured in kilobytes, megabytes, and gigabytes. A **kilobyte** (abbreviated *KB*) equals

---

central processing unit (CPU)

electronic circuits that perform essential tasks to handle and manipulate data

microprocessor chip

circuits densely etched onto a silicon wafer

arithmetic/logic unit (ALU)

the CPU element that performs mathematical calculations and makes logical comparisons to execute program instructions

control unit

the CPU element that accesses program instructions sequentially and coordinates the flow of instructions and data into and out of the ALU, the registers, primary storage, and even secondary storage and output components

primary storage

the memory that holds program instructions and data for the CPU to process (also called random access memory [RAM])

random access memory (RAM)

same as primary storage

bits

pulses of electricity (short for *BInary digiTS*)

bytes

groups of eight bits

kilobyte

approximately 1,000 bytes

Processing Hardware 41

approximately 1,000 bytes (actually 2^{10} or 1,024); early personal computers included 640 KB of RAM, so they could hold 640 × 1,024, or 655,360 bytes of data in main memory.

Similarly, 1 **megabyte** (abbreviated *MB*) equals approximately 1,000 KB, or 1 million bytes (actually 1,024 × 1,024 = 1,046,516). Today's applications and systems programs can require 16 to 32 MB or more of RAM to operate effectively, especially if you run multimedia or other graphics programs. Finally, 1 **gigabyte** (abbreviated *GB*) equals approximately 1,000 MB or 1 billion bytes (1,024 × 1,024 × 1,024 = 1,073,741,824 bytes). Today's personal computer systems usually include at least 1 gigabyte of secondary storage, and this requirement is growing.

CPU Characteristics: Speed

To achieve the critical goals of efficient processing and timely output, people who use a computer need to be able to measure and compare CPU processing speeds. These measures include the time required to complete one machine cycle, clock speed, and others.

Machine Cycle Time. A computer executes instructions so quickly that machine cycle times are measured in fractions of a second. (A machine cycle is the process of fetching and executing an instruction.) Less powerful computers achieve machine cycle times ranging from milliseconds (one 1-thousandth of a second) and microseconds (one 1-millionth of a second). More powerful ones complete machine cycles in nanoseconds (one 1-billionth of a second) and picoseconds (one 1-trillionth of a second).

Users have trouble understanding such tiny periods of time. They may more easily grasp a measure of machine cycle time that divides their practical tasks into individual instructions and then calculates how many instructions the computer can execute in a second. This process gives a measure called **MIPS** (for *Millions of Instructions Per Second*) to state speeds for computer systems of all sizes.

Clock Speed. Each CPU produces electronic pulses at a predetermined rate, called the **clock speed,** that affects machine cycle time. The control unit of the CPU triggers the various stages of the machine cycle by following instructions built into the CPU known as *microcode.* The control unit executes microcode in time to pulses of the CPU clock, taking at least as long to process each micro-code instruction as the interval between pulses. Therefore, a CPU with a shorter interval between pulses can more rapidly execute each microcode instruction.

Clock speed is often measured in megahertz. A *hertz* is one cycle or pulse per second. A **megahertz (MHz)** value indicates millions of machine cycles per second. Clock speeds for personal computers can range from about 20 MHz to over 200 MHz.

Unfortunately, the different measurements of processing speed do not exactly correspond. Computers can require different numbers of microcode instructions to execute a single program instruction to complete a task, such as performing a calculation or printing a result. This difference in the number of instructions prevents any direct comparison between clock speed (in megahertz) and machine cycle time (in MIPS and milliseconds).

Wordlength and Bus Line Width. The computer system must move groups of bits through its circuitry to complete processing tasks. Therefore, overall system performance—particularly speed—depends heavily on the number of bits

megabyte
approximately 1,000 KB

gigabyte
approximately 1,000 MB

MIPS
a measure of speed for computer systems of all sizes (stands for *Millions of Instructions Per Second*)

clock speed
the predetermined rate at which the CPU produces electronic pulses

megahertz (MHz)
a measurement for clock speed that indicates millions of machine cycles per second

FIGURE 2.2

Bus Line Width
A 32-bit bus line can carry more data between devices at one time than a 16-bit bus line can carry.

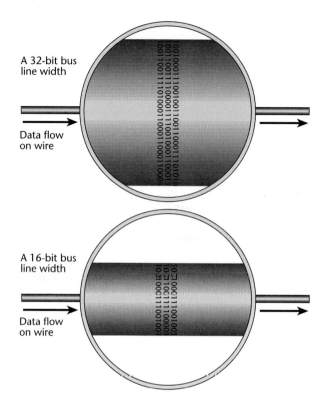

A 32-bit bus line width

Data flow on wire

A 16-bit bus line width

Data flow on wire

wordlength

a measure of the size of the CPU

bus line

electronic circuits that connect processing components

bus line width

the measurement that determines the number of bits a bus line can transfer at any one time

the CPU can process at any one time. The **wordlength** of the CPU is a measure of its size. A CPU with a wordlength of 32 bits can process 32 bits of data in one machine cycle.

Data moves from the CPU to other system components via **bus lines,** the electronic circuits that connect processing components. The **bus line width** determines the number of bits a bus line can transfer at any one time. For example, a 32-bit bus line can transfer 32 bits of data at a time (see Figure 2.2).

Table 2.1 summarizes some important performance characteristics of common personal computer CPUs. Wordlengths and bus line widths range from 16 to 64 bits. Notice that bus line width *usually* matches wordlength in personal computers. This match helps to balance the capabilities of different components for optimal system performance.

TABLE 2.1

	Common Machine Cycle Speeds, Wordlengths, and Bus Line Widths		
MICROPROCESSOR	CLOCK SPEED (MHZ)	WORDLENGTH (BITS)	BUS LINE WIDTH (BITS)
386SX	8–28	16	16
386DX	16	32	16
68030	16–40	16–32	16–32
486SX	25	32	32
486DX	66	32	32
68040	40–80	32	32
Pentium	100	64	64
Pentium Pro	150–200	64	64

In CPUs that maintain compatible wordlengths and bus widths, larger word-lengths provide more processing power. Computers with larger wordlengths can process more data in the same machine cycle. Larger data-handling capabilities allow a CPU to address more locations in RAM, so it can draw data from larger segments of primary memory. Systems that need especially large amounts of memory must also include CPUs with large address bus widths and wordlengths to take advantage of available RAM. Once again, components must balance capabilities to create a smoothly functioning system.

CISC and RISC Processors. You may have heard recently about "power" chips and wondered what that meant. Most of the processors shown in Table 2.1 share a standard method for including basic processing instructions. This standard, *complex instruction set computing (CISC)*, includes electronic circuitry in a central processing unit for as many basic microcode instructions as possible. In the mid-1970s, John Cocke of IBM recognized that most of a CPU's operations involve only about 20 percent of the available microcode instructions. He thought that a CPU might gain speed if the design could reduce unneeded microcode instructions.

This insight led to a new standard for chip design: *reduced instruction set computing (RISC)*. RISC microprocessors include circuitry only for essential microcode instructions. That difference allows them to complete processing tasks based on this core set of instructions faster than CISC chips can perform the same tasks. The less sophisticated microcode instruction sets also make RISC chips less expensive to produce than CISC chips, and they still provide reliable processing performance. Both IBM and Apple offer RISC-powered computers, called Power PCs and Power Macs.

Additional Forms of Memory

The layout of a computer's processing components locates random access memory (RAM) close to the CPU to minimize access time and maximize processing speed. Recall that this type of memory provides the CPU with a working storage area that gives rapid access to program instructions and data.

A computer system includes other types of memory in addition to RAM. **Read-only memory (ROM)** provides a nonvolatile storage area for data and instructions that do not need to change. ROM serves primarily to store programs and data that support the computer's internal functions. ROM chips maintain fixed circuit states, so they do not lose data when the computer loses power.

Cache memory provides an area for high-speed primary storage from which a processor can access data more rapidly than from RAM (see Figure 2.3). Cache memory functions somewhat like a personal phone list. While a person's private phone list may contain only 1 percent of all the numbers in the local phone directory, the person will very likely call a number from his or her own list next. Cache memory works on the same principle. It stores frequently used data in easily accessible, extremely fast memory rather than in slower RAM. The CPU can access a desired item of data or instruction more quickly from the limited selection in cache memory than it could from the larger set in main memory. The CPU first searches cache memory for data. If the CPU cannot find the needed data in cache memory, it then goes to main memory. Because cache memory is updated frequently, the CPU can often find what it needs from cache memory. The CPU can thus fetch instructions faster, raising the overall performance of the computer system.[3]

read-only memory (ROM)

memory that provides a nonvolatile storage area for data and instructions that do not need to change

cache memory

memory that provides an area for high-speed primary storage from which a processor can access data more rapidly than from RAM

FIGURE 2.3

Cache Memory
A CPU can access cache memory even faster than it can read data from RAM. A cache controller determines how often the CPU needs data from RAM. It transfers frequently used data to cache memory and deletes data that goes out of use. The CPU can access the limited data in cache memory more rapidly than it can read the larger selection in RAM.

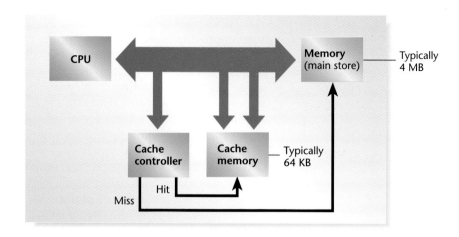

multiprocessing

processing activities completed by more than one central processing unit

coprocessor

an element that speeds processing tasks by executing specific types of instructions while the main CPU circuitry works on other types

parallel processing

a form of multiprocessing that speeds the computer's data handling and manipulation by linking several general-purpose processors to operate at the same time

massively parallel processing (MPP)

processing that combines a large number of powerful processors to operate together

system unit

a cabinet in the computer system that houses its processing components

Multiprocessing

As the term implies, **multiprocessing** refers to processing activities completed by more than one central processing unit. In one form of multiprocessing, a **coprocessor** speeds processing tasks by executing specific types of instructions while the main CPU circuitry works on other types. A computer system can include coprocessors internal or external to the CPU, and they may run at clock speeds different from those of the CPU. Particular types of coprocessors perform specific functions. For example, a math coprocessor chip speeds mathematical calculations, while a graphics coprocessor chip decreases the time that a CPU needs to manipulate graphics.

Parallel Processing. Another form of multiprocessing, **parallel processing,** speeds the computer's data handling and manipulation by linking several general-purpose processors to operate at the same time (in parallel). Parallel processing poses a stiff challenge to make the processors work effectively together on separate parts of a processing task. This difficult feat requires software that allocates, monitors, and controls multiple, simultaneous processing jobs. Parallel processing divides a task, such as a business problem to calculate performance limits for the components of a new product, into several parts. A separate processor then solves each part of the problem. Finally, the system assembles results from each processor to get the final output (Figure 2.4).

Massively parallel processing (MPP) combines an even larger number of powerful processors to operate together. One computer manufacturer, for example, achieves MPP capabilities by building about 16,000 processors into a single computer system. In the past, massively parallel processing helped users to solve only complex scientific and engineering problems. As prices of processing power come down, businesses will begin to apply MPP to their problems, as well.

To give you our idea of the different speeds, sizes, and costs of the computer system presented at the beginning of the chapter, see Figure 2.5.

System Unit: Housing for Processing and Memory Hardware

The computer system houses its processing components—the CPU and RAM—in a cabinet called the **system unit** (see Figure 2.6). All other devices, such as the disk drives, monitor, and keyboard, are installed inside the system unit or linked to it.

FIGURE 2.4

Parallel Processing
This method breaks down a problem into various subproblems or parts for separate processing. Parallel processing creates challenges not to complete simultaneous processing of the subproblems but rather to logically structure the problem into independent subproblems or parts.

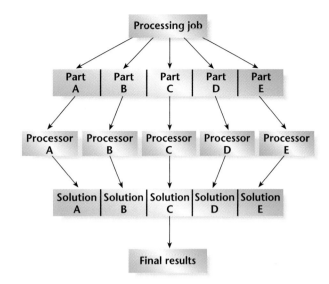

Characteristic	Personal computer	Workstation	Minicomputer	Mainframe	Supercomputer
Processor speed	30 MIPS	120 MIPS	150 MIPS	250 MIPS	60 billion–3 trillion instructions per second
RAM size	4–64 MB	16–192 MB	32–256 MB	64–1,024 MB	8,192 MB+
Physical size	Desktop	Desktop	Filing cabinet	Refrigerator	Automobile
Cost	$1,000 to over $5,000	$4,000 to over $20,000	$20,000 to over $100,000	$250,000 to over $2 million	$2.5 million to $35 million +

Types of Computer Systems
(Source: Photos courtesy of IBM Corporation and Cray Research.)

FIGURE 2.6

System Unit
The system unit is the case, usually metal or plastic, that contains the processing and memory hardware.

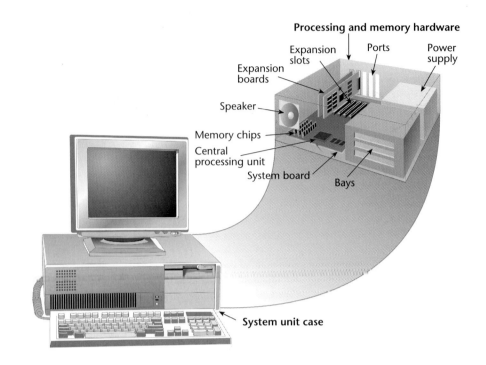

system board

a single, complex circuit board within the system unit into which the processor and memory chips normally plug

motherboard

same as system board

expansion slots

slots on the system board that accept add-on circuit boards

expansion boards

add-on circuit boards that plug into the system board to enhance system functions

ports

parts of the system board through which additional hardware components connect

serial port

a port that transmits data to an external device in series (one bit at a time)

parallel port

a port that transmits data in parallel (eight or more bits at a time)

power supply

the element that provides electrical power to the entire computer

Within the system unit, processor and memory chips normally plug into a single, complex circuit board called the **system board** or the **motherboard.** System board manufacturers usually leave space for later additions of memory or processors to increase the power of the computer. For example, you can increase RAM capacity by plugging a *single in-line memory module (SIMM)* into the system board.

The system board also contains **expansion slots** that accept add-on circuit boards—**expansion boards**—which plug in to enhance system functions. These boards might include a sound board to allow the computer system to play stereo music and a fax/modem board to send and receive fax transmissions and to connect the computer to other computer systems through a telephone line.

Additional hardware components connect to the system board through **ports.** A **serial port** transmits data to an external device in series (one bit at a time). Communications devices often connect to computers through this kind of port. A **parallel port** transmits data in parallel (eight or more bits at a time), usually to connect a printer to the computer. Other ports at the back of the system unit can connect the computer to monitors, a keyboard, a telephone, and a network (see Figure 2.7).

A **power supply** provides electrical power to the entire computer. One or more speakers provide sound output. Bays in the system unit house additional devices, such as the secondary storage devices discussed in the next section.

SECONDARY STORAGE HARDWARE

The size of random access memory plays an important part in determining the overall power of a computer system. Still, it provides only a small part of the storage required for the large sets of data and instructions that most computer systems use to complete their processing functions. Also, a computer system needs a place to store data, instructions, and information in a more permanent form than RAM can offer. Your computer system needs to retain large amounts of data even after you turn off the power; secondary storage hardware meets this need.

FIGURE 2.7

Ports
Ports like these connect the
system unit to other devices.

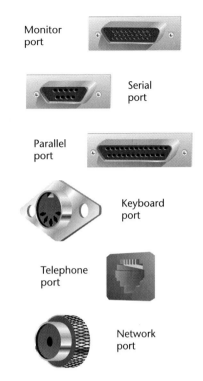

Monitor
port

Serial
port

Parallel
port

Keyboard
port

Telephone
port

Network
port

secondary storage

computer memory that offers a
nonvolatile and relatively
economical way to store large
amounts of data

Secondary storage offers a nonvolatile and relatively economical way to store large amounts of data. Most secondary storage devices save data by magnetizing selected spots on various surfaces, although some devices employ other methods. They differ primarily in the ways they access data and also in their capacity and portability characteristics. Typical costs for various secondary storage alternatives are shown in Figure 2.8.

Sequential and Direct Access

A secondary storage device can retrieve desired data through either sequential or direct access. A **sequential-access storage device (SASD)** must review and retrieve data in the same order in which they were stored. The device might arrange groups of data about specific employees by employee number. If a payroll clerk issued a command to retrieve information on Employee 125, the storage device would have to read through all the data relating to Employees 1 through 124 first.

A **direct-access storage device (DASD)** can move directly to the storage location for desired data without reading through other data in sequence. For this reason, direct-access devices usually perform faster than sequential-access devices in comparable storage and retrieval tasks. Magnetic disks and optical disks provide direct access. Figure 2.9 shows a variety of secondary storage devices that are explained in the following sections.

Magnetic Tape Drives

Magnetic tape drives, the most common sequential-access storage devices, store data by magnetizing spots to represent data bits on reels of Mylar film coated with iron oxide. Music cassettes and videocassettes store sounds and video images in a similar way.

**sequential-access storage
device**

a storage device that must review
and retrieve data in the same
order in which they were stored

direct-access storage device

a storage device that can move
directly to the storage location for
desired data without reading
through other data in sequence

magnetic tape drives

sequential-access storage devices
that store data by magnetizing
spots to represent data bits on
reels of Mylar film coated with
iron oxide

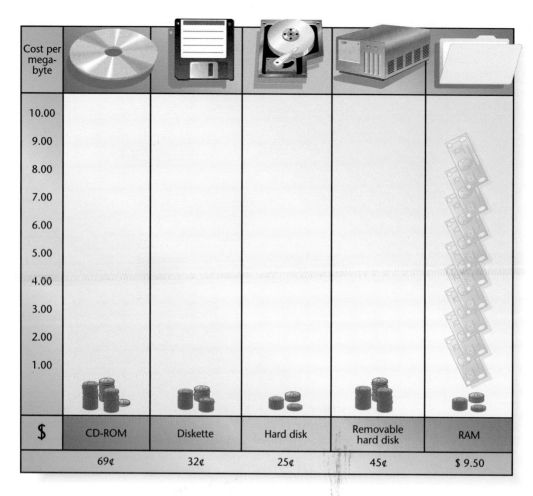

Cost per mega-byte	CD-ROM	Diskette	Hard disk	Removable hard disk	RAM
10.00					
9.00					
8.00					
7.00					
6.00					
5.00					
4.00					
3.00					
2.00					
1.00					
$	69¢	32¢	25¢	45¢	$ 9.50

FIGURE 2.8

Cost Comparison for Various Forms of Data Storage
Most forms of secondary storage cost considerably less per megabyte of capacity than RAM, although they have slower access times. A CD-ROM costs about 69 cents per megabyte, while RAM can cost around $10 per megabyte, 15 times more.

magnetic disks

secondary storage devices that store data bits by magnetizing small areas on circular storage media coated with iron oxide

hard disks

magnetic disks that store large amounts of data on thin, steel platters permanently housed in closed, metal cases

The tape drive can read data from the middle of a reel of tape only by scanning sequentially through all of the tape before the location of the desired piece of data. This disadvantage has led computer users to replace magnetic tape drives with faster direct-access devices.

Magnetic tape is often less costly than other storage media, though. This cost difference gives it an advantage in some applications, such as regular payroll processing, that require sequential access to all or most data on the tape. For example, firms generally run their payroll programs every week or two in batches, called *batch processing*. They have to produce paychecks and other payroll documents and reports for every employee, so sequential access provides data needed for this job about as effectively as direct access does.

Still, today's information systems rely on tape drives primarily to hold backup copies of information stored on magnetic disks. In this role, the tapes provide a way to replace data lost in a disk drive malfunction, fire, theft, or other mishap.

Magnetic Disks

As their main secondary storage devices, most computer systems rely on **magnetic disks,** which store data bits by magnetizing small areas on circular storage media coated with iron oxide. **Hard disks** store large amounts of data

FIGURE 2.9

Types of Secondary Storage
Secondary storage devices such as magnetic tapes and disks, optical disks, and CD-ROMs are used to store data for easy retrieval at a later date. (Source: Courtesy of Imation.)

diskettes

magnetic disks that store small amounts of data on circles of Mylar film protected in hard plastic or flexible paper covers

on thin, steel platters permanently housed in closed, metal cases; **diskettes** store smaller amounts of data on circles of Mylar film protected in hard plastic or flexible paper covers. (Flexible, paper-covered diskettes are sometimes called *floppy disks*.)

A hard disk typically remains within the system unit or connected to it by a cable. Early hard disks could hold about 20 MB of data; today's computer systems need 500 MB to over 3 GB of hard disk capacity, and that requirement is expanding at a dramatic pace. (Fortunately, prices are falling just as dramatically.)

Diskettes store fewer data than hard disks, usually 1.44 MB, but they offer the advantage of portability between systems; you can copy data from your system's hard disk onto a diskette and then read the data from another system's diskette drive. Without the protection of a hard disk's metal case and the larger system unit case, diskettes are more prone to damage and resulting loss of data. To safeguard your valuable data, observe some rules for proper care of diskettes:

1. Keep diskettes in a storage box when not in use.
2. Keep them away from food, drinks, and smoke.
3. Do not touch the diskette surface.
4. Keep diskettes away from magnets, direct sunlight, and extreme temperatures.
5. Insert a diskette into the drive's slot with care; remove it carefully as well.

read/write heads

heads that can move directly to any spot on the storage media to retrieve or store data

The **read/write heads** of both hard disk drives and diskette drives can move directly to any spot on the storage media to retrieve or store data, creating the direct-access capability of these devices (see Figure 2.10). Direct access to data allows a company's information system to respond quickly to an unpredictable series of requests. For example, suppose that the manager at Music Emporium needs to verify a customer's credit card to approve a sale of a new stereo system. The credit card company can provide information over telephone lines in a few seconds if it stores data on a hard disk. If it were to store data sequentially on magnetic tape, the drive might have to spin for a long time to locate data about a particular customer.

FIGURE 2.10

Hard Disk
Hard disks give direct access to stored data. The read/write head can move directly to the location of a desired piece of data, dramatically reducing access times, as compared with magnetic tape. (Source: Courtesy of Quantum Corporation.)

disk cartridges

high-capacity hard disk platters within removable cartridges

fragmentation

a process that spreads related data over different locations on the disk surface

defragmentation

a process that relocates parts of files to create more efficient layouts of disk space

Access times and costs vary for different types of magnetic disk devices. Diskette drives have slower access times than hard disks, and they cost more per megabyte of capacity. In addition, hard disks give quicker access to data. But the overriding factors in choosing diskettes or hard disks are portability, storage requirements, and security of data.

Disk Cartridges. Typical hard disk drives cannot match the portability of diskettes. The introduction of removable hard disks, or **disk cartridges,** has changed this relationship by placing high-capacity hard disk platters within removable cartridges. A drive unit connected to the computer's system unit accepts the cartridges, and compatible drives on other systems can accept them, as well.

Although they cost more than fixed hard disks and have much slower access times, disk cartridges combine the storage capacities of hard disks with the portability of diskettes. Current cartridges can store from 44 MB to 1 GB of data. In addition to other benefits, this portability can enhance security, since computer users can remove the cartridges and lock them up to control access to the data. (Fixed hard disks must remain with their computer systems, so unauthorized users could more easily access the stored data.) Cartridges also provide added safety for backup because they can be stored off-site. Some common cartridges in use are Syquest, Zip, and Jaz.

Redundant Array of Inexpensive Disks (RAID). The falling prices of hard disks have created another alternative for disk storage. By combining two or more inexpensive disk devices, a computer system can set up an array with a primary storage area and a backup area that stores copies of the data from the primary drive. If the primary disk drive malfunctions, the system can continue to function using the backup drive.

Applications of Magnetic Disks. Disk drives store data without much attention or intervention by the user. You must understand something about how these devices function to ensure efficient and reliable performance by your computer system, however.

When you first save a word processing document for a term paper on your hard disk, the read/write heads move in an arc to place parts of the file in locations that make access efficient for the heads. (See Figure 2.11.) As you save modified versions of the original document and store and delete other files, the disk drive may place parts of many document files at multiple locations. Over time, this **fragmentation** spreads related data over different locations on the disk surface.

While the computer system always keeps track of your data, fragmentation can dramatically slow down its retrieval and storage functions. It forces the disk drive's read/write heads to complete inefficient motions to access widely spaced locations on disk, sometimes impairing performance by over 30 percent. **Defragmentation** software can dramatically speed up computer operations on older hard disks by relocating parts of files to create more efficient layouts of disk space.

FIGURE 2.11

Fragmentation on a Hard Disk
(a) The read/write head locates parts of a file in a smooth spiral on the disk surface. (b) After the user stores modified versions of the file and adds a couple of new ones, the disk becomes fragmented. (c) Defragmentation software rearranges parts of all files in more efficient layouts.

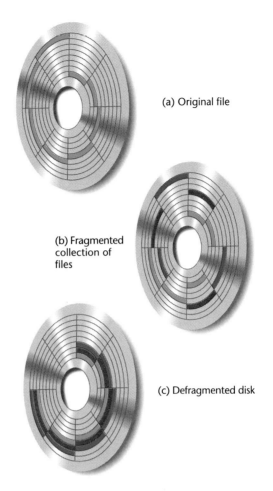

(a) Original file

(b) Fragmented collection of files

(c) Defragmented disk

data compression

a process that allows storage of more data on a given disk by completing reliable procedures to substitute sophisticated codes for original data

Data compression software allows you to store more data on a given disk by completing reliable procedures to substitute sophisticated codes for original data. For a simplified example, substitute the following codes into the sentence below: ! = disk # = store $ = data

Data compression software allows you to store more data on a given disk by completing reliable procedures to substitute sophisticated codes for original data.

The compressed version of the sentence would occupy less storage space:

Data compression software allows you to # more $ on a given ! by completing reliable procedures to substitute sophisticated codes for original $.

Disk compression can double your storage capacity without any change in hardware. It usually slows down the computer system, however, because processing steps must code the data when you store it and then decode it when you retrieve it. In addition, data compression can complicate the process of retrieving data from a damaged hard disk.

One of the most popular file compression programs is PKZIP. This shareware program is often used to compress files that are stored on a computer or sent from one computer to another. Using PKZIP can save disk space and time in sending files between computers. The compressed files have .ZIP as an extension, such as WORK.ZIP or PAPER.ZIP. Before you can use a ZIP file, it has to be decompressed (or unzipped) using the PKUNZIP program.

Optical Disks

optical disk

a rigid plastic disk permanently encoded with data

In addition to magnetic disk storage hardware, some computer systems can read data from another type of secondary storage medium—the **optical disk**. These disks function somewhat like ROM chips, since most systems cannot write data (store it) on optical disks. Instead, specialized equipment permanently encodes data on a rigid plastic optical disk by targeting lasers that physically burn pits into the coated surface.

Like a music CD player, the optical disk drive's direct-access mechanism reads data by shining a low-power laser on the surface and measuring the differences in reflected light as the beam passes over pitted areas and unpitted areas. Each pit represents a 1 bit; each unpitted area (called a *land*) represents a 0 bit (see Figure 2.12).

compact disk–read-only memory (CD-ROM)

a form of optical disk that can hold about 650 MB of data

A form of optical disk called **compact disk–read-only memory (CD-ROM)** has become a standard part of the secondary storage hardware of personal computer systems alongside hard disks and diskettes. Users benefit from vast libraries of data prerecorded on CD-ROMs. The typical disk, the size of a music CD, can hold about 650 MB of data, although new CD designs are under way that will hold 4,700 MB. Sales of CD-ROMs and hardware to read them exploded from a few thousand units in the mid-1980s to about 15 million units in 1993.[4] Newer erasable CD disk drives (CD-E) allow people to change what is stored on a CD disk. And with the introduction of CD-R (for *recordable*) drives, you can "burn" your own CD. (See "Business Bits: You Can Make Your Own CD.")

write-once, read-many (WORM) disks

optical disks on which special drives control high-powered lasers to record customized data and information

Businesses have adopted a similar technology that allows them to record data on optical disks for repeated reading. **Write-once, read-many (WORM) disks** are optical disks on which special drives control high-powered lasers to record customized data and information. Hardware with a lower-powered laser measures reflected light to read the data. Organizations use WORM disks

FIGURE 2.12

Optical Disk Storage
Lasers encode data by burning pits into the coated surface. Unburned areas are called lands. Pitted areas are read as 1 bit, lands are read as 0.

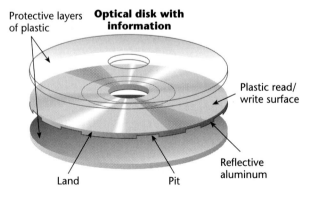

BUSINESS BITS

You Can Make Your Own CD

You've just figured out the advantages of optical disks (they are widely readable, they cost about a penny per megabyte, they have plenty of storage capacity, and they're portable). You think that your business could benefit from their use, but the CD-ROMs out there don't quite offer the content that you need. You want to make your own. The good news is that you can—through CD-R (compact disk-recordable) technology. But until recently, the cost was prohibitive ($3,000 to $7,500 for the drives and about $30 per disk, which was easily damaged during the recording process). Now the cost is more reasonable—about $1,000 for a drive and $7 per disk, with less instance of damage.

To make your first CD, experts advise that you decide what type of CD-ROM application you want to make. Does your company need a buyers' guide for products? A training disk? A product demo? Next, you must collect the content elements that will go into the CD—bitmaps, text files, video and audio clips, and so forth. If you are building a complex application such as a multimedia presentation, you'll create an overview with links among screens, objects, and data. Your CD-R drive will most likely contain premastering software that will help you image the files you want on your CD. "Burn" the disk on your CD-R drive, writing complete data in one pass. When your creation is complete, you can copy it one disk at a time through your drive, or send the master to a production company for more copies (say, more than a dozen).

These steps are designed simply to give you an idea of what the process entails. For now, go back to thinking about the decisions surrounding the uses of CD-R technology. For instance, if you plan to use CD-R for

publishing, you'll need to investigate the logistics and expense of producing multiple copies. (Some mail-order companies have discovered that distributing electronic versions of illustrated catalogs *does* make sense.) Choose a business field that interests you—finance, travel, manufacturing, health care, whatever—and begin thinking about how, as an IS professional, you could use CD-R technology to benefit your company. As you think in these terms, answer the following questions.

1. What specific CD-R project would you choose to benefit your company? How would you describe it to your boss?
2. How would you go about investigating the best hardware for your project? (Try getting on the Internet to see what you can find.)

Source: Jim Seymour, "Create Your Own CD," *PC Magazine,* April 9, 1996, pp. 99–104. Photo courtesy of Hewlett-Packard Company.

---

as a relatively inexpensive way to record data and information that users need to access repeatedly in its original, unaltered form.

A hybrid between magnetic disks and optical disks combines some of the strengths of both media. When a laser beam strikes a **magneto-optical (MO) disk,** it rearranges the molecules of a magnetic substance on the surface, creating a visual spot. A photodetector in the MO disk reader senses a reflection of a laser beam; the presence or absence of a spot indicates a bit. Demagnetizing the substrate removes the spots, effectively erasing the disk and preparing it to accept new data. Some MO drives can store more than a gigabyte of data on each removable disk.

magneto-optical (MO) disk

a hybrid between magnetic disks and optical disks

In addition, ultra-high-capacity optical disks called DVDs (for *digital video disk*) are now becoming available. DVD drives, now being developed for home entertainment systems, can store about four times the amount of material compared with a standard CD. In the future, DVD may become a popular way to store data on computers.

Since optical disks offer huge storage capacities compared with other secondary storage media, they can store large applications and programs that contain graphics and audio data. They also allow users to store data that they do not need immediately for possible later use without tying up essential system resources like hard disk capacity. Service technicians for many companies read technical data from CD-ROMs to help them locate problems and determine needed repairs.[5]

Optical disks do suffer from some minor inconveniences, such as slow access times compared with hard disks. Those who first adopted the technology had to wait for publishers to offer large amounts of materials in this format. That problem has diminished substantially, and the extensive collection of information stored on CD-ROMs—encyclopedias, home repair manuals with video demonstrations, hundreds of video games, graphics clip files—has made them important components of today's information systems.

Other Storage Alternatives

A *flash chip*, also called *flash memory*, carries electronic circuits on a silicon wafer that retain data without continuous electrical power, unlike volatile RAM. Flash chips are small and can be easily modified and reprogrammed, which makes them popular in computers, cellular phones, and other electronic products. Compared with other types of secondary storage hardware, these devices can access flash memory more quickly, they consume less power, and their smaller size helps to enhance portability. The primary disadvantage of flash memory is cost. Nonetheless, the market for flash chips exploded in the early 1990s.[6]

PC memory cards, formerly called *PCMCIA cards,* are devices the size of a credit card that contain memory chips. They fit in adapters or slots in many personal computers and function like hard disks. Although they generally cost more than traditional hard disks, these easy-to-use devices augment storage capacity without inhibiting portability. Also, they fail less often than hard disks.

Secondary Storage in the Information System

In a strong trend, business computer systems have moved away from sequential-access secondary storage devices and toward direct-access devices because it gives them speed and flexibility. In addition, both firms and individuals need large and growing capacity for data storage. Finally, the need to access data in varying situations has increased the importance of portability.

A company should choose storage hardware that supports the needs of its information system. A large manufacturer might retain an otherwise outdated magnetic tape system if that equipment could support cost-effective processing of payroll, inventory records, and customer payments. A retail store could fit all of this information on a single hard disk. To provide quick customer service, both companies would want fast disk drives in their information systems to gain direct access to large amounts of information. The manufacturer's sales representatives may need portable storage devices in laptop computers so that they can access data in their client's offices while making a sales call. A home-based business owner may need to access data for presentations to customers at their offices.

Of course, cost affects the choice of storage hardware for every computer system. Computer users can generally gain faster access to their data only by spending more money to buy faster storage devices. Portability also raises cost.

In addition to cost, security issues also influence the choice of storage hardware. Users must decide how to control secondary storage devices so they can limit access to important data and programs to authorized people.

Furthermore, a computer system may require complex memory-management programs to access and manipulate data in large secondary storage areas. An information system needs storage hardware that takes full advantage of its other components without imposing demands that the rest of the system cannot meet.

INPUT AND OUTPUT HARDWARE: GATEWAYS TO A COMPUTER SYSTEM

A user interacts most directly with a computer system through its input and output hardware. These gateways to the computer system allow people to contribute data and instructions for action by the computer's processing hardware, and they return the results of processing to the people who need that information. Input and output devices form part of the system's overall user interface, along with other hardware and software, that allow people to apply the resources of a computer system to their practical problems.

Like other computer system components, the selection of input and output devices depends on organizational goals and information system objectives. For example, suppose that the owner of Papa's Pizza wants to lower operating costs at the small chain's three restaurants by stocking only as much of each ingredient as each restaurant needs to meet customer demand. To achieve this objective, Papa's information system needs to produce reports on peak sales at each restaurant. So, Papa's computer systems must allow for easy input of data about kinds of pizza sold and provide the desired output (the reports).

To gather the proper input, waiters might enter each order at computer terminals. The system could then break down input about the orders for each restaurant to determine the items that it should keep in inventory. The output can help the owner to avoid both wasting money by storing unneeded ingredients (say, anchovies) and disappointing customers by running out of popular ones (Italian sausage).

As customers order new kinds of pizza, the information system can quickly inform the chain's owner to help speed the correct ingredients to the restaurants that need them. So, two primary information system needs—speed and functionality—determine the input and output devices that Papa's should select for its computer system.

Speed and Functionality of Input and Output Hardware

The needs of business information systems often emphasize fast results. To fulfill this requirement, a computer system needs input functions that can rapidly collect data and output functions that quickly disseminate information after processing.

To ensure accurate input into a system, a company's computer system should place input devices near the location of the transaction. Restaurants use computer systems to speed orders and collect data on inventory and sales. (Source: Courtesy of the Squirrel Companies, Inc.)

Also, specific businesses require certain kinds of output from their information systems, and those systems must gather particular kinds of input data to generate this output. These conditions create important functional demands for input and output hardware in each firm's computer system.

For example, several reporters for the *New York Times* dictate stories to computer-input devices that understand human speech.[7] This specialized hardware speeds input of a particular kind of data to the newspaper's information system, and it also allows reporters to input late-breaking stories with minimal stress. The more relaxed pace in the newsroom at the weekly *Naperville* (Illinois) *Sun* allows the paper's reporters to type their stories at general-purpose keyboards. As the needs of the information system become more specialized, the computer system must incorporate more specialized input and output devices.

Automating Input. Any business information system should capture data as close as possible to its source—that is, close to the activity that creates the data. This important principle prevents distortion of input from workers forgetting correct values before they enter data (or forgetting to enter data at all). For this reason, a company's computer system should place input devices near the locations of its transactions.

Source data automation collects input through devices that automatically capture data as transactions occur without special data-entry activities by system personnel. This method ensures accurate and timely input for the information system, while it frees workers to concentrate on customer service and other functional responsibilities. In a source data automation system, a sales clerk can enter input for the information system as customers place orders. Instead, the clerk could write out paper documents for orders to be input later at a keyboard, but this arrangement would risk loss of the documents, and the data entry could not easily verify questionable data (such as indecipherable handwriting) from the order slips. If the clerk enters data about the order while serving the customer, the information system has needed data immediately, and the clerk can confirm its accuracy from fresh memory.

Lufthansa, a German airline, uses source data automation to speed data input for its company car program. As each employee drives a company car out of the parking lot, a sensor on the gate records mileage and gas gauge data transmitted by computer equipment on-board the car. This system not only gathers input quickly and accurately, but Lufthansa estimates that it has saved the company about $20 million a year.[8]

A small restaurant like Papa's Pizza might place a special keyboard in the dining room, at which waiters would punch preprogrammed keys to indicate specific toppings and combinations. The computer system would then display order information on a screen in the kitchen. At the same time, it would add the order to the accumulated total, so the owner could later determine how much of what ingredients to keep in stock.

Input Hardware

Computer systems collect input—including audio, video, image, and text data—through literally hundreds of devices. Some special-purpose devices capture specific types of data. Almost all computer systems include some more familiar, general-purpose input devices. A keyboard and a mouse are standard devices for inputting text, numbers, and commands.

Keyboards have provided effective support for a wide range of data-entry needs (see Figure 2.13). Besides familiar alphabetic characters and a numeric keypad, a basic keyboard includes Control, Alt or Option, and sometimes Command

source data automation

a process that collects input through devices that automatically capture data as transactions occur without special data-entry activities by system personnel

keyboard

a standard device for inputting text, numbers, and commands; includes Control, Alt or Option, and sometimes Command keys that alter the functions of certain other keys

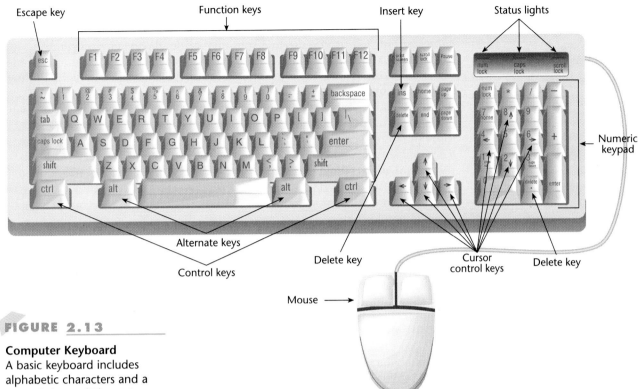

Escape key

Function keys

Insert key

Status lights

Numeric keypad

Alternate keys

Control keys

Delete key

Cursor control keys

Delete key

Mouse

FIGURE 2.13

Computer Keyboard
A basic keyboard includes alphabetic characters and a numeric keypad.The status lights show whether the user has activated the numeric keypad, Caps Lock, or Scroll Lock functions. Arrow keys and other cursor-control keys move the user to different locations in the currently displayed document file.

mouse

a standard device that allows the computer user to point to elements on the display screen and select them or issue commands

keys that alter the functions of certain other keys. A particular combination might trigger a series of program commands or display an unusual character like ç. Preprogrammed function keys (labeled F1 through F12 or F15) also trigger program commands defined by certain software packages or by users themselves.

Extended periods of typing sometimes cause health problems like backaches and carpal tunnel syndrome (a painful problem of the hands and wrists). Many companies are developing more comfortable, adjustable keyboards to alleviate this problem. Some of these devices also permit faster data entry.

A **mouse** allows the computer user to point to elements on the display screen and select them or issue commands. For many application software packages, clicking the mouse button, dragging the mouse, and then releasing the button selects a section of the screen display for later action or moves something to a different part of the screen. For example, clicking on a symbol, icon, menu, or command on the screen activates certain program functions. This causes the computer to take desired actions, such as checking for spelling errors, printing, and saving data on the hard disk.

Logitech's MouseMan Sensa line of mice features mice with different patterns and textures. (Source: Used by permission. © 1996 Logitech.)

trackball

a device that does essentially the same things as a mouse; the user rotates a ball to move the cursor on the computer screen

joystick

a device through which computer game players enter input to control the movements of on-screen characters

voice recognition devices

devices that allow users to enter data through microphones; in this way, the computer system records and converts the sound of the human voice into digital input

digital cameras

cameras that record and store images and video in digital form

A **trackball** does essentially the same things as a mouse. The user rotates a ball to move the cursor on the computer screen. In fact, a mouse is essentially a trackball turned upside down. Computer game players enter input through **joysticks** to control the movements of on-screen characters. For example, some flight simulation games use a joystick to control your imaginary flight. Pulling the joystick back puts you into a sharp climb, which you see immediately on the flight instruments and your view shown on the display screen.

Voice recognition devices and special software allow users to enter data through microphones. In this way, the computer system records and converts the sound of the human voice into digital input. On the factory floor, voice recognition allows equipment operators to give basic commands to automated machines while their hands are busy performing other operations. Security systems include voice recognition devices to allow only authorized personnel into restricted areas.

Some personal computers work with **digital cameras** that record and store images and video in digital form. One type takes still photos like a regular camera, storing electronic versions of the images. Graphics software allows users to import the images, modify them, and include them in other applications.

Digital video cameras like the one shown in Figure 2.14 allow computer systems to record and play back full-motion video. Using systems like these, people at distant locations can conduct videoconferences in which each participant's picture appears on everyone's computer screen. This technology often eliminates the need for expensive travel to attend physical meetings, increasing face-to-face contact and supporting effective teamwork between people at separate locations.

terminals

devices that connect to computer systems over some distance to support data input functions, and sometimes output, but not processing or storage

point-of-sale (POS) terminals

terminals used by retailers to enhance customer service and data collection at the same time

Terminals. Inexpensive and easy-to-use **terminals** connect to computer systems over some distance to support data input functions, and sometimes output, but not processing or storage. A terminal lacks its own processing hardware or RAM, so it must connect to a complete computer system, usually through cable or telephone lines. It allows the user to interact with the distant computer to enter general commands, text, and other data on a general-purpose keyboard or specialized keypad. The terminal may provide a display screen or other output device to show the results of data entry and remote processing. In this way, terminals can extend the reach of a computer system throughout a company's offices, warehouses, and manufacturing facilities.

Retailers use specialized **point-of-sale (POS) terminals** to enhance both customer service and data collection at the same time. Scanning devices built into the terminals read bar codes printed on product labels and tags. Based on this input, the computer system to which the POS terminal is connected identifies the item and returns information about price, sales tax, and total due to the terminal. At the same time, the computer system subtracts the sold item from inventory and adds it to management reports about sales trends. Retail POS terminals often combine other types of input and output devices like numeric keypads, receipt printers, screens, and automatic cash drawers. One survey showed that almost half of all business expenditures on computer technology pay for POS terminals.[9]

Originally envisioned for the physically impaired, voice recognition devices are a relatively new type of input device that promise to greatly change the nature of computing in the future. Decreased costs and increased availability have helped them to find their place both in the office and at home. (Source: Used by permission. © 1996 Logitech.)

FIGURE 2.14

Camera Input for Computer Systems
Digital video cameras make it possible for people at distant locations to conduct video-conferences, thereby eliminating the need for expensive travel to attend physical meetings. (Source: Courtesy of PictureTel.)

automated teller machines (ATMs)

special-purpose input/output terminals used by banks

optical mark recognition (OMR) readers

optical data readers that automatically score tests and interpret data recorded on other types of forms after people fill in boxes using No. 2 pencils

optical character recognition (OCR) readers

optical data readers that sense reflected light to recognize various characters

Banks use their own special-purpose input/output terminals called **automated teller machines (ATMs).** Customers can withdraw cash and complete other banking transactions at almost any time that suits them and usually without waiting in line. ATMs include display screens and receipt printers for output along with magnetic card readers and numeric keypads for input.

Lately, ATMs have begun to outgrow their original role dispensing cash and handling banking needs. Companies other than banks use various ATM-like devices to support their own business processes. The travel agency Fila USA dispenses tickets for airline flights, concerts, and soccer games through machines that work like ATMs. Colleges now use these kinds of terminals to output transcripts.[10]

Scanning Hardware. Special scanning devices play important roles in POS terminals, interpreting information coded on product labels and tags to gather input for retailers' computer systems. More general-purpose scanners can input image and character data to a computer system. Full-page and handheld scanners can convert monochrome or color pictures, forms, text, and other images into machine-readable, digital data. Individuals and businesses import scanned images of drawings and photos to enhance documents and screen displays of all kinds. Many of the graphic images that enrich sites on the World Wide Web represent scanned versions of hand-drawn art or conventional photographs.

U.S. enterprises use scanners to cut down on the high cost of storing and handling the estimated one billion or more pieces of paper that they generate every day. Many companies scan incoming documents and store the images within their computer systems in large-capacity secondary storage hardware instead of accumulating bulky stacks of paper. Mobil Oil employed such a system to reduce the massive burden of government-required paperwork that must remain immediately accessible at all times. Using a scanner to convert the documents to digital images both increased the ease of document access and decreased Mobil's document storage costs.[11]

Special scanning devices called *optical data readers* can also help people to rapidly input data from paper documents. One category of optical data readers, **optical mark recognition (OMR) readers,** automatically scores tests and interprets data recorded on other types of forms after people fill in boxes using No. 2 pencils. Another category of optical data readers, **optical character recognition (OCR) readers,** senses reflected light to recognize various characters. In combination with special software, OCR readers can convert handwritten or typed documents into digital data. Once entered, this data can be shared, modified, and distributed through computer systems.

Magnetic Ink Character Recognition (MICR) Hardware. The banking industry had to confront an avalanche of paper checks, loan applications, and bank statements as early as the 1950s. The development of **magnetic ink character recognition (MICR)** helped banks to speed processing of routine documents by encoding data in magnetic ink on the bottom of a check or other form. Both people and appropriately equipped computer systems can read data printed with this ink (see Figure 2.15).

Networks. Individual computers in today's business environments often receive input and disseminate output through network connections with other computers. These kinds of systems have become critical to business today, and they have made possible such new trends in work as telecommuting, work groups, and others.

Output Hardware

Computer systems provide output to decision makers in a business to help them solve problems or capitalize on competitive opportunities. The needs of the information system may require a computer system to provide visual output, printed paper, sound, or even digital data. Output from one computer system can become input for another computer system within the same information system. Whatever content or form an information system requires for output, the computer system needs hardware that functions to provide this information to decision makers and other computer systems in a timely and understandable way.

magnetic ink character recognition (MICR)

a process by which data are encoded in magnetic ink on the bottom of a check or other form

FIGURE 2.15

MICR Hardware
Coded data printed in magnetic ink at the bottom of a check, utility bill, or other form speeds processing since magnetic sensors can automatically capture input. Banks and other businesses still make effective use of this aging technology. (Source: Courtesy of NCR.)

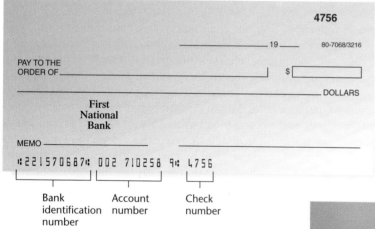

Bank identification number   Account number   Check number

Display Screens. As businesses move away from cumbersome paper handling, many decision makers read output directly from their **monitors,** glass screens that display images of text and graphics by contrasting bright and dark areas. Most personal computer monitors employ cathode-ray tube technology like that of television sets.

Even this standard output device can powerfully affect the functional effectiveness of a computer system. For example, upgrading from a 14-inch screen to a 17-inch monitor has led to a 9 percent productivity increase for managers working with certain applications. The larger display allows for easier, more precise control of detailed reports.[12] Monitor quality has shown remarkable progress since the early personal computers. Today's wide selection of monitors offers tremendous choices of price and quality.

The quality of a monitor image is often measured in **pixels,** individual points of light on a display screen. A larger number of pixels per square inch gives an image with higher **resolution,** or clarity and sharpness. For example, a resolution of 1,024 × 768 (786,432 pixels) gives a sharper display than one with a resolution of 640 × 350 (224,000 pixels).

Monitors can present either monochrome or color displays. Monochrome monitors typically show output in one of three colors: gray, green, or amber. Color monitor displays range from a few shades to thousands. A monitor's ability to display color depends on the quality of the monitor, the amount of RAM in the computer system, and the graphics adapter card. Early personal computers met the **color graphics adapter (CGA)** standard with eight colors and resolution of 320 × 320 pixels. Today's standard **super video graphics array (SVGA)** provides vastly superior color and resolution. Another standard, extended graphics array (XGA), was developed by IBM. This standard, however, is not as popular as SVGA.

Liquid crystal displays (LCDs) provide an alternative to television-type monitors, usually for portable computers. These flat-screen monitors trap liquid crystal—an organic, oil-like material—between two polarizers. Applications of electricity cause this material to form characters and graphic images on a backlit screen. One of two technology options for LCD monitors, passive-matrix displays, typically give dimmer, slower pictures at lower cost. Active-matrix displays give bright, clear pictures visible over wider viewing angles, but they cost and weigh more.

Advances in monitor technology have allowed display screens to provide input as well as output. By touching certain parts of a **touch-sensitive screen,** you can choose a program command or cause the computer to take an action. Touch-sensitive screens are popular input devices for some handheld personal computers and personal digital assistants (PDAs) such as the Newton because they eliminate other input devices, which consume space in storage and in use. These screens also appear in information kiosks like those at airports and department stores, allowing customers to select output about local restaurants and hotels or gift ideas.

Printers and Plotters. Printed paper, or *hard copy,* remains among the most useful and popular forms of computer system output. **Printers** generate most hard copy, operating at different speeds with different features and capabilities. Some can accommodate preprinted forms such as blank checks and invoices.

Printer manufacturers typically state output speeds as numbers of pages printed per minute (ppm). They state levels of quality, or resolution, as numbers of dots printed per inch. A printer that produces 600 dots per inch (dpi) prints more clearly than one that produces 300 dpi.

monitors
glass screens that display images of text and graphics by contrasting bright and dark areas

pixels
individual points of light on a display screen

resolution
clarity or sharpness

color graphics adapter (CGA)
a color graphics standard of eight colors and resolution of 320 × 320 pixels

super video graphics array (SVGA)
a display standard that provides color and resolution vastly superior to that of CGA

liquid crystal displays (LCDs)
flat-screen monitors that trap liquid crystal between two polarizers; applications of electricity cause this material to form characters and graphic images on a backlit screen

touch-sensitive screen
a display screen that allows the user to touch certain parts of it to choose a program command or cause the computer to take an action

printers
devices that generate most hard copy, operating at different speeds with different features and capabilities

Printers produce images on paper through either impact or nonimpact technologies. The printing components of an impact printer strike the paper during the printing process; the print components of a nonimpact printer do not. An ink-jet printer is a nonimpact printer that sprays tiny dots of ink on the paper, generating quality levels up to 600 dpi. Laser printers achieve 600 dpi quality by creating electrostatic charges on paper that attract grains of special ink; the printers then bond the ink onto the paper using heat, much as photocopying machines do. Figure 2.16 shows a laser printer and an example of its output.

plotters

hard-copy output devices that draw smooth curves and precise angles without jagged edges

Plotters, another type of hard-copy output device, support design work by drawing smooth curves and precise angles without jagged edges. Some plotters physically move pens across paper or acetate; others employ electrostatic processes similar to those of laser printers. Businesses typically use these devices to generate hard copy of blueprints, schematics, and other drawings.

Computer Output Microfilm (COM) Hardware. Many companies require their information systems to meet the output needs of decision makers without the burden of producing, handling, and storing stacks of paper documents. Their computer systems often include **computer output microfilm (COM) devices,** which record computer system data directly onto microfilm for future reference using microfilm readers. This kind of hardware streamlines the traditional procedure for storing information compactly on microfilm, which requires photographing and then destroying printed hard copy. Newspapers and journals typically output their publications on microfilm using COM in addition to printing them. Readers can then view past articles and news items in concise, convenient form.

computer output microfilm (COM) devices

hardware that records computer system data directly onto microfilm for future reference using microfilm readers

Special-purpose Output Devices. Many additional input and output devices meet specialized or unique needs of particular information systems. Special-purpose listening devices can detect problems with equipment functions. Georgia Institute of Technology has developed a hardware device that can monitor equipment sounds and detect wear or damage to important parts.

voice output devices

devices that allow computers to send output-synthesized speech over speakers and phone lines

Voice output devices, also called *voice response devices,* allow computers to send output-synthesized speech over speakers and phone lines. Some banks and financial institutions use voice recognition and response systems to give account information to customers over the phone. The Denver Better Business

FIGURE 2.16

Laser Printer and Hard Copy
Laser printers produce high-quality printed output. With a wide variety of speeds and price ranges, these output devices offer many features, including color capabilities.
(Source: Courtesy of QMS, Inc.)

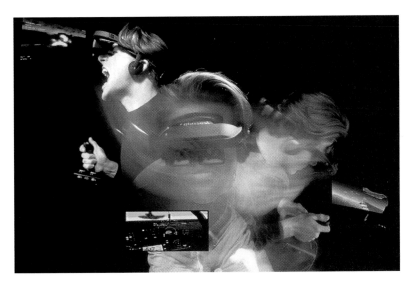

Using special hardware and software, plus vision glasses, the virtual reality system places the participant into an artificial, three-dimensional, entertaining experience. (Source: Courtesy of Virtual I-O, Inc. Seattle, WA.)

data projectors

output devices that project monitor images onto large screens

virtual reality

a system that incorporates both input and output hardware to simulate real-world experiences

Bureau serves its customers through an automated system named FRED, short for Free Reports for Educated Decisions. Callers can obtain reports by following the instructions of the synthesized voice.

Computer systems in many classrooms and training centers output instructional displays through **data projectors,** which project monitor images onto large screens. An instructor teaching a class on a word processing program can use a data projector to show a large group of students what should happen on their own computer screens.

Multifunction devices for personal computers often combine a printer, scanner, fax, and copy machine into one box. Multifunction devices are typically less expensive than buying the devices separately, and they take less room on a desk. These devices, however, do not always have the features and quality of stand-alone devices, and if one component, such as the fax, breaks and you have to take the unit to be repaired, you give up your printer, scanner, and copy machine as well.

A **virtual reality** system incorporates both input and output hardware to simulate real-world experiences. A headset fills the user's visual field with three-dimensional color images and plays sound over attached earphones. Spatial sensors in the headset, and sometimes a glove also worn by the user, act as input devices. The computer changes the images and sounds in the headset in response to the user's movements.

Virtual reality hardware adds a powerful new dimension to computer games. In business settings, it allows architects and their clients to simulate walking through finished buildings before construction even begins. Physicians can practice surgical techniques through virtual operations, and pilots can experience realistic simulations of flights without ever leaving the ground.

In Detroit, General Motors has developed what some believe is the first commercial-scale virtual reality center. The center can simulate three-dimensional environments to help automotive engineers, manufacturers, architects, geologists, and medical experts envision the results of potential decisions. They can then recognize problems early and avoid expensive mistakes. This technology should support business goals of developing better products, streamlining procedures, improving efficiency, and reducing costs.

EQUIPMENT UPGRADES: RESPONDING TO CHANGE

To keep up with needed business or personal tasks, companies and individuals must upgrade formerly effective computer systems. The ability to upgrade system components can be an important criterion for selecting computer hardware.

Typical upgrades include installing additional memory, supplementing original processors with coprocessors for specific tasks like math, and adding hard-disk capacity. A hardware upgrade may change the original configuration of a computer system, forcing changes in other hardware, software, and user routines to accommodate the new devices. Established **standards**—performance guidelines approved by accepted industry groups—often simplify system

standards

performance guidelines approved by accepted industry groups

plug and play

a standard used by Microsoft in its Windows 95 operating system software that eliminates much of the complexity of reconfiguring a personal computer system

upgrades, though. Microsoft uses a standard called **plug and play** in its Windows 95 operating system software that eliminates much of the complexity of reconfiguring a personal computer system. The goal is for a computer owner to be able to install (plug in) a new device and use it (play) immediately.

Owners of small computer systems can easily attach CD-ROM drives, scanners, additional hard disks, tape drives, and other devices thanks to a standard called the *Small Computer System Interface (SCSI)*. Any storage, input, or output device that meets SCSI (pronounced "scuzzy") standard can connect to any system with the correct port. SCSI adapters can connect "daisy chains" of up to eight SCSI devices.

Finally, the Personal Computer Memory Card International Association (PCMCIA) has set standards for PC memory and communications cards. Like SCSI, the PCMCIA standard helps to ensure compatibility between existing computer systems and new cards.

Standards provide critical protection for computer owners by limiting the costs of integrating new components, making their systems function effectively for longer periods. In addition, standards reassure developers of new products that their devices will work effectively with existing systems. Industrywide agreement on performance guidelines expand users' options and reduce the complexity of upgrading equipment.

Of course, a computer system, like the functions of individual components, should support fundamental objectives of the larger information system. The computer system must carry out its current processes and offer flexibility to meet future needs. Each computer system component—processing hardware, RAM, and storage, input, and output devices—makes a critical contribution to the successful operation of the computer system, the information system, and the organization as a whole. The more you know about both broad information system goals and hardware characteristics, the better you will be at creating and maintaining effective computer systems. See the "Eye on the Web" box for how to use the Internet to locate product information.

HARDWARE BUYER'S GUIDE

Many students purchase personal computers while at school. If you are thinking about buying a PC, the tips in this section may help you to make a good decision. Also, Appendix A at the end of the book contains tips to help you determine what hardware to purchase when buying a personal computer.

1. *Carefully decide how you will use your personal computer.* The power and type of personal computer you need will depend on the work you want it to do. If you need portability, perhaps to take notes in class, buy a laptop or notebook computer. If a stationary system will meet your needs, a desktop computer usually provides given capabilities, including hard-disk and RAM capacity, more cheaply than a portable unit. If you expect to perform a large number of sophisticated calculations (e.g., for engineering), buy a computer with a fast processor.

2. *Determine your total budget.* Don't forget to include software, a printer, and other components that you may need.

3. *Review reports in magazines before you make any purchase decisions.* The magazines described in the section of Chapter 1 on literacy resources can help you to determine the best systems for you in your price range.

EYE ON THE WEB

You want to research the latest hardware developed by IBM, Dell, Compaq, or other companies. Or you want to shop around for the best price on a new personal computer. In either case, the World Wide Web (WWW) is the place for you to start.

Companies have benefited from corporate access to the Internet. Posting information on the Internet makes it readily available to scores of potential customers. For example, IBM can display up-to-date product information about its Power Series personal computers. Effectively using a product line display, the company can highlight the benefits gained from its PowerPC architecture, which is based on RISC technology. Dell provides a search screen for users to locate a "DellWare Vendor" convenient to them. Dell is also able to outline in detail the many different levels of service available to both individual and corporate customers. Compaq has assembled an information page that permits users to point and click on different Compaq models to obtain product details.

Customers can benefit from current information about products. For example, when Intel released the Pentium microprocessor chip, a floating point calculation error was discovered. Bulletin board postings allowed Internet users to be among the first to learn of this problem. (You can find a summary of documents concerning the floating point "bug" by entering "Pentium" as a search keyword.)

The displays go far beyond information concerning major brands of PCs, however, to cover input and output devices of all types. Interested shoppers can review the specifications for different products ranging from monitors to speakers to laser printers. And you don't

have to just take the vendor's word, either. Reviews and reports are available, as well. In fact, for consumers who wish to conduct their own testing, a list of different benchmarking programs is available for browsing. (A benchmark test would, for example, show performance measures for different brands of PCs, each running the same tests under the same conditions. This allows users to compare directly the performances turned in by several machines.)

Once you choose a model, you can search for a good buy via the WWW. You can easily compare prices of different products without leafing through magazines or spending hours on the telephone collecting the information. You can even make purchases on-line. As hardware vendors find a home on the Internet, comparison shopping will become easier and easier. It's a great two-way medium working to the benefit of all: hardware vendors sell hardware to hardware users who can use hardware to eliminate the hard sell!

WEB EXERCISES

1. Locate and list several of the specifications of the new line of IBM Power Series PCs. Do the same for Power Macs.
2. List two different information sources from the Internet that discuss the floating point bug discovered in Intel's Pentium chip.
3. Find prices on-line for the same monitor and system unit (or any hardware components that you are personally interested in buying) from at least two different vendors. Use a spreadsheet program to enter these prices, and calculate the lowest cost for your PC.

4. *If in doubt, get additional processor, hard-disk, and memory capacity.* If you are not sure how much power and capacity you need, favor your most powerful option. You will usually spend more money and time adding RAM, hard-disk capacity, and processing hardware than you would spend to buy a well-equipped computer system in the first place. Try to anticipate future needs and buy a PC that will satisfy them.
5. *Price is only one criterion.* Base your decision on price along with warranty terms, availability of local service, the reputation of the manufacturer, and other information about the quality of the PC and its components. A local dealer may offer a multiyear service contract.
6. *Try to get needed system resources bundled with the PC.* Many manufacturers market bundles that include multimedia equipment, software, and more. Determine what you need and look for a PC manufacturer that offers such a system. Again, you can probably buy everything you want more cheaply in one package than as separate components.

7. *Seek recommendations and advice.* Ask your instructor, advisor, lab administrator, fellow students, friends, and family for recommendations. Your instructor, advisor, or lab administrator may know what type of computer would work best with those of your school.

8. *Weigh several purchase options.* You can purchase a PC directly from the manufacturer, through a mail-order company, or at the store of a local dealer. If you will need help with initial setup, training, and installation of additional equipment, consider buying from a dealer or manufacturer that can offer local service. Determine the service you want, and identify the vendor that can offer the best package for the best price.

9. *Evaluate the reputation of the manufacturer.* Good computer companies offer good prices, long and comprehensive warranties, and good service. Check these features before you buy.

10. *Consider buying a used computer.* Classified ads in the newspaper and school bulletin boards list used computers for sale. Remember, however, that buying a used computer can be like buying a used car—the price may seem low, but you may buy someone else's problems.

11. *Pay with a credit card.* You can challenge the charge on a credit card if the product you buy does not work or arrives damaged. Some card companies even insure your purchase against loss or theft. After you have purchased your PC, it is usually a good idea to pay off your credit card bill as soon as possible to avoid high interest charges.

- A computer-based information system serves the needs of the larger organizational information system by combining components with capabilities to complete essential input, processing, output, and storage functions.

- Many personal computer systems serve individual users, but more and more of them are connected in powerful networks to support information system needs that formerly required larger computers. The main categories of general-purpose computers are personal computers (desktop, laptop, handheld), workstations and minicomputers, and mainframes and supercomputers.

- Computers store and process pulses of electricity called *bits;* patterns of bits represent data and instructions with meaning to the user.

- Secondary storage devices use either sequential or direct access to data. Many types of secondary storage are available: magnetic tape, magnetic disk, cartridge, and optical disk.

- A business information system should automate input as much as possible to capture data close to the transaction or other activity that creates the data.

SUMMARY

1. *Explain the contribution of technology to a business information system.* A computer system needs hardware components that help it satisfy the demands of the larger information system and the organization as a whole. Computer system components perform input, processing, output, and storage functions similar to those of a person in a paper-based office.

2. *Distinguish among types of computer systems.* Embedded computers control the operations of many products. Businesses use stand-alone, special-purpose computers for specific tasks like providing information at kiosks and diagnosing equipment malfunctions. Among general-purpose computers, the category of personal computers includes desktop computers and portable computers like laptops, notebooks, and handheld units. Workstations and minicomputers perform more sophisticated processing tasks than PCs, although that gap is closing as PCs gain more power. Mainframes and supercomputers meet the intensive data-processing needs of large companies and other organizations.

3. *Describe the power, speed, and capacity characteristics of processing and memory devices.* Within the central processing unit, the arithmetic/logic unit performs mathematical calculations and makes logical comparisons to execute program instructions. The control unit sequentially accesses program instructions and coordinates the flow of instructions and data into and out of the ALU, the registers, primary storage, and even secondary storage and output components. Registers are high-speed storage areas within the CPU that temporarily hold small units of program instructions and data immediately before, during, and after execution by the CPU. Random access memory (RAM) holds program instructions and data in volatile storage areas immediately before they enter the registers and immediately after they exit. Bits are pulses of electricity (either 0 or 1). Each byte represents eight bits. Read-only memory (ROM) provides a nonvolatile storage area for data and instructions that do not need to change. Cache memory is a high-speed primary storage area for frequently used data.

4. *List the access methods and capacity and portability characteristics of secondary storage devices.* Secondary storage offers a nonvolatile and relatively economical way to store large amounts of data. Sequential-access storage devices must review and retrieve data in the same order in which it was stored; direct-access storage devices can move directly to the storage location for desired data without the need to read through other data in sequence. Magnetic tape drives store large amounts of data by magnetizing spots on relatively portable reels of Mylar film coated with iron oxide. Hard disks store large amounts of data by magnetizing spots on thin, steel platters permanently housed in closed, nonportable, metal cases. Diskette drives store smaller amounts of data by magnetizing spots on easily portable circles of Mylar film protected in hard plastic or flexible paper covers. Optical disks store large amounts of data permanently encoded by specialized equipment that physically burns pits into the coated surfaces on rigid plastic disks.

5. *Demonstrate the functions and contributions of input and output devices.* A keyboard supports a wide range of data-entry needs; the user types alphabetic characters and numbers and enters program commands through special keys. The user moves a mouse or trackball and clicks adjacent buttons to control the cursor or pointer on the computer screen, select elements for later actions, and enter program commands. Many computer systems get some input from various kinds of terminals (e.g., point of sale, ATMs). Scanners allow users to input graphics for computer processing or detect coded information printed on product labels or tags. Output hardware comes in many forms. Monitors display computer system output on glass screens. Liquid crystal displays are used for portable computers. SVGA (super video graphics array) is the standard for color display monitors. Printers and plotters produce hard copy of computer system output, varying from impact printers, ink jets, and laser printers to pen plotters and other specialized output.

Key Terms

computer system 34	supercomputer 38	kilobyte 40
embedded computer 35	central processing unit (CPU) 40	megabyte 41
personal computer (PC) 36	microprocessor chip 40	gigabyte 41
desktop computer 36	arithmetic/logic unit (ALU) 40	MIPS 41
laptop computer 37	control unit 40	clock speed 41
handheld (palmtop) computer 37	primary storage 40	megahertz (MHz) 41
workstation 38	random access memory (RAM) 40	wordlength 42
minicomputer 38	bit 40	bus line 42
mainframe computer 38	byte 40	bus line width 42

read-only memory (ROM) 43
cache memory 43
multiprocessing 44
coprocessor 44
parallel processing 44
massively parallel processing (MPP) 44
system unit 44
system board 46
motherboard 46
expansion slot 46
expansion board 46
port 46
serial port 46
parallel port 46
power supply 46
secondary storage 47
sequential-access storage device 47
direct-access storage device 47
magnetic tape drive 47
magnetic disk 48
hard disk 48
diskette 49

read/write head 49
disk cartridge 50
fragmentation 50
defragmentation 50
data compression 51
optical disk 52
compact disk–read-only memory
   (CD-ROM) 52
write-once, read-many (WORM) disk 52
magneto-optical (MO) disk 53
source data automation 56
keyboard 56
mouse 57
trackball 58
joystick 58
voice recognition device 58
digital camera 58
terminal 58
point-of-sale (POS) terminal 58
automated teller machine (ATM) 59
optical mark recognition (OMR)
   reader 59

optical character recognition (OCR)
   reader 59
magnetic ink character recognition
   (MICR) 60
monitor 61
pixel 61
resolution 61
color graphics adapter (CGA) 61
super video graphics array (SVGA) 61
liquid crystal display (LCD) 61
touch-sensitive screen 61
printer 61
plotter 62
computer output microfilm (COM)
   device 62
voice output device 63
data projector 63
virtual reality 63
standards 63
plug and play 64

 Concept Quiz

1. Identify the following acronyms:
   a. CPU
   b. RAM
   c. bits
   d. RISC
   e. ROM
2. A kilobyte equals approximately _____ bytes; a megabyte equals approximately _____ kilobytes; a gigabyte equals approximately _____ megabytes.
3. _____ unify many diverse processing functions in a single location or facility to offer an organization the highest degree of control.
4. What type of printer produces output by electrostatic charge?
5. All of the following are connected to a computer via ports *except:*
   a. keyboard
   b. telephone
   c. monitor
   d. hard drive

6. Music cassettes and videocassettes store sounds and images in a way that is similar to
   a. direct-access storage
   b. magnetic tape drives
   c. secondary storage
7. To care for diskettes, do all of the following *except:*
   a. avoid touching the diskette surface
   b. keep them away from food and drinks
   c. store them in a light, airy area
   d. insert them into the drive carefully
8. Disk cartridges have all of the following advantages *except:*
   a. they have faster access times than hard disks
   b. they provide added safety for backup
   c. they can enhance security
   d. they are portable

Mark "true" or "false" after each of the following statements.

9. Defragmentation software can dramatically speed up computer operations in older hard disks. _____

10. CD-ROM has become a standard part of secondary storage hardware of personal computer systems, alongside hard disks and diskettes. ———

11. Liquid crystal displays are used most frequently on mainframe computers. ———

12. Business computer systems have recently begun to move away from sequential-access secondary storage devices, toward direct-access devices because the latter give them speed and flexibility. ———

13. Most business information systems focus on low cost rather than accuracy and speed. ———

14. Advances in monitor technology have allowed display screens to provide input as well as output. ———

15. An ink-jet printer is an example of an impact printer. ———

Discussion Questions

1. What factors must an IS person consider when choosing a computer system for his or her organization?

2. In what ways might a global travel agency use distributed processing?

3. What type of businesses might benefit from the use of optical disks in their systems? Why?

4. Think of as many different uses for the Xybernaut Mobile Assistant (chapter opening photo) as you can, both for businesses and individual consumers.

Team Activity

1. Home-based businesses and larger organizations need to be able to select a computer system that meets current and future needs. Suppose your team is made up of staff members who are charged with selecting a computer system for Golden Fleece, a company that manufactures outdoor clothing made of synthetic fleece. The company is headquartered in Colorado, but it has manufacturing plants in the South and overseas. Its dealers are located nationwide, and it just launched a mail-order catalog.

2. As a team, try to determine generally what types of processing hardware, secondary storage hardware, and input and output hardware would be best for Golden Fleece headquarters (and, if you have time, for its manufacturing plants and mail-order operations).

Applying IT

1. Every day, you come into contact with different types of computer system terminals (for instance, your bank's ATM). In your mind, walk yourself through a typical day, trying to think of all the different terminals you use or are affected by. List them and describe how you use them, as well as in what ways they benefit (or hamper) you.

2. Imagine that your boss wants you to find out about the latest technology in optical disks, possibly to use as part of your organization's computer system. Access the Internet to find out what different companies offer, their product specifications, and prices. Compile the information in a spreadsheet so that your boss can compare alternatives easily.

CASE

IBM

IBM is changing. Recently, Chairman Louis Gerstner, Jr. announced that it was OK for the company's thousands of employees to relax their uniform—white shirt, dark tie (or white blouse, dark skirt)—to pressed chinos. And mainframes are back. They never really disappeared, but IBM suffered major losses during the early 1990s because it missed the boat on PC technology, and its mainframes were just too big and expensive to appeal to many customers. But the new mainframes—like chinos—are lighter, smaller, and less expensive to build and maintain; and customers who need this type of computer have been lining up to buy them.

The new mainframes, called complimentary metal oxide semiconductor (CMOS) machines, do everything the old bipolar mainframe computers could do, and more. Plus, they occupy only 100 square feet instead of 600 square feet; they weigh about a ton instead of 15 tons; they require less testing time (a week, as opposed to three weeks); and they cost $18,000 per MIPS instead of $23,000 per MIPS. Despite the explosive increase in PC users, some users still need mainframes like the new CMOS: banks, insurance companies, and airlines, to name a few. So far, companies in these industries have been eager to order the new mainframes.

But IBM must be careful not to miss the boat again; this time, it must do a better job of anticipating the types of hardware that organizations want and need. There will be competition, as well. For instance, Amdahl and Hitachi will be introducing their own new lines of CMOS mainframes, which puts pressure on IBM to lower its prices. One expert predicts that these new mainframes will be selling for less than $5,000 per MIPS within the next few years. And just as the new machines are less expensive to build and buy, so they are less expensive to maintain. "If an old machine that had a $15,000-a-month maintenance charge is replaced by a CMOS machine with maybe a $1,500-a-month maintenance charge, this is a big deal," notes Charles Burns, director of research for datacenter strategies at Gartner Group. Both of these situations translate to fewer dollars for IBM.

What will be the future of mainframes? So far, the expense of converting from mainframe software to PC software is so great that businesses have avoided the risk of doing so. But what if, ultimately, that cost is greatly reduced? IBM is already looking for new ways for companies to use mainframes, such as adapting popular software programs to run on mainframes and searching for ways to make use of the Internet. But so far, no one has come up with a sure bet. "The dogs aren't eating the dog food," warns Charles Burns. Still, IBM is unlikely to turn back. And its workers are even more unlikely to go back to those white shirts and dark ties. (For your information, IBM's Web site is www.ibm.com.)

Questions

1. Based on what you now know about hardware—and mainframes—can you foresee a new direction for IBM's CMOS? If so, what might it be?
2. What uses does a university have for a mainframe?
3. What advice would you give to a company that is considering buying a mainframe?

Sources: David Churbuck and Gary Samuels, "Can IBM Keep It Up?" *Forbes*, June 3, 1996, pp. 142–144; Barbara DePompa and Dan Brinzac, "Mainframes in the Making," *Information Week*, May 27, 1996, pp. 52–58; http://techweb.cmp.com/iw.

Answers to Concept Quiz

1. a. central processing unit b. random access memory c. binary digits d. reduced instruction set computing e. read-only memory **2.** All three answers are the same: 1,000. **3.** centralized systems **4.** laser printer **5.** d **6.** b **7.** c **8.** a **9.** true **10.** true **11.** false **12.** true **13.** false **14.** true **15.** false

CHAPTER
3

Software: Systems and Applications Packages

CHAPTER OUTLINE

Software Overview
Systems Software
    Operating Systems
    Current Operating Systems
    Initiating the Operating System: The Boot Process
    Utility Programs
Applications Software
    Proprietary Applications Software
    Off-the-Shelf Applications Software
    Support Provided by Applications Software
Programming Languages
    Generations of Programming Languages
    Classes of Programming Languages
    Language Translators
Software Buyer's Guide

Levi Strauss & Co. uses a special computer program to offer their individually fitted, Personal Pair™ jeans for women. A trained sales associate uses an in-store computer kiosk to enter a customer's measurements. The computer program interprets the data and suggests a prototype jean for the customer to try on. Once the fit is determined, the final measurements are sent via modem to the LS&CO factory, where a pattern is generated and cut using laser technology. When ready, the customer can either pick her jeans up at the Original Levi's® Store or have them delivered to her doorstep. Photo courtesy of Levi Strauss & Co.

LEARNING OBJECTIVES

After completing Chapter 3, you will be able to:

1. Differentiate systems software from applications software.
2. Describe the function of an operating system and list some operating systems.
3. Explain the capabilities that utility programs add to computer systems.
4. Describe the kinds of applications software packages that support users' processing needs.
5. Show how programming languages allow people to control the operations of computer hardware.

In the 1950s, businesspeople and researchers regarded computer hardware as exotic and expensive luxuries, and almost no one else had ever seen or used it. The high cost of hardware overshadowed the importance of software, because hardware consumed so much more of the total budgets for computer-based information systems.

That situation has dramatically changed. Software can account for 75 percent or more of the total cost of a particular information system. One reason for this change is that advances in hardware technology have driven hardware costs continually lower over time. Also, software has come to perform increasingly complex tasks; developers need more time to create more complicated programs, and this investment in labor raises the cost of new software. At the same time, demand for programming skills has grown, and the short supply of programmers has propelled salaries sharply upward for software developers.

Software will probably continue to command more information system resources than hardware does. In fact, Figure 3.1 shows an even more pronounced imbalance in the future—software will consume an even greater portion of the overall budget of a typical information system than its current share.

SOFTWARE OVERVIEW

documentation

written material that describes the program functions to help the user operate the computer system

systems software

the set of programs designed to coordinate the activities and functions of the hardware and various programs throughout the computer system

Recall from Chapter 1 that software consists of programmed sequences of instructions for the computer. These instructions control input, processing, output, and storage activities of the computer hardware. **Documentation** describes the program functions to help the user operate the computer system. The program displays some documentation on-screen, while other forms appear in external resources like printed manuals.

The general category of software includes two kinds of programs: systems software and applications software. **Systems software** is the set of programs designed to coordinate the activities and functions of the hardware and various programs throughout the computer system. A particular systems software package works only for a specific CPU design and class of hardware. The combination of a specific hardware configuration and systems software package is sometimes known as a *computer system platform*.

FIGURE 3.1

Balance between Software and Hardware Costs
Since the 1950s, businesses have spent ever-larger portions of their information system budgets on software and smaller portions on hardware.

To carry out the tasks of the computer system, systems software works together with **applications software**, which consists of programs that help users to solve particular computing problems. Applications software earns its name because it *applies* the power of the computer to help users perform specific tasks and solve well-defined problems. The needs and priorities of an overall information system determine the capabilities that applications software must give to a computer system. As with hardware, software capabilities should create a balanced set of essential functions within performance, cost, control, and complexity limits.

applications software

programs that help users to solve particular computing problems

SYSTEMS SOFTWARE

Systems software controls the basic operations of computer hardware and supports the applications programs' problem-solving capabilities. For example, one common type of applications program helps the user to create and edit written documents (this class of software is called *word processing programs*). This document-handling capability needs some way to allow a user to save document files on disk. The applications program accomplishes this and similar basic operations by activating systems software commands.

Of course, it would be possible to design an applications program that included its own sequence of instructions to operate the disk drive and keep track of stored files. But that arrangement would waste vast amounts of system resources because every application for a particular hardware configuration would have to include the same instructions. Systems software avoids this unnecessary duplication by providing a centralized source for instructions like these.

The part of systems software that translates commands of users and applications programs into hardware activities is called the *operating system*. Systems software also includes utility programs.

Operating Systems

operating system

a set of computer programs that control hardware devices to support users' computing needs

An **operating system** is a set of computer programs that control hardware devices to support users' computing needs (Figure 3.2). The operating system forms a sort of interface between the hardware and applications software and between the hardware and the user. It works like a chauffeur, who operates automotive hardware as instructed by an important passenger; the operating system takes instructions from an applications program (and sometimes directly from the user) and controls hardware to carry out those instructions.

Many of the collection of programs that make up the operating system enter RAM immediately when a computer starts to operate ("boots up," in computer terminology). These basic instructions remain stored in RAM until the user turns off the power switch, carrying out essential computer system tasks:

- Performing common hardware functions
- Providing a degree of hardware independence
- Managing system memory
- Managing processing tasks
- Providing a user interface

Common Hardware Functions. All applications programs must perform basic tasks like capturing input from the keyboard or some other input device, retrieving data from disks, storing data on disks, and outputting information to the monitor screen and printer. Hardware devices may require many,

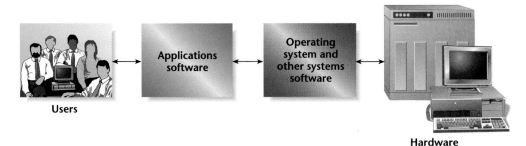

Users

Hardware

FIGURE 3.2

Role of the Operating System
Along with other systems software, the operating system acts as an interface between applications software and computer hardware and between the hardware and the user.

detailed instructions to complete even such basic functions. The operating system converts a simple, basic instruction from an applications program like "read a file from disk" into the complex sequence of instructions that the hardware requires.

For a simplified example, suppose that an application needs to read a piece of data from disk. It may command the operating system to:

◆ Retrieve Product$ from Drive C:.

The operating system might translate this simple command to the hardware into a longer sequence, as follows:

◆ Check for Drive C: on the computer system.
◆ If no such drive exists, inform the applications program; otherwise, continue.
◆ Start up Drive C:.
◆ Find the block of data that represents Product$.
◆ Read this block of data.
◆ Send the data to the billing application.
◆ Stop Drive C:.

The operating system simplifies the basic task of reading a block of data from a disk so that the applications program can complete the task by issuing one basic instruction rather than a sequence of more detailed instructions. In this way, the operating system acts as an intermediary between the applications program and the hardware. It allows applications to perform hundreds of such functions by translating each one into one or more instructions for system hardware.

Actually, the operating system does not interact only with applications programs; the user can issue commands directly to the operating system, as well. The most common direct commands from users to operating systems act to launch selected applications programs. Users also issue direct commands to prepare diskettes to store data (called *formatting*, or *initializing*, diskettes), to copy files between disks, and to display listings of the files stored on particular disks. Still, an operating system does most of its work at the direction of applications programs, unseen by the user.

Hardware Independence. The operating system saves applications software from the wasteful requirement to include detailed instructions for basic computer functions. It also provides another, similar benefit—it allows for updates in those detailed instructions in response to differences and changes in hardware without any need for changes in applications software. Therefore, it reduces the dependency of applications on particular hardware configurations.

Suppose that a disk drive manufacturer designs a new hard disk that can operate much faster than earlier versions. This new hard disk functions differently from the old hardware, however, so it requires different instructions to perform certain tasks. Without the ability to update operating systems, publishers of applications software would have to revise all of their programs to take advantage of the new, faster hard disk.

Fortunately, simpler changes in the operating system can make the new capabilities available to many existing applications programs. The revised operating system can convert commands from old applications to the new sequences of instructions for the improved hardware (the concept behind plug and play mentioned in Chapter 2). This buffer helps software designers to make their applications somewhat independent of particular hardware characteristics.

Memory Management. Another important function of operating systems, **memory management,** allows software to use the storage capacity in RAM. The operating system controls how programs access memory, and it maximizes memory capacity. Efficient memory management works to promote effective execution of program instructions and to speed processing.

This memory management function is important because computer systems include many types of memory. For example, the operating system MS-DOS, which runs on many personal computers, divides RAM into four categories:

1. Conventional memory takes up the first 640 KB of RAM.
2. Upper memory goes from 640 KB, where conventional memory stops, to 1 MB (1,024 KB).
3. Extended memory goes from 1 MB to the upper physical limits of the CPU, anywhere from 16 MB to 4 GB.
4. Finally, expanded memory is RAM capacity that exceeds the processor's normal retrieval and storage abilities. To access expanded memory, the computer uses a special program within the operating system called the *expanded memory manager (EMM).*

Some operating systems offer a **virtual memory** capability, which allocates space on disk to supplement the immediate, functional memory capacity of RAM. Virtual memory then swaps segments of program instructions as needed between memory and one or more disks. The number of program segments held in RAM depends upon the sizes of those segments and the computer's RAM capacity.

Virtual memory can speed overall processing activities by keeping instructions for essential program functions in relatively fast RAM and leaving instructions that the CPU needs less frequently on disk to be called as needed. Assume that the written instructions for a computer program would fill ten pages. If the computer were to store only a segment of this program, perhaps the first few pages, in RAM, it might also be able to store another program segment from some other program there. Virtual memory allows the computer to store currently needed pages of a number of programs in RAM, while the rest of these programs wait on the disk—a concept called *paging.*

Processing Task Management. An operating system must also include instructions for managing all processing tasks. This task-management function allocates computer system resources to make the best use of those assets. Task-management software can permit one user to run several programs or processing activities at one time (multitasking and multithreading). It can also allow several users to share a single computer (time-sharing).

memory management

a function of operating systems that allows software to use the storage capacity in RAM

virtual memory

a capability offered by some operating systems that allocates space on disk to supplement the immediate, functional memory capacity of RAM

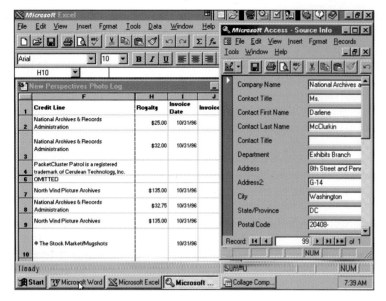

An operating system with **multitasking** capabilities allows a user to run more than one application at the same time. For example, the manager at a Benny's Bagels store might need to create a report on that outlet's purchases of ingredients for bagel dough. The manager could complete this work effectively if the computer could run an inventory control program to provide data, a spreadsheet program to carry out calculations, and a word processing program to write the report text, all at the same time. Multitasking would allow all three programs to share data and results. Important tables and analysis from the inventory control program could provide input directly into the word processing program.

Multithreading is basically multitasking within a single application, so that several parts of one program can work at once. Multithreading might allow the manager at Benny's to work on two different spreadsheets at once, possibly printing one while entering data in another.

Multitasking and multithreading can save users considerable time and effort. By offering these capabilities, an operating system allows a user to keep a number of programs open and running together. Each application can affect the output of the others by sharing data and results, and the user can easily make changes.

Time-sharing allows access to a computer system by more than one user at a time. For example, the computer system at the Benny's Bagels headquarters might allow the managers of all 15 outlets to enter data about weekly sales at the same time. In fact, time-sharing allows thousands of people to simultaneously use an on-line computer service to get various types of information, from valuable business news to recipes for carrot cake.

Operating systems for large computer systems, like mainframes, usually allow for time-sharing. Because personal computer operating systems usually serve the needs of single users, they do not require capabilities for managing multiple-user tasks.

User Interface. One of the most important functions of any operating system is to provide a **user interface,** which incorporates the routines that give one or more individuals access to and command of the computer system. The user interface of an operating system has a powerful effect on the experience of using applications software. A simpler, more intuitive user interface helps more people to make effective use of a computer system.

Early computer systems offered only **command-based user interfaces,** which require users to enter text commands to direct the computer to perform basic activities. For example, the MS-DOS command ERASE FILE1 would cause the computer system to erase a file called FILE1 from a particular disk. More complicated tasks require longer, more involved commands. For example, this command

```
COPY C:\DOCUMENTS\MINUTES.JUN A:
```

would locate a file named MINUTES.JUN within a subdirectory called DOCUMENTS on Drive C: and duplicate it on a diskette in Drive A:. Omission or misplacement of a single backslash, space, colon, or period would leave the

multitasking

a capability offered by some operating systems that allows a user to run more than one application at the same time

multithreading

multitasking within a single application, so that several parts of one program can work at once

time-sharing

a capability offered by some operating systems that allows access to a computer system by more than one user at a time

user interface

an element of operating systems that incorporates the routines that give one or more individuals access to and command of the computer system

command-based user interface

an interface that requires users to enter text commands to direct the computer to perform basic activities

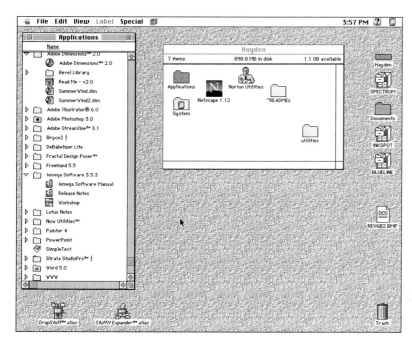

Macintosh System 7.5 provides an easy to use graphical interface that other operating systems are striving to emulate.

graphical user interface (GUI)

an interface that displays pictures called *icons* on the screen to represent document files and application programs

operating system completely unable to interpret the command. The user must learn and conform to the often-confusing demands of a command-based user interface.

In contrast, a **graphical user interface (GUI),** pronounced *goo-ey,* displays pictures called *icons* on the screen to represent document files and application programs. The user can control and launch applications and send other commands to the computer system simply by pointing and clicking with a mouse. Many people find that GUIs are easier to learn and use than command-based user interfaces, because the users intuitively grasp the functions represented by the icons. They often prefer to select choices from menus than to type complicated commands.

Alan Kay and his colleagues at Xerox's Palo Alto Research Center pioneered techniques of displaying overlapping windows and icons in a user interface. Today, the most widely used graphical user interface is Windows by Microsoft. As the name suggests, Windows dedicates a window, or a portion of the display screen, to a specific application. Windows offers a multitasking capability, running and displaying several windows, and therefore several applications, at once. Following this reasoning, some people refer to all GUIs, even those not developed by Microsoft, as *windows* interfaces. Microsoft's Windows owes its popularity in part to the many advantages of all graphical user interfaces, listed in Table 3.1.

Applications written for graphical user interfaces cannot run under command-based user interfaces, but applications written for command-based systems often can run in GUIs. However, a program can maximize the capabilities of a GUI only if it includes the graphics and point-and-click command routines of that kind of interface.

Current Operating Systems

Early computer operating systems provided adequate support for basic functions required by users and their applications. These systems software packages could accept keyboard input and store files on disk, but they offered few

TABLE 3.1

Advantages of Graphical User Interfaces

- Easy multitasking—All open applications can be viewed in separate windows.
- Intuitive operations—To open a file, you click on a simple icon; to delete a file, you drag it to a trash can icon. Users generally do not need detailed manuals, and icons represent useful support functions.
- Consistent application interfaces—All applications share similar icons and menus; once you learn one application, you know a lot about how to run others.
- Flexible applications—You can provide mouse or keyboard input and save files in different formats with different options.
- Confirmation messages—Boxes appear asking users to confirm that they want to take important or potentially dangerous actions like erasing disks.

of the functions and features that today's users expect. A modern operating system must provide flexible ways to organize and control files. In particular, it must include an attractive user interface based on intuitive, easily understandable actions.

PC-DOS and MS-DOS. IBM released its Personal Computer in 1981 with an operating system called **Personal Computer Disk Operating System (PC-DOS).** Microsoft developed PC-DOS and released its own nearly identical operating system for IBM-compatible microcomputers under the name **Microsoft Disk Operating System (MS-DOS).** Since the 1980s, these operating systems have been popular for IBM PCs and compatible systems.

MS-DOS and other command-based operating systems perform functions for users in response to typed commands. Users enter commands like COPY to duplicate files, RENAME to change file names, DIR to generate a listing of files in a directory, and FORMAT to prepare a new disk to store files.

Windows. Microsoft eventually recognized that many users would prefer a GUI's point-and-click operations over the sometimes complicated command strings of MS-DOS. In the mid-1980s, personal computers began to gain new hardware capabilities, including faster CPUs and larger RAM capacities, that would need to run GUIs, and Microsoft released **Windows.** The original version of this software (Windows 2.0) ran together with MS-DOS. It created a shell that converted user input through a graphical interface into MS-DOS commands. Windows 3.0 and 3.1 gained rapid acceptance in the industry and are still popular.

Newer versions of Windows, including Windows 95 and Windows NT, are fully functional operating systems; they interact directly with computer hardware without any need for MS-DOS commands. The user initiates actions by clicking icons with a mouse button. Windows 95 also has plug and play capabilities, as described in Chapter 2; the operating system makes any necessary changes to the system configuration to accommodate new hardware. (See Figure 3.3.)

Windows NT provides a complete, GUI-based operating system that can run DOS or Windows applications on networks of personal computers connected through telecommunications links. Microsoft developed Windows NT primarily for business users. It offers portability to a variety of hardware platforms, including powerful workstations and multiprocessing systems. Its centralized security system helps IS administrators to monitor various system resources.[1] Windows CE has been developed to be used with handheld personal computers.

OS/2. In 1988, IBM announced a new operating system called **Operating System 2 (OS/2)** to compete with Windows and to take advantage of the expanded capabilities of more powerful personal computers. OS/2 requires at least 8 MB of RAM, at least 5 MB of hard-disk capacity, and a powerful CPU. These hardware resources allow it to offer functions like system monitoring, multitasking, and virtual memory. OS/2 also features a graphical user interface, and it even performs some functions of applications software like communications and database management. It can run applications written for MS-DOS and Windows in addition to those designed specifically for OS/2. More recently, IBM introduced OS/2 Warp, which adds excellent multitasking and memory management capabilities along with strong technical support.

Personal Computer Disk Operating System (PC-DOS)

the operating system developed by Microsoft and released by IBM with its Personal Computer in 1981

Microsoft Disk Operating System (MS-DOS)

the operating system released by Microsoft for IBM-compatible microcomputers

Windows

the GUI released by Microsoft to run with MS-DOS

Operating System 2 (OS/2)

an operating system released by IBM in 1988 to compete with Windows and to take advantage of the expanded capabilities of more powerful personal computers

Windows Explorer provides a view of the PC with as little or as much detail about files, folders, drives, and print jobs as you need.

Because of the architecture of Windows 95, a newly installed plug-and-play device is automatically identified and configured.

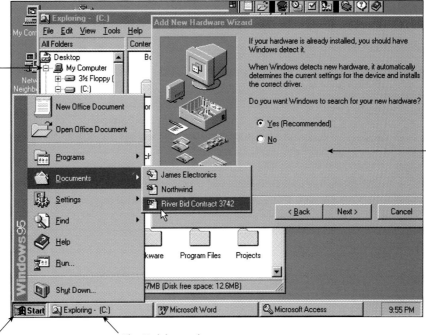

The point of access to the system is the Start button. The Start button and the Task bar are always visible—even when applications are open full screen.

The Task bar makes switching between applications easy. Every new window you open automatically gets its own button.

Windows 95 supports true multitasking among applications. With multithreading, a single application can even perform several tasks simultaneously.

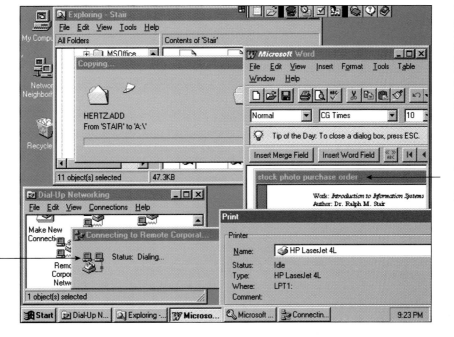

Longer, less cryptic file names make it easy to find what you're looking for.

Dialing remotely into network services.

FIGURE 3.3

Innovations of Windows 95
(Source: Courtesy of Microsoft Corporation.)

Apple Computer Operating Systems. IBM Personal Computers and compatible platforms traditionally use processors manufactured by Intel Corporation and DOS or Windows as operating systems. In contrast, personal computers from Apple Computer typically use Motorola processors and a proprietary Apple operating system. Although IBM and compatible computers hold the largest share of the business PC market, Apple computers also have attracted loyal users. Apple computers have especially strong followers in the graphics, design, and publishing industries.

Apple introduced the Macintosh computer in 1984, offering the first commercial availability of a graphical user interface and a mouse in addition to a keyboard. Other computers at the time ran under command-based interfaces with only keyboards for input. The rest of the industry quickly moved to offer GUI capabilities because of their ease of use. The Macintosh remains the most popular Apple system for business applications.

System 7.5

the current version of the Macintosh operating system

System 7.5, the current version of the Macintosh operating system, supports sophisticated control of computer system resources within a simple, graphical interface that users find easy to learn and use. The Macintosh operating system offers many outstanding capabilities to handle graphics and color, virtual memory, and multitasking. The *toolbar* gives access to useful features like database access simply by clicking icons with a mouse. Some powerful business applications run under the Macintosh operating system, among them Microsoft Word word processing, Excel and Lotus 1-2-3 spreadsheet programs, Illustrator and Freehand art design programs, and Photoshop photo editor. Networking and Internet access are also easily accomplished.

Multiple Virtual Storage/Enterprise Systems Architecture. Mainframe computer manufacturers have traditionally provided proprietary operating systems software for their specific hardware. For example, larger IBM mainframe computers run *Enterprise Systems Architecture/370 (ESA/370)* and *Multiple Virtual Storage/Enterprise Systems Architecture (MVS/ESA).* A staff of thoroughly trained IS professionals would run such a large, demanding system.

Unix

an operating system developed by AT&T in the 1970s for minicomputers

Unix. In the 1970s, AT&T developed a powerful operating system called **Unix** for minicomputers. At that time, federal government regulations prohibited AT&T from competing in the computer marketplace, so it could not market Unix. That limitation changed in the 1980s, when suspicion against monopolies led to the breakup of AT&T and the elimination of many federal regulations on its activities. Since then, Unix has gained some support as an operating system.

Unix is a portable operating system with versions that can run on many computer platforms from personal computers to mainframe systems. Unix benefits companies using both small and large computer systems, because it provides compatibility with different types of hardware. Also, it allows users to operate many kinds of computers while learning only one operating system.

Initiating the Operating System: The Boot Process

booting up

the essential step completed by the computer immediately after the power switch is turned on; this step loads the operating system software into RAM

A computer cannot run any operating system until it loads that software into RAM. Following instructions in read-only memory (ROM), it completes this essential step immediately after you turn on the power switch. This is called **booting up** the computer system. Different systems perform different operations, but systems that run MS-DOS boot up in a five-step sequence:

1. *The user turns on the power.* Turning on the power switch starts the process.
2. *The CPU checks the BIOS chip.* Instructions programmed into a ROM chip called the *Basic Input/Output System (BIOS)* direct the CPU to perform a number of diagnostic checks of system hardware and then look for the operating system files. Usually, the boot-up routine directs the CPU to check the main diskette drive (Drive A:) first; it checks the hard disk if it finds no appropriate file there. This sequence allows the user to boot from an original diskette to bypass the boot-up files on the hard disk if necessary.
3. *The operating system is loaded into memory.* Once the CPU finds the operating system files, instructions in ROM direct it to load those files into memory. After this point, the operating system controls the rest of boot up and subsequent system operations.
4. *The operating system checks for important files.* The boot-up process next follows instructions in a file named CONFIG.SYS to specify the system's hardware configuration, including CD-ROM drive and expanded memory. The file named COMMAND.COM then loads into RAM to provide the command language interpreter for the operating system. This piece of software interprets basic operating system commands and carries out the appropriate activities. (The CONFIG.SYS and COMMAND.COM files form part of the computer's original operating system package. Users should never delete these files, although changes in the system configuration do often require modifications to their contents.) After loading COMMAND.COM, the computer checks for an optional file named AUTOEXEC.BAT that automatically launches programs specified by the user. For example, someone who runs Windows in combination with MS-DOS should usually include a command in the system's AUTOEXEC.BAT file that launches the Windows program.
5. *The screen displays the operating system prompt or a graphical user interface.* The boot-up process for MS-DOS finishes by displaying a graphical user interface screen or a prompt, such as C:/>, at which the user can issue an operating system command. At this point, you can start applications software to write term papers, make calculations, or perform other tasks.

Utility Programs

utility programs

systems software programs that perform useful functions like merging and sorting sets of data and keeping track of computer jobs as they run

Along with the functional capabilities of the operating system, systems software also includes **utility programs** to perform additional useful functions like merging and sorting sets of data and keeping track of computer jobs as they run. New computer systems often include some installed utility programs. You can purchase additional utility programs after you begin working with your computer and recognize your needs.

Some utilities help with system management needs. *Diagnostic utilities* help personal computer users to identify the causes of problems with their systems and to optimize the functions of RAM, disk drives, and other components. One popular diagnostic utility package is Norton Utilities. This program can help identify disk problems and suggest solutions. It also offers a defragmentation program, which will optimize system performance by rearranging blocks of data on the hard disk for quick retrieval.

Another category of utilities is *antivirus utilities.* They protect against infection by known computer viruses (destructive programs that can destroy data, programs, or even operating systems). Virus utilities check hard disks, diskettes, and computer memory for viruses and remove them when found. Symantec and Virex are two leading antivirus utilities.

FIGURE 3.4

Desktop Organizer
A desktop organizing utility activates functions when called by the user; it does not appear on-screen or disrupt the activities of other programs. (Source: Courtesy of Starfish Software.)

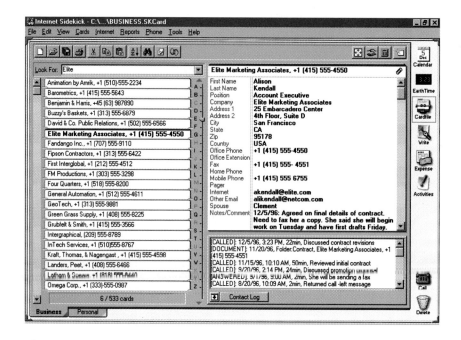

Many *desktop organizers* pop up as needed to make calculations, store notes, make phone calls, schedule appointments, and more without disrupting the functions of other applications. (See Figure 3.4.) While working in your other programs, you can call up a desktop organizer, perform a desired task, and then return to your initial application.

File management utilities help users of some computers to display the full contents of files created on completely different computer systems and software packages. For example, Outside In for Windows, published by Systems Compatibility Corporation, allows an IBM-compatible system to view a file created on a Macintosh. The Macintosh operating system provides the reverse function through its MacLink extension.

Data compression utilities help take advantage of available storage capacity. Compressed files take up less space on disks, so they take up less memory. When a compressed file is needed, the utility's decompression routines place the expanded versions in RAM. Data compression utilities can almost double the amount of data you can store on a disk, increasing capacity without additional hardware costs.

Many other types of utilities are also available. File synchronization utilities update files stored on different computers to ensure that all versions match. Screen capture programs such as PixelPop, from Imageset Corp., save a current screen display to a disk file or print it. Backup utilities automatically allow you to back up your hard disk. One utility, from Eloquent Technology, can even translate text to speech. The software can be programmed to convey emotions like excitement and boredom by varying pitch level and other variables. It can also simulate accents, such as a Southern drawl or a Midwestern twang.

APPLICATIONS SOFTWARE

A computer system will not run normally without an operating system to control basic hardware functions, and utility programs support basic computing activities. Still, users need applications software to apply the power of the computer in a way that helps them solve problems and perform specific tasks. Users of all kinds run applications programs to make computers do a wide range of useful work.

In a business setting, applications software provides especially valuable support for decision making. Suppose that a manager suspects that some employees are working more than 40 hours each week, while others are working less than 40 hours. The company must pay 1½ times normal wage rates for hours over 40 per week, so it may be able to achieve the same production at a lower cost by ensuring that all employees work 40 hours at their regular wage rates and none work overtime. To assess this possibility, the manager might ask for a list from the firm's payroll program of all employees who worked significantly more or less than 40 hours per week over the previous three months.

Applications programs also perform more routine transaction processing tasks like completing sales orders, controlling inventory, paying bills, writing paychecks, and providing regular information to managers and executives. In fact, applications programs carry out most of the computer-related business activities discussed in this book. Table 3.2 lists other possibilities.

A company can obtain applications software in three ways:

1. Develop its own programs
2. Customize an existing program for its own application needs
3. Use an existing program without changes

In the first two choices, the company creates **proprietary software;** in the third, it purchases **off-the-shelf software.**

proprietary software

software developed by a company for its own needs

off-the-shelf software

general-function software that buyers can literally pull off the shelves of retail stores

Proprietary Applications Software

Some companies, especially large ones or those with unusual processing needs, assign internal IS personnel to develop custom applications packages. A company gains important advantages by completing such a project:

1. *Conformance with user requirements.* Custom software can do exactly what its users need. It can provide essential features, reports, and other output that fully support transaction processing and decision-making needs. By sponsoring the development project, a firm can maintain full control over the results. At the same time, the organization need not pay for features that it does not require and would never use.

TABLE 3.2

Business Functions of Applications Software

Accounts receivable	Freight routing
Accounts payable	Order entry
Airline ticketing	Payroll
Automated teller machines	Human resources management
Cash-flow analysis	Electrical power management
Check processing	Textbook editing
Loan processing	Purchasing
Credit card administration	Real estate management
Newsletter production	Receiving
Distribution control	Restaurant management
General ledger	Retail operations
Health care scheduling	Hotel management
Inventory control	Shipping
Invoicing	Investment management
Production scheduling	Tax planning and preparation

Customized Software has helped OTR Express to track its loads, destinations, and rates. (Source: Courtesy of OTR Express, Inc.)

2. *Flexibility during use.* Since the firm owns the software that it develops itself, company personnel can suggest and carry out changes to better suit current practices. The same staff members who develop a program can alter or supplement it as the company's needs change.

3. *Accommodation of unique problems.* Customized software can address processing needs unique to one company. In contrast, an off-the-shelf application must meet more general needs of a larger market to justify the software publisher's investment in its development. A company with extremely unusual needs may have to develop its own applications or do without any.

Of course, the company must pay for this close match between its processing needs and its software's capabilities. In-house development can cost much more than buying software off the shelf.

OTR Express, a Kansas truckload carrier, provides one example of successful in-house software development. This company developed distribution control software to track its loads, destinations, and rates. These custom application programs help to organize lists of customers, recent shipping requests, and routes. The system updates data daily and reprocesses everything every 30 days. OTR's software then lists customers in order by the profitability of their shipping requests. OTR's loadplanners use this list to target the firm's best prospects and plan schedules to keep them satisfied.[2]

Recall that a company need not employ its own programmers to obtain proprietary software. External vendors can often supply custom software less expensively than a company can maintain a staff of programmers. A firm that specializes in software development, often called a *value-added software vendor,* may develop or modify an application to meet the needs of a particular company. As an alternative, the vendor might create an application to perform processing common in an industry and then modify the program for individual companies.

Off-the-Shelf Applications Software

Computer users can purchase or lease needed applications if they lack the expertise or funds required for development projects. Some software developers concentrate on producing and selling programs that meet the processing needs of many computer users and organizations with little or no alteration. These general-function packages get the name *off-the-shelf software* because buyers can literally pull the packages off the shelves of retail stores.

Many companies find that off-the-shelf applications supply adequate support for their business processes. The owner of a video arcade probably cannot afford to hire a programmer to create an application that will help manage the inventory of game machines, repair parts, and other supplies. But a software retailer in the same mall probably sells a program that will process inventory records and perform many other functions, as well. Even the giant aeronautics manufacturer and defense contractor Northrop decided to implement a standardized application to track inventories of 256,000 components and ensure prompt delivery of needed parts.[3]

Companies decide to purchase or lease off-the-shelf software to gain a number of advantages:

1. *Low cost.* A software publisher spreads development expenses over a large number of customers, reducing the cost of the application to any one customer.
2. *Low risk.* Potential users can accurately analyze the features and performance of a package before they buy it. Early users identify problems, or "bugs," with new software, so later users can expect their software to work as intended. In contrast, when a company develops a custom application it takes more risk that the final package will fail to offer planned features and performance.
3. *High quality.* Many companies offer high-quality off-the-shelf packages for common processing tasks. Of course, retail success does not give an iron-clad guarantee of high quality, particularly for unusual applications targeted to small markets.
4. *Quick response.* A company can quickly buy and install off-the-shelf software; a project to develop and install custom software can take years.
5. *A handle on resource limitations.* A firm may need a complete staff of IS personnel to develop or customize a proprietary application. Small firms without these kinds of resources may have no choice but to rely on off-the-shelf software.

Support Provided by Applications Software

Whether a firm develops applications software internally or buys the latest package from a software company, such as Microsoft or Claris, it can find programs that support many, widely varied processing needs. Different applications apply the computer's processing power to specific organizational and personal activities, so choices of specific packages have powerful effects on the effectiveness of a computer's support for the user's needs. Individuals, groups, and organizations should carefully analyze their specific processing goals and needs before they decide what applications software they will use and how they will acquire it.

Most personal computer users rely heavily on software from a category called **personal productivity tools.** These general-purpose programs support a number of processing activities common among individual users:

personal productivity tools

general-purpose software programs that support a number of processing activities common among individual users

- Word processors for writing tasks
- Spreadsheet programs for numerical calculations
- Database management systems to track essential information
- Communications tools to link PCs with outside resources
- Presentation graphics software to produce attractive, persuasive displays for meetings and other events

In addition, businesspeople now regularly rely on applications software for more advanced functions like project management, financial management, desktop publishing, and creativity enhancement (see Table 3.3).

PC users can buy personal productivity software off the shelf in single, stand-alone packages, integrated packages, or suites. **Integrated packages** combine the processing functions of several applications into one software package. A **software suite** is a bundle of single applications designed to function together and share data.

integrated packages

personal productivity software packages that combine the processing functions of several applications into one software package

software suite

a bundle of single applications designed to function together and share data

Integrated packages like Microsoft Works and ClarisWorks usually include some combination of the tools listed earlier. They allow the user to shift easily between word processing documents, spreadsheets, and databases, carrying data from one to another. Different functions work in compatible ways to meet the user's processing needs without unnecessary concern for barriers between

TABLE 3.3

Advanced Applications in Business

TYPE OF SOFTWARE	FUNCTION
Project management	Planning, scheduling, allocating, and controlling people and resources (money, time, and technology) needed to complete a project on schedule
Financial management	Tracking and reporting income and expenses related to company finances and budgets, including management of investment portfolios
Desktop publishing	Creating high-quality documents featuring complex mixes of text and graphics with elaborate page layouts
Creativity enhancement	Generating innovative ideas and solutions to problems within a framework conducive to thought

different applications. Individual functions within integrated packages usually provide less powerful capabilities than users could get from comparable stand-alone packages, though. Also, advances in operating systems have simplified the important ability to shift between different applications. This change has allowed separate programs to provide seamless support for a user's processing needs similar to that of an integrated package. For these reasons, software suites are quickly replacing integrated packages.

Software suites can combine many individual applications into full-functioned systems. Word processors, spreadsheets, database management systems, graphics, communications tools, organizers, and other kinds of tools can all work together. A user with specialized needs can often select which stand-alone packages to include as part of the suite. Some common suites are Microsoft Office 95, Lotus SmartSuite 96, and ClarisWorks 4.0. One software company, for example, lets customers select from eight packages; all of them work similarly, so you can learn the basics for one application and then apply the same techniques to carry out similar functions in the other applications. Also, programs usually cost less in a bundled suite than the total of their individual prices. Unfortunately, one software publisher's suite may include one or more weak applications, so some people still prefer to buy separate packages.

Integrated Software packages combine several tools such as word processing, spreadsheet, and database programs.
(Source: Courtesy of Microsoft Corporation and Claris Corporation.)

groupware

applications software that helps to link separate computer systems in a way that helps a team of managers and employees to share ideas and produce joint output

New Kinds of Support: Groupware. Along with familiar personal productivity functions, business users rely on applications software to support a continuously expanding list of company activities. **Groupware** has emerged recently as an important tool for helping groups of people to work efficiently and effectively together. Groupware helps to link separate computer systems in a way that helps a team of managers and employees to share ideas and produce joint output. Individuals working from their homes hundreds of miles apart could work together to jointly develop a World Wide Web site or a radical design for an ultralight airplane. Groupware can support people's efforts to expand their potential interactions with others far beyond traditional boundaries. Similarly, new applications tools emerge regularly; as they do, they create new possibilities for the lives of users. The most well-known groupware program is Lotus Notes.

shareware

software that can be used without paying anything

freeware

same as shareware

Shareware. As software costs consume ever-larger chunks of information system budgets, users hunt for inexpensive alternatives. Some PC users find the processing functions they need in low-cost **shareware** or **freeware,** which they can use without paying anything. Small groups of programmers or individuals working alone often produce these applications and sell them at very low prices. The functions of many shareware packages mimic those of much more expensive and popular applications. They may not offer all the options of more traditionally developed software, but some managers and executives get what they need at good prices from shareware.[4] Many Internet sites maintain large collections of these programs that users can download for free; they can try a software package to confirm that it performs well, after which most shareware developers expect people to pay small fees for regular use.

Shareware applications perform all kinds of processing functions.[5] Packages include word processors, spelling checkers, grammar checkers, and fill-in-the-blank business correspondence programs. For under $30, you can buy software to help make a business plan and schedule important business meetings. Shareware desktop publishing and graphics programs can help you to produce documents with color and design features similar to those available in high-priced applications. Some excellent shareware communications programs allow you to connect to other computers and the Internet. (The popular Web browser Netscape originated as a shareware program.) Shareware utility programs can help you back up your hard disk and manage files.

PROGRAMMING LANGUAGES

Many users carry out all kinds of activities on their computers without ever understanding or caring about how their software came to offer essential capabilities for their systems. These people may miss an important opportunity to improve their own effectiveness. By understanding general programming basics, users can enhance their own control of their computer systems.

Specialists controlled the earliest computers. They manually flipped switches to open and close electrical circuits within the processing hardware. This complex procedure allowed them to enter both data and processing instructions in the correct sequences to complete the most basic operations and

TABLE 3.4

Evolution of Programming Languages

GENERATION	LANGUAGE	APPROXIMATE DEVELOPMENT DATE	SAMPLE STATEMENT OR ACTION
First	Machine language	1940s	00010101
Second	Assembly language	1950s	MVC
Third	High-level languages	1960s	READ SALES
Fourth	Query languages	1970s	PRINT EMPLOYEE NUMBER IF GROSS PAY > 1000
Fifth	Natural languages	1980s	IF certain medical conditions exist, THEN make specific diagnosis

generate even limited output. Today's computers, however, store and process entire blocks of data and long sequences of instructions to control the CPU's activities and the physical states of digital circuitry.

A programmer can choose among several common languages to find the one that provides the best tools for solving a particular computing problem. As Table 3.4 shows, programmers typically think of the range of available programming languages as successive generations.

Generations of Programming Languages

First Generation: Machine Language. The binary digits of the CPU actually form a kind of computer language called **machine language.** Machine language for a simple operation to multiply two numbers could require several strings of 0s and 1s. One string might cause the CPU to retrieve the first number from RAM. A second string might retrieve the second number. A third might multiply the two numbers, and a fourth might place the result back into another memory location (see Figure 3.5).

Machine language is considered a **low-level language** because its binary symbols (1 and 0) resemble the way the computer works (circuits on and off). For instance, **American Standard Code for Information Interchange (ASCII)** defines machine-language representations of letters of the alphabet. Since CPUs can process machine language, they can process binary translations of text files.

Unfortunately, people can understand machine language only with extreme difficulty. Therefore, programmers need a way to convert instructions that they can understand into binary code to create machine language that will control the CPU as desired. **Programming languages** perform this essential task by assigning terms that programmers can recognize and remember for sets of machine-language instructions that direct a computer's CPU to accomplish certain functions. This substitution sacrifices some processing speed, but it vastly simplifies the programming process.

machine language

computer language formed by the binary digits of the CPU

low-level language

computer language whose binary symbols (1 and 0) resemble the way the computer works (circuits on and off)

American Standard Code for Information Interchange (ASCII)

the code that defines machine-language representations of letters of the alphabet

programming languages

computer languages that assign terms that programmers can recognize and remember for sets of machine-language instructions that direct a computer's CPU to accomplish certain functions

FIGURE 3.5

Simplified Machine-language Instruction
A machine-language instruction consists of all 0s and 1s to carry out an operation.

00100101	00000010	00001101
Operation code (i.e., multiply)	Address location 1 (i.e., first number)	Address location 2 (i.e., second number)

assembly languages

the second generation of programming languages, which replace binary digits with symbols that people can more easily understand

high-level languages

the third generation of programming languages, which use more symbolic code than do assembly languages

COBOL

a high-level language developed as a procedure-oriented, business-focused language to develop batch-processing applications

Second Generation: Assembly Language. The second generation of programming languages, **assembly language,** resulted from initial attempts to overcome difficulties of programming in machine language by replacing binary digits with symbols that people could more easily understand. Assembly languages use codes like *A* for an addition operation, *MVC* for a data movement, and so on.

Third Generation: High-level Languages. Languages in the third generation continued the trend toward more symbolic code and away from basic hardware operations. Statements and commands in these **high-level languages,** including BASIC, COBOL, and C, resemble English words. Programmers can learn and use these languages more easily than they can master machine and assembly languages, because program statements more closely resemble everyday human communication and understanding. High-level languages use sensible-sounding statements such as

```
PRINT TOTAL_SALES, READ HOURS WORKED
```

and

```
NORMAL_PAY=HOURS_WORKED*PAYRATE.
```

Business organizations rely heavily on programs written in an important example of a high-level language: **COBOL,** short for *COmmon Business-Oriented Language.* COBOL was developed in the late 1950s as a procedure-oriented, business-focused language to develop batch-processing applications. Today's COBOL programs can complete either batch processing or real-time processing.

COBOL's developers designed the language to give programs the appearance and structure of business reports written in English with sentences, paragraphs, sections, and divisions. As Figure 3.6 illustrates, COBOL programs are generally long, requiring up to seven times more instructions than other high-level language programs that produce similar output. Companies have found, however, that COBOL's powerful file processing capabilities offset the drawback of program length. For another advantage, COBOL programs written according to accepted standards can typically run on many computer platforms.

Despite its age, COBOL continues to dominate business computing. An estimated 80–90 percent of today's business software is written in COBOL. Because companies have such vast financial investments in their current COBOL programs, many hesitate to switch to less complex software. A new version of COBOL, COBOL 97, will also help to keep it current with today's business needs.

C

a high-level, general-purpose language that supports programming for real-time processing in both business and scientific applications

Another high-level programming language, known as **C,** was written in the 1970s by Dennis Ritchie of Bell Laboratories. This general-purpose language effectively supports programming for real-time processing in both business and scientific applications. It has evolved into a largely standardized version for many computer platforms, which helps to make applications portable between different systems. Unlike many high-level languages, C gives extensive access to many basic functions of the processor. This similarity to assembly language suits it to programming for critical systems software as well as applications for businesses and other users.

fourth-generation languages (4GLs)

high-level programming languages with less emphasis on processing procedures and a closer resemblance to English than third-generation languages

Fourth-Generation Languages. Observers dispute the boundaries that define generations of programming languages after the third. Most agree that a **fourth-generation language (4GL)** is a high-level programming language

FIGURE 3.6

COBOL Program to Compute the Total of 15 Numbers

```
IDENTIFICATION DIVISION

PROGRAM-ID.   TOTAL-OF-15-NUMBERS.
ENVIRONMENT DIVISION.
CONFIGURATION SECTION.
SOURCE-COMPUTER.   CYBER-74.
OBJECT-COMPUTER.   CYBER-74.
INPUT-OUTPUT SECTION.
FILE-CONTROL
      SELECT DATA-FILE ASSIGN TO DISK.
      SELECT TOTAL-FILE ASSIGN TO PRINTER-FZ.
DATADIVISION.
FILE SECTION.
FD    DATA-FILE
      LABEL RECORDS ARE OMITTED.
      DATA RECORD IS DATA-CARD.
01    DATA-CARD.
      02  DATA-VALUE  PICTURE IS 9(6)V99.
      02  FILLER      PICTURE IS X(72)
FD    TOTAL-FILE.
      LABEL RECORDS ARE OMITTED.
      DATA RECORD IS TOTAL-LINE.
01    TOTAL-LINE.
      02  TITLE       PICTURE IS X(12).
                      VALUE IS "THE TOTAL IS."
      02  FILLER      PICTURE IS X(2).
      02  TOTAL-VALUE PICTURE IS 9(13)V99.
      02  FILLER      PICTURE IS X(102).
WORKING-STORAGE SECTION
77    RUNNING-TOTAL  PICTURE IS 9(13)V99.
                     VALUE IS 0.
PROCEDURE DIVISION.
BEGIN-JOB
      OPEN INPUT DATA-FILE.
      OPEN OUTPUT TOTAL-FILE.
MAIN-LOOP
      READ DATA-FILE AT END GO TO PRINT-ROUTINE.
      ADD DATA-VALUE TO RUNNING-TOTAL.
      GO TO MAIN LOOP.
PRINT-ROUTINE.
      MOVE SPACES TO TOTAL-LINE.
      MOVE RUNNING-TOTAL TO TOTAL VALUE.
      WRITE TOTAL-LINE.
END-OF-JOB.
      CLOSE DATA-FILE.
      CLOSE TOTAL-FILE.
      STOP RUN.
```

with less emphasis on processing procedures and a closer resemblance to English than third-generation languages. A 4GL emphasizes the desired output more than the program statements that produce that output. As a result, many managers with little or no training can create their own programs using fourth-generation languages.

Some 4GLs allow users to specify simple commands or procedures to retrieve information from databases (organized collections of related data). Users can state these commands in the form of simple questions or queries. For example, a billing database written in a 4GL might allow a user to click on the variable AMOUNT and enter ">$250" to get a listing of all customers whose bills exceed $250. Fourth-generation languages also allow for more sophisticated queries like these:

```
PRINT EMPLOYEE NUMBER IF GROSS PAY>1000
PRINT CUSTOMER NAME IF AMOUNT >5000 AND IF TIME DUE >90
PRINT INVENTORY NUMBER IF ON HAND <50
```

Some 4GLs offer code-generation features that automatically produce many of the programming statements and instructions required to produce specific output. Code generators can sometimes create 90 percent or more of all statements for a particular programming project.

Because these languages allow users to ask questions in sentences that resemble human language, they have been called **query languages.** Many of them operate only within organized databases, so they are also called *database languages.* One popular fourth-generation language is a standardized system for searching and manipulating databases called **Structured Query Language (SQL).** Businesspeople have found 4GLs extremely helpful in developing programs for expert systems. They have also found SQL to be extremely helpful in getting useful information like this:

```
SELECT OCCUPANT FROM ROOM_CHG
   WHERE ROOM_CHG>1000
```

In this SQL statement, OCCUPANT refers to patients at a hospital, and ROOM_CHG refers to the total room charges for that patient. The SQL statement selects all patients who stayed in the hospital with total room charges greater than $1,000.

Fifth-Generation Languages. Finally, **fifth-generation languages (5GLs)** also support creation of programs for expert systems and even artificial intelligence, in which computers imitate the reasoning capabilities of humans. Fifth-generation languages are sometimes called **natural languages** because their syntax so closely approaches human language. Fifth-generation programming languages allow programmers to communicate with computers as they would with other people (see Figure 3.7).

For example, programs written in fifth-generation languages can respond correctly to queries like: "How many athletic shoes did our company sell last month?" Although many fifth-generation languages are experimental and development continues, database programs have already implemented 5GLs. Other 5GL programs have the potential to predict the weather, diagnose diseases based on input about symptoms, and guide exploration for oil and natural gas. Table 3.5 lists some natural programming languages and their uses.

Object-oriented Programming Languages. In an even newer development, **object-oriented programming (OOP) languages** group program instructions and data into modules called *objects* that perform individual processing tasks. By grouping, or **encapsulating,** relevant program steps and data, an object captures a routine for performing a particular function or task. The

query languages

programming languages that allow users to ask questions in sentences that resemble human language

Structured Query Language (SQL)

a popular 4GL that is a standardized system for searching and manipulating databases

fifth-generation languages (5GLs)

programming languages that support creation of programs for expert systems and artificial intelligence

natural languages

programming languages whose syntax closely approaches human language

object-oriented programming (OOP) languages

programming languages that group program instructions and data into modules called *objects* that perform individual processing tasks

encapsulating

grouping relevant program steps and data to capture a routine for performing a particular function or task

FIGURE 3.7

Sample Natural Language Program

```
GIVE MF A SORTED LIST OF
ALL SALES REPRESENTATIVES
LIVING IN DENVER AND
EARNING OVER $47,500
```

TABLE 3.5

Software Packages with Natural Language Capabilities

PRODUCT	USE OR AREA
Clout	Interfacing with R-base database
RAMIS II English	Interfacing with RAMIS II
STRAIGHT TALE	Word processing
EXPLORER	Map display and generation
BROKER	Interfacing with Standard & Poor's database
MARKETEER	Interfacing with market analysis
LADDER	Ship identification and location
NATURALLINK	Interfacing with Dow Jones News/Retrieval Service
INTELLECT	Interfacing with mainframe databases

object can then become part of many different processing routines that require that function. For example, one company uses OOP to computerize the way companies sell and deliver their products without shutting down entire programs (see "Who's Who: Joe Liemandt/Trilogy Development Group").

In effect, each object represents a limited-function application program. A complete object-oriented program combines objects with desired characteristics to perform processing required by the user (see Figure 3.8). Objects in such a group can work effectively together because they acquire some characteristics of other objects in the same group through a process called *inheritance*.

Programmers create applications using object-oriented programming languages in much the same way that construction crews assemble buildings using prefabricated parts like window and door units. A carpenter adds an entry and exit capability to a wall by installing a complete door-and-jamb assembly, saving the trouble of making a door on-site and hanging it in a site-built jamb. In much the same way, a programmer can give a data-input capability to a payroll program simply by including an object with the required instructions. By combining existing objects for much of a program's processing steps, the programmer can avoid the time and expense of writing new instructions for those tasks. An object can even direct a computer to execute programs or to retrieve and manipulate data from outside that object.

FIGURE 3.8

Object-oriented Programming
Programmers can combine new program objects with existing ones, either purchased from vendors or previously developed internally, to easily and efficiently develop programs that accomplish desired processing.

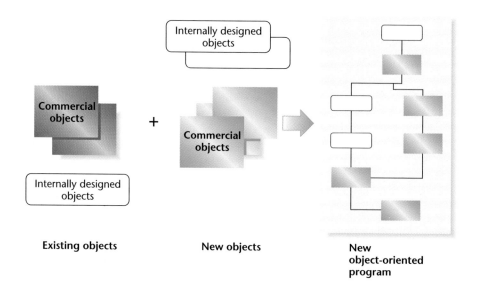

WHO'S WHO

Joe Liemandt/Trilogy Development Group

Joe Liemandt's business goal is simple: he wants to "change the way things are bought around the world." When Liemandt was a senior at Stanford, through research he discovered that, while companies had begun to use applications software in a variety of ways, they still hadn't figured out how to computerize the way they sold and delivered their products. Most sales orders were still handwritten, with reference to cumbersome product catalogs and confirmations between salespeople, engineers, customers, and so forth. There had to be a better way, thought Liemandt.

He found it. The trouble was, he found it during the second semester of his senior year, and he wanted to drop out of college. "My market window's closing!" Liemandt exclaimed to his father. "You're a moron," replied his father, the late Gregory Liemandt (who worked with Jack Welch at General Electric before starting his own company). But Joe believed that if he didn't move fast on his idea, he'd be lost. Hewlett-Packard and IBM were already researching proprietary projects.

"I knew when I got to college I was going to start a software company," explains Liemandt. "I started doing tons of research. I'd sit in the library going through lists of the top 50 software companies." He researched Hewlett-Packard's development of a rule-based programming package, which consisted of a series of if/then constructions that HP salespeople could use to determine price structures. But while rule-based programming had its advantages, it also had its limits, most notably the cumbersome number of if/then equations needed to make it work. So he took a look at Xerox's constraint-based programming, a type of programming already in use by airlines to track passenger yields. But it just wasn't able to handle huge volumes of data.

So Liemandt quit college and, along with several classmates, founded Trilogy Development Group. "Their parents hated me," he recalls. But the group spent thousands of hours programming until they finally hit on a combination of rule-based programming, constraint-based programming, and object-oriented programming. Object-oriented programming would allow programmers to add new information (for instance, about new product lines) or make other changes without shutting down the entire program. Then the group moved to Austin, Texas, to lure David Franke, a prominent programmer, aboard. The result of all these efforts was Trilogy's Selling Chain software—and it was a hit.

Selling Chain allows companies to generate product and service solutions sales orders by computer. For instance, a manufacturer can load into the program all the products, specifications, and options that it offers to customers. Once all this information is in the program, a salesperson can ask it questions such as: What if my customer wants to link one workstation with another printer? What would that do to the price? Does this customer need new cables? And so forth.

Shortly after David Franke joined Trilogy, Hewlett-Packard signed a $3.5 million agreement for Trilogy's sales-configuration software and support services. Companies like Chrysler, Boeing, and IBM have followed. "I'm not afraid of big business," says Liemandt, rather proudly. "I love big business." Big business has certainly noticed him—not only customers, but competitors. Germany's SAP ($1.9 billion in sales) and Baan of the Netherlands ($216 million) are developing similar, competing products. So Liemandt can't rest on his accomplishments. But he has no intention of doing so. "It's a land grab," he notes. "Whoever gets the market share and partners first, wins. We've got two years until it is over." After that, who knows? But it's certain that Liemandt will have something up his sleeve; change is inherent in the IS business. "Six months from now, whatever you're doing, you will have to do something different," he predicts. Those aren't prophetic words; they're just the facts.

Sources: Josh McHugh, "Holy Cow, No One's Done This!" *Forbes*, June 3, 1996, pp. 122–128; Janice Maloney, "So You Want to Be a Software Superstar," *Fortune*, June 10, 1996, p. 11. Photo courtesy of Trilogy Development Group.

reusable code

the sequence of programming instructions that can be reused within an object for a variety of applications

A single object can provide a set of capabilities for many kinds of programs. This possibility creates one of the primary advantages of object-oriented programming: **reusable code.** The programmer can reuse the sequence of programming instructions within an object for a variety of applications, just as the carpenter can install one type of prefabricated door in many different houses. A payroll application, a billing program, and an inventory control program could all include the same object to provide data-input capabilities. Reusable code speeds programming and maintains reliability, since the programmer

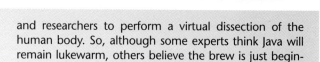

BUSINESS BITS

Sun Microsystems' Java 1.0

Sun Microsystems has a new brew. It's called Java 1.0, and it already has a HotJava browser and JavaScript, the next generation of Netscape's LiveScript. Java allows developers to write miniapplications, or applets, that are distributed over the Internet and can work across a range of browsers, although Java can also handle large applications. It has a variety of features, including an interpreter, a debugger, a compiler, and a viewer for running applets without a Web browser.

Much of Java's structure comes from the C++ programming language, but there are some significant differences. For instance, the programming syntax of Java is simpler than that of C++, making it easier to use for some people. But Java is also much slower than native C++ code. "It's about ten times slower than C right now," notes Kim Polese, marketing manager for products at Sun Microsystems. Some reviewers point to the fact that Java's reliance on C++ could be a turn-off for users. "Many programmers are already conversant with C++, making for an easy transition to Java. But those without extensive C or C++ programming experience may have a difficult time," writes Kevin Richard in *PC Magazine*.

But for those who get the hang of it, Java can be an excellent tool. One company is using Java to create an on-line financial service—called Wall StreetWeb—that can give immediate stock quotes. Another has developed the Visible Human Viewer, which allows medical students

and researchers to perform a virtual dissection of the human body. So, although some experts think Java will remain lukewarm, others believe the brew is just beginning to get hot.

1. Do you think lack of speed will eventually become an issue for Java users? Why or why not?
2. In addition to the examples discussed, what types of applets could you imagine being created by Java?
3. Access one of the following Web sites and see what you can learn about Java's potential: http://java.sun.com; or http://www.surinam.net/java/jars.

Sources: Kevin Richard, "Java 1.0: Something New Is Brewing on the Web," *PC Magazine*, April 9, 1996, p. 51; James Staten, "Java House Opening on Mac in January," *MacWeek News*, www.macweek.com/mw_12-04-94/java.html. Photo courtesy of Sun Microsystems/Java.

need not check for errors in instructions within an object known to function correctly in other applications. One IBM manager has predicted that the change from writing a new set of instructions for every function in a program to object-oriented programming will yield productivity gains similar to those of the industrial revolution.[6]

Wall Street leaders Bear Stearns and Salomon Brothers have implemented object-oriented programs to replace their old systems and quickly create new investment programs for mutual fund and stock investing. The new applications enhance the capabilities of existing programs without having to rewrite those instruction sets from scratch. In the fast-paced world of Wall Street, the reusable code of object-oriented programming allows faster responses to volatile markets and higher investment returns.[7]

Harley-Davidson used an object-oriented programming language to develop the software in its information system. Each time the company markets a new motorcycle or other product, managers use this language to quickly modify the tracking software to reflect the change. The programming language helps all company personnel to support the larger information system objective of providing timely and accurate product information and the organizational goal of merchandise tracking.[8]

Smalltalk

an object-oriented language for use on desktop computers

Alan Kay developed **Smalltalk** at Xerox's Palo Alto Research Center in the 1970s. For more than a decade, the language found few applications in business settings. Its implementation on desktop computers has begun to change this. Today, companies such as Texas Instruments and Citicorp are using Smalltalk for a variety of business applications.[9]

Emerging object-oriented languages include C++ and Java. C++ is an enhancement of C, discussed earlier, that adds capabilities for object-oriented programming. C++ maintains the strengths of C as a real-time, general-purpose language for business and scientific applications, and it simplifies and speeds the programming process.[10]

Java

an object-oriented language that automates procedures to incorporate video, audio, and 3-D animation into applications software

Java is a newer object-oriented programming language developed by Sun Microsystems that automates procedures to incorporate video, audio, and 3-D animation into applications software. (See "Business Bits: Sun Microsystems' Java 1.0.") Along with HotJava, a World Wide Web browser, Java gives programmers a powerful programming environment in which to develop almost any conceivable type of application that will work across the Internet.

The power of object-oriented programming has also led to efforts to convert more traditional programming languages to take advantage of the new methods. For example, since many organizations have millions of dollars invested in COBOL-based information systems, they do not want to abandon COBOL altogether. Instead, modified versions of COBOL seek to implement object-oriented programming within that language. One project is working toward creating a *Common Object–Oriented Language,* or *COOL.*

visual programming languages

languages that allow a programmer to use a mouse, on-screen icons, and pull-down menus to create programs in traditional languages

Visual Programming Languages. Another new development has produced many programming languages that work in visual or graphical environments. Often called **visual programming languages,** these languages allow a programmer to use a mouse, on-screen icons, and pull-down menus to create programs in traditional languages. This visual environment can create an easier and more intuitive user interface for programming.

Visual Basic, PCCOBOL, Visual PCCOBOL, and Visual C++ are examples of visual programming languages (see Figure 3.9). Despite their similar names, languages with a visual or graphical environment usually differ substantially from those based strictly on character-based and text-based programming.

Classes of Programming Languages

batch processing languages

languages that support programming for routine processing tasks that handle large sets of data at regular intervals

real-time processing languages

languages that must support programming to generate immediate output on demand for less predictable processing tasks

The developers of programming languages envisioned them as tools for solving particular kinds of problems. Therefore, each language displays attributes that suit it to a certain class of computing problems. **Batch processing languages** support programming for routine processing tasks that handle large sets of data at regular intervals. For example, a payroll application must collect data for all of a company's employees and produce paychecks every one or two weeks. In contrast, **real-time processing languages** must support programming to generate immediate output on demand for less predictable processing tasks. A ticketing agency must run a program in real time to determine seat availability for a rock concert every time someone wants to buy a ticket. Different languages suit the programming routines required for these kinds of processing.

FIGURE 3.9

Visual Language Translator for COBOL
Changes can be implemented efficiently by graphically analyzing and debugging COBOL programs. (Source: Courtesy of Computer Associates International.)

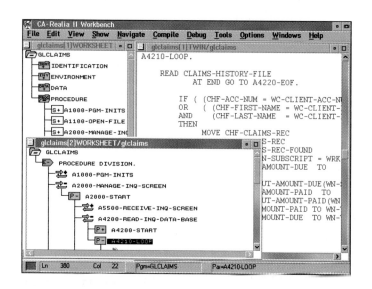

language translators
the interfaces between high-level programming languages and machine languages

interpreter
a language translator that translates one program statement at a time, as the program is running

compiler
a language translator that converts a complete program into machine language to produce a program that the computer can process in its entirety

FIGURE 3.10

How an Interpreter Works
An interpreter translates each program statement or instruction in sequence. The CPU then executes the statement, erases it from memory, and translates another statement. An interpreter does not produce a complete machine-readable version of a program.

Language Translators

As already discussed, programmers would have a hard time writing in machine language's 0s and 1s. Instead, they write programs using higher-level languages. But computers cannot execute the program instructions without translation. The interfaces between the high-level programming language and machine language are called **language translators.** Language translators convert the programmer's source program into its equivalent in machine language so that the computer can process the instructions. There are two types of language translators, interpreters and compilers.

An **interpreter** translates one program statement at a time, as the program is running. It will display on-screen any errors it finds in the statement. (See Figure 3.10.) This line-by-line translation makes interpreters ideal for those who are learning programming. But it does slow the process.

The other type of language translator, a **compiler,** converts a complete program into machine language to produce a program that the computer can process in its entirety. Once the compiler has translated a complete program into machine language, the computer can run the machine language program as many times as needed. A compiler creates a two-stage procedure for program execution (see Figure 3.11). First, it translates the program into machine language; then the CPU executes that program.

Because a CPU can run a complete compiled program faster than it can interpret a program line by line, programmers usually choose compilers to translate frequently run business programs. Compiled programs offer another advantage, since they can often run on different computer system platforms, as

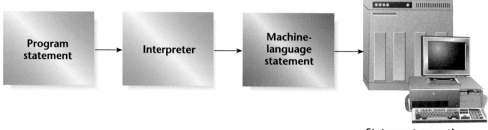

Statement execution

FIGURE 3.11

How a Compiler Works
A compiler translates a complete program into a complete set of binary data (Stage 1). The CPU can then execute the converted program in its entirety (Stage 2).

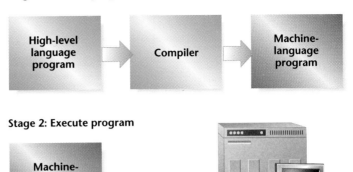

Stage 1: Convert program

High-level language program → Compiler → Machine-language program

Stage 2: Execute program

Machine-language program →

Program execution

long as those systems share a CPU and operating system. Still, an interpreter may give satisfactory results for infrequently run programs.

Programmers use compilers and interpreters for a variety of programming languages. Just as you observe the rules of grammar when writing a report in English, a programmer must conform to the **syntax** of a computer language when writing a computer program. The syntax of a language dictates how the programmer can combine symbols and terms into program statements that convey meaningful instructions to the CPU. Although programmers follow some standard practices while working in any language, they must deal with variations in required syntax between different languages and even between versions of a single language.

syntax

the element of language that dictates how the programmers can combine symbols and terms into program statements that convey meaningful instructions to the CPU

SOFTWARE BUYER'S GUIDE

Computer users frequently make purchase decisions about applications software. They buy systems software less often, since computer hardware purchases usually include operating systems and some utility programs. Still, upgrades sometimes require such a purchase, and users who want to write their own applications must choose language translator packages. The list in this section summarizes some important considerations to guide purchases of software for your personal computer. The "Eye on the Web" box also helps you explore the Internet as a source of product information.

1. *Analyze what you want to do with your computer.* Before you buy software, decide what functions you need it to accomplish. Do you want to use your computer for word processing, keeping track of expenses, paying bills? If you will use your system for your job or courses at a college or university, find out what software your company, school, or other organization uses. Organizations often choose certain standard packages to help users share data and work.

2. *Try to buy software bundled with a computer purchase.* In addition to systems software, computers often come with some applications. Many users get integrated packages in this way. Software already loaded on a new computer saves both money and time required for installation. (See the "Hardware Buyer's Guide" at the end of Chapter 2.)

EYE ON THE WEB

Suppose one afternoon, while leafing through a magazine, you come across a reference to some interesting software. Or maybe a friend has recommended a software package to you. Perhaps you've had a chance to use a certain package at school or on the job. Otherwise, you probably enter into the software-buying decision without much information about the package. You may wonder if the software has the functions you want, or if it is user friendly. Unfortunately, many packages are sold with labels that warn you that only unopened packages may be returned.

The Internet may provide you with a useful alternative. Much as you would be able to read descriptive information about a software package in a magazine, you can search and find similar information on-line, through a WWW query. But that's just the beginning.

When you access a software company's page on the Web, you might discover that it is possible to download a demonstration copy of the software. This feature gives you the ability to explore the software's capabilities and its interface prior to making a purchase decision. For example, Nisus, a company that produces mailing list coordinators and calendaring software, permits the user to download scaled-down, demonstration versions of some products. You might wonder if there are any differences between the full package and the demonstration package; the Nisus Web page alerts you of these differences in advance, even before the software has been downloaded.

Those who are already licensed users of a package may want to browse the Web periodically for updated products. Often, a patch—an incremental change to an existing version of a software package—can be taken directly off the Internet.

Software companies find the Web to be a useful means of alerting the public to upcoming events. Microsoft, for example, allows users to query the Web for upcoming Microsoft events. In fact, the user may narrow the query down to a specific type of software (e.g., word processing software). The name and phone number of a contact person are also provided for those who want more information.

The Web allows the user to browse for answers to standard software questions, such as system requirements (e.g., disk space or memory requirements), as well as characteristics and suggested prices. In addition, companies are beginning to take advantage of the Internet to announce software news. Because software announcements can be posted in real time, users can acquire the latest information.

The types of software that can be accessed through the Web seem limitless. The Internet abounds with information concerning word processing, spreadsheets, databases, and other software. Corporate users may browse through groupware or presentation software titles and Internet browsers like Netscape. Individuals considering a purchase for entertainment or home use may select from numerous games. There are also sites for games that are actually played on the Web, requiring only a graphics-equipped browser.

WEB EXERCISES

1. Browse the Web to find the price of one word processing package, one spreadsheet software package, and one database package.
2. Perform a query to see if you can locate demonstration versions of games that can be played on the Web. Write down the name and the URL for at least two such sites.
3. Locate information concerning at least one groupware package. Jot down the name of the package, as well as some descriptive information concerning the software.

3. *Set a total budget.* Before you start evaluating software packages, look at your total budget. Determine what you really need and set priorities that reflect your most important needs.
4. *Consider price as only one criterion.* In addition to price, a software purchase decision should reflect the capabilities that you need for your computer system and the applications that support those functions. Also, consider ease of use, support from the software publisher, documentation, availability of training programs and materials, compatibility with other programs, and speed of operation. These characteristics can be just as important as price.

5. *Consider the hardware requirements of all software in your system.* Your computer will need the right CPU and enough memory and storage capacity to accommodate all of the software you want to run. Confirm that your machine has sufficient RAM to run one or more programs. Does your hard disk have enough free space to store all program files? Can your CPU run the software at a reasonable speed?

6. *Review magazine reports.* Before you buy a software package, read reviews of it in popular magazines listed in Chapter 1. Most of those publications regularly review and evaluate both system and applications packages.

7. *Verify that your operating system will work with your applications.* Most hardware purchases include operating systems software. Applications that run on those systems must work with the installed systems software. Avoid the mistake of buying a word processing program designed for Windows 95 if your system runs MS-DOS along with the Windows 3.1 shell. In the same way, any decision to upgrade or change your operating system should consider whether you will continue to use current applications. This match between operating system and applications should balance your computing needs, your experience, the needs of other systems at work or school, and the types of capabilities you need in your computer system.

8. *Look for student discounts.* Some software publishers, such as IBM's Lotus, offer their software to students at reduced prices. Check with your instructor, advisor, or lab assistant.

9. *Consider buying a suite of applications.* If you will need a number of applications—including word processor, spreadsheet, graphics package, and database manager—evaluate suites that contain all of them. You will pay less for a software suite than you would spend to buy separate packages. Also, because all of the applications work in similar ways, you can more easily learn how to use the software.

10. *Try to find freeware or shareware packages that do the work you need.* The low cost of freeware and shareware makes them seem like attractive choices, but be sure that you can get the service and features you want.

11. *If you are an IS specialist or plan to become one, or if you want more control over your applications, choose and learn a programming language.* Programming languages like Visual Basic and C allow you to control exactly how your applications work.

- An operating system works like a chauffeur, who operates automotive hardware as instructed by an important passenger; the operating system controls processing hardware to carry out the instructions of the user and his or her applications software.

- Users can obtain applications software in three ways: (1) by developing programs, (2) by customizing existing programs for special needs, and (3) by using an existing off-the-shelf program.

- Object-oriented programming techniques group program instructions and data into modules that perform individual processing tasks; users can compose their own sequences of objects to create complete applications programs.

- The cost of applications software can often be reduced by buying integrated programs, called *suites*. In suites, separate applications programs are designed to work together and to share data.

SUMMARY

1. *Differentiate systems software from applications software.* Systems software includes programs that support activities throughout the computer system by coordinating the functions of the hardware and various other programs. Applications software consists of programs that help users to solve particular computing problems.

2. *Describe the function of an operating system and list some operating systems.* An operating system performs common hardware functions, provides a degree of hardware independence, manages system memory, manages processing tasks, and provides a user interface. MS-DOS and PC-DOS, two early operating systems for personal computers, present command-based user interfaces that require users to accurately type sometimes-complex instructions to carry out basic system activities. Windows, OS/2, and the Macintosh operating system offer graphical user interfaces, in which users control basic activities by pointing at icons and menu choices using a mouse and then clicking mouse buttons. Unix is a portable operating system, which allows compatibility with different types of hardware.

3. *Explain the capabilities that utility programs add to computer systems.* Utility programs supplement operating system functions by performing additional, useful activities. Many users include disk compression and defragmentation utilities in their computer systems.

4. *Describe the types of applications software packages that support individual users' processing needs.* Businesses create or customize proprietary applications or purchase off-the-shelf applications to support many kinds of decision-making and transaction-processing needs. Common functions for these programs include word processing, spreadsheet calculations, database management, communications, and creation of presentation graphics. Integrated packages and software suites combine these and other functions into unified applications or sets of applications that help users share data and work together in many other ways.

5. *Show how programming languages allow people to control the operations of computer hardware.* Programming languages convert statements resembling human language into strings of 1 and 0 bits that cause hardware to execute desired functions. Machine language defines strings of 1s and 0s that represent the on/off pulses of electricity that computers process. Popular high-level languages include COBOL and C. Query languages and natural languages help users create their own processing routines to search databases and perform other useful tasks without the help of programming specialists.

Key Terms

documentation 74
systems software 74
applications software 75
operating system 75
memory management 77
virtual memory 77
multitasking 78
multithreading 78
time-sharing 78
user interface 78
command-based user interface 78
graphical user interface (GUI) 79
Personal Computer Disk Operating System (PC-DOS) 80
Microsoft Disk Operating System (MS-DOS) 80

Windows 80
Operating System 2 (OS/2) 80
System 7.5 82
Unix 82
booting up 82
utility program 83
proprietary software 85
off-the-shelf software 85
personal productivity tools 87
integrated package 87
software suite 87
groupware 89
shareware 89
freeware 89
machine language 90
low-level language 90

American Standard Code for Information Interchange (ASCII) 90
programming language 90
assembly language 91
high-level language 91
COBOL 91
C 91
fourth-generation language (4GL) 91
query language 93
Structured Query Language (SQL) 93
fifth-generation language (5GL) 93
natural language 93
object-oriented programming (OOP) language 93
encapsulating 93

reusable code 95
Smalltalk 97
Java 97
visual programming language 97

batch processing language 97
real-time processing language 97
language translator 98

interpreter 98
compiler 98
syntax 99

Concept Quiz

Fill in the blanks of the following statements.

1. There are two main types of software programs: _____ and _____ .
2. The set of computer programs that control hardware devices to support a user's computing needs is called _____ .
3. BASIC, COBOL, and C are examples of _____ program languages.

Answer the following questions briefly.

4. What is the most important feature of a good, current operating system?
5. What product did Microsoft launch to offset the difficulties many users encountered with the complicated command strings of MS-DOS?
6. What is the first step completed by the computer as soon as the power switch has been flipped on? What does this step accomplish?
7. What type of software package converts an entire program resembling human language into strings of 1 and 0 bits that cause computer hardware to execute desired functions?

Choose the best answer for each of the following.

8. All of the following are types of utility programs except:
   a. antivirus program
   b. file management program
   c. word processing program
   d. diagnostic program
   e. data compression program

9. All of the following are examples of third-generation, or high-level languages, except:
   a. MVC
   b. COBOL
   c. BASIC
   d. C
10. One of the primary advantages of object-oriented programming is:
    a. being able to predict the weather
    b. reusable code
    c. decision making
    d. the CPU can execute it without translation

Mark "true" or "false" after each statement.

11. Applications software can provide very valuable support for decision making in a business setting. _____
12. Off-the-shelf applications software usually costs more than propriety software and may be of dubious quality. _____
13. Most personal computer users rely heavily on a category of software called personal productivity tools. _____
14. If you are considering buying applications software, avoid buying software that is bundled with your computer purchase. _____
15. Shareware is free to users. _____

Discussion Questions

1. Why is it important for an IS person (as well as other computer users) to understand programming languages and techniques?
2. How might applications software provide valuable support for a human resources department?
3. Why might a large company choose to develop its own applications programs?
4. How does the applications software for Levi's Personal Pair jeans shown in the chapter opening photo offer greater value to Levi's customers? How might this software help create loyalty to the Levi's brand?

Team Activity

The class should divide into teams. Imagine that another classmate or friend came to you and asked what type of software he or she should buy. Using the software buyer's guide in this chapter, determine what your classmate should buy. Role play and use different needs each time. (You can also use the research you conducted for "Eye on the Web"; conduct more, if necessary.) Become familiar with current software packages and their advantages and disadvantages. Share information with your team members.

Applying IT

1. Learning to "think like a computer"—in other words, learning to understand software programming—will enhance your IT capabilities. Just for fun, try translating the following command into an operating system sequence. Doing this will help you "think" the way an operating system does.

   ```
   Retrieve Sneakers$$ from Drive B
   ```

2. Thus far in software history, fifth-generation languages most closely resemble human language. To find out more about the capabilities of specific fifth-generation software programs, access the Web using a personal computer. Browse until you find something interesting. Download your information and share it with classmates. If you do not have access to the Internet, research the information at the library and bring a copy of it to class for possible discussion.

CASE

TestDrive

This chapter's "Eye on the Web" tells you that you can search for and download software "demos" from the Internet. TestDrive, so far a small company in California, has a different way for you to try out software before you buy it. The method is just what the company's name suggests: a test drive.

TestDrive offers an electronic "shrinkwrap"—like the packaging you see on diskettes in the stores—to software publishers who want to allow consumers to preview their products. To test drive a software program, a customer may go to the publisher's storefront on the Web and download the program. TestDrive's software allows the customer to use the product, free of charge, for a set period of time determined by the publisher. At the end of the free period, the customer either clicks a button to reach the Web site again, where a credit card transaction can take place (after which the TestDrive shrinkwrap automatically disappears from the program), or indicates lack of interest, upon which TestDrive deletes the software from the hard drive.

TestDrive seems to have some advantages over demos. For instance, some demos are so altered that customers don't get the full picture of what the software is capable of (and thus may decide not to buy it). Some demos have embedded timers that trigger automatic self-destruction after a certain period. (When some of these programs explode, traces of code may land in the user's hard drive.)

TestDrive is also looking forward to the day when most software is sold via the Internet. Retailers will be able to carry far more titles, and software developers will not have to spend the money they now allocate for packaging. Some experts also believe that Internet users will be less apt to return software than buyers who purchase diskettes at retail stores. Edward Lauing, TestDrive's chief executive, waves away critics who warn that TestDrive technology simply isn't ready to handle large jobs. "People talk about bandwidth as if it is insurmountable," he argues. "When I do my laundry, I don't sit and watch it go around. I go do something else." In fact, he's already doing something else. He plans to license TestDrive technology to on-line services, existing Web-based companies, and retailers (such as Egghead and Babbages) that have cyberspace outlets. He'll be charging Web-based stores an upfront fee to help them get their preview software running, and he'll be taking a cut of the transactions that TestDrive launches. By the time Lauing gets back to his laundry, he may decide to buy a whole new wardrobe, instead.

Questions

1. The success of TestDrive has depended on Lauing's combination of IS knowledge and marketing savvy. Name one or two other software companies whose success you think has depended on this combination of knowledge. Explain why.
2. Can you envision any other uses for TestDrive's technology? If so, what might they be?
3. Browse the Internet for a publisher's Web site that offers software previews with TestDrive. Download the software and try it out. Did you find TestDrive a convenient way to preview the software? Why or why not?

Source: Nikhil Hutheesing, "Try It, You'll Like It," *Forbes*, July 1, 1996, p. 78.

Answers to Concept Quiz

1. systems software; applications software **2.** an operating system **3.** high-level **4.** An attractive user interface that is based on intuitive, easily understandable actions. **5.** Windows **6.** Booting up; This loads the operating system software into RAM. **7.** A compiler **8.** c **9.** a **10.** b **11.** True **12.** False **13.** True **14.** False **15.** False

CHAPTER 4

Telecommunications and Networks

CHAPTER OUTLINE

Overview of Communications Systems
Capabilities of Telecommunications Systems
    Types of Telecommunications Signals
    Transmission Capacity
Types of Communications Media
    Physical Cables
    Microwave and Satellite Transmissions
    Other Transmission Options
Telecommunications Devices
    Modems
    Facsimile (Fax) Hardware
    Multiplexers
    Communications Processors
    Integrated Services Digital Network (ISDN) Technology
Communications Software and Protocols
    Functions of Communications Software
    Network Operating Systems
    Communications Protocols
Network Configurations and Classifications
    Local-area Networks
    Larger Networks
    The Internet
    Intranets
    Criteria for Successful Networking
Communications Buyer's Guide

Thumbing through the card catalog or poring over pages in periodical guides used to be the only way to research a topic or locate a particular title in the library. Today, most libraries are served by large networks accessed through computer terminals. One such network is the CARL System (Colorado Alliance of Research Libraries), a library management system that includes an on-line catalog and one of the largest databases available for public access in the world. More than 14,000 terminals are connected to CARL either directly or through computer-to-computer network connections. CARL is installed in over 450 libraries and is used by nearly 50,000 people each day. (Photo courtesy of CARL Corporation, a Knight-Ridder Information Company.)

LEARNING OBJECTIVES

After completing Chapter 4, you will be able to:

1. Outline the basic capabilities of a telecommunications system, including signal types and transmission capacities.
2. Describe available transmission media for telecommunications signals.
3. List the hardware needed for a telecommunications system.
4. Show how communications software and protocols control the functions of a telecommunications system.
5. Lay out network resources in configurations that support specific applications.
6. Mention several criteria for successful networking.

Scientists estimate that most of the circuitry in the human brain performs processing related in some way to communication. People spend vast amounts of time and energy gathering input from others, evaluating and analyzing that input, and formulating and delivering responses. Technology has enhanced human communication by linking people instantaneously whether they are across the street or around the globe. Computers create powerful and flexible systems of new connections between people that allow them to share information, work, and play together.

Communications technology has allowed progressively larger numbers of people to communicate over continually expanding distances at ever-faster rates. Early computer systems carried out all input, processing, and output functions within single, centralized locations. All hardware devices then shared one room, exchanging data over short cables. Improvements in communications technology have allowed computer systems to reach locations where people need their resources. Early users carried processing jobs to a computer room. Today's computer systems reverse the process, bringing computing resources to the users wherever they are—from homes, the factory floor, or the facilities of customers and suppliers.

Computers extend companies' information systems over electronic links within a single building, across town, or around the world. Distant resources can then enhance an information system and provide better support for efficient transaction processing and effective decision making. For example, the manager of a local Speedy Mart can receive an emergency shipment of soft drinks by entering an order directly into the computer system of a distant warehouse. Similarly, an inventory manager must decide how many cases of soft drinks the warehouse should stock to supply many stores without holding more than customers will buy over a certain period. Direct communication between store and warehouse computer systems can provide information about each store's daily sales to support this decision.

In fact, networks of computers can even create entirely new business opportunities and help companies to achieve otherwise impossible goals. The Internet can function as a global storefront, spreading product information and attracting customers throughout the world. A small hobby store can sell model trains to customers anywhere simply by connecting its desktop PC to the Internet.

OVERVIEW OF COMMUNICATIONS SYSTEMS

communication

the transmission of a signal through a medium from a sender to a receiver

telecommunications system

collections of resources that support electronic transmissions of communication signals

Communication is the transmission of a signal through a medium from a sender to a receiver (Figure 4.1). The signal carries a message composed of data and information.[1] Note that the sender does not deliver the message directly to the mind of the receiver; rather, a signal transmits the message from one to the other. Also, the signal itself moves through some communications medium. Many kinds of media carry communication signals, including the air, copper wires, and waxed strings stretched between paper cups.

Remote computer devices communicate with each other via **telecommunications systems,** or collections of resources that support electronic transmissions of communication signals. These resources include several kinds of telecommunications media and specialized hardware devices, along with users, software, and databases. In telecommunications, the sender uses hardware (such as a computer) to send an electronic signal (such as e-mail) over a transmission medium (such as a cable), which the receiver's hardware picks up. Telephone, radio, and television networks are examples of telecommunications systems. A

FIGURE 4.1

Elements of Communication
The sender transmits a signal through the transmission medium to carry a message (data and information) to the receiver. Air functions as a medium for sound signals; cables carry signals between telephones and computers.

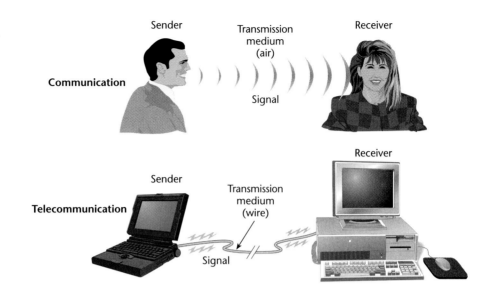

data communications system

a kind of telecommunications system for electronic collection, processing, and distribution of data, typically between computer systems

data communications system, one kind of telecommunications system, employs this technology for electronic collection, processing, and distribution of data, typically between computer systems.

Figure 4.2 shows a general model of a telecommunications system. The sender (1), such as a person, computer system, terminal, or other source, originates the message. The system transmits the sender's signal (2) to a device (3), which may convert the signal into a format that suits the telecommunications medium (4). Another telecommunications device (5) receives the signal and passes it to the receiver (6), perhaps after converting it to a different format. The same system can carry messages in the opposite direction from the receiver (6) to the original sender (1).

CAPABILITIES OF TELECOMMUNICATIONS SYSTEMS

FIGURE 4.2

Elements of a Telecommunications System
Telecommunications devices relay signals between computer systems and transmission media.

The functions of a telecommunications system determine how it can help a business to take advantage of opportunities and solve problems. For example, the capability to send a software upgrade over telecommunications lines to buyers may create an opportunity to improve customer service. Telecommunications may help a firm to solve a problem with delivery speed by allowing customers to place orders directly on the information system at the firm's warehouse.

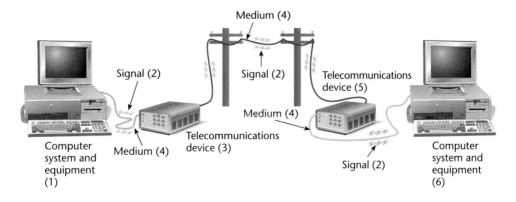

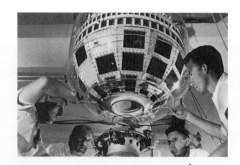

1876	1889	1927	1948	1951	1961	1962
Alexander Graham Bell invents the telephone	First public coin telephone	First international telephone call (New York to London)	First microwave relay system between New York and Boston	Direct long-distance dialing	Wide-area telephone service (WATS) for toll-free calls	First international telephone call and television program relay by Telstar satellite

FIGURE 4.3

The History of Telecommunications
Telecommunications began in 1876 when Alexander Graham Bell invented the telephone. Advances in technology continually add new milestones to the timeline. (Sources: Property of AT&T Archives. Reprinted with permission of AT&T; Ariel Skelley / The Stock Market.)

analog signal
a telecommunications signal represented by continuously varying voltage

digital signal
a telecommunications signal represented by discrete voltage states

The capabilities of a telecommunications system depend on the types of signals, transmission capacity, and transmission modes that its components can accommodate. In particular, these functional characteristics determine a critical system capability: transmission speed. Figure 4.3 shows how telecommunications systems have progressed through the years.

Types of Telecommunications Signals

Traditional telephone wires carry transmissions as continuous variations in electrical voltage, creating a pattern like that in Figure 4.4(a). In contrast, the voltage on a cable that connects PC components resembles the discrete on/off pattern in Figure 4.4(b).

The continuously varying voltage in Figure 4.4(a) represents an **analog signal.** A sound wave traveling through air creates the same kind of continuous variation in air pressure. Thus, people communicate by analog signals when they speak directly to one another. Since telephones were designed to communicate human speech, they employ this kind of analog signal to carry messages.

In contrast, the discrete voltage states in Figure 4.4(b) represent a **digital signal.** The on/off pulses of such a signal provide a convenient way to

Integrated
cellular systems
and digital
networks

1963	1970	1978	1979	1984	1996
Touch-Tone replaces rotary dialing	Picture Phone service to allow users to see as well as talk to each other	Mobile cellular phone service started in Chicago	Local-area networks (LANs)	Court-ordered breakup of the Bell System	Telecommuni-cation Reform Act

transmit the 1/0 bits that computer hardware devices process. Therefore, computer systems generally communicate by exchanging digital signals. Computers need specialized hardware that converts digital signals to analog signals and back again to transmit messages over traditional telephone lines.

FIGURE 4.4

Analog and Digital Signals

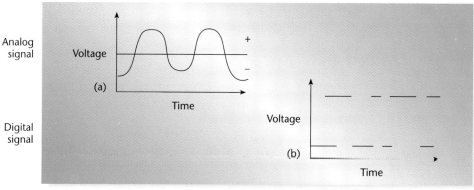

Transmission Capacity

For either signal type, the speed of a telecommunications link affects information system effectiveness. Some applications, such as sending large graphics files from an Internet site's host computer in Milwaukee to a PC in Amsterdam, can require very fast transmission speeds. A sales representative does not need such a high-capacity communications link to send weekly sales data from a desktop computer at home to the office minicomputer. The needs of a business problem or opportunity determine the required transmission speed.

In turn, speed requirements determine the transmission capacity needed for a telecommunications link. The explanation of this capacity measurement begins with frequency. **Signal frequency,** stated in hertz (Hz), measures the number of times per second the transmission medium cycles between high and low voltage to carry a signal. Different media can simultaneously carry different numbers of frequencies. The range of signal frequencies that a given medium can carry at one time is known as the medium's **bandwidth,** so this measure reflects its capacity for transmitting different signals. A medium with a bandwidth of 100 hertz (100 cycles per second) can transmit ten times as much data as a medium with a bandwidth of 10 hertz. The capacity, or bandwidth, of a medium determines its transmission speed, measured in **bits per second (bps),** the number of data bits that it can transfer in one second.

Transmission capacity can vary from about 300 bps (baseband) to over 10 million bps (broadband or wideband). Transmission from a PC over standard telephone lines is typically done at 14,400 bps or 28,800 bps, although faster speeds are possible.

signal frequency

transmission capacity stated in hertz (Hz) that measures the number of times per second the transmission medium cycles between high and low voltage to carry a signal

bandwidth

the range of signal frequencies that a given medium can carry at one time

bits per second (bps)

the number of data bits a medium can transfer in one second

TYPES OF COMMUNICATIONS MEDIA

Data and other transmissions move over various types of telecommunications media, each with its own transmission capacity, speed, and other characteristics. A telecommunications system might transmit data by electrical pulses along a copper wire or microwave pulses through the atmosphere depending on the purposes of the information system and its role in ensuring the organization's success. The proper media will help a company to link its functional subsystems in a way that maximizes effectiveness and efficiency.

Different communications media connect systems in different ways. Some move signals along physical cables, like copper wire, while others send light and radio waves through the air. The choice of media should identify the least expensive way to support essential goals of the information and organizational systems, while allowing for future changes.

twisted-pair wire cable

a type of cable that moves signals over one or more pairs of twisted, copper wire bundles

noise

distortion to a signal caused by unintended fluctuations

Physical Cables

Generally, three types of cables supply physical connections between data communication devices. They are twisted-pair wire cable, coaxial cable, and fiber-optic cable.

Twisted-pair Wire Cable. **Twisted-pair wire cable** moves signals over one or more pairs of twisted, copper wire bundles (Figure 4.5). The twist helps to prevent the signal from "bleeding" into the next pair. Insulation around the twisted-pair wires allows a cable to package them close together in one group without creating **noise,** or distortion to the signal caused by unintended fluctuations. A large cable can include literally hundreds of wire pairs.

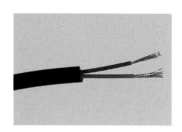

FIGURE 4.5

Twisted-pair Wire
(Source: Fred Bodin.)

FIGURE 4.6

Coaxial Cable
(Source: Fred Bodin.)

coaxial cable

a type of cable that consists of a dielectric surrounded by a conductive shield

fiber-optic cable

cable that transmits signals as pulses of laser-generated light over extremely thin strands of glass or plastic bound together in a jacket similar to that of a coaxial cable

FIGURE 4.7

Fiber-optic Cable
Traditional telephone lines relied on twisted-pair wire cables. Newly installed fiber-optic cables will enrich the capabilities of this common telecommunications link in exciting and surprising ways. (Source: Greg Pease / Tony Stone Images.)

The low cost of buying and installing twisted-pair wire cable gives it its primary advantage. Because cable often consumes over half of the budgets of many telecommunications installations, this advantage provides a significant benefit. Almost all U.S. homes and businesses receive telephone service over twisted-pair cable networks. These connections can give access to many other benefits, like direct links to other companies and the resources of the Internet, at low cost. Unfortunately, twisted-pair wire cable does not support data transfer rates as high as those of other kinds of cables, and it takes up more space. Because of the increasing need for more capacity, twisted-pair wire will no doubt become obsolete.

Coaxial Cable. Figure 4.6 shows a typical **coaxial cable,** similar to those used in cable television installations. This kind of cable consists of a dielectric, an inner conductor wire covered by insulation, surrounded by a conductive shield (usually a layer of foil or braided metal wire). A layer of nonconductive insulation called the *jacket* surrounds the entire cable.

Coaxial cable falls in the middle of the cost and performance spectrum for data transmission cables. It costs more than twisted-pair wire cable but less than fiber-optic cable. Coaxial cable offers cleaner analog transmissions than twisted-pair wire cable gives, because two layers of insulation provide more protection against noise. Coaxial cable also beats the transmission speeds of twisted-pair cable. Cable television providers may soon offer Internet access, interactive shopping, and other services over their coaxial cable systems.

Fiber-optic Cable. When telecommunications systems need extremely fast and reliable transmissions, they send data over fiber-optic cables. Twisted-pair and coaxial cables transmit signals by variations in electrical voltage over copper or other metal wires. **Fiber-optic cable** transmits signals as pulses of laser-generated light over extremely thin strands of glass or plastic bound together in a jacket similar to that of a coaxial cable (Figure 4.7). A thin coating over individual fibers, called *cladding,* works like a mirror, preventing one fiber's light from interfering with the signals carried by other fibers.

Because it carries digital pulses of light rather than electricity, fiber-optic cable has some extraordinary abilities compared with other kinds of cables. Table 4.1 compares its advantages and disadvantages. Its high speed and extreme safety of data create possibilities for a vast array of new services and capabilities. In addition to voice transmissions, fiber-optic cables can carry video transmissions. Many new information services will soon be able to send movies, graphics, and vast quantities of other kinds of data over fiber-optic phone lines to your computer system or television.

Microwave and Satellite Transmissions

While cables create physical connections between telecommunications devices, microwave and satellite transmissions send data through the atmosphere and beyond. Although these media allow users to avoid the expense of laying cable, they require extremely expensive transmission devices. Therefore, they meet the needs of large companies that must transmit enormous amounts of data and can afford the substantial investment. (Even though satellite communication is expensive, the farming industry has begun to bank on it. See "Business Bits: Global Positioning Systems.")

TABLE 4.1

Advantages and Disadvantages of Fiber-optic Cable

Advantages

- *Tremendous data transfer rates* A single cable can carry data at more than 2.5 billion bps with a bandwidth of at least 200 trillion hertz. This speed allows it to handle 32,000 simultaneous long-distance calls. Fiber-optic cables can move some transmissions that take a little less than an hour over copper wires in less than 1 second. This speed brings important benefits for data-intensive businesses.
- *Smaller size than traditional cables* Fiber-optic cables fit easily where bulky copper wires would not. When new wiring must fit within existing conduits or other spaces, fiber-optic cables often prove more cost-effective than rebuilding to accommodate larger conduits.
- *Reliable transmission over long distances* Fiber-optic cables are immune to electrical interference that would disrupt signals on traditional cables. Also, copper wires often require amplification devices at intervals along the transmission path; fiber-optic media do not require these expensive and troublesome devices.
- *Safety in hazardous environments* Fiber-optic connections do not emit accidental sparks as metal cables sometimes do, so they eliminate one source of fire risk.
- *Resistance to corrosion* Fiber-optic cables do not degrade in hostile environments that would corrode metal cables.
- *Security of transmissions* Would-be data thieves and eavesdroppers can tap into traditional cables anywhere along their length; with the right equipment, virtually no one can make an undetected and unauthorized connection with fiber-optic cable.

Disadvantages

- *Cost* Fiber-optic cable and related hardware cost more than comparable installations of twisted-pair wire and coaxial cable. Developing technology is shrinking the difference, though.
- *Complex installation* Fiber-optic cable requires more sophisticated installation techniques than traditional cable.
- *Splicing difficulty* Since later installers cannot simply tap into existing fiber-optic cable, costs for later system revisions also rise.

microwave transmission

transmission that sends messages through the air as high-frequency radio signals

line-of-sight signal

a signal that requires an unobstructed straight line between the sender and receiver

Microwave transmissions, also called *terrestrial microwave,* send messages through the air as high-frequency radio signals (Figure 4.8). This technology allows only a **line-of-sight signal,** which requires an unobstructed straight line between the sender and receiver. In favorable conditions, microwave transmissions can carry signals through the air as far as 30 miles. They might carry messages between an office building and a warehouse some distance away.

FIGURE 4.8

Microwave Transmissions
Line-of-sight transmissions require microwave stations in relatively high locations such as mountaintops, towers, and tall buildings.

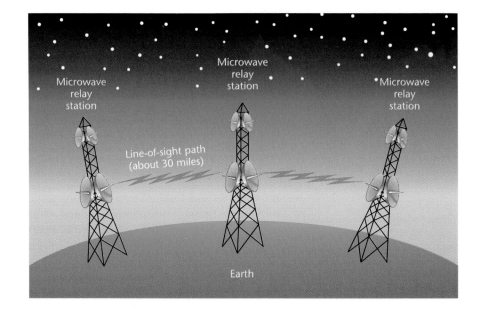

BUSINESS BITS

Global Positioning Systems

It's no news that high-tech has come to the farming industry; in fact, agribusiness has been driven by technology for many years. But satellites that tell farmers exactly where the best soil is and what fertilizer to use? That piece of technology is new; and it still sounds, to some, too good to be true. Or at least, it is too expensive.

Several computer companies now build and sell computers designed to meet every need the farmer may have. The result is called precision farming. For instance, Douglas Harford, a farmer in Illinois, uses the system, which includes a monitor on his combine and a personal computer, both of which collect necessary data. The monitor receives data from the satellite-borne Global Positioning System (GPS), which pinpoints exactly where he is on his property while driving the combine. With the system, he can determine variations in elevation, soil composition, moisture and wind exposure, and so forth. His computer program determines which fertilizers, herbicides, and insecticides—and in what amounts—to apply to every little sector of his property. The idea is to get the most out of his land. So far, Harford has used his system to create test plots to determine how changing a single variable could affect a crop.

Harford has spent $20,000 on the technology, including $3,500 for the Global Positioning System receiver. Is the cost worth it? He says that he's broken even, saving about $20,000 on unnecessary chemicals and other expenditures. But more important, he says, "I am confident that this will give me a tremendous advantage."

Harford's example illustrates how important it is for businesses (and individuals) to buy the computer system that meets their needs. Furthermore, consider how volatile variables in the farming industry are; farmers can't control the weather or the price of chemicals and grain. And it takes a year to accumulate enough data on a plot of land to make it worthwhile. Thus, the payoff on these computer systems is slow, at a time when farmers don't have extra money to spend.

Still, engineers like Allen Myers, founder of Ag Leaders Technology, are banking on precision farming systems to be the coming wave. His systems sell for $3,400, and he expects to sell 3,000 of them this year. Rockwell Corp, already a leader in GPS technology for aircraft, now offers integrated systems to farmers for $6,000 to $8,000.

If farming computer technology drops in price and becomes more available to the average farmer, it could be the beginning of a new age in farming. Farmers won't be able to start or stop the rain, but they'll be better able to respond to the forces of nature.

1. Why is it so important for a precision farming system to meet the needs of average farmers?
2. In addition to the features mentioned above, what other types of data might be able to help farmers?
3. What steps might computer manufacturers and dealers take to train farmers how to use their systems? Why is this important?
4. Access the Web site of UNAVCO at http://www.unavco.ucar.edu to search for other types of fields in which GPS is used.

Source: Christine Lutton, "Cyberfarm," *Forbes*, July 15, 1996, pp. 86–87. Photo of the Tokyo electronics district courtesy of Ben Simmons / The Stock Market.

Microwave systems can achieve longer transmission distances by placing relay stations in series; one station receives a signal, amplifies it, and retransmits it to the next. Strings of towers with microwave stations carry long-distance telephone calls in some areas with suitable terrain. Weather and other atmospheric conditions can affect the quality of a microwave signal, but microwaves can carry literally thousands of channels at a time.

A **communications satellite** is basically a microwave station that orbits the earth (Figure 4.9). A satellite receives a signal and then rebroadcasts it at a different frequency. (Many people incorrectly believe that the signal simply

communications satellite

a microwave station that orbits the earth

FIGURE 4.9

Satellite Transmissions
Communications satellites are microwave relay stations that receive signals from one earth station and rebroadcast them to another.

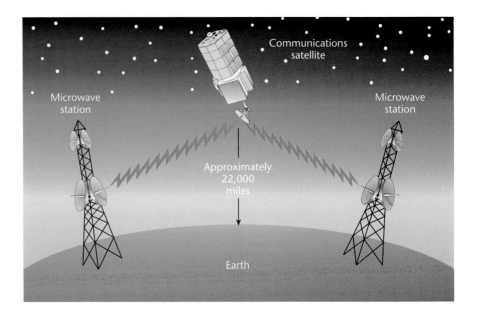

bounces off of the satellite.) From its position high above the surface of the earth, a satellite can quickly transmit data over a long distance. This provides an important link for large companies that need high-speed transmissions over large geographic regions. While mountains, structures, and even the curvature of the earth block line-of-sight microwave transmissions, satellites easily avoid these obstacles.

Specialized companies own most satellites. They generate revenue by renting or leasing the capabilities of these devices to other companies. Some large retail chains, for example, use satellite transmissions to connect their main offices to retail stores and warehouses throughout the country or the world. Holiday Inn has used satellite transmissions to improve customer service by sending the latest room and rate information to reservation desks throughout Europe and the United States.[2]

In addition to standard, fixed satellite stations on the ground, small, mobile systems add flexibility to a telecommunications system. A dish that measures a few feet in diameter can operate on battery power anywhere in the world. Television news organizations use systems like these to transmit reports from locations far from their studios.

A TV "satellite city" remained outside the Davidian ranch in Waco, Texas, during the siege, allowing media organizations to transmit pictures and reports to the world watching. (Source: Robert E. Daemmrich / Tony Stone Images.)

Other Transmission Options

In addition to physical cables and microwave and satellite transmissions, some organizations employ additional resources to enhance the portability and flexibility of their telecommunications systems. These supplemental options include infrared and cellular transmissions.

Infrared Technology. **Infrared transmissions** used with TV controllers and computer systems work somewhat like microwave technology, but they send low-frequency light waves rather than microwaves through the air. Line-of-sight infrared links require short, unobstructed transmission paths. Under these conditions, infrared transmissions can connect computer systems and various remote devices within a range of a few hundred yards. Approximately 80 percent of notebook computers shipped in 1996 will contain an infrared port. New infrared data transfer standards recently adopted allow transfer speeds of 1.152 to 4 megabits per second (Mbps), which allows PC-to-PC transfer, printing, and network access.[3]

A lumberyard's information system might use infrared transmissions to link handheld computers of yard workers with a central computer in the main office. Similar systems could carry messages within a factory building or between separate systems in adjacent buildings. Some special-purpose phones also use infrared technology.

Cellular Telephones. **Cellular telephone service** overcomes the range limitations of radio transmissions by dividing an area, such as a city, into cells. A radio receiver accepts signals from mobile phones and other devices within each cell and integrates them into the regular phone system. As a cellular device moves from one cell to another, the system automatically channels input from the new receiver into the existing phone-system link to maintain a continuous call (Figure 4.10). Cellular phone users can contact anyone who has access to regular phone service, like a child at home, a business associate in London, or another cellular phone user.

The expansion of cellular transmissions has streamlined mobile communications as prices of cellular phones, equipment, and services have declined. Some police and firefighters use cellular phones along with or instead of their radios. Businesspeople of all types use cellular phones to maintain voice

infrared transmission

transmission that sends low-frequency light waves rather than microwaves through the air

cellular telephone service

telephone service that divides an area into cells; a radio receiver accepts signals from mobile phones and other devices within each cell and integrates them into the regular phone system

FIGURE 4.10

Typical Cellular Telephone Call
The caller dials a number from a cell phone installed in a car (1). The phone broadcasts the resulting signal, and the low-powered antenna in the same cell (2) receives it. The system retransmits the signal to the regional cellular phone switching office (3), which forwards it to the local telephone company switching station nearest the call's destination (4). Now integrated into the regular phone system, the call automatically rings at the correct phone (5), all without operator assistance.

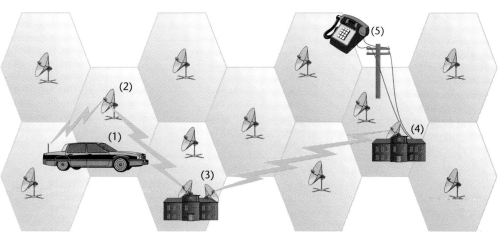

contact with their offices from remote locations. Portable computers like hand-held and laptop units can contact cellular networks through special hardware to allow data communications independent from physical connections to telecommunications systems.

All of these users risk problems with signal interference and distortion. Eavesdropping represents an even more serious problem. Because cellular devices broadcast radio waves, anyone with the right receiver can listen to a cellular phone conversation.

TELECOMMUNICATIONS DEVICES

Computers cannot read or process fluctuations in voltage over twisted-pair cables or patterns of microwaves. These and other telecommunications media can communicate with computers only through specialized hardware. Telecommunications devices convert signals carried by transmission media into data that computers can process and vice versa.

Businesses match their hardware to their communications needs. Virtually every office, whether home based or traditional, needs standard communications equipment like modems and fax machines. Larger organizations include multi-plexers and dedicated communications processors in their systems to control heavy signal flows. High-end information systems employ resources like ISDN switches to integrate telecommunications fully into users' basic work routines.

Modems

modem

a device that converts telecommunications messages back and forth between the analog signals of phone lines and the digital signals of computers

Despite the emergence of other options, telephone lines easily remain the most common medium for telecommunications and data communications. Recall that a traditional, twisted-pair telephone cable typically transmits voice and data using an analog signal. A **modem** converts telecommunications messages back and forth between the analog signals of phone lines and the digital signals of computers (Figure 4.11). Translating data from digital to analog is called *modulation,* and translating from analog to digital is called *demodulation.* Thus, these MOdulation/DEModulation devices received the name *modems.*

Fiber-optic cables can carry faster, digital signals, but they usually do not reach the telephone wiring inside buildings to which modems connect. Twisted-pair wire cables usually carry signals over short distances between fiber-optic back-bone cables outside users' facilities and the computers inside. Therefore, the new technology still needs modems to convert between analog and digital signals.

FIGURE 4.11

How a Modem Works
The sending modem modu-lates the computer's digital signals to produce analog signals for transmission over traditional phone lines. The receiving modem demodu-lates these analog signals back into digital signals for process-ing by the receiving computer.

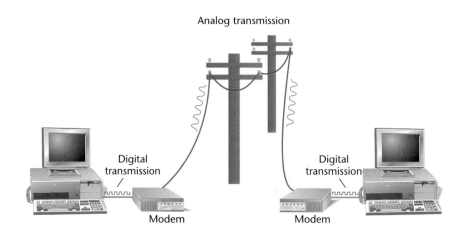

Analog transmission

Digital transmission

Modem

Digital transmission

Modem

An internal modem is a circuit board inside the computer's system unit; it creates the connection to telephone lines through a port that accepts a standard telephone cable. An external modem is a separate device linked to the computer and to phone lines by cables. A cellular modem plugs into a socket on a laptop or other portable computer to modulate and demodulate data for transmissions over cellular telephone networks.

A modem performs several communications functions in addition to translating data for transmission across telephone lines. It dials telephone numbers, originates new messages, and answers incoming calls under the direction of communications software. Modems can also perform diagnostic tests to evaluate their own operations and ensure accurate transmissions.

Most modems can vary their transmission rates to match the signals of other systems. As mentioned earlier, today's standard transmission speeds run at either 14,400 bps or 28,800 bps. These speeds push the capacity limits of existing telephone cables, but rapid advances in technology will allow ever-faster communications. The spread of fiber-optic technology will promote dramatic acceleration in telecommunications.

Facsimile (Fax) Hardware

facsimile (fax) machine

device that transmits images of documents via standard telephone lines

fax board

a device that uses a circuit board to send document files in electronic format to other personal computers or standard fax machines without first printing hard copy

Facsimile (fax) machines transmit images of documents, including text, graphs, photographs, and other visual elements, via standard telephone lines. The hardware scans the hard copy and then converts the scanned image to analog data for transmission. The receiving fax machine reconverts and prints out the document.

A **fax board** provides similar capabilities at lower cost through a circuit board that fits into an empty expansion slot inside a computer's system unit. The fax board can send document files in electronic format to other personal computers or standard fax machines without first printing hard copy. In effect, it allows the computer to print the document on the remote fax machine or computer system. The add-on board cannot, however, send a previously printed document until someone scans the hard copy using separate hardware.

Note that the computer receives a fax as an image rather than a document file, so it cannot complete further processing of the faxed information. Newer fax boards avoid this limitation by working in conjunction with optical character recognition software to convert an incoming fax image into ASCII text. The resulting text file can then become input for another program, like a word processing program. The receiver can carry out further editing and perhaps retransmit the new version of the document back to the sender.

A fax/modem allows a user to send and receive faxes through a computer. (Source: Courtesy of Diamond Multimedia Systems, Inc.)

fax/modem

a device that combines faxing capabilities with the telecommunications functions of a modem

A **fax/modem** combines these faxing capabilities with the telecommunications functions of a modem. This powerful tool helps to integrate separate information system functions into a single, compact system. As you work on one task, perhaps writing a report in a word processing program, your fax/modem can answer an incoming call and receive a fax with minimal disruption to your other work. Fax/modems generally offer high transmission rates, usually 14,400 bps, 28,800 bps, or faster.

Multiplexers

multiplexer

a device that helps control the cost of transmission by transmitting several telecommunications signals over a single medium at a time

As a firm's message traffic grows, so does the cost of transmission media to carry the signals. A **multiplexer** helps to control this cost by transmitting several telecommunications signals over a single medium at one time. Multiplexers group and condense signals so they can be transmitted more quickly and so save time and money.

Communications Processors

front-end processor

a device that performs processing tasks related to sending and receiving telecommunications transmissions

As message traffic increases on a firm's telecommunications system, the burden of related processing tasks on the computer's central processing unit also grows. To prevent this work from slowing performance, some information systems include **front-end processors**, which perform processing tasks related to sending and receiving telecommunications transmissions. These dedicated computers get their name because they operate in front of the main system CPU. They relieve the main system CPU of these tasks, so the main system CPU can process work more efficiently (Figure 4.12).

FIGURE 4.12

Front-end Processor
This dedicated computer assumes the burden of communications management to free the main system processor for other work.

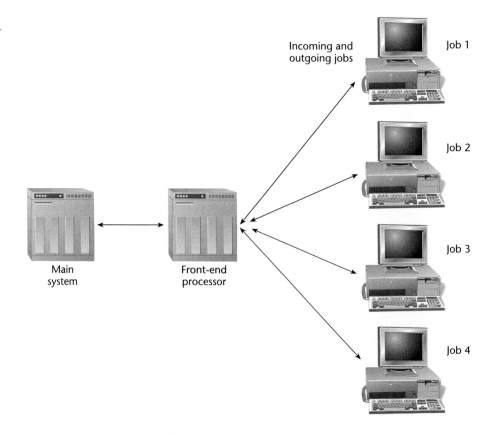

Main system

Front-end processor

Incoming and outgoing jobs

Job 1

Job 2

Job 3

Job 4

Like a receptionist greeting visitors at an office complex, the front-end processor directs the flow of incoming and outgoing jobs. This general task involves a number of vital functions, beginning with controlling connections between a large computer and literally hundreds or thousands of communications lines. The front-end processor regularly **polls** terminals and other devices to identify and accept new messages. It also performs some system maintenance routines:

- Controlling automatic answering and calling procedures
- Checking circuits
- Monitoring transmission errors
- Maintaining logs of communications traffic
- Editing basic data entering the main processor
- Assigning message priorities and processing them in sequence from most to least important
- Automatically routing signals over the most efficient of many alternative communications paths
- Ensuring general data security for the main system CPU

Integrated Services Digital Network (ISDN) Technology

The most advanced telecommunications systems move beyond hardware to control message transmissions. They coordinate communications tasks to integrate diverse resources into comprehensive, organizationwide information systems. **Integrated Services Digital Network (ISDN)** technology helps to implement this high standard. It maximizes the capacity of existing transmission media to simultaneously carry voice, video, and image data in a digital format at high speed. An ISDN system can transmit a 22-page document in a single second!

ISDN achieves this impressive performance because it need not convert digital signals to analog ones and back. Instead, **ISDN switches** connect digital communications services directly to computer systems. In this way, a single network can combine local and long-distance phone service, video and voice displays, fax transmissions, and an expanding list of other resources (Figure 4.13). A private branch exchange (PBX) may serve as an interface between diverse company resources and the ISDN network, or computers and other devices may connect directly through ISDN switches.

ISDN typically supports faster transmission speeds and larger signal capacities than more traditional analog networks can offer; they are about four times as fast as the speediest modem. This speed and capacity helps users to routinely share images, multimedia presentations, and other complex data across telephone lines. AT&T and other phone companies offer ISDN service that

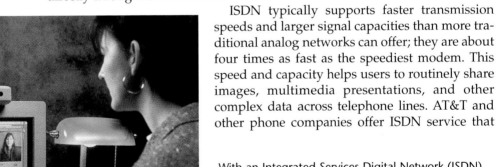

With an Integrated Services Digital Network (ISDN) computer connection, special cameras and high-capacity phone lines are utilized so that two users in separate locations can not only see and hear each other on-screen, but also share information and work on information simultaneously. (Source: Courtesy of vis a vis Communications, Inc.)

FIGURE 4.13

ISDN Resources

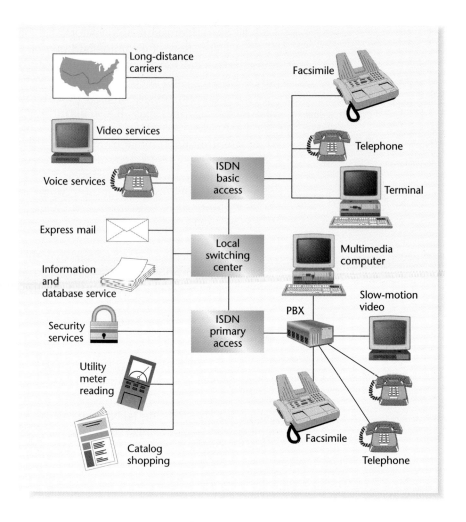

allows business users to transmit full-motion video and data files while voice communications continue at the same time. But ISDN service is not available in all areas and is costly; recent fees ranged from $25 to $100 per month, plus usage charges of approximately 10 cents a minute.[4]

A service like this can transform the most basic business routines, however. For example, an advertising agent could transmit a draft of a full-motion TV commercial while talking with the customer on the phone about suggested changes. The ISDN system could later return the customer's modified version to the agency. Growing numbers of companies regularly send large amounts of video and multimedia data like these over phone lines. ISDN can offer cost-effective and efficient ways for these firms to connect with customers, consultants, and colleagues to expand the boundaries of their business processes.

COMMUNICATIONS SOFTWARE AND PROTOCOLS

In business telecommunications systems, many kinds of devices send expanding numbers and types of messages over varying transmission media. Computers manage this complex traffic of electronic signals the same way they perform other useful tasks: by running software. Communications software functions like glue, joining diverse components into a unified telecommunications system. In particular, it controls the actions of hardware devices to ensure accurate and efficient exchanges of data.

The procedures embedded in software that unify hardware functions are commonly called *communications protocols.* Communications software typically sets these protocols.

Functions of Communications Software

Communications software performs a number of important functions in a telecommunications system. First, it sets the basic format for the number and sequence of data bits that identify each character or other element in a message.

Format of Communications. The sending and receiving computers can accurately interpret transmitted data only if they agree on a common format and other specifications. Communications software allows users to set these conditions. Also, if the systems fail to agree or other errors arise, the software can often indicate the nature of the problem and suggest possible solutions.

Additional functions vary depending on the sophistication of the telecommunications system. The following paragraphs discuss some common ones.

Communications Log. Communications software can maintain a log listing all data exchanges over a specified period of time. The system manager might refer to this log to evaluate current system usage and plan for changes. This information helps to ensure that the telecommunications system effectively supports the larger information system.

Micro-to-mainframe Links. Some businesses need software that allows personal computers to connect to mainframes. This function creates a flexible information system in which desktop computers both meet the processing needs of individuals and give access to more powerful, centralized resources shared by everyone in the organization.

Control and Coordination. Communications software controls access to system resources to prevent conflicts. The system could not function if several devices attempted to use the same communications line at the same time. Software coordinates competing demands for system resources based on job priority levels to maximize overall efficiency.

Security. Software carries out important security procedures. Most systems assign unique identification numbers and passwords to permit these users to do their work while blocking others from interfering. Similar procedures guard against unauthorized copying, modification, or downloading of software.

Network Operating Systems

Formerly isolated personal computer users gained important benefits when communications software allowed their systems to share data through telecommunications links. This possibility quickly led these individual users to envision more elaborate **networks** of computer systems linked electronically in a way that allows them to share wider ranges of hardware and software resources. To achieve this ambitious goal, they needed a way to coordinate access to those resources.

Recall from Chapter 3 that operating systems coordinate access to hardware and applications software in all individual computer systems. When an application program requires data from a disk drive, it issues a command to the operating system, which controls the drive's actions to read the appropriate

network

groups of computer systems linked electronically in a way that allows them to share wider ranges of hardware and software resources

network operating system (NOS)

an operating system for large disk drives, printers, and other hardware connected to a telecommunications network

spot on the disk. A **network operating system (NOS)** performs the same control function for disk drives, printers, and other hardware connected to a telecommunications network. An applications program running on a networked computer requests data from a disk drive in another part of the same network by issuing a command to the network operating system.

This component of systems software also performs memory management, task management, and other operating system functions throughout a network. Two examples of NOSs are NetWare from Novell and Windows NT from Microsoft.

Communications Protocols

protocol

a summary of certain communications standards that allow any computer system or network to communicate effectively with any other system or network

To share still larger pools of computing resources, system users must agree on extremely detailed sets of communications standards called *protocols*. A **protocol** consists of standards that allow any computer system or network to communicate effectively with any other system or network. Companies and organizations of all sizes adopt widely recognized communications protocols to avoid wasting time agreeing on individual specifications for information system exchanges. Computers of different types from different manufacturers can easily communicate simply by operating within a single protocol.

Most protocols specify many kinds of standards and procedures in various layers. *Open Systems Interconnection (OSI)*, a protocol endorsed by the International Standards Committee, includes the layers illustrated in Figure 4.14. Separate layers set specifications for:

1. Physical connections between pieces of equipment
2. Methods of transforming data for transmission (e.g., for asynchronous or synchronous communication)
3. Paths for data flows between locations in a network
4. Data flows between separate networks, including security precautions
5. Access to devices and other resources within a network, including user priorities

FIGURE 4.14

Seven-layer OSI Model
Different computers from different manufacturers using different operating systems can communicate if they all conform to this Open Systems Interconnection (OSI) model.

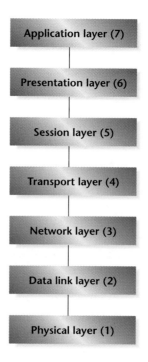

Application layer (7)

Presentation layer (6)

Session layer (5)

Transport layer (4)

Network layer (3)

Data link layer (2)

Physical layer (1)

6. Formats and appearance features of monitor screens and other displays
7. Available applications software on a network

In the 1970s, the U.S. government pioneered the development of the *Transmission Control Protocol/Internet Protocol (TCP/IP)* to govern links between computers at its defense research agencies. This protocol created the original model for today's Internet. Since then, the government has adopted OSI standards, but schools and businesses continue to rely on TCP/IP.

The popularity of IBM systems has led many other computer manufacturers and communications companies to make their systems compatible with IBM's communications protocol, *Systems Network Architecture (SNA)*. Many international companies, on the other hand, prefer the *X.400 protocol* and *X.500 protocol*. International acceptance makes these protocols important as businesses try to simplify their increasingly global telecommunications.

NETWORK CONFIGURATIONS AND CLASSIFICATIONS

A network configuration determines a unique combination of telecommunications media, devices, software, and protocols that meets the needs of a particular information system. One situation might call for a small network that connects a few personal computers and related devices within a single room. Another network may have to connect literally thousands of computers of many different kinds in locations spread around the world.

nodes

individual computers and other connection points within networks

Common sets of needs have created a few basic classifications or types of networks. The boundaries between them depend on the physical distances between **nodes,** or individual computers and other connection points, along with their communications methods and services. Standard classifications include:

- Local-area networks, which connect equipment in a building or other limited area
- Regional networks, which span larger areas
- Wide-area networks, which join systems across different regions
- International networks, which carry telecommunications signals between countries

Local-area Networks

local-area network (LAN)

a network that connects computer systems and devices within a small geographic area

A **local-area network (LAN)** connects computer systems and devices, usually by physical cables, within a small geographic area. Typically, local-area network cables form part of the wiring of an office building or factory (Figure 4.15) alongside the hardware for electrical, telephone, and alarm systems.

file server system

a system in which the file server transfers the necessary files and programs to a node or an individual PC on the network

Local-area networks can include many kinds of computers, from basic personal computers through powerful microcomputer workstations and minicomputers to mainframes. File server systems and client/server systems are two popular systems for coordinating the resources of a LAN. With a **file server system**, the file server transfers the necessary files and programs to a node or an individual PC on the network. The node or PC on the network does the actual processing. To get a list of all students in an introductory computer class, the file server would transfer all of the necessary programs and files to an individual PC or node on the network. The PC or node on the network then does the necessary processing and generates a list of all students in the class.

FIGURE 4.15

Typical LAN Configuration
All of these computers connect to each other and to both printers for rapid communication. Everyone can access data and applications software from the server. Someone in the office can print out a work order in the shop, while the shop foreman prints out a letter to a different customer on the laser printer.

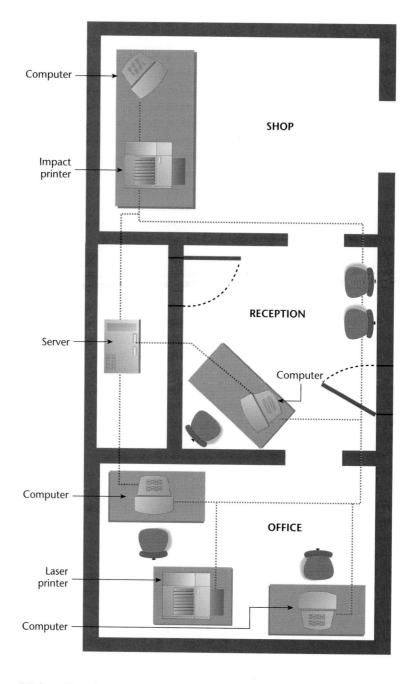

client/server system

a system in which the server does all or most of the processing

With a **client/server system (CSS)**, the server does all or most of the processing (Figure 4.16). The server then transfers the results to the individual PC or node on the network, called a client. To get a list of all students in the introductory computer class, a PC on the network (the client) requests the information from the server. The server does all of the necessary processing and develops a list of the students in the class. The results are then transferred from the server to the client. The amount of information flowing through a LAN can be reduced with a client/server system because only the needed results are transferred from the server to the client. In addition, less expensive individual client computers can be used because the server is doing all or most of the processing.

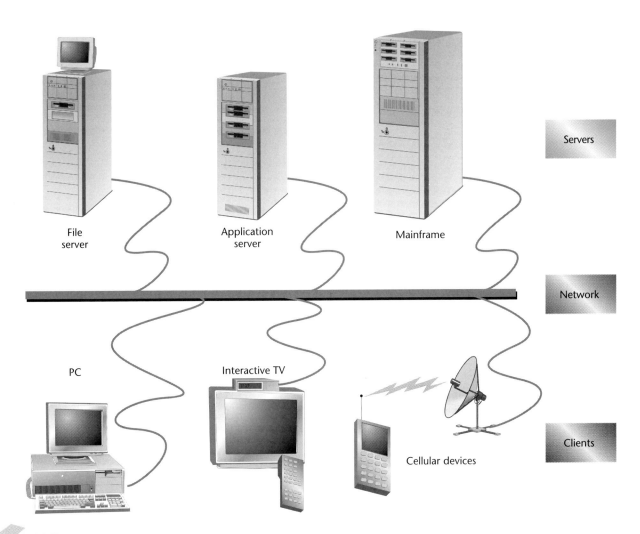

FIGURE 4.16

Client/Server System
A client/server system ties personal computers, larger computers, databases, and various other resources into one flexible, integrated, and powerful network.

network interface card

a device through which an individual PC usually connects to a LAN

bridge

hardware that connects two or more networks that use similar protocols

gateway

hardware through which networks based on dissimilar protocols can communicate

An individual personal computer usually connects to a local-area network through a **network interface card.** This circuit board fits in an expansion slot and includes a port that accepts the network cable.

Many LANs also include hardware and software resources that allow them to communicate with other networks. A **bridge** connects two or more networks that use similar protocols. Networks based on dissimilar protocols can communicate through a **gateway**. Both of these connections further expand the resources available from individual nodes on a LAN. A user on any of these systems can access programs and data across vast geographic regions simply by clicking an icon or typing a few simple commands. The communications software on the user's computer and the communications software on the LAN's file server automatically perform the tasks needed to establish the link to the other network.

Estimates suggest that over 60 percent of business PCs in the United States are connected to one or more local-area networks. As LANs gain new capabilities and power, demand for connections (including related hardware and software) will soar. LANs provide excellent support for information systems that require mainly internal communications or connections within small areas. As these needs expand, however, organizations expand their networks to support essentially internal communications across larger areas.

Larger Networks

regional network

telecommunications systems that join resources within specific geographic regions

wide-area networks (WANs)

networks that expand telecommunications links to encompass resources spread over large geographic regions

international (global) networks

networks that link systems between countries

Regional networks are telecommunications systems that join resources within specific geographic regions. Local phone companies provide typical examples of these kinds of networks. A cellular phone system also works through a regional network.

Wide-area networks (WANs) expand telecommunications links even farther to encompass resources spread over large geographic regions. These links may employ microwave and satellite transmissions in addition to telephone lines. When you make a long-distance phone call, you are using a wide-area network run by AT&T, MCI, Sprint, or another company. (See Figure 4.17.)

A particular user might access similar resources through connections between LANs, but larger networks allow more direct control. The LAN node can access a system outside its own network only when that system will accept the connection and limits that it imposes. A large organization may set up its own regional network or WAN instead to ensure full access to needed resources.

Networks that link systems between countries are called **international (global) networks.** As growing numbers of companies, even many small businesses, serve global markets, the functions of international networks must expand. Communications carriers are working hard to secure part of this $88 billion market.

International telecommunications networks encounter special problems. For one, the volume of signal traffic requires sophisticated equipment and software. More important, international networks must comply with complex national and international laws that regulate electronic exchanges of data

FIGURE 4.17

Wide-area Network
WANs join computing resources across vast regions. Any combination of satellite, microwave, or cable transmissions may provide the actual connections between nodes (shown by dashed lines).

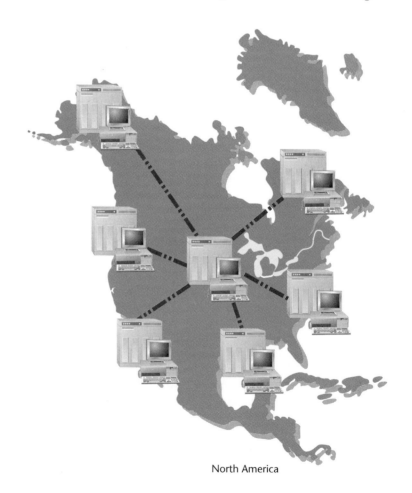

North America

across national borders, often called *transborder data flow.* Some countries impose severe restrictions on the applications of telecommunications and databases; these laws can inhibit or completely prevent normal business transactions such as payroll processing. Other countries place few limits on uses of telecommunications and databases. These countries, sometimes called **data havens,** allow foreign governments and companies to avoid their native laws by processing data within the borders of less restrictive neighbors.

Companies have overcome obstacles like these to create numerous private and public international networks. United Parcel Service, for example, has invested in its own international network, UPSnet. Over this network, drivers using handheld computers send real-time information about pickups and deliveries to centralized data-processing facilities. In addition to these 77,000 handheld units, UPSnet encompasses five mainframes, 60,000 personal computers, several satellite dishes, and enough fiber-optic cable to wrap around the earth 25 times. Customers can access the huge network directly to track packages, and it helps the company to speed billing, plan fleet deployment, and maintain effective customer service.[5]

The Internet

The **Internet** is the largest public international network. Originally started by the U.S. government to link defense researchers, the Internet has become a vast, hybrid network of networks. No one now owns or controls the Internet; instead, operators of computer systems at universities, government agencies, business firms, commercial services, and other organizations essentially agree to host information on their systems and to give access to other users. People and organizations in over 100 countries draw regularly on the amazingly diverse pool of information, software, and other resources made available by this unique, cooperative enterprise. Some observers estimate that the number of Web pages has grown from a few thousand five years ago to over 50 million today. In fact, the amount of traffic on the Internet threatens to choke the system's capacity, creating gridlock.[6]

Resources and Applications of the Internet. In 1991, the Commercial Internet Exchange (CIX) Association was established to help businesses fully connect to the Internet. This event marks the real beginning of the Net's commercial use. Since that time, businesses have found a number of applications for their Internet connections. Computer software companies, for example, distribute documentation, technical information, and software upgrades over the Internet. An independent telecommunications consultant can keep track of the most current technical information through company and university reports that might be published nowhere else or only after long delays. Home users can download weather maps, check airline ticket availability, or play video games. The Internet brings resources to a computer monitor that users could otherwise obtain only after extensive searches and perhaps even foreign travel.

Electronic mail (e-mail) is a major application of the Internet for most companies. In one month, IBM employees exchange close to 60,000 messages with people or organizations outside the company using the Internet.[7] Used-book dealers display catalogs and sell their wares over the Internet to collectors worldwide. Customers can place orders by keying in payment information and shipping addresses or simply by mailing orders to addresses they see on the Net. Table 4.2 shows part of a list of business applications that grows constantly as innovative firms develop new uses.

data havens

countries that place few limits on uses of telecommunications and databases

Internet

the largest public international network

electronic mail (e-mail)

mail that is sent and received via computers

TABLE 4.2

Business Applications of the Internet

- Exchange messages electronically with employees, customers, and suppliers
- Send and receive documents around the world
- Find information using bulletin boards on a wide array of topics
- Follow technological developments and industry information for a variety of areas
- Market products to other businesses and individuals
- Provide customer support and respond to customer concerns
- Conduct market research by posting queries about product interest on bulletin boards (but beware of unwritten rules about selling in certain noncommercial forums)
- Download inexpensive shareware and freeware applications
- Read journal articles and reports on academic and government-sponsored research published in electronic form
- Subscribe to news services like United Press International or The *Wall Street Journal Interactive* for comprehensive information about current events
- Review information published by government agencies like the Bureau of Economic Analysis, Bureau of the Census, Federal Reserve Board, Bureau of Labor Statistics, and the General Accounting Office
- Monitor government grant opportunities published in the *Commerce Business Daily*
- Review proposed federal laws discussed in detail in the *Federal Register*
- Locate books, articles, and other materials cataloged by the Library of Congress

File Transfer Protocol (FTP)

utility software that allows users to transfer files back and forth between Internet sites and their own computers

Using the Internet. Internet users gain access in a number of ways. Most universities and government agencies already have Internet connections, and students, faculty, and staff members can usually connect free of charge. Private companies and individuals can connect through the facilities of commercial companies that generate their revenues by providing Internet access. Information services like America Online, CompuServe, and many smaller, regional companies sell connect time at fees ranging from about $10 to $30 per month.

Early Internet users employed a number of software tools for connecting with specific sites and finding desired resources. **File Transfer Protocol (FTP)** is a type of utility software that allows users to transfer files back and forth between Internet sites and their own computers.

Users control these and similar tools by specifying the Uniform Resource Locators (URLs) of desired Internet sites. For example, the URL for the White House home page on the World Wide Web is http://www.whitehouse.gov. URLs for Web pages usually begin with the characters "http://," which refers to the hypertext transfer protocol. The next part of the URL, "www.whitehouse," refers to the specific World Wide Web site, and "gov" (short for *government*) indicates the domain, or the type of organization that hosts the Web site. Similarly, http://www.sprint.com is the URL for Sprint, and http://www.fsu.edu is the URL for Florida State University. The domain "com" indicates a commercial organization and "edu" refers to an educational institution.

Many Internet users dislike the extensive typing required to specify sites. In addition, they often must add long strings of characters to specify directories and file names. But a newer set of tools has created an even simpler process.

World Wide Web (WWW)

a huge and rapidly expanding collection of electronic documents that can combine text, still and moving images, sounds, and automatic links to other documents

The Web. Perhaps the most exciting part of the Internet is the **World Wide Web (WWW),** a huge and rapidly expanding collection of electronic documents that can combine text, still and moving images, sounds, and automatic links to other documents. Developed by the European Laboratory for Particle Physics (known as CERN) in 1991, the Web distributes "pages" of information over the Internet. A "home page" on the Web provides information about an individual,

Jason and Matthew Olim: CDnow

One evening a few years ago, Jason Olim was sitting at a bar with a couple of friends, trying to figure out what he wanted to do with his life. He knew that whatever it was, it would involve computers. And he wanted his own business. But on this particular occasion, an idea struck him: Why not open a music shop on the Internet? Customers could browse through CD titles or go straight to what they wanted, without ever setting foot in a crowded shopping mall. The Web site could include more than just titles—maybe album reviews, information on upcoming concerts, and the like. And Jason could fulfill orders just as easily as he received them; all he had to do was link himself to the inventories of distributors. "I was imagining three people. We were going to manage a computer and eat pizza," he recalls. Soon he would learn how naive this image was.

Jason realized that creating a "cyberstore" meant writing a lot of computer code. He was proficient at it, but his twin brother, Matthew, was the wizard. So Matthew took over constructing the necessary software to manage the Web site while Jason covered business matters, such as making connections with music wholesalers. Within months, the new company—called CDnow—sold its first album. Then came cassettes and T-shirts, and within a year, CDnow's sales topped $2 million. A review in the May 1995 issue of *NetGuide* exclaimed, "CDWOW! might be a better name."

As other entrepreneurs realized the vast commercial possibilities offered by the Internet, competition entered the race for CDnow's market. Music Boulevard, now part of N2K, a large multimedia development company, and MCI's phone order business, 1-800 MUSIC NOW, are both strong contenders (the latter now has a Web site). Still, "CDnow is by far the biggest and the best, the one we like the most," notes Barney Cohen, chairman and chief executive of Valley Records, which fulfills orders for CDnow.

One obstacle that the twins must overcome is consumers' unwillingness to give their credit card numbers over the Internet, but they believe that this will disappear as shoppers become familiar with the practice. In the meantime, the Olims are forging ahead. They now accept advertising, and they were recently selected by Microsoft to test on-line ads for the Microsoft Network. "Every week is a revolution," says Jason. Even in the virtual world of cyberspace, the revolution is real.

Source: John Grossman, "Nowhere Men," *Inc.*, June 1996, pp. 63–69. CDnow can be found at www.cdnow.com. Photo courtesy of CDnow, Inc.

group, or organization with text, graphics, and video. Many business firms use this technology as a powerful new advertising medium. (One new company, CDnow, which sells music over the Web, was selected by giant Microsoft to test on-line ads for its network. See "Who's Who: Jason and Matthew Olim: CDnow.") A home page for a gardening business, for example, could contain attractively laid out pages describing the company, its products, a listing of current seeds and bulbs with prices, and a gardening tip for the month.

hypertext

links within Web pages that permit easy navigation to new information

Hypertext links within Web pages permit easy navigation to new information; you simply click the mouse on words or images to call a new page with the indicated information to your screen. A hypertext link is usually underlined and in color on-screen (see Figure 4.18). If you click on those underlined words, you activate a hypertext link that automatically retrieves another page with additional information. Other links can be graphic images; clicking the mouse on them will also retrieve more information or take you to another Web site.

Hypertext links allow you to surf almost effortlessly between Web pages to find information on products and services offered by companies, the names and addresses of people you want to contact, a new joke every ten minutes, real-time video of a street corner in Los Angeles, and much more. Developers define the text, links, and other contents of their home pages by creating document files using a language called *Hypertext Markup Language (HTML)*.

FIGURE 4.18

White House Home Page on the World Wide Web
Individuals and diverse government, educational, and commercial organizations set up home pages on the Web to provide information about themselves over the Internet.

web browsers

applications software packages that allow users to navigate and search through resources on the Internet and the Web

Web Browsers. Several **web browsers** are available. Browsers are software packages that allow users to navigate and search through resources on the Internet and the Web. Browsers provide 3-D animation, sound, and video capabilities. Three popular web browsers are HotJava by Sun Microsystems, Netscape by Netscape Communications, and Internet Explorer by Microsoft.

search tools

large electronic indexes that catalog Web pages and information on the Internet

Search Tools. **Search tools** are essentially large electronic indexes that catalog Web pages and information on the Internet. To find information, you select progressively more specific topics from a series of menus or enter one or more key words. Once you enter your key word, the search tool examines its vast listing of Internet resources and displays links to items that match your criteria. These tools can often find and display hundreds or even thousands of Internet references related to a topic of the user's choice. Search tools are sometimes called *spiders* because they search the Web. Some common search tools are Yahoo, Magellan, Lycos, Webcrawler, AltaVista, and InfoSeek. See the "Eye on the Web" box for some information about searching the Web.

Intranets

intranet

a small-scale Internet

An **intranet** is essentially a small-scale Internet. Intranets use the same technology and tools as the Internet to link computers within an organization. Employees can share information and work over an intranet easily. Since computers users may already be familiar with the workings of the Internet, training time can be minimal. Intranets take the advantages of e-mail one step further, allowing multimedia access to press releases, company policies, and benefits information. Users can view graphics, see videos, hear audiotapes, and read documents. Work can also be done collaboratively, with input from many different sources.

Company use of intranets is expected to skyrocket in upcoming years. One recent study projected that the intranet market will grow to more than $13 billion by 1999. Another predicts that by 2000, 180 million workers will be using intranets

EYE ON THE WEB

Telecommunications and networks are integral to the Internet. The Internet is, after all, a network of networks! And, while on one level telecommunications can be considered no more complicated than calling a friend on the telephone, at another level it represents limitless possibilities.

If the idea of computer communications seems to complex, take a moment to browse a user-friendly explanation of what happens when two computers are "talking" to each other. Using *telecommunications* as a keyword for a Web search, you can find information about how both digital and analog transmission are used. Other Web sites detail topics such as how modems work and why data compression techniques can save an organization both time and money.

If you are searching for product information, perhaps before purchasing a new modem, you'll easily find documentation on the Internet (such documentation is available for downloading; in fact, you can even choose from a variety of formats, such as ASCII text, PostScript printer files, or even files compatible with your favorite word processing package).

Technology and telecommunications are changing rapidly; the Internet provides a means for users to keep abreast of current events. Students and professionals alike may access Web sites devoted to detailing the latest Congressional rulings or regulations. Bell Atlantic, for example, has posted corporate reactions to regulatory news on the World Wide Web.

The WWW presents companies with a unique opportunity to obtain valuable customer information. Bell Atlantic allows users the opportunity to participate in a company survey (participants receive a thank-you note from actor James Earl Jones in return for taking the few moments to complete the requested information).

As the Internet gains prominence, many groups have begun to recognize the potential of educating users to comfortably access the Web. One exciting project currently under way is Blacksburg Electronic Village. This project, begun through a cooperative effort between a university, a Bell operating company, and the citizens of Blacksburg, Virginia, links the entire town to the Internet. Contained within the services provided are electronic shopping, mailing lists, and e-mail communications with other townspeople. An on-line village mall, for example, provides information on almost 100 local businesses. The electronic village extends far beyond commerce, however. A calendar of events alerts the locals to arts and entertainment programs, while information is provided on senior citizens activities as well.

In short, telecommunications can open entire new worlds for many people. Researchers, students, and industry professionals can stay current on topics of interest. Electronic publication can open the doors to more efficient sharing of news. Several newswire services exist to bring same-day, accurate, spot news of events to users. Plans are currently being implemented to offer on-line "yellow pages" to customers, and perhaps one day soon you'll consult your PC, rather than a listing in your newspaper, when deciding which program you would like to view.

WEB EXERCISES

1. Query the Web for some information concerning the Blacksburg Electronic Village. Write down the name of the university and the phone company that cooperated with the citizens of Blacksburg in establishing this project.

2. Why might some companies consider it advantageous to provide Internet and/or Web training to school children or customers?

3. Telecommunications can be a great aid in completing homework assignments. Access the Rockwell Web site, and browse for information explaining the difference between analog and digital communication. Then, using a word processing package, write two or three paragraphs explaining what you've discovered. Finally, use e-mail to submit your assignment electronically.

around the globe.[8] Large companies such as AT&T, Turner Broadcasting, and Tyson Foods are already using intranets, but the technology can be applied easily in small firms also.

Criteria for Successful Networking

The needs of an organization and its information system should determine the components included in a network, their layout, and the transmission media that carry signals between them. A successful network design must ensure reliability, security, acceptable response times, privacy, and ethical use. Success also depends on effective services and support from hardware and software vendors. As with other IS components, a network's design must balance cost, control, and complexity in a way that suits its users.

Reliability. A network must perform reliably—that is, consistently in the way users expect it to perform. No network can effectively support the processing needs of its users if it suffers from excessive breakdowns or downtime and distortion of signals during transmission. As the complexity of a network's design increases, so does the probability of breakdowns and poor connections or other problems that cause signal distortion.

Security. A secure network protects data from unauthorized access, interception, or disruption. The network operating system and user procedures must maintain adequate control of access to data flows through the network. Security measures must also protect disk drives and other secondary storage devices. In addition, viruses can be quickly spread throughout a network, infecting many computers. So users of networked computers must take extra precaution to avoid viruses.

Response Time. Users usually measure response time (the time they must wait to receive messages over a network) in seconds. Most users want average response times of less than 10 seconds. A network can annoy users, perhaps including important customers, if its response time exceeds 30 seconds. Response time depends on the complexity of the network configuration and the sophistication of its transmission media, devices, and software.

Privacy and Ethical Use. Network users share communications and storage resources, so they often worry about privacy and control of sensitive data. E-mail users have complained when supervisors monitored their transmissions. One person may store files intended to remain private on his or her personal computer, but other network users may gain access to these files. Along with security to guard against unwanted outside access, a network needs clear standards for private and shared information. In addition, a strong code of ethics should promote and enforce those standards.

Vendor Services and Support. Vendors sell, rent, or lease telecommunications media, hardware, and software to an organization when it sets up a network. Besides the initial products and installation services, these outside suppliers usually provide important, ongoing support services like training, maintenance, and repair. Both fixed and variable costs become critical in purchase decisions. Fixed costs include the prices of equipment, line jacks or terminals, and wire or cable. Variable costs include additional personnel to run the network, equipment rental, rent or lease payments for communications lines, and so on. Like most other decisions, the network must balance cost against potential benefits.

COMMUNICATIONS BUYER'S GUIDE

Getting on-line requires both hardware and communications software. Review the buyer's guides for hardware and software in Chapters 2 and 3 for guidance on evaluating purchases of these elements. In addition to those suggestions, some additional tips should affect purchases of resources to connect a PC to an on-line service:

1. *Decide what network services you want.* Do you need only e-mail capabilities, or do you want full access to the Internet, stock prices, news stories, travel information, and so on? These needs determine the speed you need from a modem and the software you should buy.

2. *Check out what your college or university offers.* Most colleges and universities offer e-mail, access to the Internet, and other services to students free or at nominal fees. A particular class may include access to certain on-line services.

3. *Investigate commercial on-line services.* Many commercial networks compete to provide access to national and regional groups of customers. CompuServe, America Online, Prodigy, and the Microsoft Network lead the field with national scope. All offer e-mail, Internet connections, and a variety of other services. Most charge fixed monthly fees for selected amounts of connect time with additional charges for further usage and services.

4. *Get an adequate modem.* Get a modem that can interface with your chosen on-line service. Transmission speed dominates this decision. If you are unsure about the speeds you will need, consider getting a faster modem. As industry standards increase, on-line applications take advantage of the new technology; people with old equipment soon will have to wait while their modems handle larger and larger transmissions. Speeds of 14.4 kbps and 28.8 kbps are common now, but the future will bring faster modems.

5. *Consider a fax/modem.* When buying a new modem, consider one with fax capabilities. You may need special fax software to take full advantage of these capabilities, but this feature adds a valuable improvement to your PC.

6. *Review PC journals and Internet books.* Take full advantage of the Internet and on-line services by actively looking for interesting sites. Books on the Internet provide information about stable, long-standing sites. The popular magazines listed in Chapter 1 may include more up-to-date information about the rapidly changing on-line landscape. The commercial on-line services themselves provide new references, usually categorized to help you find what you want.

- Early users carried processing jobs to a computer room. Today's systems bring computing resources to the users—wherever they are.

- The choice of transmission media should identify the least expensive way to support essential goals of the information and organizational systems, while allowing for future changes.

- Communications media are cables (twisted-pair wire, coaxial cable, and fiber-optic cable), microwaves, and satellite transmission. Infrared and cellular technologies are also being applied to telecommunications.

- Virtually every office, whether home based or traditional, needs standard communications equipment like modems and fax machines, along with the software to make them work; larger organizations need more complex telecommunications systems.

- Communication formats must be consistent between the sending and receiving devices. Some common protocols are OSI, TCP/IP, and SNA.

- Common network types are local-area networks, regional networks, wide-area networks, and international (global) networks.

- No one owns or controls the Internet; instead, operators of computer systems maintain this unique, cooperative enterprise to provide access for all. An intranet is essentially a small-scale Internet, used within an organization.

SUMMARY

1. *Outline the basic capabilities of a telecommunications system, including signal types and transmission capacities.* The sender's computer delivers a digital signal to a telecommunications device, which transmits it over an appropriate medium, perhaps after converting it into an analog signal. Another telecommunications device receives the signal and passes it to the receiver's computer, if necessary converting it back to a digital signal. The bandwidth of a transmission medium determines its signal capacity and speed, measured in bits per second (bps).

2. *Describe available transmission media for telecommunications signals.* Twisted-pair wire cables move analog signals over one or more pairs of twisted, copper wire bundles. A coaxial cable consists of an inner conductor wire covered by insulation, surrounded by a conductive shield (usually foil or braided metal wire), all covered in a jacket of nonconductive insulation. A fiber-optic cable transmits signals as pulses of laser-generated light over thin strands of glass or plastic bound together in an insulating jacket. Microwave transmissions send messages in line-of-sight, high-frequency radio signals. Satellites orbit the earth, receiving microwave signals and rebroadcasting them at different frequencies. Additional transmission media include infrared transmissions and cellular phone technology.

3. *List the hardware needed for a telecommunications system.* A modem converts telecommunications messages back and forth between the analog signals of phone lines and the digital signals of computers. Facsimile (fax) machines transmit images of documents via standard telephone lines. Multiplexers transmit several telecommunications signals over a single medium at one time. Front-end processors perform processing tasks related to sending and receiving telecommunications transmissions to relieve a computer system's main CPU of this burden. An Integrated Services Digital Network connects traditional media with digital switches to simultaneously carry voice, video, and image data at high speed.

4. *Show how communications software and protocols control the functions of a telecommunications system.* Communications software controls telecommunications signals so that sending and receiving systems agree on the patterns and lengths of data bit strings. A network operating system controls the functions of disk drives, printers, and other hardware connected to a telecommunications network, just as an operating system controls hardware in an individual computer. Communications protocols summarize certain standards that allow any computer system or network to communicate effectively with any other system or network. Popular protocols include Open Systems Interconnection (OSI), Transmission Control Protocol/Internet Protocol (TCP/IP), and IBM's Systems Network Architecture (SNA).

5. *Lay out network resources in configurations that support specific applications.* A local-area network (LAN) connects computer systems and devices, usually by physical cables, within a small geographic area. Client/server systems link individual computers (clients) with a computer with large storage capacity (server) so that nodes can access document files and applications programs. It can also connect any node to other LANs through bridges or gateways. Regional and wide-area networks (WANs) form telecommunications links between computing resources spread across entire regions or even countries. They often employ microwave and satellite transmissions in addition to telephone cables. An international, or global, network connects nodes in different countries. The Internet is a public, international network of networks. Educational institutions, government agencies, business organizations, and individuals use it to exchange e-mail and share vast pools of information. The World Wide Web (WWW) forms part of the Internet devoted to displaying a huge and rapidly expanding collection of electronic documents that can combine text, still and moving images, sounds, and hypertext links to other documents.

6. *Mention several criteria for successful networking.* A successful network design must ensure reliability, security, acceptable response times, privacy, and ethical use. Also, vendors must provide effective services and support for the hardware and software they sell.

Key Terms

communication 108	digital signal 110	twisted-pair wire cable 112
telecommunications system 108	signal frequency 112	noise 112
data communications system 109	bandwidth 112	coaxial cable 113
analog signal 110	bits per second (bps) 112	fiber-optic cable 113

microwave transmission 114
line-of-sight signal 114
communications satellite 115
infrared transmission 117
cellular telephone service 117
modem 118
facsimile (fax) machine 119
fax board 119
fax/modem 120
multiplexer 120
front-end processor 120
polling 121
Integrated Services Digital Network
   (ISDN) 121

ISDN switch 121
network 123
network operating system (NOS) 124
protocol 124
nodes 125
local-area network (LAN) 125
file server system 125
client/server system 126
network interface card 127
bridge 127
gateway 127
regional network 128

wide-area network (WAN) 128
international (global) network 128
data haven 129
Internet 129
electronic mail (e-mail) 129
File Transfer Protocol (FTP) 130
World Wide Web (WWW) 130
hypertext 131
web browser 132
search tool 132
intranet 132

Concept Quiz

1. Which of the following are examples of telecommunications systems?
   a. telephone
   b. radio
   c. data communications
   d. all of the above
2. Computers generally communicate by exchanging
   a. analog signals
   b. digital signals
   c. continuous varying voltage
   d. traditional telephone lines
3. All of the following are types of cables that supply physical connections between data communication devices *except*:
   a. alternate-pair wire cable
   b. twisted-pair wire cable
   c. coaxial cable
   d. fiber-optic cable

Write "true" or "false" after each of the following statements.

4. Microwave transmissions allow only a line-of-sight signal. _____

5. Radio communications systems still fill a wide range of information needs for different types of companies. _____
6. Although the expansion of cellular transmissions has streamlined mobile communications, prices of cellular equipment and services have skyrocketed. _____
7. Telephone lines still remain the most common medium for telecommunications and data communications. _____

Fill in the blanks in the following statements.

8. In addition to translating data for transmission across telephone lines, a modem performs the functions of _____, _____, and _____.
9. A front-end processor regularly _____ terminals and other devices to identify and accept new messages.
10. Integrated Services Digital Network (ISDN) technology is able to maximize the capacity of existing transmission media because _____.

Answer the following questions briefly.

11. What are the three main functions of communications software? What are four additional functions?
12. What does a protocol do?
13. What are the standard classifications of networks?

14. What is the name of the largest public international network? Who started it, and why?
15. What is the World Wide Web? Who developed it?

Discussion Questions

1. As an IS professional working for a state university system, what type of media would you choose for your telecommunications system? Why?
2. How has the Internet changed the way you communicate? If it hasn't, why not?
3. As an IS professional, what criteria would you use to determine the components that should be in your company's network? Why would these criteria be important?
4. Does your university library have a system similar to the CARL system shown in the chapter-opening photo? If so, in what ways do you use it? If your library does not have such a system, do you think it needs one? Why or why not?

Team Activity

Divide the class into groups of three or four. Each team should choose an organization—a company that interests them, a professional athletic team, or a nonprofit organization. Then, using the "Communications Buyer's Guide" in this chapter (as well as any applicable points made in the discussion questions above), each IS team should decide on the best type of telecommunications network for their organization. Teams can present their findings to the class or in writing. An alternative activity can include a discussion of future uses of telecommunications networks. Students can brainstorm ideas of what uses they can be put to—home, business, entertainment—as well as the different forms they may take.

Applying IT

1. To support your team activity, access the Internet and browse through the Web to find the telecommunications link that has the best transmission capacity for your objectives. If you do not have Internet access, locate the information in your library. Use a spreadsheet to compile the information that you obtain (for instance, note whether the medium is baseband or voiceband).
2. Make an inventory of the telecommunications devices that you use on a regular basis. Do they meet your own criteria for effectiveness? Why or why not?

CASE

Reed Elsevier

For a long time, the European publisher Reed Elsevier had a good thing going. The firm, a joint venture between Britain's Reed International Plc. and Holland's Elsevier N.V., publishes more than 1,000 academic journals (making it the largest publisher of this type in the world).

Academic publishing works like this. Scholars write and submit articles for free; publication in the "right" journals helps them gain tenure, grants, and status in their fields. School libraries automatically subscribe to necessary journals. And the publisher can charge whatever it wants for a subscription because it has a captive audience; for instance, a single-year subscription to *Neuroscience* (one of Reed Elsevier's journals), published semiweekly, costs $3,775.

All that may be changing, however, with the Internet. Now, journals as well as individual articles are available on-line. A recent *Directory of Electronic Journals* catalogs nearly 700 titles, including 142 peer-reviewed journals.

These electronic publications are a lot cheaper than print ones. For instance, Louisiana State University's library is able to offer whatever its professors and students want electronically, for about $25,000 per year in copyright and delivery fees. Compare that cost with the $446,000 it spent each year on print subscriptions. (Reed Elsevier does offer electronic information—but at 110 percent of the print version.) Electronic publications are also a lot more quickly available. More recently, LSU eliminated the library's role altogether, allowing professors and grad students to log on to the Internet and simply browse through the tables of contents of 17,000 journals; they can retrieve the publications directly from UnCover Co., an electronic retrieval company, at a cost of about $13 per article. "We're a little bit ahead of where the rest of the country is going," says LSU library's assistant dean, Chuck Hamaker.

Turnaround time for an electronically published manuscript is about three months; it can take two years for a scholarly manuscript to make its way into a print journal. Software for publication via the Internet is also flexible. Several years ago, Paul Ginsparg, a high-energy particle theorist at the Los Alamos National Laboratory, wrote a program that allows the 200 researchers in his field to post manuscripts on the Internet. The software has now expanded to include 30 other disciplines in which the speed at which information can be disseminated is crucial. Soon, Ginsparg will launch a plan for a formal review process that can be conducted electronically. Since this is perhaps the most important step in academic publishing, it is the one barrier to electronic publishing that must be removed before electronic publishing is universally accepted. Stevan Harnad, a psychology professor at the University of Southampton in England and the founding editor of the journal *Psychology*, has proposed having scholars post their manuscript drafts as well as their final, peer-reviewed publications on the Internet. If academia accepts this proposal, scholarly publishers like Reed Elsevier will have to completely change the way they bring the work of academics to the public eye.

Questions

1. Do you think electronic publishing will entirely replace print publishing in the academic world? Why or why not?
2. What can a company like Reed Elsevier do to compete with the new information technology?
3. Access Reed Elsevier's Web site at www.reed-elsevier.com/reglance.html and learn what you can about the company's publications. Are there some that might lend themselves more readily to electronic publishing than others? Why?

Source: John R. Hayes, "The Internet's First Victim?" *Forbes*, December 18, 1995.

Answers to Concept Quiz

1. d **2.** b **3.** a **4.** True **5.** True **6.** False **7.** True **8.** dialing telephone numbers; originating new messages; and answering incoming calls with the direction of communications software **9.** polls **10.** it does not need to convert digital signals to analog ones and back again. **11.** It sets the basic format for the number and sequence of data bits that identify each character of other elements in a message; it determines whether each byte carries a parity bit to allow error checking; it specifies how the combinations of bits indicate the divisions between bytes of data. Four additional functions are: communications log; micro-to-mainframe links; control and coordination; security. **12.** It summarizes certain standards that allow any computer system or network to communicate with any other system or network. **13.** Local-area networks; regional networks; wide-area networks; international networks **14.** The Internet; the U.S. government, to link defense researchers **15.** The WWW is a huge, expanding collection of electronic documents that can combine text, still and moving images, sounds, and automatic links to other documents. It was developed by the European Laboratory for Particle Physics (CERN).

CHAPTER
5

Word Processing and Spreadsheet Applications

CHAPTER OUTLINE

Word Processing Programs
    Basic Features of a Word Processor
    Supporting Features
    Integration with Other Applications
Suggestions for Using Word Processors
Spreadsheet Programs
    Spreadsheet Basics
    Changing a Spreadsheet
    Supplemental Features
Dynamic Use of Spreadsheets

Whether they have feathers, fins, or fur, pets require a great deal of care. Daniel Matson of Animal House Pet Shop in Norwich, Connecticut, uses his word processing software to produce information sheets about the care and feeding of each animal he sells. Every new pet owner leaves the store with an information sheet so they'll have an at-home reference on animal care. Matson also uses desktop publishing software to produce a newsletter that provides additional tips on pet care, offers solutions to common animal problems, and contains coupons for pet supplies. Customers appreciate the information and keep coming back. Photo courtesy of Animal House, Inc.

LEARNING OBJECTIVES

After completing Chapter 5, you will be able to:

1. Describe the basic and supporting features of word processing programs.
2. List important suggestions for effective use of word processing programs.
3. Explain the basic and supplemental features of spreadsheet programs.
4. Detail some guidelines for dynamic applications of spreadsheets.

When computer users describe their most important information processing needs, writing and revising documents usually ranks at the top of the list. Completing error-free numerical calculations often represents a close second. These functions are truly critical for business users, who spend much of their work time corresponding with others and drafting written reports. They also work hard to track and project income, expenses, inventory levels, and other numerical data.

Computers, especially personal computers, revolutionized these information processing functions by offering word processing and spreadsheet applications. Businesspeople (and many other groups of users) welcomed these powerful computing tools and the huge gains in efficiency and effectiveness that they allowed.

Typists no longer have to meticulously correct typographical errors in completed documents with messy erasers and correction fluid; word processors allow them to proofread their work and make needed changes before printing a clean copy. They can produce revisions and generate many copies of standard documents simply by opening document files, making needed changes, and printing out the new versions.

Before word processing, a typist began with a blank sheet for each document, even if it required only minor changes from another version.

Spreadsheet programs similarly automate many tedious calculation and recordkeeping functions. Computers manipulate columns of numbers and formulas much more quickly than people can, and their calculations produce far fewer errors. Spreadsheets took over the basic arithmetic of number-intensive processing for business, science, statistics, and other ventures. This change freed people to concentrate on the formulas necessary to represent specific events and the real-life implications of numerical calculations.

In particular, spreadsheet software transformed business decision making by allowing managers to imagine changes in input and immediately estimate the resulting effects on important outputs (for example, if sales increase by 10 percent next year, how many more employees will the company have to hire?). Planners can change the input numbers and then observe changes in the output numbers to quickly and easily foresee the likely results of various decisions. This information helps them to prepare effective responses well in advance.

Word processors and spreadsheets reinforce one anothers'

strengths. Together, these applications allow people to compile and communicate the results and assumptions of sophisticated analysis through many channels. Documents prepared in word processing programs can incorporate data from spreadsheets to present the latest, most accurate information about company activities. Organization members can distribute these vital messages as reports, memos, letters, and e-mail messages. The distinctions among the applications programs are increasingly being blurred as users focus more on integrating different applications in each document for whatever their needs are. This approach to work is called the *document-centric approach*. Keep in mind that what once were separate applications are being merged to make work easier. We will discuss the different applications separately so that you can understand each program's strengths and the elements they bring to the complete computing task.

This chapter explains the functions through which word processing programs support document creation and revision. It then gives some practical suggestions for using word processors. Later sections discuss the mechanics of working with spreadsheets and some practices that enhance their effectiveness.

WORD PROCESSING PROGRAMS

Computers are not the first devices people have used to capture the written word. Early printing presses revolutionized human communication and vastly expanded people's ability to share and transfer knowledge. Typewriters improved the efficiency of creating and distributing legible, standardized written material. The first book to be prepared with a typewriter and submitted to a publisher was Mark Twain's *Adventures of Tom Sawyer,* in the 1800s.

Typewritten texts were not trouble free. Correcting typewritten mistakes takes considerable effort, and large errors require the typist to start over from scratch. To prevent key jams, the keyboards of typewriters were designed intentionally to slow typing. This QWERTY layout (named for the letters at the upper left of the keyboard) remains standard in today's computer keyboards despite the disappearance of its original justification.

Word processing applications apply the computer's power to the tasks of creating, revising, and distributing written documents. Common types of documents include letters, business reports, memos, advertising brochures, student research papers, textbook manuscripts, church bulletins, and many others. In addition to standard text, word processing documents can include a wide range of other elements, such as equations, graphics, tables, and footnotes. After the user inputs these elements via the keyboard or another method, the application provides powerful tools for editing the document and formatting its appearance. The computer can also check for errors in spelling and even grammar before you distribute the finished document. In fact, current word processing programs, such as Word 6.0 for Macintosh, can detect and correct your common and repeated typing errors instantaneously. Besides paper-based output, word processing software supports preparation of documents for distribution by fax, e-mail, and the World Wide Web, among other channels.

word processing

a function that applies the computer's power to the tasks of creating, revising, and distributing written documents

word wrap

a word processing feature that starts a new line as the text characters reach the right margin

Basic Features of a Word Processor

All word processing programs share some standard features that allow you to input, revise, format, and output documents. Most documents begin as text input by someone typing at a keyboard. The word processor can also read completed files from a diskette or download them across some telecommunications medium, but someone had to input the original files, probably by typing. (Other, more exotic, alternatives include scanning printed material using optical character recognition software and dictating out loud to a speech recognition program.)

As the text characters reach the right margin, the computer automatically starts a new line, a feature called **word wrap.** Unlike a typewriter, the word processor does not require the typist to press the return key at every line to indicate a line break. Most other typing conventions work with a word processing program, including the Tab, Shift, and Caps Lock keys. (For text that will become a printed publication, do not space twice between sentences, as typists traditionally do. The word processing program

Text and pictures can be input into a document using a scanning device. (Source: Courtesy of Logitech, Inc.)

can automatically produce double, triple, or other spacing. The computer keyboard also includes additional choices, some of them discussed in Chapter 2:

* Cursor-control keys (Page Up, Page Down, Home, End, and the arrows) control where typed characters will appear. (If you use a mouse, you may not use these keys often.)
* The Delete and Backspace keys eliminate characters to the right or left, respectively, of the cursor.
* Insert usually switches the program between insert mode, in which new typing adds to existing text, and typeover mode, in which new typing replaces old characters.
* Function keys activate program functions that vary between applications packages, as do combinations of keys pressed together with Control, Alt (or Option), and Shift.

Editing Text. Word processing applications allow you to change the existing contents of a document easily. This capability is the primary advantage of computer-based writing over typing; a typist must retype every word of a document to incorporate any significant revisions, while a computer user can simply open the document file, make the desired changes, and print out a new copy.

You edit a word processing document by placing the cursor (usually indicated on the screen by a flashing underline or vertical line, called an I-bar) at the point in the text where you want to make a change and then inserting or deleting the appropriate material. More involved editing techniques give truly outstanding capabilities to word processing users:

* *Block operations.* You can define a block of text in most word processing programs by placing the mouse pointer at the beginning of the passage, holding down the left mouse button, and dragging the pointer to the end of the passage; the location of the pointer when you release the mouse button defines the end of the block. A block could be one character, a single word, a paragraph, or several pages. After defining the block of text, you can manipulate it without affecting the rest of the document. This technique gives a simple way of deleting a lot of text at once, moving the selected text to another spot, saving it in its own document file on the disk, and formatting it. See Figure 5.1.

FIGURE 5.1

Blocking and Moving Text
Once you select a block of text, you can delete it, cut it from one place and move it to another, copy it and insert it at another location, save it separately from the rest of the document file, and manipulate it in many other ways.

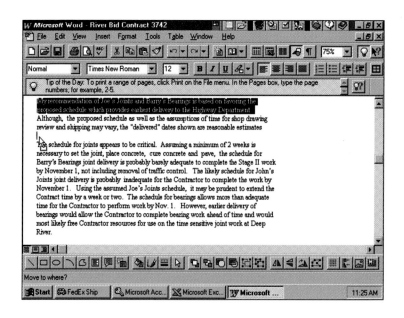

cut

to remove a block of text and place it in the clipboard

copy

to duplicate a block of text and place it in the clipboard

paste

to move the contents of the clipboard from one location to another

global search

a word processing function that allows you to specify a string of characters and then direct the computer to locate them anywhere in your document

search and replace

a word processing function that allows you to specify one string of characters for the computer to find and another to replace them

zoom

a word processing function that allows you to magnify parts of your document on-screen to get a closer look without affecting the finished product

fonts

styles of type

- *Cut and paste.* Using the **cut** and **copy** features of a word processor, you can remove or duplicate a block of text and place it in the clipboard. You can then move the cursor to another location, perhaps in another document or even another applications program, and **paste** (insert) the contents of the clipboard there.
- *Search and replace.* The **global search** function of a word processor allows you to specify a string of characters (perhaps a word or phrase) and then direct the computer to locate them anywhere in your document. In the **search and replace** function, you specify one string of characters for the computer to find and another to replace them. You can choose to make this kind of blanket revision automatically or approve each change as the computer finds the search string.
- *Zoom.* A word processor's **zoom** function allows you to magnify parts of your document on-screen to get a closer look without affecting the finished product. For example, you might zoom in to enlarge a small graph or table and confirm that it will look right in the final output. After studying the chosen element, you can zoom out again to view the whole document.
- *Multiple document editing.* A word processor's multiple document capability allows you to work with two or more documents at one time. You can go back and forth between them, perhaps copying text from one and pasting it into the other. You can often display both documents in separate windows on-screen for easy comparisons.

Formatting Documents. A word processing application allows you to alter the appearance of a document in many ways, both while you input data and after you complete data entry. You can choose among many **fonts,** or styles of type, to give your characters a desired look. A computer system's font collection usually includes many different typefaces and sizes. (See Figure 5.2.) Two examples of personal computer font collections are True Type (scalable) fonts and Adobe Type Manager PostScript fonts (used in professional publications). Also, you can use **bold,** *italic,* or underlined fonts, among other choices, to highlight specific characters, words, or passages. In the course of a writing and revision sequence, you can use ~~redline~~, or ~~strike-out~~, fonts to indicate text proposed for deletion before you make a final decision.

FIGURE 5.2

Font Choices
Word processing applications allow great flexibility in text fonts and other formatting features.

Twelve point Helvetica type.
Nine point Helvetica type.

Twelve point Palatino type.
Nine point Palatino type.

Twelve point New Berolina MT type.

Twenty-four point New Berolina MT type.

Twelve point Gill Sans Condensed type.

Twenty-four point Gill Sans Condensed type.

A full-featured word processor allows you to give your text exactly the look you want. In addition to fonts, you can specify many other aspects of your document's appearance:

- *Paper size and margins.* Unless you specify other measurements, most word processing programs assume that your document will fit on paper 8½ by 11 inches with 1-inch or 1½-inch margins on all sides. You can choose other standard page sizes (8½ by 14 inches, business envelope size, etc.), instead. Margins can vary continuously, depending on the capabilities of your printer. You might specify a wide margin at left, perhaps extending headings into the empty space, or alternate margins at left and right on successive pages to create facing pages with empty space at the outside edges. You may want to keep wider margins at the insides of facing pages if the document will be bound in some way. This precaution prevents the binding from hiding any text.
- *Line spacing.* You can specify standard choices of single, double, or triple spacing between lines or (usually) enter a measurement of your own.
- *Justification.* A word processing program allows you to **justify** text left or right to align all characters at the left or right margin. As an alternative, you can center each line on the page width or specify **full justification,** in which the computer varies spaces between words as needed to align characters at both margins.
- *Tab and indent.* Most applications automatically set tab and indent stops every ½ inch unless you change them. A hanging indent starts the first line at the left margin and aligns subsequent lines indented one stop (or another measurement you specify) from that point. This format helps to give a neat appearance for both numbered and unnumbered lists (like this one).
- *Multicolumn text.* A word processor normally arranges text in a single column defined by the left and right margins. You can also choose to divide that horizontal space into two or three (or more) columns to create a layout similar to that of a newspaper. When text reaches the bottom of one column, it automatically starts again at the top of the next.

You need not detail all of these conditions for every document. Any word processing program assumes **default settings** for many of these formatting choices until you change them. The ability to determine these characteristics gives you a powerful tool to control the appearance of your document.

Spelling, Grammar Checking, and Thesaurus. Everyone makes typographical errors when inputting text, and many misspell words. A word processing program's **spelling checker** detects these mistakes by comparing every word in a document against a huge dictionary file of allowable words. If it finds no match for a particular string of characters, the computer displays the questionable word and allows you to correct it, bypass it, or add it to the dictionary so later spelling checks will not highlight it again (see Figure 5.3). Abbreviations such as *RAM, ROM,* or *CPU* will not be recognized as words, but they can be added to the dictionary.

Note that this comparison does not consider the meanings of words, only whether each character string matches a list of acceptable strings. For example,

it wood knot under stand any of the err ores in this sent ants.

---

justification

a word processing function that allows you to align text at the left or right margin

full justification

justification in which the computer varies spaces between words as needed to align characters at both margins

default settings

formatting choices that do not change until you change them

spelling checker

a word processing feature that detects spelling mistakes by comparing every word in a document against a huge dictionary file of allowable words

FIGURE 5.3

Spelling Checker Function
A word processing application's spelling checker compares character strings in a document against a list of allowable strings and highlights any differences for the user's action.

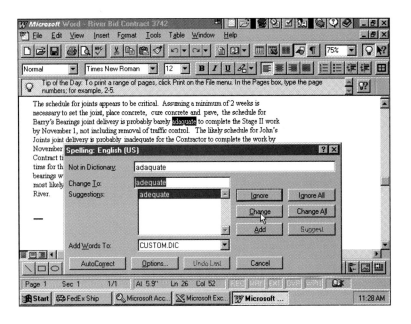

grammar checker

a word processing feature that detects grammatical mistakes

thesaurus

a word processing feature that lists alternatives to selected words

This potential problem illustrates an important limitation of word processors and all applications software. The computer processes patterns of electrical pulses; only the user's interpretation gives them any meaning as words, numbers, or other information. Therefore, the spelling checker and other software functions do not relieve users of responsibility for the accuracy and quality of their systems' input and output.

Grammar checkers detect more complex mistakes. Did you enter an opening parenthesis but forget a closing parenthesis? Do you have a run-on sentence or overuse passive voice? A grammar checker will highlight errors like this and suggest changes. This capability often comes from a separate program rather than being an internal function of a word processing application.

The **thesaurus** feature of a word processor lists alternatives to selected words. For example, you may decide that you have written the word *leadership* too frequently in a paper, but you cannot think of a substitute. In most word processing programs, you place the cursor before the word you want to replace, or you highlight it as a block. Then, when you give the appropriate command, the computer will display a number of words for you to consider as replacements, such as *direction*, *guidance*, and *administration*. Another command will automatically replace *leadership* with the alternative word you selected. A thesaurus may also display words with opposite meanings (antonyms).

File Management in Word Processing. It is important to save your document files frequently while working so that you do not lose them during power fluxes. This general principle applies with particular force in word processing, because this application focuses on revising documents to create and save new versions. If you do not save regularly, you risk losing the results of hours of work polishing text and devising an elaborate format. The program's automatic save function will help you to guard against a power failure or other problem by interrupting your work briefly to back up your document file every few minutes or as frequently as you desire.

When you first save a document file, the computer will allow you to specify a file name and a folder or directory in which to place the file. If you try to save later with the same name and location, the computer may ask you to confirm that you want to replace the version on disk. If not, you can give a Save As command to save the document with a new name and/or location. This choice allows you to keep different versions of a file. As you revise, you may specify new file names for later versions and still retain earlier drafts for comparison. For example, you could save Term Paper Revision 1, Term Paper Revision 2, and so on, if you are unsure of changes or need to keep backups. Save As also allows you to place a document file on a diskette or in a different folder or directory.

The file management features of some applications can convert files to the formats of other word processing programs or other versions of the same program. For example, this convenient capability allows a program like Microsoft Word to read and manipulate document files created in WordPerfect or an earlier release of Word.

Finally, some word processors provide a last-open-file feature that quickly opens the files with which you most recently worked. This saves you some time by automating the procedures needed to open those files.

Printing Documents. Word processing programs provide many flexible printing options. You can print an entire document or only a selection, perhaps a few pages. You can print a file on disk without opening it for editing. You can even direct the computer to print in the background, while you continue working on something else.

Both Windows and Macintosh applications allow you to specify your printer choice for all applications through the operating system rather than requiring separate instructions within the word processing software. Applications that run under MS-DOS, however, require you to specify a printer as part of their internal printing functions. The word processors then print by activating utility programs called *printer drivers*. (The files for these programs come with your word processing program or a new printer.) In all applications, once you have specified a printer, you can print hard copy simply by clicking a few icons or giving simple commands.

Supporting Features

Many additional features expand the basic capabilities of today's word processing programs to enhance their power and at the same time make them easier to use. For one important example, you can include many *special characters* that do not appear on the standard keyboard in your text. You can place bullets, stars, or boxes in the margin to highlight particular text, such as list items. In addition, you can place mathematical symbols, Greek characters, monetary symbols, and many other special symbols in your documents. (See Figure 5.4.)

FIGURE 5.4

Special Characters
A word processing document can include many valuable symbols and characters in addition to normal letters and numbers.

$$\text{å ß } \partial \text{ } f \text{ © ˙}\Delta \text{ ° ¬ } \ldots \text{ æ}$$

$$\text{œ } \Sigma \text{ ´ ® † ¥ ˆ ø } \pi \text{ ʺ ʹ}$$

$$\Omega \approx \text{ ç } \sqrt{} \int \text{ ˜ } \mu \le \ge \div$$

special effects

a word processing feature that
alters fonts to condense or expand
the letters, outlines characters,
and draws simple drop shadows

Fancier **special effects** alter fonts to condense or expand the letters, and you can do outlines of characters and simple drop shadows (see Figure 5.5). If you also use a page makeup program, you can curve and shape the text. For example, the title of a document could follow a sweeping curve with smaller type at the beginning and end. Text could even wrap around a graphic or a large initial letter.

Regular Bodoni MT Ultra font.

You can condense the characters so they're closer together.

Or you can expand them so they're farther apart.

Fonts can be outlined in word processing documents.

Fonts can have a heavier background shadow.

Do companies that people love to work for do things differently? And does it really make a difference when it comes to quality and productivity?

FIGURE 5.5

Special Effects for Word Processing Fonts
Some easy special effects can add interest to your word processing documents. Page makeup programs give you even more flexibility with design.

Managers are being forced to develop new skills and attitudes to effectively get things done, and pressure is mounting.

Some observers believe the much-maligned middle manager is poised for a comeback after almost a generation of being leaned to near extinction. In the meantime for those "lucky" enough to still have a management job, the rewards can sometimes seem few and far between. The new increasing number are saying they need to pay

The new reality for many managers in the '90s means longer hours, little or no opportunity for advancement, and fiercer-than-ever pressure.

more attention to their personal and emotional lives in order to make it work back at the office. This can mean anything from exercising and eating better to finding new ways to mentally "get away" from the stress.

This awareness of the nonwork self is an attempt to retain balance and sanity under the strain of overwhelming performance expectations. A manager today is supposed to be both a visionary and a coach, skilled at the touchy-feely side of getting...

bookmark

a word processing tool that helps you reach sections that require more work or contain information you want to review or reread without scrolling through screen after screen of text

You can place **bookmarks** anywhere in a document and then move quickly to those locations. This tool helps you to reach sections that require more work or that contain information you want to review or reread without scrolling through screen after screen of text. The bookmarks do not appear in the finished document; they work only to help you find desired materials.

Features that Automate Program Functions. Certain word processing features speed up and simplify the work of writing and revising.

- *Icons and toolbars.* Like other applications running under graphical user interfaces, word processing programs present icons and toolbars to help you quickly and easily perform many complex functions. For example, Microsoft Word for the Macintosh (Version 6.0.1) allows the user to display up to ten different toolbars with icons to print, save, open, and merge files; set font choices, paragraph formats, margins, and borders; check spelling; and perform many more tasks. Some word processors' toolbars offer icons for almost every function the programs can perform. If you need different options, you can often customize the toolbars so their icons activate functions of your choice.

macro

a word processing feature that automates combinations of keystrokes

- *Macros.* A **macro** performs a similar automating function based on combinations of keystrokes instead of mouse clicks. You can create a macro that performs a sequence of menu commands, perhaps to choose a left-justified, indented, single-spaced paragraph format, and assign it to a key combination like Control–L. Then every time you hold down the Control key and press *L*, the word processor automatically sets the paragraph single-spaced, aligned at the left, and indented from the margin.

  In another common use of macros, you can assign a long character string to a single key combination. Suppose, for example, that you are writing a report on computer applications in business. You might have to type the term *management information systems* more than 20 times. Instead, however, you could define a macro that assigns the term to a couple of keys, perhaps Alt–M. Then, when you need to add the term *management information systems*, you could just hold down the Alt key and press *M*. This use of macros greatly speeds text input, and it also reduces typographical errors.

style sheet

a word processing feature that summarizes a wide range of formatting choices

- *Style sheets.* A **style sheet** summarizes a wide range of formatting choices, including fonts, margins, justification, line spacing, and more, for all elements in a particular kind of document. You need not separately carry out all of these formatting decisions for each text paragraph, heading, footnote, and other element in your document. Instead, you can simply apply the style sheet and designate the various elements, and each one takes on the formatting choices you have previously specified. This tool saves considerable time and effort otherwise required to develop a complex document. It also allows you to impose a standard look for all documents of a particular type.

wizards

smart document development tools that work like predefined style sheets

- *Wizards.* Many word processing applications come with smart document development tools, often called *wizards*, that work like predefined style sheets. A word processing **wizard** automatically assigns fonts, margins, and other features for some common types of documents. You simply answer a few questions, and the wizard defines formatting commands for letters, calendars, faxes, reports, and many other types of documents. This tool can give you professional-looking documents without taking the time to create a style sheet. You can change or override any settings made by the wizard and still benefit from the rest of its blanket formatting.

BUSINESS BITS

Lotus SmartSuite 96

Shortly after IBM swallowed up Lotus, the progressive, trendy company could easily have hung a sign reading "Lotus Doesn't Live Here Anymore" outside its Cambridge, Massachusetts, headquarters. Key executives and creative people quickly departed from the ten-year-old company, despite promises from its new, conservative parent that nothing would change. After weeks of splashy headlines in the business pages, Lotus seemed to disappear.

But the Lotus division of IBM has a new product, and the computer industry has taken notice of it. The program is called SmartSuite 96 for Windows 95, and it is fighting to become a major competitor to Microsoft's Office 95. SmartSuite 96 focuses on giving teams of employees ways of working together on documents and spreadsheets. For under $400, SmartSuite 96 offers six applications: the Lotus 1-2-3 spreadsheet, Approach database, Freelance Graphics presentations package, Organizer information/calendar manager, ScreenCam screen capture utility, and Word Pro word processor. (Office pro offers only four applications for $100 more.)

Among SmartSuite's flashy features is the SmartCenter, which allows users to organize and access data from a single location via four separate "file drawers" in which programs, documents, and notes applications can be stored. SmartSuite 96 is streamlined in that it has the same "look and feel" across its different applications, so users can travel back and forth comfortably. There is also LotusScript, an object-oriented programming language available in Word Pro, Approach, and Freelance. The Team Mail feature lets users send an entire file or just selected pages for others to read and review. Finally, TeamConsolidate streamlines the process of managing document revisions by several people.

According to initial reviews, SmartSuite 96 has some inconvenient glitches; for instance, 1-2-3 and Organizer can't handle long file names. There is also the uncertainty in the business and computer industry about what IBM plans to do with Lotus, not to mention why the company bought Lotus in the first place. This uncertainty translates to what kind of identity Lotus software products will have in the future. But Lotus, which has traditionally organized its workers into teams, has built a reputation for products that foster teamwork. Can this team make it to the playoffs against Microsoft (which has 90 percent of the Windows suite market), never mind win?

1. List some advantages to buying and using a software suite. How could suites help foster teamwork in an organization?
2. What steps might Lotus take to increase its market share of the Windows suite market?
3. Access the Web site for Lotus at http://www.lotus.com/ and see what you can learn about SmartSuite 96.

Source: "Lotus SmartSuite 96: Back in the Ring Again," *PC World,* January 1996, pp. 40–45. Photo courtesy of Lotus Development Corporation.

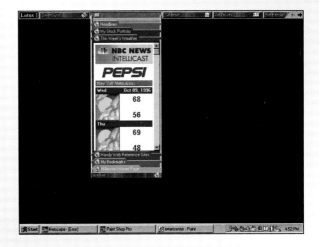

---

on-the-fly correction

a word processing function that monitors your input and automates the process of bringing it in line with quality standards

- *On-the-fly correction.* Of course, you still have to input the text, graphics, and other elements of the word processing document. To support this function, a word processor's **on-the-fly correction** function monitors your input and automates the process of bringing it in line with quality standards. Like an automatic spelling and grammar checker, this feature fixes common errors in spelling or grammar (or notifies you of the errors) as you type. For example, you can direct the program to change *teh* to *the* without any specific instructions from you. The program probably lists some typical errors, and you can specify your own most frequent mistakes.

mail merge

a word processing function that allows you to prepare hundreds or thousands of personalized letters simply by incorporating selections from an address file to be merged with a word processing document file

Mail Merging. Another popular word processing function is the ability to combine the text of a letter written in a word processor with a list of names, addresses, and other information. This **mail merge** function allows you to prepare hundreds or thousands of personalized letters simply by incorporating selections from an address file to be merged with a word processing document file. This combination adds headings with names and addresses, personalized salutations, and perhaps other variations to a standard letter suited for individual recipients. Figure 5.6 shows a sample of a mail merge.

Cooperative Word Processing. Successful applications often reinforce today's team-oriented business environment by offering functions designed specifically to support collaboration and cooperative work. (For example, the Lotus division of IBM offers a new product that focuses on giving teams of employees ways of working together on documents and spreadsheets; see "Business Bits: Lotus SmartSuite 96.")

work group

a word processing feature that helps to integrate the contribution of several people to a document

- *Work group support.* The **work group** feature of a word processing program helps to integrate the contributions of several people to a document. The application displays changes made by each person in a different color, so that all can determine who suggests which modifications. At the end of the revision process, the program incorporates approved changes and automatically eliminates others.
- *Internet support.* Many word processing applications support production of documents for the Internet. They can save files in the hypertext markup language (HTML) format required for pages on the World Wide Web.

FIGURE 5.6

Mail Merge
During mail merging, a form letter in a document file can be merged with multiple names and addresses in a data file to create individualized letters.

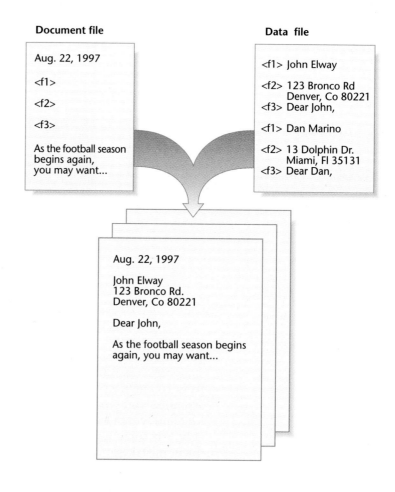

Document file

Aug. 22, 1997

\<f1\>

\<f2\>

\<f3\>

As the football season begins again, you may want...

Data file

\<f1\> John Elway

\<f2\> 123 Bronco Rd
        Denver, Co 80221
\<f3\> Dear John,

\<f1\> Dan Marino

\<f2\> 13 Dolphin Dr.
        Miami, Fl 35131
\<f3\> Dear Dan,

Aug. 22, 1997

John Elway
123 Bronco Rd.
Denver, Co 80221

Dear John,

As the football season begins again, you may want...

Additional Elements to Enhance a Document. Besides sophisticated capabilities for inputting, revising, and formatting text, word processors help you to include many other elements in your documents.

- *Headers and footers.* All popular word processors allow you to enter and format information to appear at the top or bottom (or both) of every page in a document. These elements often include page numbers, dates, and other information, and they help readers to locate where they are in a document and identify which document they are reviewing.
- *Graphics.* Market-leading word processing applications can also import graphics like charts, photos, and drawings to illustrate and enhance your text. You can adjust the sizes of these pictures, add borders around them, and give them captions. The program's page makeup function places graphics, perhaps wrapping text around them, according to your instructions.
- *Footnotes and endnotes.* Word processors support creation of footnotes and endnotes through built-in features that automatically number and place these references at the appropriate positions in larger documents. If you delete a footnote, the program automatically renumbers all remaining ones. Its page makeup function allows space at the bottom of the appropriate pages and inserts footnote text.
- *Sorted elements.* A word processing application can also sort references or other elements in list formats. This feature can arrange these elements either alphabetically or numerically in ascending or descending order. It provides a useful tool for handling lists as well as reference information.
- *Outlines.* The **outlining** feature of a word processor arranges text in a different way. It helps you to create and manipulate a logical hierarchy of statements and then tie text selections to this structure. If you rearrange the outline, the associated text changes place, as well. The program imposes a numbering system to define levels of an outline in any of several formats, including roman numerals for main points, capital letters for the next level down, then Arabic numbers, lowercase letters, and so on.
- *Table of contents and index.* A table of contents provides a similar kind of reference to help readers understand the structure of a long document. After creating the document, you indicate materials that you want to appear in the table of contents. You then specify the location and appearance of this element and command the application to generate it. The resulting table of contents carries the page numbers for the listed materials, and the computer revises these page references if the positions of the materials in the document change. An index lists document elements in alphabetical order rather than their sequence in the text, but you define entries and the application assigns page numbers just as for a table of contents.
- *Mathematical elements.* Some word processors have built-in mathematical functions that allow you to make simple calculations in a document. For example, suppose that you want to illustrate a point in a letter by including a column of numbers with a total. Your word processor may be able to automatically recalculate the total if you change a number in the column.

  Documents like a statistical report or a paper for a calculus class require a more complex mathematical tool called an *equation editor*. This feature extends the ability to include special symbols so you can add simple or complex equations and mathematical statements to your documents. You can easily place symbols for mathematical calculations like square roots and calculus operators by giving simple commands or

outlining

a word processing feature that helps create and manipulate a logical hierarchy of statements and then ties text selections to this structure

FIGURE 5.7

FIGURE 5.7

Equation Editor
Equation editors extend the
capabilities of word processing
by allowing special symbols to
be included in the document.

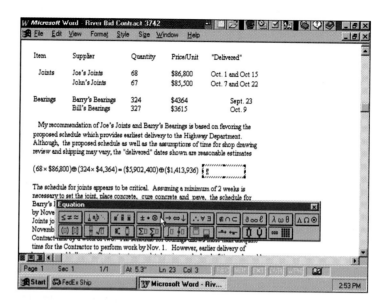

choosing options from a menu. The computer formulates the equation
based on your instructions (Figure 5.7).

- *Tables.* The advanced mathematical tools of some word processing programs
  give them limited spreadsheet capabilities. Such a program can manipulate
  values, formulas, or procedures placed in cells of a table created within a
  word processing document. You define the table by specifying the number
  of rows and columns. This automatic format feature allows you to place borders around table cells and align entries left, right, or centered. The computer then spaces the columns evenly across the page width and generates
  the appropriate number of rows in your specified format. You can revise this
  layout to make columns wider or narrower depending on the data that you
  will input, and you can make other formatting choices to achieve the desired
  appearance. When you enter data (numbers or characters) into a cell, the
  application automatically extends the cell's depth and wraps the data to the
  next line, if necessary. You can also highlight a cell, row, or column with
  shading, different types of borders, and other special features, depending on
  what you want to emphasize.

Integration with Other Applications

Some calculations become too complex to complete within a word processor's
built-in functions. Some draw on data already created and stored within a
spreadsheet program. In such a situation, you can create a document most
effectively and take full advantage of your applications by importing tables
and other numerical data from a spreadsheet or another program.

Today's full-featured word processors can easily incorporate spreadsheet
data along with graphics, database information, and files from many other
applications into all kinds of documents (see Figure 5.8). You can accomplish
this integration by cutting and pasting, linking, or embedding objects from
other applications. In a report on the market for a new product, for example,
you might include a detailed financial analysis from a spreadsheet program
and a list of likely dealers from a database program. One German software
company, Star Division, offers a suite that allows users to move information
easily from the World Wide Web to text documents and spreadsheets and to
write e-mail in HTML.[1]

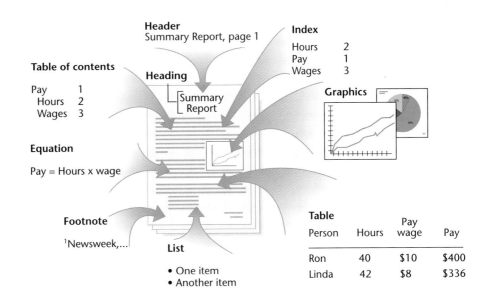

FIGURE 5.8

Functions within a Word Processing Application
Many functions within a word processing program begin to blur the boundaries between separate applications. You can insert tables, lists, graphics, footnotes, and equations in a document. In addition, you can use the program's table of contents and indexing features to automate contents pages and indexes.

Incorporating Spreadsheets and Graphics into Word Processing Documents. You can pick up existing numerical data by borrowing a small section of a spreadsheet, perhaps a few columns and rows of data with sales projections for a new product. To integrate such a limited selection of data, you can simply launch the spreadsheet, open the appropriate file, define a block with the desired data, and execute a Copy command. You then return to your word processing application, place the cursor in the document where you want the data to appear, and issue a Paste command. If you later want to make a change, you have to redo the process.

With linking, a connection is established between the word processing document and another document, such as a spreadsheet program. Once the link is established, you can edit the spreadsheet result inside the word processing document. With embedding, the spreadsheet file is included within the word processing document. You can also edit the spreadsheet result inside the word processing document. Embedding, however, results in larger file sizes.

A *document-centric* approach allows you to concentrate on the documents you are developing instead of the computer programs or technology you are using. In Windows 95, for example, you can place document icons on your desktop. To work on a document, you select the document icon and press the Enter key. You don't have to go through a series of menus to first start the application and then open the document. You can also have the results from several applications in one document. Spreadsheet analysis and tables from a database, for example, can be placed in a company report developed with a word processing program.

Spreadsheet programs include functions to display their data in charts such as pie charts, bar graphs, and line graphs. You can import these graphics into your word processing document, rather than raw data, from your spreadsheet program (Figure 5.9). After importing a chart, you can add arrows, circles, boxes, annotations, and more through the word processor's internal drawing tools. You can also easily change the size and positioning of an imported graphic.

In the same way, you can import a more complex drawing or other illustration created in a dedicated graphics program to help reinforce written information and improve its appearance. If a small, simple drawing will do, word processors include many pieces of clip art.

FIGURE 5.9

Spreadsheet Graphic in a Word Processing Document Graphics generated from a spreadsheet, such as this pie chart, can be imported into word processing documents.

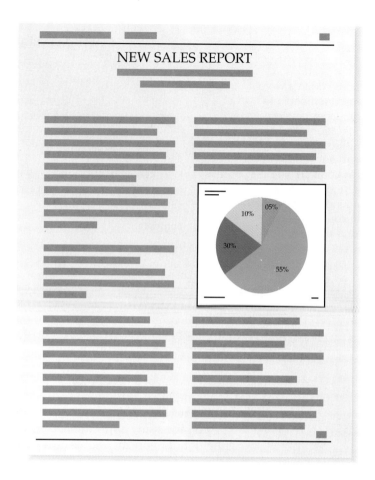

SUGGESTIONS FOR USING WORD PROCESSORS

A word processor can ease the burden of writing compared with older methods, and it can help you to produce superior finished documents. A few suggestions can help you work as productively as possible with a word processing program:

- *First, develop a good outline.* Most writing instructors suggest developing a detailed outline of any complex document before beginning to compose the text. A thoughtful sequence of major, secondary, and lower-level topics allows you to concentrate on appropriate wording without confusion about what should come next. You can simply write text for each section of the outline in sequence.
- *Finish stating your ideas and then edit.* Many people have trouble starting to write. If they stop repeatedly to change text and correct spelling, they often lose momentum and have to begin all over again. To avoid this kind of diversion and distraction, successful writers focus on producing a first draft while their ideas are fresh, planning to improve their text in later revisions.
- *If you doubt whether you should include some material, do not delete it.* After completing a first draft, you may be tempted to delete sentences or major blocks of text in editing. If you are not sure about a deletion, consider marking it in some way or cutting and pasting to move it to the end of the manuscript or to another file. Then, if you decide you really want to

EYE ON THE WEB

Hypertext markup language (HTML) is a new coding system used to transform documents into Home Pages and other World Wide Web documents. Many Web surfers visit Web pages without realizing how they are created. Once complicated, the process is now becoming easier. For many nontechnical users, the idea of generating HTML code is daunting. Using these numerous codes correctly will transform a document into something to share with the world via the World Wide Web. Misplacing an ending delimiter, however, may turn that Web document into a disaster! The average user just might consider having to embed HTML codes into a text passage too close to programming for comfort.

"HTML Writer" (software programs) take a giant step toward alleviating these fears. An HTML Writer allows a user to import a document from a word processor and easily place HTML codes around text passages. For example, suppose you have written a paragraph but wish to emphasize a phrase by using boldface type. With an HTML Writer and your mouse, you can highlight the phrase and simply click on the appropriate button for boldface type. No coding is necessary. It's that easy! Advances like this one are making the unknown world of HTML code more and more accessible for the average Web user.

Microsoft has ventured a step further toward eliminating "HTML anxiety." The company has developed the Internet Assistant for Word (as well as another comparable add-in for Excel) which permits Windows 95 users to prepare Web-ready documents using these popular word processing and spreadsheet packages. Rather than attempting to structure HTML tables, numbered lists, and so on, Internet Assistant permits the user to transform the word processing document into a Web-ready document simply by pointing the mouse and clicking on the appropriate button. Additionally, the Internet Assistant add-ins allow the user to view the document as it will appear on the Web without having to load a browser and switch applications. In this "preview" mode, the user has the option of making additional modifications or embellishments before posting the finished HTML document to a Web site.

The developers of the World Wide Web brought the Internet within reach of casual computer users. This downward evolution and demystification has continued with the development of HTML Writer and packages such as Microsoft's Internet Assistant. Rather than limiting one's involvement with the Web to viewing, anyone who can use a word processor can now create impressive looking Web documents quickly and easily without having to master the intricacies of HTML.

WEB EXERCISES

1. Consult your instructor or your school's computer lab assistants to discover whether an HTML Writer (possibly Microsoft's Internet Assistant add-in software) is available at your facility. Compose a small paragraph describing your dream vacation. Using one of these tools, transform your paragraph into a Web-ready document.
2. If your computer lab facility has an HTML Writer software package, try to explore some of its capabilities. Does it allow the user to format tables? Describe the steps necessary to center a title in a document. Does your software package permit you to "nest" the HTML codes which you embed into your document?

include the text later, you can simply return it to its original location (or a new one). Consider using the word processor's redline or strikeout font to designate questionable deletions; you can then return and actually delete the material before completing the document, if you like. Many programs will automatically mark all revisions, after which you can make a final decision about each one after completing your initial edits.

- *Save and reuse page and document layouts.* As mentioned earlier, style sheets can save you setup time. Many word processing users require a few basic layouts for most of their papers or documents. To avoid spending time duplicating these standard choices, you can save the specifications for each kind of page layout in a separate file. Rather than initiating a new document every time, you can create a style sheet, open this existing file, and begin inputting text within the standard layout. Style sheets help standardize complex formatting specifications.

- *Break up large documents into smaller files.* As you work with an extremely long document, the large document file may become difficult to manipulate. You may have to wait for the computer to perform basic editing tasks, such as searching for a word or changing a format throughout a document. Also, editing sessions usually focus on limited sections of a long document rather than skipping through the entire file. To avoid problems and narrow the focus of the work, save major sections (such as chapters in a book) as separate files. You can later combine the sections for final printing, if necessary.
- *Frequently save your work.* This advice cannot be overemphasized. Set the automatic save feature of your word processor to back up your document file regularly, perhaps every few minutes.

SPREADSHEET PROGRAMS

spreadsheet

a program that automates numerical calculation tasks by processing user-defined data according to specified formulas

The earlier discussion of integrated computing described the benefits of importing numerical data from a spreadsheet application rather than creating a separate table within a word processor. A **spreadsheet** program automates numerical calculation tasks by processing user-defined data according to specified formulas. The spreadsheet provides its most important benefits when it recalculates values, either automatically or at the user's command, to reflect changes in data. (To read about one of the first spreadsheet programs, see "Who's Who: Dan Bricklin/VisiCalc.") This powerful capability supports many critical information system needs, especially in business firms. A planner can vary the input data for projected sales, for example, and immediately view the effects of these changes on costs and profits.

Spreadsheet Basics

cells

the intersections of a spreadsheet's rows and columns

The intersections of a spreadsheet's rows and columns define **cells,** which store numbers, formulas, and labels. Letters identify columns, and numbers identify rows. Each cell has an *address;* Cell A1 lies at the top left, with B2 one column to the right and one row down, C3 one more column right and one more row down, and so on. (See Figure 5.10.)

FIGURE 5.10

Spreadsheet Program Display
The spreadsheet's matrix of rows and columns stores numerical data, formulas to carry out calculations, and labels to document the significance of data and formulas.

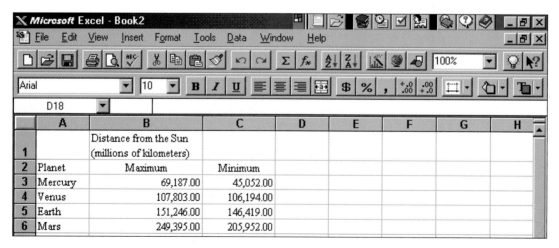

	A	B	C	D	E	F	G	H
1		Distance from the Sun (millions of kilometers)						
2	Planet	Maximum	Minimum					
3	Mercury	69,187.00	45,052.00					
4	Venus	107,803.00	106,194.00					
5	Earth	151,246.00	146,419.00					
6	Mars	249,395.00	205,952.00					

WHO'S WHO

Dan Bricklin/VisiCalc

Dan Bricklin was a revolutionary during a decade when people were tired of revolutionaries. In a sense, the country was in a lull during the 1970s. But Dan Bricklin wasn't. After graduating from MIT, he went to work for Digital Equipment Corporation (DEC), where he wrote programs for an interface between newswire services and typesetters; perhaps more important, he wrote about 25 percent of DEC's first word processing program. After several years, Bricklin left DEC and entered Harvard Business School to pursue an MBA.

As he learned about business theory and practices, Bricklin began to grow frustrated with the time and labor required to perform business calculations. He knew that computers could help—but no one had yet found a way. He wanted applications software to be able to do for calculations what word processing software had done for document writing. He wanted users to be able to input numbers and other variables, change them around, and have the results calculated. Businesses could then make rapid sales forecasts, control inventory, and predict human resource needs. So Bricklin began to write his own program. He teamed up with Bob Frankston, a friend from MIT, and together they began to form the program into a useful product that just might sell. They started their own company, called Software Arts, Inc.

The duo had to buy computer time on a time-share basis (no one had his own computer at that time); Frankston wrote during the night, when computer rates were lowest, and Bricklin finished his MBA. Soon, although it was a tough sell, Apple bought a version of the new program for its Apple II computer. The program was called VisiCalc (for *Visible Calculator*). Shortly thereafter, Tandy, Commodore, and Atari all had versions of VisiCalc. When VisiCalc reached computer stores, it sold for $100.

VisiCalc had no huge, splashy launch. It just quietly appeared. But what it did was ultimately change the way businesses operated, all around the world. The VisiCalc spreadsheet allowed company managers to enter variables such as costs and revenues, change them around, and see immediately how the changes would affect a product's performance and the company's bottom line. VisiCalc reduced the cost of building spreadsheets by 80 percent (they were no longer time and labor intensive), and small businesses could now compete with larger ones by making the same complex financial calculations as their competitors. VisiCalc, which was inexpensive to buy and easy to use, also changed the computer industry itself; in a sense, it lent credence to the personal computer. In fact, because the first version of VisiCalc was written for the Apple II (an early PC), people bought the Apple II specifically so they could use VisiCalc. Once VisiCalc was established, so was the PC.

Lotus eventually bought Software Arts, having already introduced its own Lotus 1-2-3 spreadsheet. Bricklin worked with Lotus for awhile but went off on his own again to start another company, called Software Garden, Inc. He introduced more programs, such as Dan Bricklin's Demo Program and Demo II (the latter provides customized demos, prototypes, and other components necessary for building computer basic training). Bricklin's perspective on his career is philosophical. "I'm not rich because I invented VisiCalc, but I feel that I've made a change in the world. That's a satisfaction money can't buy." Most people would love to be able to say the same thing about their own work.

Sources: Paul Stranahan, "Dan Bricklin," *Jones Telecommunications and Multimedia Encyclopedia*, www.digital century.com/encyclo/update/bricklin.html; "The Father of the Spreadsheet: Dan Bricklin," http://mbhs.bergtraum.k12.ny.us/. (Photo: Ira Wyman.)

title bar

a spreadsheet feature that states the name of the document file for the currently displayed spreadsheet

content bar

a spreadsheet feature that reveals the formula, number, or label stored in the current cell

Like other applications, a spreadsheet's screen display shows a menu bar, toolbar, and other program-control features. In addition, the **title bar** states the name of the document file for the currently displayed spreadsheet. The **content bar** reveals the formula, number, or label stored in the current cell; as you edit or input new data, the changes appear here.

You can easily move around a spreadsheet to view and change its contents. The arrow keys move your display up, down, left, or right one cell at a time. Other cursor-control keys move it one screen forward or backward. In addition, most spreadsheets present scroll bars, function keys, and icons that move you to various parts of the spreadsheet. A GoTo command allows you to display a specific cell by entering its address.

formulas

spreadsheet equations that perform calculations based on specific data or the contents of one or more cells

Formulas. Each **formula** in a spreadsheet performs a calculation based on specific data or the contents of one or more cells. The formula =42/7 would divide 42 by 7 to return the value 6. (The equals sign indicates to the application that the cell contents represent a formula.) The formula =B3/7 would divide the contents of Cell B3 by 7, while =J5 + E5 + F5 + G5 would sum the specified cells. When new input changes a number in one cell, the cells that depend on that one also change, and the recalculation function proceeds to update the entire spreadsheet.

Of course, the cells specified in a formula could also contain formulas, so the results of one calculation can become input for others. This possibility allows a potentially serious logical problem in a spreadsheet's design. A spreadsheet application allows you to define a series of formulas, each taking input from others earlier in the series. If you fail to keep careful track of this string of calculations, you may create a *circular reference,* in which one cell takes input from another that takes input from the first. As Figure 5.11 illustrates, you might enter the formula =J8/H8 in Cell L5. If either J8 or H8 requires input from L5, you have created a circular reference. The spreadsheet cannot complete the calculation in L5 until it calculates J8 and H8, but it cannot complete those steps until it completes L5. The conflict often becomes less obvious in the longer sequences of formulas that spreadsheets commonly require. (Perhaps J8 receives input from G6, which receives input from I4, which receives input from L5.) Fortunately, applications check for these conflicts as you enter formulas, but you still must resolve the problem and create logically consistent formulas yourself.

functions

spreadsheet elements that complete certain standard calculations

Functions. Spreadsheet programs simplify the process of specifying common formulas by offering **functions** that complete certain standard calculations. (These are often called @ *functions,* pronounced "at functions," because the @ symbol precedes the function names.) Spreadsheet functions basically give short names to represent complex, preprogrammed formulas. Table 5.1 lists some useful functions.

range

a spreadsheet rectangle that encompasses one cell, a row, a column, or rows and columns of adjoining cells

Ranges. Many spreadsheet operations affect groups of cells. A **range** is a rectangle that encompasses one cell, a row, a column, or rows and columns of adjoining cells. A formula can complete a calculation based on the values for all cells in a range (e.g., E5 through G5). A function, for example, can complete a calculation based on the values for all cells in a range. The function =SUM(A1:A10) would add, or sum, the values in Cells A1 through A10. In addition, you can assign names for specific ranges and then specify those names in formulas and other operations to instruct the application to retrieve the contents of those groups of cells.

FIGURE 5.11

Circular Reference
No formula in a sequence can take input from another that takes input, however indirectly, from itself.

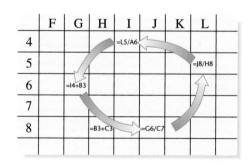

TABLE 5.1

Popular Spreadsheet Functions	
@ABS	Computes an absolute value [e.g., ABS(–5) is 5]
@AVG	Computes the average of a range
@COUNT	Counts the number of blank cells in a range
@DAY	Displays the day component of today's date (e.g., on December 15, 1997, @DAY would give 15)
@INT	Displays the integer value of a number [e.g., @INT(4.5) would return the value 4]
@MAX	Computes the maximum value in a range
@MIN	Computes the minimum value in a range
@NPV	Computes the net present value of a range
@PMT	Computes the payments for a loan given the interest rate, the amount borrowed, and the repayment time.
@ROUND	Rounds numbers with desired precision [e.g., @ROUND(34.1264,2) gives 34.13; the addition of ",2" indicates the desired number of decimal places]
@SLN	Computes depreciation by the straight-line method
@SUM	Computes the sum of a range of values
@TODAY	Displays today's date
@YEAR	Displays the year component of today's date (e.g., on December 15, 1997, @YEAR would give 97)

Note: An at symbol (@) indicates to the application that the following information represents a function rather than a text label or some other element.

Cell Formats. Spreadsheets can track all kinds of numerical data, including amounts of money, percentages, time measures, and so on. Cell formats control how labels, values, and formulas appear in the screen display and other output. For example, one format adds a dollar sign and perhaps two decimal places to show an amount of money. Another format shows an interest rate as a percentage rather than a decimal. Most spreadsheets offer several formats for dates. For example, they can show the date December 31, 1997, as 31-Dec-97, 31-Dec, Dec-31-97, Dec-31, 12/31/97, and 12/31.

Names for Cell and Range References. Traditional spreadsheets specified cell addresses in all formulas. For example, a formula in Cell M45 might compute a company's profits by subtracting data for costs in Cell J45 from revenues in Cell F45. The user would have to remember that =F45 – J45 represented revenues minus costs. Today, some spreadsheets allow you to assign natural language descriptors to cell contents and then refer to these descriptors in formulas. For example, the contents of Cell M45, designated as PROFITS, might read = REVENUES – COSTS, where these words refer to Cells F45 and J45, respectively. Another calculation for the firm's tax payment might take PROFITS as one input.

File Management. Like other applications, a spreadsheet program allows you to save and retrieve document files to preserve your work. You can also combine two or more document files into a single, larger spreadsheet. An application's extract feature allows you to copy part of one spreadsheet to another.

A spreadsheet's print capabilities allow you to generate a hard copy of your data. You can print selected pages or parts of the spreadsheet, including graphics associated with it. Some spreadsheet programs allow you to preview the printed output and change the format and layout of the hard copy.

Changing a Spreadsheet

After you have entered labels, values, and formulas, you can change a spreadsheet to improve its ability to support your information needs. Typical changes include revising cell contents and ranges, inserting and deleting rows and columns, and customizing the screen display.

Editing Cell Contents. Inputting new data replaces the current contents of a cell with a new number or label. You can also enter a new formula to replace an incomplete or erroneous one. Highlight the desired cell using the cursor-control keys or the mouse and then double-click, click the appropriate icon, or press the editing function key.

Editing a Range. Changes often affect rectangular ranges of cells rather than individual ones. Moving cell contents to another area of a spreadsheet allows for large-scale changes. The program moves all of the formulas within the range, as well as the data. In the process, it changes the cell addresses so all formulas continue to draw input from the correct cells.

This automatic adjustment of cell addresses makes possible one of the most powerful spreadsheet capabilities: copying. For example, you might make 12 copies of a range with formulas for a monthly budget, one for each month in the year. Many spreadsheet tasks repeat certain calculation sequences. You can quickly and accurately duplicate a single sequence to complete the necessary spreadsheet, and the application will automatically adjust your cell addresses so the formulas continue to work as expected.

Revising the Row-and-Column Structure. If you decide to add a calculation to your spreadsheet after constructing it, you can insert a row or column to store the required data and formulas. If existing rows and columns no longer provide valuable information, you can delete them. In either case, the program will automatically change the addresses of cells that move to accommodate the new material or fill the gap left by the deleted material. It will also update formulas that refer to the cells whose addresses have changed.

Controlling the Display. You can customize a spreadsheet's display in a number of ways:

- Increase or decrease the length or width of a column through automatic or manual options
- Hide columns from view if you want to omit information from the display but retain it in the spreadsheet; this option allows you to keep certain information confidential or just to condense the display
- Freeze rows and columns at the top and left to keep headings on the screen; other cells can scroll separately, allowing you to view all data in the spreadsheet along with labels that explain their meanings
- Split a large spreadsheet into different windows to view two areas at the same time
- Specify fonts and typestyles, margins, and other formatting for your final output

Supplemental Features

Supplemental features of spreadsheets vary from version to version. Some typical features are presented here. As in other applications, spreadsheet programs provide help commands to display on-screen documentation about program controls. As in word processors, wizards work like built-in tutors to help you perform program tasks instead of just explaining how they work (see Figure 5.12). These step-by-step sequences lead you through complicated tasks or activities as you complete them.

Macros and Templates. Like word processors, spreadsheet programs allow you to define macros for frequent command sequences. One macro might assign a single command, such as Control–S, to activate a series of operations that sort a database section of a spreadsheet. These user-defined tools allow you to customize your spreadsheet to support your unique information processing needs.

Another time-saving tool, a **template,** supplies a matrix of spreadsheet cells with all of the formulas needed to perform a standard set of calculations but no numerical values. When you input your data in the appropriate cells, the template becomes a fully functional spreadsheet. Leading applications include a variety of templates, and you can buy others wherever you purchase software. By customizing commercially produced ones, you can quickly and easily develop your own templates.

Fill Down/Fill Right. Spreadsheet applications include important tools designed to speed input of repeated data. The **fill down/fill right** feature duplicates data and/or formulas in a specific cell throughout a row, column, or block of rows and columns. Fill right might help you to complete your monthly personal or business budgeting spreadsheet, for example. Each column would represent one month's expenses and each row would report expenses in a certain category. You could select the row for your rent expense and then copy the same amount in each column, since you would pay the same amount to your landlord every month. These features automate data entry and save you keystrokes.

In a more elaborate data-input tool, some spreadsheets can anticipate later entries based on the first one and suggest complete cell contents for a row, column, or other block. You enter the first number or name in the series, and the

template

a spreadsheet tool that supplies a matrix of spreadsheet cells with all of the formulas needed to perform a standard set of calculations but no numerical values

fill down/fill right

a spreadsheet feature that duplicates data and/or formulas in a specific cell throughout a row, column, or block of rows and columns

FIGURE 5.12

Spreadsheet Wizard
Wizards provide step-by-step guidance as you complete program activities.

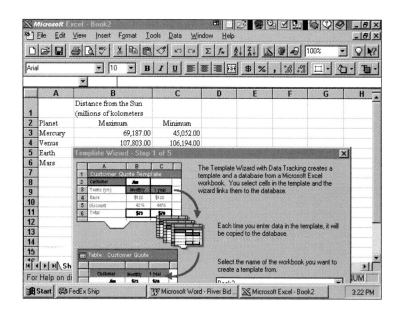

fill by example

a spreadsheet feature that can anticipate later entries based on the first one and suggest complete cell contents for a row, column, or other block

program's **fill by example** feature generates the rest of the series. This tool can help with routine data entry like a series of years (1997, 1998, 1999, etc.) or months (January, February, March, etc.). You type the first entry (1997 or January) in the appropriate cell, and the spreadsheet fills in the rest of the series in different cells.

Graphics and Mapping. By producing graphs and charts that illustrate numerical data, a spreadsheet application contributes an important set of tools to an information system. (See Figure 5.13.) After you have entered the data and structured formulas to produce the desired calculations, a few commands will produce pie charts, line graphs, bar graphs, and more. These nicely formatted illustrations, including options with three-dimensional effects, present data in compelling, eye-catching ways that powerfully reinforce their significance. You can also add lines, rectangles, circles, boxes, text blocks, arrows, and freehand drawings to explain and enhance a graph. You can print the graph or insert it into a document file from another application, such as a word processing report.

Some spreadsheets expand their graphics abilities to include built-in maps of the world, the United States, Canada, and other countries and areas. By integrating spreadsheet data with these maps, you can create strong visual images of sales trends, population growth, and so on, for different areas or regions (see Figure 5.14).

Additional drawing features allow you to place boxes, circles, ellipses, shaded rectangles, arrows, freehand drawings, and text blocks throughout the spreadsheet. These elements add documentation to supplement or replace explanatory text labels.

Database and Reference Tools. Most spreadsheets can apply their file and table management capabilities to create and manipulate databases of text information as well as numerical data. You can input text labels in spreadsheet cells in the same way that you input numerical data to create a table listing names, places, or other text. Then you can sort the table alphabetically, search for certain information, and even automatically replace specified information with something else.

FIGURE 5.13

Graphing Capabilities of Spreadsheet Applications
Spreadsheet programs can generate many kinds of graphs and charts to illustrate changes in numerical data and their significance.

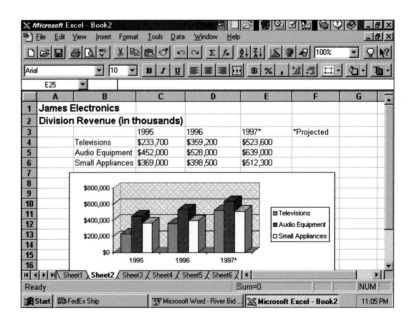

FIGURE 5.14

Map-based Spreadsheet Graphics
As part of their graphics abilities, many spreadsheets can generate maps that display data by region.

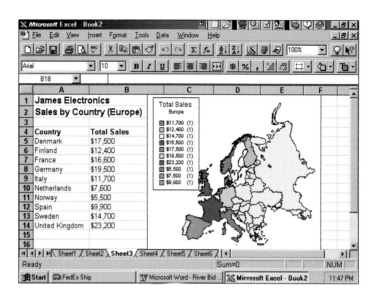

You can extract information from the database table and place it in other parts of the spreadsheet (see Figure 5.15). A numerical spreadsheet to track sales might include a section with customer names, addresses, and other information. Transaction processing routines in the numerical formulas could then draw input from the database section to produce invoices.

To meet similar needs, a spreadsheet application's **table lookup** feature pulls certain standard, unchanging values from separate tables within the spreadsheet. For example, an instructor's grading spreadsheet might include a table of numerical scores and the equivalent letter grades. Using table lookup, the spreadsheet can compare a student's average score for coursework, such as 89, with a table of standard values and determine the appropriate letter grade, such as A–.

table lookup

a spreadsheet feature that pulls certain standard, unchanging values from separate tables within the spreadsheet

Linking Spreadsheets. Dynamic links between spreadsheets allow them to use other spreadsheets as reference tools, as well. A large spreadsheet typically organizes its cells in pages or sheets. Although the application saves all of these pages together in a single document file, each page represents a separate spreadsheet, starting with Cell A1 at its upper, left-hand corner. A page can

FIGURE 5.15

Database Manipulation within a Spreadsheet
Database capabilities allow a spreadsheet to combine internal text and numerical data in documents like invoices.

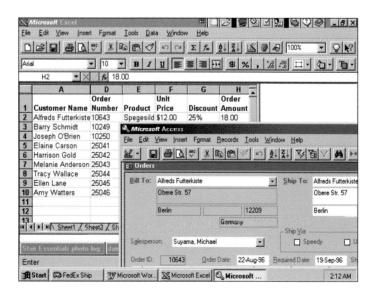

conduct its calculations independently, or it can draw data and formulas from other pages by referring to their cell addresses. These links between pages effectively create a compact, three-dimensional matrix of cells that you can easily view and navigate. Without linked pages, you would have to move far across a large, flat surface to find a particular cell, creating a much more unwieldy tool.

In the same way, dynamic links can join completely separate spreadsheets saved in different document files. The application then automatically updates all linked spreadsheets to reflect changes in one of them. This feature resembles the capability, mentioned earlier, to link spreadsheet data with word processing documents.

Versions and Scenarios. One of a spreadsheet program's most powerful benefits comes from its ability to display the likely effects of potential events and assumptions. A built-in **version** feature of some spreadsheet programs allows you to carry out spreadsheet calculations with different values for key variables to gauge the impact of different possibilities on the entire spreadsheet. For example, a planner might create a version of a cost-and-revenue spreadsheet to reflect a low cost for maintaining equipment. Similarly, a second version might show a high cost for equipment, a third version might show high revenues, and a fourth might show low revenues. Each version illustrates the impact of a varying circumstance on the company's overall costs and revenues.

By combining versions, a decision maker can create more complex **scenarios.** For example, one scenario's spreadsheet might reflect the best case with a combination of low maintenance costs and high revenues. Another could show the worst case with high equipment costs and low revenue. As the assumptions change, the spreadsheet shows the likely effect on companywide operations, allowing planners to decide whether to proceed with a project or how to respond to potential developments.

Cooperative Work on a Spreadsheet. Work groups consult to make most business decisions. A spreadsheet program includes features designed to support this cooperative work by allowing a group of people to share a single spreadsheet. The application keeps track of who worked on certain parts of the spreadsheet and when. In addition, some spreadsheet applications create document files that integrate easily into other groupware applications, such as Lotus Notes. A spreadsheet program's **data protection** features prevent unwanted changes to cell contents.

These applications support flexible distribution options to allow multiple users to share data without barriers. Colleagues can send entire spreadsheets or selected cells as faxes, through local-area or wide-area networks, or via electronic mail without leaving their spreadsheet program. You might use this feature to distribute your version of a spreadsheet showing your expectations for future data. (You can also send graphs through the same communication links.) The people who receive your version can make their own changes and return the spreadsheet for your consideration. Everyone can exchange spreadsheet data, modify it, and return it numerous times in less than an hour, so that everyone understands the others' expectations. Together, workers can reach a decision that reflects input from all parties.

To fulfill a need for wider communication, a spreadsheet program can automatically send a complete or partial spreadsheet to a group of people. For example, an accountant at a company with seven branches might distribute a spreadsheet showing companywide sales, revenues, and costs to all branch managers at once simply by clicking a few icons or giving a few simple commands.

---

version

a spreadsheet feature that allows you to carry out calculations with different values for key variables to gauge the impact of different possibilities on the entire spreadsheet

scenarios

combined spreadsheet versions

data protection

a spreadsheet feature that prevents unwanted changes to cell contents

Backsolver. Many spreadsheets offer a feature that reverses the normal sequence of analysis. The *backsolver* starts with certain outcome data and helps you to work backward to determine needed input values to produce that output. For example, a real estate broker might develop a spreadsheet program to analyze the percentage gains on investments in certain types of commercial real estate. The spreadsheet would include formulas for complex tax, depreciation, and expense calculations. Its normal analysis would process inputs about prices, financing, and other data to calculate returns, but the broker might want to determine the price a client should offer to generate a 10 percent return on a property. The backsolver would support this analysis by calculating the needed input, given the target output (the return percentage).

Internal Programming. Some spreadsheets can incorporate external processing tools, such as Visual BASIC applications, to perform powerful, programmed calculation routines in combination with spreadsheet formulas. Supplemental programming tools might control a spreadsheet as it performs sophisticated manipulations like executing a sequence of commands, executing a number of commands repeatedly, and branching to specific commands depending on the results of other processing steps.

DYNAMIC USE OF SPREADSHEETS

A spreadsheet application can effectively support transaction processing tasks like income and expense reporting, especially when changing conditions require frequent updates to data. Still, the real power of this kind of program comes from its decision support abilities. In this role, data in output cells show the effects of specific inputs on an entire set of numerical calculations. A carefully formulated and organized spreadsheet helps people foresee the likely effects of changes in certain conditions so they can plan responses well in advance.

what-if analysis

a spreadsheet practice in which data in output cells show the effects of specific inputs on an entire set of numerical calculations

Decision makers call this practice **what-if analysis.** They change the data in spreadsheet cells to create different versions based on potential real-life events. The program then recalculates all formulas, and the new output shows the effect on every variable that depends on the changes. With reliable answers to important questions ("What if sales increase 10 percent next year?"), decision makers can begin preparing for likely future conditions.

Spreadsheet programs provide extremely powerful and versatile tools for performing almost any calculation or mathematical analysis. To realize this potential, however, a spreadsheet's data, formulas, and structure must suit its processing tasks. Popular magazines often print tips for effective spreadsheet use. This section summarizes some suggestions to help you produce effective spreadsheets:

- *Plan before you start filling cells.* Before you start entering data and formulas, plan the general appearance and features of your spreadsheet. Lay out the design on paper to indicate the numbers of rows and columns, leaving space for column headings and other explanations of the data.
- *Devote one part of the spreadsheet to input data.* If you will revise your spreadsheet or add data, try to group all input values that could change in one place. Otherwise, you may have to search the entire spreadsheet to find where to enter new data. Of course, formulas can find data anywhere in the spreadsheet as long as you specify the right cell address, so you need not place input data near the formula that will need it for a calculation.

- *Summarize results in a single location.* Experienced spreadsheet users often place a summary section near the top (or in another convenient location), where others can easily find the results of the calculations. The summary section can be created by copying results into a convenient location.
- *Gather formulas and macros in one location.* Spreadsheet users often do not need to see the formulas and macros that produce the results they need. On the other hand, the person who updates the spreadsheet may have to change formulas sometimes. By grouping all formulas and macros in one location, you can avoid cluttering the output display and simplify efforts to revise the processing routines.
- *Include many explanatory titles and extensive internal documentation.* For example, instructional text like "ENTER INTEREST RATE AS A DECIMAL" might appear above a cell that stores an interest rate. Without these instructions, someone might enter "10" for an interest rate of 10 percent instead of the correct amount (0.10). The mistake would lead to output 100 times larger than it should be.
- *Document any assumptions at one location in the spreadsheet.* For example, spreadsheet formulas might compute depreciation by the straight-line method. This formula reflects an assumption about the appropriate method that people who use the spreadsheet may need to understand. Grouping text labels that describe important assumptions helps users to interpret a spreadsheet's data.
- *If you revise the same spreadsheet repeatedly, identify each version with internal labels.* Clear titles help you to remember the conditions for each version of your spreadsheet. For example, you might develop a spreadsheet that analyzes the terms of car loans. Each time you change the spreadsheet to evaluate the terms of a different lender, record a date and explanation in the spreadsheet (e.g., JANUARY 15, LOAN FOR RED FORD EXPLORER, FIRST NATIONAL BANK). This technique provides a useful history if you save each version and analyze them all together.
- *List or print formulas.* It is easy to make mistakes in constructing formulas that cause a spreadsheet to calculate the wrong information. To ensure that you can easily review your formulas, you should always print or list all of them. (Most programs generate this kind of record through a built-in feature.) Some companies insist that all personnel follow this procedure and send listings of their spreadsheet formulas and documented templates to a central office for review and storage.
- *Use data protection.* Once you have developed and completely tested a spreadsheet, protect data in all cells that contain formulas. This precaution prevents accidental changes that would make the spreadsheet produce incorrect results.
- *Use templates frequently.* Once you have developed a spreadsheet that you will use regularly, save it as a template before entering data. Later, you can create a similar spreadsheet much more quickly by customizing the existing template than by developing a completely new one. Before you spend time developing your own templates for various applications, look for commercial ones that you can more easily revise.
- *Test your spreadsheet with values that give known results.* You should always test a new spreadsheet by inputting values that activate all formulas, cells, IF functions, and other processing routines. The test data should generate known results so you can determine whether the spreadsheet performs as expected.

- Default settings, style sheets, and wizards automate many formatting choices and greatly simplify the process of creating valuable word processing documents.

- Today's word processors can easily incorporate spreadsheet data, graphics, database information, and document files from many other applications to provide a unified system for recording and distributing information.

- Style sheets can speed the creation of repeatedly used word processing document formats.

- Functions simplify spreadsheet formulas, sometimes even replace them, by automating common calculations.

- Ranges specify rectangular groups of cells and may include a row, a column, or rows and columns of adjoining cells.

- Whenever possible, develop spreadsheets by customizing existing templates rather than creating new ones.

SUMMARY

1. *Describe the basic and supporting features of word processing programs.* Word processing applications facilitate text entry (usually via keyboard), text editing, text formatting, spelling and grammar checking, file management, and printing. Supporting functions include access to special characters and symbols, icons and toolbars, macros, style sheets, wizards, on-the-fly correction, support for work groups and networks, headers and footers, footnotes, lists, outlines, table of contents and index, mathematical equations, and multicolumn tables. Word processors offer valuable opportunities to integrate applications by importing spreadsheet data and graphics and merging documents with database files.

2. *List important suggestions for effective use of word processing programs.* Develop an outline before writing, finish inputting text before beginning to edit, delete material only when certain that it will not be useful later, reuse and customize page and document layouts, break up large documents into smaller files, and save your document file frequently.

3. *Explain the basic and supplemental features of spreadsheet programs.* The basic features of spreadsheet programs begin with rows and columns of cells, which store data, formulas to manipulate that data, and labels to document their significance.

Functions replace or enhance formulas to complete standard calculations. A range encompasses a series or block of cells to allow similar data entry, formula references, or other activities like moving and copying. A spreadsheet program provides flexible alternatives for editing cell and range contents, adding rows and columns, and controlling the display. Supplemental features include macros and templates, fill down and fill right, graphics creation, database manipulation, links between spreadsheet pages and separate spreadsheets, versions and scenarios, support for cooperative work group activities, backsolver analysis, and internal programming.

4. *Detail some guidelines for dynamic applications of spreadsheets.* A spreadsheet application can effectively support transaction processing tasks, but its real power comes from what-if analysis. Spreadsheet programs prove especially effective if you plan before inputting data and developing formulas; devote part of the spreadsheet to input data; summarize results, formulas, and macros in separate locations; document elements with text labels; state assumptions; identify different versions; list or print formulas; protect data; save and use templates; and test calculations with data that give known results.

Key Terms

word processing 145	grammar checker 149	title bar 161
word wrap 145	thesaurus 149	content bar 161
cut 147	special effect 151	formula 162
copy 147	bookmark 152	function 162
paste 147	macro 152	range 162
global search 147	style sheet 152	template 165
search and replace 147	wizard 152	fill down/fill right 165
zoom 147	on-the-fly correction 153	fill by example 166
fonts 147	mail merge 154	table lookup 167
justification 148	work group 154	version 168
full justification 148	outlining 155	scenario 168
default setting 148	spreadsheet 160	data protection 168
spelling checker 148	cell 160	what-if analysis 169

 ## Concept Quiz

Answer each of the following questions briefly.

1. In what way did spreadsheet software transform business decision making?
2. To what business tasks do word processing applications apply a computer's power?
3. Besides paper-based output, what other channels of distribution (e.g., electronic transmissions) does word processing software support?
4. Name five complex editing capabilities of a word processing program.
5. Name five ways a full-featured word processor allows you to alter the look of your text.

Mark "true" or "false" after each of the following statements.

6. The thesaurus feature in a word processor lists alternatives to selected words. _____

7. Many word processing applications come with smart document development tools, which are called wizards. _____
8. If calculations become too complex for a word processor's built-in functions, a user can import tables and other numerical data from a spreadsheet program. _____

9. Spreadsheet programs do not include display functions for charts and graphs; the user must add these with another applications program. _____
10. A spreadsheet program automates numerical calculation tasks by processing user-defined data according to specified formulas. _____

Fill in the blanks to complete the following statements.

11. The intersections of a spreadsheet's rows and columns define its _____ .
12. Each _____ in a spreadsheet performs a calculation based on specific data or the contents of one or more cells.
13. _____ control how labels, values, and formulas appear in the screen display and other output.
14. The automatic adjustment of cell addresses makes possible one of the most powerful spreadsheet capabilities: _____
15. A built-in _____ feature in a spreadsheet program allows the user to carry out spreadsheet calculations with different values for key variables to gauge the impact of different possibilities on the entire spreadsheet.

Discussion Questions

1. Why is it important for computer users not to rely solely on spelling checkers to confirm the accuracy of documents? What consequences might this have in a business setting?

2. The suggestions for using word processors mentioned in this text are suggestions you can apply as you write research papers and other documents in college. Do you practice any of these now? Are they effective? Would you add any other suggestions? How do you think these suggestions might apply to business documents?

3. How might an insurance company use the version and scenario features of a spreadsheet to gauge the impact of natural disasters (such as floods and hurricanes) on its business?

4. How could the owner of Animal House Pet Shop (chapter-opening photo) use word processing features such as mail merging or other applications programs to offer even more or better services to its customers?

Team Activity

Divide the class into teams of three or four members. Each team should choose an existing company that interests them and whose products with which they are familiar (say, Microsoft, General Motors, Coca-Cola, Trek Bicycles, or the like). Then the team should work on developing a spreadsheet that will perform calculations or analyses for some aspect of the business (use the suggestions for effective spreadsheets listed in the chapter). Conduct at least one what-if analysis to see how effectively the spreadsheet could help the decision-making process for company managers. Present the spreadsheet, along with the what-if analysis, to the class, explaining how they work.

Applying IT

1. Using your word processor, write down your ideas from Discussion Question 3. Next, build a spreadsheet to illustrate one or more of your ideas. Determine whether your word processor's built-in functions can handle this; if not, try integrating items from other applications through cutting and pasting, linking, or embedding objects.

2. Access the Internet and search for different word processing or spreadsheet software applications that are available. Then create your own spreadsheet illustrating the name, price, features, and other characteristics of each product.

CASE

Spreadsheets Come of Age

Computer spreadsheets have been around for 20 years now, since Dan Bricklin's invention of VisiCalc. They are part of almost every business. What have they accomplished? Do businesses still use them in the same way? And are businesspeople happy with the products that software developers offer them?

Spreadsheets have accomplished a lot. They have helped businesses cut costs, make predictions, and stay competitive. "If you compare the capabilities of spreadsheets now to five years ago, they are so much more powerful today," says Bryan Fukuda, an analyst at Dataquest Inc. "With all the sorting, it is almost like a database tool."

As the use of spreadsheets has become standard operating procedure for most businesses, managers, IS staff, and other employees have found creative ways of using them. First Albany Corp. uses Lotus Notes and 1-2-3 to help deliver current investment analyses to its customers. By using the two applications, First Albany can compile data on past and future financial performance of profiled companies in a single spreadsheet that is easy to review. It's also fast. "Now it takes 15 seconds instead of a half hour," says Barry McCurdy, senior vice president and director. Employees at Occidental Petroleum Corp. in Dallas use Excel and Sinper Corp.'s TM/1 on-line analytical processing software to review the corporate database to learn where and how product lines can be consolidated. Individuals can now use spreadsheet software to figure out how much money they should contribute to flexible spending accounts for medical expenses or dependent care, excluded from taxable income. Local governments use spreadsheet software to help with budget planning.

Are users happy with what they have? "I like some features from different products," answers David Burkleo of the Oklahoma City PC Users Group. "I'd like to have them all together—roll the best of each into one." This is where third-party add-in tools have come into play. For instance, an add-in tool might track all worksheet versions. Another might provide advanced graphics display. These tools customize the applications to the needs of the user. And just as in any other industry, what the user wants, the user eventually gets.

Questions

1. Describe some spreadsheet software with which you are familiar. In what ways have you used it or how could you use it? Have you used it in any unconventional ways? If so, describe them.
2. If you were to request features for the ideal spreadsheet software, what would they be?
3. Access the Internet and locate the Web sites for First Albany Corp. (http://www.fac.com/) and Occidental Petroleum Corp. (http://www.oxy-chem.com/) to see what you can learn about the companies. Why are their businesses so suited to spreadsheet use?

Sources: Tim Ouellette, "Spreadsheets Mature into Sophisticated Business Tool," *Computerworld*, April 3, 1995, pp. 41–42; Don Lobley, "Software Can Make Hard Decisions Easy," *American City & Country*, May 1996, p. 10; Sidney J. Baxendale et al., "Spreadsheet Allows Making the Best Choices in an FSA," *Taxation for Accountants*, March 1992, pp. 182–185.

Answers to Concept Quiz

1. It allowed managers to imagine changes in inputs and immediately estimate the resulting effects on important outputs. **2.** Creating, revising, and distributing written documents **3.** Fax, e-mail, the World Wide Web (students may add others if they know of any) **4.** Block operations, cut and paste, search and replace, zoom, multiple document editing **5.** Through paper size and margins, line spacing, justification, tab and indent, multicolumn text (students may also add others) **6.** True **7.** True **8.** True **9.** False **10.** True **11.** cells **12.** formula **13.** Cell formats **14.** copying **15.** version

CHAPTER
6

Database, Graphics, On-line Information, and Other PC Applications

CHAPTER OUTLINE

Database Programs
    Basic Elements of a Database
    Manipulating a Relational Database
    Designing a Database Structure
    Building a Database
    Modifying an Existing Database Structure
    Reports, Documents, and Other Output
    Role of a Database in the Information System
    Integration with Other Applications
    Hints for Using a Database
Graphics Programs
    Paint and Draw Programs
    Presentation Graphics
    Hints for Using a Graphics Package
On-line Information Services
    News and Features
    Business and Finance
    Travel
    Internet Shopping
Other Personal Computer Applications
    Project Management
    Reference Software
    Specialized Productivity Software

Do you want anchovies on that? Don't ask. Mi Amore Pizza & Pasta already knows the answer thanks to an extensive customer database. Gary Mead, owner of Mi Amore, uses a marketing database that tracks customers and purchases. Customers are identified by their phone number, which is entered into the cash register at the time of purchase. The computer automatically builds the database. If a regular customer hasn't stopped by in two months, the database automatically generates a postcard with a discount coupon to get them back. Every Christmas, Mead queries the databases for his best customers and sends them personally signed cards. (Photo: Alan Levenson.)

LEARNING OBJECTIVES

After completing Chapter 6, you will be able to:

1. Describe principles for organizing and manipulating databases.
2. Explain how graphics programs create charts and other illustrations.
3. Describe the resources available through on-line information services.
4. List some common special-purpose applications.

Whether we are at work or at home, we are surrounded with information. Using that information wisely and efficiently is key to success. Business activities today center more and more on processing information than on processing raw materials. Even our personal lives often seem dominated by complex collections of facts—telephone numbers, dates for distant events, personal identification numbers for ATM cards, lists of friends and acquaintances, and so on. Just as a computer can convert words and numbers to its own code, process them, and turn out valuable documents and spreadsheets, it can also provide a digitized memory that records essential facts and produces them on demand.

Database programs give computers this powerful capability. Files can store almost any amount of information—from a few phone numbers to a complete set of transaction data without which a business cannot function. These applications support business processes like bill paying, recordkeeping, inventory control, sales ordering, personnel records, and many more. Without these tools, many companies could not process routine transactions at all, and decision makers would stumble in the dark for lack of information.

Supplementing the alphabetic and numeric information of databases are graphics and on-line services. It is often said that a picture is worth a thousand words. Attractive graphics and illustrations can dress up the text of a word processing document or the rows and columns of a spreadsheet. They can often present information in an easier-to-understand format to show trends and patterns. Drawings can even become essential links between pages of information in a company Web site. These visual tools can also convey meaning in ways that words and numbers cannot.

On-line services, especially through their Internet access capabilities, allow any computer system with a modem to reach vast databases and other collections of information. These services, often attractively packaged in graphically rich displays, carry e-mail messages, stock prices and other financial data, summaries of legal cases, the latest news, the opinions of other users, and many more kinds of information to computer screens around the world. They bridge the globe and end people's isolation from remote businesses, government agencies, and other people who share their interests.

This chapter continues the examination of applications programs begun in the last chapter. We turn from word processing and spreadsheets to database, graphics, on-line, and project and personal management applications. These computing capabilities are increasingly being integrated to achieve the central goal of all information systems. With the document-centric approach, people can concentrate more on developing effective and powerful documents and less on separate programs and menus. This approach has allowed users to store, sort, and reproduce information that helps businesses and people understand and interact with their world. Sometimes knowing what has happened as quickly as possible can be critical to personal and business success.

DATABASE PROGRAMS

With today's trend toward telecommuting, national business chains, and global business, a database often provides the central storehouse for data in a far-flung information system. A database is a collection of related files that usually stores a standard set of data for a number of different uses. Managers who are not on-site can access sales information for up-to-the-minute reports, customer service can immediately check on the status of an order, and human resource managers can tap into the system to see whether benefits coverage is adequate for employees.

Companies are using databases more and more to help them compete in their markets. And the databases they are using are growing in size. By creating large data warehouses, they can instantly access customer information and preferences. These large storehouses of information contain trillions of bytes of information that can be sorted and resorted. This "data mining" allows companies to search for patterns—to track and store customer buying preferences, habits, and behaviors. In that way, they can more readily offer products and services their customers need and want, when they want them. This increases sales for the companies and helps develop satisfied customers. Currently, data mining is used most frequently in retailing, financial management, commercial and mortgage loan processing, and corporate strategic planning. But it is coming to the World Wide Web, so soon you may be able to tap these large data resources, too.

Basic Elements of a Database

Companies use databases to store a variety of data, which can later be sorted and analyzed to provide up-to-the-minute information to managers and other employees. For example, an employee database would include a number of standard facts about every worker in a company, including name, address, Social Security number, hiring date, wage rate, job assignment, choice of medical insurance plan, and much more (see Figure 6.1). The structure of the database lays out a matrix of fields and records, which organizes the important information.

field

this stores one type of element (alphabetic or numeric) about each employee, customer, or other individual subject in the database

Fields. A **field** stores one type of element (alphabetic or numeric) about each employee, customer, or other individual subject in the database. Examples include employee names or Social Security numbers. Many database displays resemble tables in which columns represent fields. The employee database might show Social Security number in the first field, name in the second, address in the third, and so on.

FIGURE 6.1

Fields and Records in an Employee Database File
Each record stores a collection of fields with standard data items for each employee.

Fields

Records

Social Security Number	Employee Name	Address	Hire Date	Wage Rate	Job Assignment	Medical Plan
XXX-XX-XXXX	Juan Gomez	123 Someplace Somewhere, IL	1-2-89	$18	Sales Rep	FHP
YYY-YY-YYYY	Anne Olinski	456 E. 7th Elsewhere, IL	3-7-87	$21	Sales Manager	PHP
ZZZ-ZZ-ZZZZ	Arthur Dewann	8910 Lincoln Somewhere, IL	8-9-96	$12	Sales Trainee	FHP
⋮	⋮	⋮	⋮	⋮	⋮	⋮
⋮	⋮	⋮	⋮	⋮	⋮	⋮

record

a collection of related fields

file

a collection of related records

relational database

a collection of files

key field

a common field shared by tables

Records. A **record** is a collection of related fields. The employee record would include data fields for each employee, such as employee number, pay rate, and other data. In a table display, each row represents a record.

Files. A **file** is a collection of related records. An employee file would contain records for all company employees. An inventory file would contain all products in stock in the warehouse. Two-dimensional tables like the one in Figure 6.1 represent separate files. A business's database would likely include a number of files, one to store information about employees, another to store different information about customers, another to record items or products in inventory, and so on.

A **relational database** encompasses a collection of files—that is, a collection of two-dimensional tables of data (see Figure 6.2). When these tables share at least one common field, called a **key field,** the database program can link their data into a larger, three-dimensional structure. These links give access to desired data from several different files to develop useful reports about all aspects of the business (or other focus of the database). In other words, the links allow managers to sort and re-sort data to get a good picture of what is happening in the business. Database applications provide many powerful tools for selecting and displaying information that applies to a particular transaction, set of transactions, or decision.

Manipulating a Relational Database

A human resource director could scan the database in Figure 6.1 by eye to find needed information about employees. In practice, though, a company's databases typically store enormous collections of data. These resources can be useful only if users can separate data that relate to a particular situation from unrelated data.

Selecting the database that contains useful information may narrow the choices. For example, a human resource director probably would not need information in the company's customer database to process a medical insurance claim. The employee database would provide the required information. But a large company's employee database might contain records for hundreds or thousands of workers—far too many to scan by eye. So an electronic retrieval system can simplify the task.

Further, many processing tasks require data from several files. For example, a payroll routine would need many kinds of data:

- Workers' names, addresses, Social Security numbers, and wage rates from the employee file

FIGURE 6.2

Relational Database with Links between Files
The key field Part No. links these related files. These links create a larger, three-dimensional data structure that supports a wide range of information system needs.

Sales Database			
Part No.	Description	Amt. Sold	Sold by
34712E	Reticulated Widget	1,407	Dewann
35616R			
40312M			

Inventory Database			
Part No.	Description	Amt. in Inventory	Amt. on Order
34712E	Reticulated Widget	3,412	1,316
35616R			
40312M			

Design Database		
Part No.	Description	Design Date
34712E	Reticulated Widget	3-14-94
35616R	Convertible Widget	2-7-96
40312M	Inverted Widget	7-21-95

- The hours worked for manufacturing workers from the production scheduling file
- Sales totals from the ordering file for representatives paid by commission (percentages of total sales) rather than hourly wages
- Required tax payments from the finance file

The firm could enter all of this information in a separate payroll database, but doing so would waste information system resources. IS personnel would have to update both the individual files and the payroll file, and the duplication would fill twice as much disk space. Also, other processing tasks would require still more separate files. Instead, a relational database can link all of the company's related files, so the payroll application and other processing jobs can draw current data from them as needed.

To scan and choose data from this complex, interlinked collection, database applications include **data manipulation languages (DMLs).** These sets of commands and procedures allow users to change or manipulate the contents of databases. In Chapter 3, we discussed the use of query languages to extract information from databases. Structured Query Language (SQL) was mentioned as one example of a widely used query language. Types of queries include commands to select pertinent data for specific reports, documents, and other outputs. They also help with maintenance of the database to ensure its accuracy.

Querying a Database. Certain commands **query** the database—that is, they search for specific values in any table or combination of tables. For example, the human resource director might want to identify all records in the employee database with wage rates greater than $15 per hour. To gather this kind of information, a database program's query capabilities locate all records in one or more files that satisfy specified criteria. A **Find command,** also called a **filter,** executes such a query by quickly scanning a database to locate and display information that supports a specific processing need while overlooking the rest. You can find important information in a database by using a command or clicking on menus. An example of a command in a dBASE program is given below.

```
.LOCATE FOR PRICE>400.AND.QUANTITY<10
```

The above command will locate and list all products with a price that is greater than $400, where there are fewer than ten units of the product in inventory. Most database programs that use Windows or a graphical user interface use menus and icons to find important information. You can save useful filters for future queries if you regularly need the same kind of information.

The Find command also includes a Replace capability to locate a string of characters or values and automatically change them to another string. For example, if a college course moves from the business school to the information systems department, its course number might change from BA303 to ISM3004; the college's database administrator can execute Find and Replace commands to search the scheduling database and automatically change every occurrence of BA303 to ISM3004.

Filters and Replace commands can also specify multiple criteria for a query by linking them with the logical operators *and, or,* and *not.* A small-business owner, for example, might plan a trip to northern Michigan during which she wanted to visit all customers in that area who had bought $1,000 or more worth of product from her company in the previous year. The Find command could search the order database for all records with annual sales totals above $1,000 *and* a certain ZIP code *or* city in the address fields.

data manipulation language (DML)

sets of commands and procedures that allow users to change or manipulate the contents of databases

query

something that certain commands do to search for specific values in any table or combination of tables

Find command

a command that executes a query by quickly scanning a database to locate and display information that supports a specific processing need while overlooking the rest

filter

same as File command

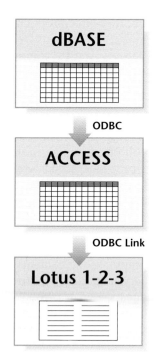

dBASE

↓ ODBC

ACCESS

↓ ODBC Link

Lotus 1-2-3

ODBC can be used to export, import, or link tables between different applications.

primary sort key

the first criterion by which the computer arranges records

secondary sort key

the second criterion by which the computer arranges records

Most newer database programs for personal computers use their own procedures or techniques for querying, although usually they do allow queries in *Structured Query Language (SQL)*. SQL is the program developed in the 1960s for mainframe computers.

Another database feature, open database connectivity (ODBC), seeks to expand the ability to link databases by defining a standardizd protocol for data storage. With ODBC, you can (1) export, (2) import, or (3) link tables and data between different applications. For example, a table in an Access database can be *exported* to a Paradox database or a Lotus 1-2-3 spreadsheet by clicking the File and Save As/Export menus in the Access database. Tables and data can also be *imported* using ODBC. For example, a table in a dBASE database or an Excel spreadsheet can be imported into an Access database using the File, Get External Data, and Import menu selections within the Access database. *Linking* allows an application to use data or an object stored in another application without actually importing the data or object into the application. The Access database, for example, can link to a table in the FoxPro database by clicking on File, Get External Data, and Link from within the Access database. Applications that follow the ODBC standard can use these powerful ODBC features to share data between different applications stored in different formats.

Sorting and Merging. Some data selection tasks may require certain information from all records in a file. A query would not help, because it selects only some records. Instead, a database program includes a feature to sort the entire database according to the contents of a specified field. For example, a small-business owner may decide to visit her firm's best customers rather than those in a certain region. To identify these customers, she could sort the customer database on the cumulative sales total field. Or, in a larger firm, a human resource director may need to sort the employee database by employee name, Social Security number, department, or another field, depending on whether he needed to prepare tax information, employment totals for race and gender, or other information.

Like a query, a sort can also specify multiple criteria. The computer arranges records first by the **primary sort key** and then by the **secondary sort key.** For example, the human resource director could direct the database program to arrange the employee table by position held and then by gender. The program would sort the records first by job titles and then by gender of the employee. A report such as this could be useful for reporting to government agencies that check on the makeup of a work force.

To create a single, larger table from two small tables, a database application can merge these tables. The small-business owner may initially create separate customer databases for two divisions of her company. If her information system later requires that she manipulate all customer records at once, she can merge these two tables. If the two divisions both sold products to some of the same customers, their databases would include duplicate records. The merge would automatically consolidate these repeated records so the finished database would include one record for each customer.

Internal Calculations and Statistical Functions. A database program can make internal calculations. The results of such calculations may be then manipulated by separate applications. The results of calculations may appear only in a printed or on-screen report, or they may define the contents of a separate field. A small company's database application can meet its payroll needs by multiplying each worker's hours from the manufacturing database times his or her pay rate from the employee database. The database program can calculate deductions based on data about benefits such as sick time and vacation pay from the employee database and tax rate data from the finance database. It can figure net pay for each employee by subtracting its own calculated figures—deductions and gross pay—and then either print out paychecks or store the data it develops in a new field or table (or both).

Database programs also have capabilities to compute averages, medians, and more complex statistics. These applications help you to produce **cross-tabulations,** statistical tables that show relationships between two variables. For example, a cross-tab like the one in Table 6.1 might show the education levels of a company's workers and their salaries. Cross-tabs combine data from separate sources to reveal important trends and characteristics that otherwise might remain hidden.

Some database programs can perform limited matrix or table manipulations. For example, you can easily transpose a table of numbers electronically to reverse the order of data in rows and columns. Some matrix manipulations require transpositions and similar manipulations.

Macros and Internal Programming. Some advanced users need more elaborate data manipulation capabilities than the database program's basic features can supply. As in word processors and spreadsheets, these applications allow you to create powerful macros that automatically perform sequences of steps when you select preprogrammed icons or pull-down lists. Macros can group repeated steps necessary to enter data, find information, and develop reports, among other functions.

In addition, these applications often include internal programming languages through which you can design extremely complex, custom features. Microsoft Access, for example, offers Visual Basic with processing tools that help sophisticated users to write programs that run within the database program to manipulate its data.

Individual information systems often must process data in unpredictable ways, so database programs offer almost limitless ways to modify and manipulate their fields, records, and files. Still, effective support for your processing tasks begins with a database design that anticipates your information needs.

Designing a Database Structure

A good database design specifies a set of tables that record data needed for particular processing tasks. It identifies the records for which each table will store data and the fields appropriate for each record. The resulting structure should organize data in a way that suits the problems the application will help you to solve and the opportunities it will help you to realize. The three-step process

cross-tabulation

statistical tables that show relationships between two variables

TABLE 6.1

Cross-tabulation

A cross-tab compares separate data to illustrate relationships among them.

EDUCATION	<$15,000	$15,001–$30,000	$30,001–$45,000	$45,001–$60,000	>$60,000
High school	22	8	2	0	1
B.A.	9	15	12	8	3
M.A.	0	2	7	12	11
Ph.D.	0	0	0	1	3

Identify goals	Determine output requirements	Determine input requirements
• Pay employees • File with tax authorities • Process benefit claims	• Printed paychecks • Periodic report filing • Claims to insurance company	• Wages • Hours • Tax rates • Benefit plan choices • Other deductions

FIGURE 6.3

Designing a Database
First, identify specific processing goals for the database. Then, determine the output that it must supply to meet those goals and the input necessary to produce that output.

of database design illustrated in Figure 6.3 moves from general goals to output that the application must supply as it reaches those goals to inputs required to produce that output.

Design Goals. The goals of database design reflect those of the organization. One company may want a database to meet payroll obligations, including paying employees and remitting tax payments to the government. A related goal may require data processing for insurance claims. In fact, even a small company's overall database would have to supply data for inventory, production scheduling, marketing, finance, and several more functions.

Output Requirements. The operating goals determine the reports, documents, and other outputs that a database must supply. The payroll function of a company's database might need to print paychecks, complete periodic filings with the tax authorities, and fill out claim forms for the insurance company. Other functions might order new stock to replenish inventories, begin production orders to fill product orders, generate invoices to bill customers for sold products, and supply financial statements to report on all of these transactions.

Input Requirements. Finally, determine what data the database must gather and store to generate the desired outputs. The payroll function would require employee name, address, Social Security number, wage rate, hours worked, applicable tax rates, insurance plan choice, and other deductions (such as retirement savings plans). The database design must then specify a field for each of these data items. It must also set a field size in characters and state the data type for each field; data type choices include text, number, currency, and date.

Next, the design groups the fields that refer to the same kind of record. Name, address, Social Security number, wage rate, and perhaps insurance plan choice all refer to each employee. Therefore, the database design needs employee records with those fields (and probably others). Hours worked might come from manufacturing records, however, which include a field indicating the employee who performed a particular job on a particular order or shift. Tax rates might come from finance records, since they apply uniformly to all employees, and financial processing would also require access to this data.

The number of different kinds of records helps to determine the number of tables needed to meet processing needs. A single table would become cumbersome if it included records for both employees and products. Instead, the database should include several data tables, one with employee records, one with product records, one with customer records, and so on. Related tables should share key fields to link them together and allow processing tasks to draw data from them as needed. A sketch similar to Figure 6.2 may help to clarify the number and relationships of different tables.

Building a Database

Once a database design specifies the facts to be collected and their field, record, and table structure, data input can proceed. Database programs require a number of procedures to assemble a complete database, and they offer many tools and features that support this process. (See Figure 6.4.)

Naming the Database. First, create a new database name. In many programs, this involves clicking an icon or giving a simple command. A box will appear on-screen in which you can enter the name of the new database that you wish to create.

Creating New Tables. Next, you create the new tables that will hold the different kinds of records determined in your design. Once again, click the New Table icon or give the appropriate command.

Defining Fields. For each new table, specify a field name, size, data type, and description of each field that your design demands. Further specifications vary for different data types—text, number, currency, or date. Number and currency fields may require a setting for decimal places (e.g., ".00" for currency fields denominated in U.S. dollars).

Most databases require that you designate a primary key field for each table. Any of the fields can serve as the primary key, but it should represent some area of overlap between tables. Two tables that share some characteristic will likely both supply data for some processing task, so a careful choice of this linking field will enhance the ability of the database to meet your information needs. For an employee database, you might select the Social Security number as the key field. That field could then link with finance for tax reporting and with separate departments for hours worked to generate payroll.

Entering Initial Data. After fully specifying the tables for a new database, you can start entering data. To start this process, click on the name of the table or give the appropriate command. The program then displays the table on-screen with blank rows and columns awaiting data. (See Figure 6.5.)

FIGURE 6.4

Building a Database
Database applications provide many tools and tricks to simplify the process of creating a database that realizes your design.

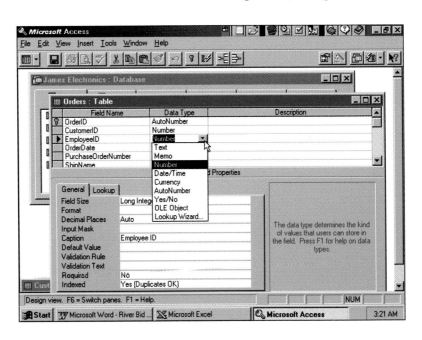

FIGURE 6.5

Data Input Display
The finished table structure now waits for you to fill it with data.

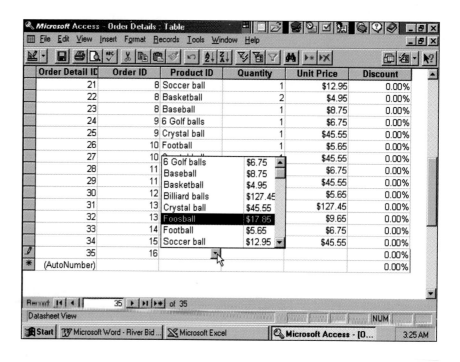

Most database programs provide several features designed to speed and simplify data input. You can usually enter data (or modify existing data) either directly into the table as it is displayed on-screen or through special data entry screens. These displays resemble forms with blank spaces for the empty fields. When you fill these spaces on one screen, you have entered a record into the database.

The program will suggest default values for certain fields. As you start to enter new data, the application anticipates your entry based on previous keystrokes and fills in the field with data that it expects. Of course, you can change any incorrect default values. A single keystroke, usually Tab, moves data entry from one field to another. As you complete the number of characters allowed in a field, some database programs automatically move to the next field.

Modifying an Existing Database Structure

Unanticipated processing needs or changing conditions often require changes to the database structure after you complete it and input data. Database applications allow for these possibilities with flexible systems for revising the structure of an existing database.

Adding and Deleting Tables. You can make major modifications by adding or deleting tables. As in a spreadsheet application, you can most easily add a table by copying a similar one and making needed changes. This can save a lot of time, even with rather extensive changes, by avoiding the need to specify every aspect of the new table, such as the number of fields and their properties. In anticipation of this process, consider saving the empty structure of all tables before inputting data.

Renaming the Database and Tables. You can change the name of the database and its tables, if you wish. Some people take advantage of this capability to specify different names for backup copies of their databases. For example, the name DB12_12 could represent a backup copy made on December 12.

Modifying Field Structures. If you discover a need for new data in a table, you can insert a new field to store it. If you find that data in a certain field does not contribute to your information system, you can delete that field. To modify the display or group fields differently, you can move columns so they appear in a different order.

Field characteristics can also change. For example, you can change a field's data type. Your database can probably track amounts of money as numeric data, but you may decide later to change those fields to currency data. You can modify field descriptions and adjust their properties, including their size (number of characters), decimal places, default values, and other properties. In some programs, you can even designate a new primary key field, but this could cause problems and so is not recommended.

Modifying Records (Rows in Tables). After you enter records in the database, you can return to change or delete them. Of course, you can always add new records—for example, as the company hires new employees. You can copy or cut a complete record and then paste it in another location.

As for data input, you can modify records either in the table display or in on-screen forms for individual records. The form display shows the fields for one record at a time and allows you to select any field, usually by clicking the mouse or pressing Tab, to make changes. When you go to the next record, you can direct the program to automatically save changes to the current record.

Reports, Documents, and Other Output

Once you set up a database structure and fill its fields with meaningful data, the application can work for you to produce desired reports, documents, and other outputs. These outputs usually appear in screen displays or hard-copy printouts. An information system can also integrate the capabilities of several applications. The next section explains this process, in which a database program serves as a front-end application to other programs. You can share database output with other computer users by sending it electronically using a modem.

The output-control features of a database program allow you to select the records and fields to appear in reports. You can also complete calculations specifically for the report by manipulating database fields. Formatting controls and organization options (like report headings) help you to customize reports and create flexible, convenient, and powerful information handling tools. The sections that follow discuss the kinds of output that a database application can produce and the program features that achieve these goals. (See Figure 6.6.)

Types of Outputs. A database program can produce a wide variety of documents, reports, and other outputs that contribute to an organization's goals. The most common reports select and organize data to present summary information about some aspect of company operations. For example, accounting reports often summarize financial data like current and past-due accounts. Many companies base their routine operating decisions on regular status reports that show the progress of specific orders toward completion and delivery. Exception and key-indicator reports highlight events that require urgent management attention. In addition, a database might help a firm to generate:

- Form letters with address labels
- Payroll checks and reports
- Invoices
- Orders for materials and supplies

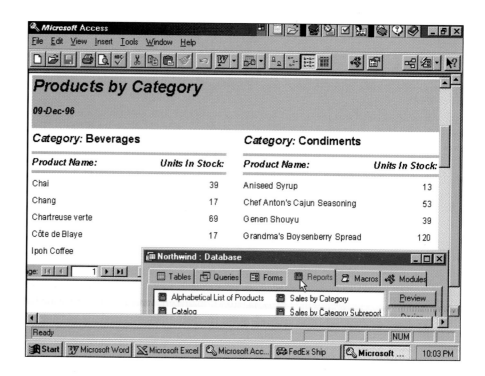

FIGURE 6.6

Database Output
A database application offers sophisticated formatting and organization options to help you customize its output to meet your information needs.

Additional kinds of output vary depending on users' individual needs.

Document Layout. Development of a database report begins with specifications for an overall **document layout**. This step determines the records and fields that supply data for the report along with its overall appearance. A typical document layout includes a **report header,** which appears only at the beginning of the document to state the title of the report, the names of the people who developed it, the date, and other information. Similarly, a **report footer** appears once at the end of the report to state any assumptions, conditions, or other qualifications that may help readers to evaluate the report.

Page Layout. A database program provides a number of features that help you to format the appearance of each page in a report. These features resemble the choices for word processing documents, like fonts, margins, page numbering, page headers and footers, and so on.

Contents Layout. A report's **contents layout** determines the information that appears in the report and its organization. You begin to specify the content layout by designating records and fields to supply data. Customizing features include **group headers and footers,** which appear before and after groups of records to document their meanings and significance. For example, an expense table might include group headers to separate expenses for advertising, travel, supplies, equipment, maintenance and repair, and inventory. A group footer might display calculated subtotals, averages, and so on, for each expense category.

Detail formatting determines exactly how the report displays each record. It specifies the order of the columns or fields, the widths of columns, and their formats (text, number, currency, or date).

document layout
the overall appearance of a report

report header
an element that appears only at the beginning of a document to state the title of the report, the names of the people who developed it, the date, and other information

report footer
an element that appears once at the end of a document to state any assumptions, conditions, or other qualifications that may help readers to evaluate the report

contents layout
determines the information that appears in the report and its organization

group header/footer
elements that appear before and after groups of records to document their meanings and significance

detail formatting
determines exactly how the report displays each record

Printing Database Results. The printed output from a database program can reflect complex manipulations along with all of the formatting and organization features discussed so far. A simple printout might list selected records from one or more databases. You can always print the entire database or selected tables to carefully evaluate the structures of the tables and the accuracy of the data. A printed report can include calculated values, such as gross pay and net pay, based on data from selected fields.

Many database programs offer print preview functions to show on-screen images of finished printouts. After studying a preview, you can return to the formatting and organization activities to fine-tune the format for your report.

Saving a Database. Never forget to save all files frequently while working with a database application. You can save a database at any stage in development, data entry, or maintenance and manipulation. In particular, you should save your database design separately before entering any data. Then, when you need a new database, you can modify the empty table structure to suit current needs rather than beginning from scratch. When entering data or making changes, save the database often. In addition, always maintain one or more up-to-date backup copies of the database.

Role of a Database in the Information System

Both word processing and spreadsheet programs can perform some of the data storage and data manipulation functions described for a database application. You can type lists, such as names and addresses, in a word processor and then store, copy, and sort them. Spreadsheet cells can store text labels and numbers and organize displays of this information in various ways. When your information needs require you to store and manipulate some collection of facts, you have to decide which type of application will most effectively meet your needs. Most situations that demand intensive storage and processing of raw facts call for a database application.

Large Amounts of Data. If you must store and manipulate a large amount of data, create a database to do the job. Spreadsheets and word processing programs cannot handle large document files as capably as database applications can.

Extensive Data Entry. If you must regularly enter new data, a database application will simplify the process. With features specifically designed to accept and process regular updates, these programs minimize the burden of this function and help to prevent mistakes. In addition, specially designed data-entry screens further simplify and speed the process.

Data Manipulations. Other applications cannot approach the excellent abilities of database programs to query, sort, merge, and edit fields, records, and tables. These programs allow you to combine tables in a variety of ways and perform a number of other useful data manipulations.

Reporting Requirements. An information system that requires a number of printed or on-screen reports should maintain the data for these tools through a database package. So, any organization that needs to manage large lists of information—sales, employees, product inventory, equipment maintenance, accounting reports—can find a database useful. Other kinds of applications require much more effort to produce complex reports and other output documents.

TABLE 6.2

Advantages of Database over Spreadsheet Applications

DATABASES	SPREADSHEETS
• *Flexibility due to data independence.* Each item is stored independently from any application that could access it.	• *Linked data.* Each item and the methods to manipulate it (e.g., formulas) are linked.
• *Centralized data storage.* In most database programs, data are stored in one place.	• *Possible data redundancy.* Data are often duplicated as they are linked to other data.
• *Consistency of data.* Changes to data are updated immediately, and all users access the same updated data.	• *Possible inconsistency of data.* Changes may be updated on only one spreadsheet. Other spreadsheet users may not be notified of the change.
• *Unlimited data sharing.* The number of users is not restricted, except by company policy. All can make concurrent updates.	• *Limited data sharing.* Data may not be able to be updated by more than one user, depending on the software.
• *Input formatting control.* Users may format input screens, thus allowing all later users to use the same input screens. This helps make data input consistent.	• *Limited input control.* More sophisticated knowledge of spreadsheet programming is necessary to ensure consistency of input.
• *Flexible reporting.* Reports can be generated as needed and need not be determined from the outset.	• *Reporting more limited.* Standard reports can be handled effectively, but unanticipated reports may require considerable programming skill to generate.

Source: Adapted from James E. Hunton and M. K. Raja, "When Is a Database Not a Database?" *Journal of Accountancy*, June 1995, p. 90.

Table 6.2 gives an overview of the advantages of database applications over spreadsheets.

Integration with Other Applications

An information system makes the most effective use of a database program when it integrates the capabilities of that application with those of other programs. A database adds power to word processors and spreadsheets by serving as a central storehouse and a front-end processor to supply them with needed data. In particular, database applications typically include excellent input routines, which help an information system to gather data that support all kinds of processing tasks. As we discussed in the previous chapter, this document-centric approach combines various types of information to allow for effective communications.

Someone who is writing a report about companywide revenues need not type in essential data about regional income and expenses; the word processor can draw those figures from the company database created in the normal course of sales and purchase transactions. A spreadsheet can provide formulas for calculations and statistical analysis of fields from the same database; the database program probably could not easily perform such complex manipulations on its own.

Processing tasks that stretch the capabilities of single applications become relatively easy when a compatible group of programs work together. For example, a marketing manager might want to report to the company president on a statistical analysis of 500 customer responses to a survey. The company's database provides the best features for inputting and storing the responses to specific questions. A spreadsheet then reads the database fields and calculates averages and more complex statistics. The word processor easily incorporates the results of these calculations (and perhaps some raw data from the database) into the final report text.

Input from Other Applications. The database program can receive input from other applications, as well as supplying its output to those programs. You can paste part of a word processing file into the report footer for a database report to duplicate some other document's explanation of company operations. You can also embed or link text and other materials from other applications to ensure that the database report includes up-to-date information. For example, a database report that lists customers by state or region can import a map or other illustration from a graphics program.

Hints for Using a Database

Careful planning and design help to ensure a complete and well-organized database at the heart of an information system for an individual or a business. Effective management of such a system can require in-depth study and experience, however. In fact, large organizations often employ full-time staff members just to create, maintain, and update the corporate database. A sophisticated user may want to take a course devoted exclusively to these activities, but the following hints suggest some fundamental principles of good database design:

- *Review goals and objectives.* Begin database design by thoroughly reviewing the data needs of your information system.
- *Use tutorials and other introductory materials that accompany your application to acquaint yourself with its features and capabilities.* Most database software packages include tutorials and other instructional materials to help you learn about the program features. Look for disks and manuals with names such as "Getting Started," "Quick Introduction," and "Guided Tour." Time spent learning about your database program will help you to build powerful databases.
- *Use wizards and other automatic development features.* Like other full-featured applications, most database programs provide wizards and other tools to automate software functions. (See Figure 6.7.) These packages include some standard layouts for data input and reporting screens to perform common tasks. Approach, a database from Lotus, offers more than 50 built-in data tables for tasks ranging from business accounting to developing a wine list.

    Some program aids present a few simple questions and then generate data input forms, screen formats, and report layouts based on your responses. Access by Microsoft uses Cue Cards, which guide your efforts to input data, find information in the database, develop reports, and perform other common activities. You can modify what the computer generates to meet your exact needs. Wizards and other automated programming features can save you time and improve your database designs.
- *Carefully design the tables and records of the database.* Effective design for tables presents a serious challenge, even to experienced users. Information system needs should determine the contents of each table and record type. Divide needed data into simple tables, each one focused on a single function or type of records. Similarly, limit the number of fields in each record to avoid duplication; rather than adding extra fields to existing records for a new information need, create a new table linked to existing ones by a common key field. Ensure that a primary key field uniquely identifies each record.

FIGURE 6.7

Database Wizard
Wizards and other automatic
programming tools provide
especially valuable help in
database applications.

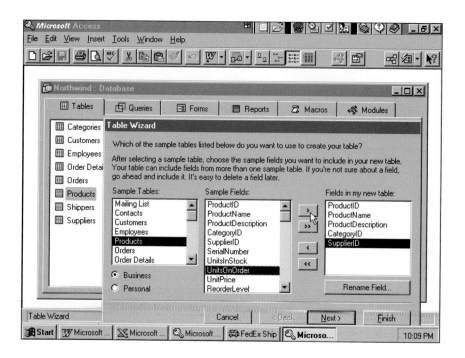

- *Practice consistent data input.* By maintaining consistent abbreviations and other styles for data, you ensure that the program can complete effective queries. For example, if you enter "ACCT," "ACC," and "ACCOUNTING" to indicate accounting majors, later queries will have to allow for all three possibilities. If you start to enter phone numbers with area codes, make sure that all phone numbers have them.

- *Keep the database current and accurate.* Make sure that your database reflects any changes that occur. Spend some time developing screens to aid effective data input and modifications, including internal documentation that describes the meaning of data in each field. Manipulate and maintain the database with care to make sure that the program returns the results you want. If you want the address and phone number of someone named Long, a query for that name would also return records for Longrace, Longfellow, Longhouser, and other variations. In a really large database, you might still have to hunt through screenfuls of unwanted records that match your search conditions to find what you want. To avoid this annoyance, frame your Find commands carefully, perhaps combining multiple conditions with logical operators (*and, or,* and *not*).

GRAPHICS PROGRAMS

Sometimes, even a thousand words cannot express the same meaning as a picture. Pictures can generate interest in other applications, and users are quickly learning the value of graphics programs. Illustrations, pictures, and graphs can often show trends and relationships more effectively than tables of numbers or written descriptions, and a moving picture with sound might replace entire volumes of printed information. Graphics programs give users the ability to quickly develop, edit, and incorporate illustrations, drawings, pictures, moving images, and sound into their information system products. This section explores the colorful, attractive, and informative world of electronic graphics.

Paint and Draw Programs

Several kinds of applications software provide tools for creating and altering different kinds of graphics. **Paint programs** produce **bitmapped graphics,** which store data about the color that the monitor should display at each point on the screen. This method of presenting and storing graphic data suits paint software for detailed illustrations with subtle variations in color. In contrast, **draw programs** generate **vector graphics** as stored sets of instructions and procedures for creating lines, circles, and other color images. They find their most common and powerful uses in specialized computer-aided design (CAD) applications that automate the precise drawing tasks of architects, engineers, and product designers. Vector graphics programs usually do not match the image clarity of bitmapped graphics, but they require less storage capacity.

In business information systems, paint and draw software packages can help users who lack advanced art skills to produce attractive graphs, illustrations, and drawings. These programs provide color palettes and tools that control where the color appears as you move the mouse or other pointing device. A paint program's brush places swaths of color on the screen; its spray-can tool places unevenly shaded circles of color. A draw program's line tool stretches a straight line between points that you define with mouse clicks; its circle tool places the center at the point where you click the mouse, and you then pull outward and release the mouse button at the desired diameter. (See Figure 6.8.)

Paint and draw programs can display a grid with a ruler on the screen to help you develop accurate drawings. If you activate the **snap on grid** feature, the program forces all lines or shapes to the nearest point on the grid so that lines, box corners, and so on, line up. The **align objects** feature perfectly lines up symbols, drawings, and the like. For example, you can create a number of boxes in perfect vertical or horizontal alignment. Graphics programs also provide some familiar display-control features like zoom in and out.

While paint and draw software provide flexible capabilities to produce almost any drawing or illustration, the work can take a long time. Also, many business needs call for standard graphics, especially pie charts and other kinds of graphs. More specialized graphics programs, called *presentation graphics*, provide libraries of charts, pictures, and images that users can customize in minutes.

paint program

a graphics program that produces bitmapped graphics

bitmapped graphics

graphics that store data about the color that the monitor should display at each point on the screen

draw program

a graphics program that generates vector graphics

vector graphics

stored sets of instructions and procedures for creating lines, circles, and other color images

snap on grid

a feature that forces all lines or shapes to the nearest point on the grid so that lines, box corners, and so on, meet

align objects

a feature that perfectly lines up symbols, drawings, and the like

FIGURE 6.8

Paint and Draw Programs
A paint or draw package presents a drawing area, a menu bar, a toolbar, and a color palette.

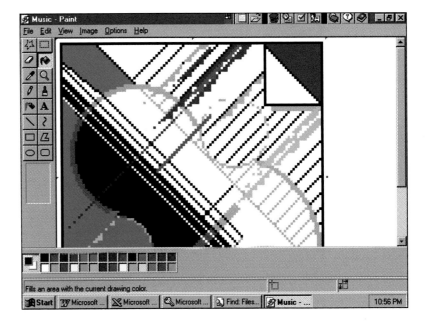

Presentation Graphics

presentation graphics program

software that helps users to develop pie charts, line drawings, bar charts, trend lines, organization charts, and a wide range of other illustrations

Powerful, easy-to-use **presentation graphics programs** help users to develop pie charts, line drawings, bar charts, trend lines, organization charts, and a wide range of other illustrations. These programs can output their images in many ways: printed hard copy, files on disk, on-screen images, and photographic slides for projection with common audiovisual equipment.

Available charts and forms meet many needs, as Figure 6.9 illustrates. You can easily create text charts like outlines and lists, varying the font size, layout, bullets or check marks, and many other details to get the appearance you want. The program generates graphs like bar charts and line charts to illustrate numerical data, perhaps in three dimensions with shading and text labels to highlight trends and certain important facts. Pie charts clearly show budget allocations and percentages, and the software can give a raised appearance to selected wedges (called an *exploded pie chart*) for emphasis. High/low/close charts are excellent graphic tools for following stock prices or other investment data; the vertical lines define the security's trading range, and the horizontal ticks show its closing price. An organization chart illustrates the hierarchy of various positions within an organization. Free-form charts combine boxes, circles, lines, arrows, symbols, and similar visual elements to represent many useful kinds of graphics, such as flow charts.

clip art

such graphics as fancy borders, pictures of famous people, decorative designs and initials, and many small drawings

Most graphics packages include many document files with existing pictures and illustrations. These **clip art** files usually include fancy borders, pictures of famous people, decorative designs and initials, and many similar drawings. You can use them in their current form or alter and combine them to make your own images.

FIGURE 6.9

Presentation Graphics
Business users rely on many kinds of charts and graphs to present and give power to their ideas.

Creating a Graph. You create a graph through a simple procedure of choosing a background and page layout and then entering data in the blank spaces presented by the program. A full-featured graphics program presents a wide selection of professionally produced backgrounds with elaborate combinations

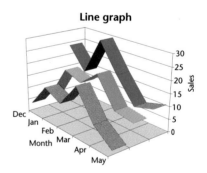

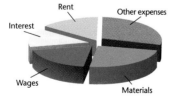

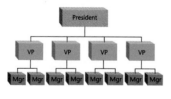

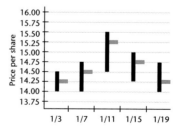

of colors and other decorative features. Page layout choices usually include bulleted lists, a number of different chart types, tables, a free-form drawing template, and more. The page layout overlays the chosen background. For example, a pie chart from the page layout might appear on a colorful background made up of flags of European countries. After you select the background and page layout, the program prompts you to enter numerical data to define the chart. You can also include special symbols and drawings in your graphic.

Smartmasters and Wizards. Wizards make it even easier to create and modify graphics. These graphics templates present some simple questions and build presentation slides based on your answers. **Smartmasters** provide entire collections of presentation slides for specific themes. For example, a business plan Smartmaster provides slides on various planning tasks, including product positioning, pricing, and risk analysis, as resources for a business planning seminar. Other Smartmasters provide graphics that illustrate a number of common business activities. As always, you can modify the graphics created by wizards and Smartmasters to suit your needs.

Changing, Printing, Saving, and Importing Graphics. A presentation graphics program also provides powerful functions for modifying completed graphics. You can enlarge, reduce, shade, move, rotate, flip, copy, and even delete selected elements of a chart. These customizing possibilities ensure that the program's output will convey the intended information in the way you want.

You can print that output, plot it, or save it as a file. In both Windows and Macintosh environments, you can cut or copy and paste graphics to transfer them between applications. Most graphics programs support a variety of printing and plotting equipment, including advanced laser printers and plotters, many of them capable of color output. If you choose to save a graphic to disk, the program can accommodate a number of different formats that allow other programs, including word processors, to import and display them.

On-screen Slide Shows. In addition to printing graphics and exporting them to other applications, many programs allow you to display your images in sequence on a computer screen to create electronic **slide shows.** During a presentation, the computer screen can show supporting illustrations in the order you specify. For larger presentations, projection devices can exhibit colorful slides on large screens. Laptops can often link with television screens or projection panels if you travel and must make presentations.[1]

Slide shows have become excellent sales tools. These slides provide many advantages over printed brochures and other static sales tools. Customized presentations can show carefully chosen products intended to appeal to particular clients. They can include moving images, such as trucks completing performance tests or skiers going down a slope.

Also, some graphics packages can incorporate sound into your presentations. You can record or import sound clips with music or narration and paste them into specific spots or screen displays. You can further enhance your presentation by incorporating **speaker notes** into the graphics to provide information and prompts as guides to the presenter.

Color Slides and Transparencies. After developing completed images, you can output them as color slides. In the simplest method, you can take a picture of the monitor display with your own camera. For better image quality, special developing labs will produce slides, transparencies, or color

---

Smartmaster

graphics feature that provides entire collections of presentation slides for specific themes

slide show

a display of images in sequence

speaker note

notes that you can incorporate into your graphics to provide information and prompts as guides to the presenter pictures from a diskette with the files from your graphics program using a color plotter. If you produce enough graphics to justify the expense, you can outfit your computer system with a special camera and produce your own slides and transparencies.

Hints for Using a Graphics Package

Graphics packages offer powerful tools for enhancing your documents and presentations with attractive and interesting illustrations. As for other applications, however, the software produces its best output under the careful control of a skillful user. Some general suggestions, along with practical experience, will help you to develop effective graphics:

- *Design your image before you start to use the graphics program.* Sketch the elements of the graphic manually on a sheet of paper. As you refine this drawing, the changes you make should guide your initial work, creating the image in the graphics program. This preparation helps you to avoid extensive revisions in later stages.
- *Do not clutter your graphic with too many words, symbols, or drawings.* A jumble of words, symbols, lines, and circles can obscure the message of your image. Include enough detail to communicate your essential image, and avoid distracting your audience with unnecessary elements. Consider the intended use—if you are generating slides for a large audience, large type and simple shapes are a must.
- *Balance your image.* Arrange the elements of your graphic to take full advantage of available space. If you place most of the drawings, symbols, and descriptions in one corner, you will create a dense, uneven look that detracts from your information.
- *Look for additional features, symbols, and images in other graphics programs.* Graphics packages have been designed to incorporate images from external sources. For example, you can buy CD-ROMs with thousands of clip art images to supplement those that come with your software.
- *Check your illustration for spelling mistakes and other errors.* Proofread your art work as carefully as you would read a written document. Some graphics programs even include spelling checkers to help you guard against mistakes in text labels. Check carefully to ensure correct placement of all lines, arrows, and boxes.
- *Output final copy for formal presentations and documents on laser printers and other professional reproduction equipment.* Output quality strongly affects the effectiveness of graphic images. Match this quality level to the importance of the communication task. You would waste your time producing elaborate graphics for a report if you were to print out the final copy on a dot matrix printer with a worn-out ribbon.

Graphics programs allow you flexibility in presenting information. Combined with other applications, they can give a wide range of options for an information system. But to expand the capabilities even further, many users are tapping outside resources to gather information and assist with personal and business activities.

EYE ON THE WEB

Enabling customers to complete business electronically has proved to be a major competitive advantage for many companies. Today, we are at another threshold—the World Wide Web. A company's presence on the Web allows consumers to become aware of its goods and services. Perhaps more important, this presence can be used to attract a larger customer base, facilitate customer queries, and even take orders and accept payments.

Bell Atlantic, for example, has constructed a directory listing service on the Web. Customers are able to search for telephone numbers through the Bell Atlantic Web site. IBM maintains a page devoted to providing consumers with information on its products and services; accessing the Chrysler page permits users to see their latest cars. Sony allows users to compare features found on different models of camcorders. Federal Express attained competitive advantage in the overnight delivery business by effectively tracking package delivery. Customers were able to contact the company and obtain status information on packages sent to any destination worldwide. Web users may access the FedEx page, enter an airbill tracking number, and perform an on-line status check of a FedEx shipment.

While the concept of a Web "page" evolved from advertisements and features in magazines, using the interactive capabilities of the Web permits companies to do more than merely present consumers with a static display. For example, Bell Atlantic requests that consumers who have browsed its page take a moment to complete some simple survey information. A California winery discovered that its Web site and on-line ordering enables it to fill customer orders more quickly and accurately.

Information concerning Web site "hits" (a "hit" occurs when a user accesses a particular Web page) can be evaluated by companies to discover whether they are effectively attracting consumers. Additionally, sites like Bell Atlantic's, which request information about a worldwide customer base, are collecting valuable information. The result? Firms are able to analyze and evaluate more precisely the geographic base and characteristics of customers.

Organizations that cater to specialized market segments can also reach out to these individuals, targeting their specific interests. The World Wide Web presents an opportunity for firms to augment, rather than to replace, their existing contacts with customers. Effective use of a Web site means information reaches a larger market, and companies can communicate with a wider consumer base. In the end, that can translate into a serious competitive advantage.

WEB EXERCISES

1. Access the World Wide Web and perform a search to locate information about a product in which you have some interest. Does the Web page that you accessed permit you to enter your name and address to request that additional information be sent to you? (If not, access the Bell Atlantic page to get the flavor of on-line information input.)
2. Perform a search to access Web sites for two different companies. How do the two sites differ from one another? What are some distinctive features of each of the pages that you have visited?

ON-LINE INFORMATION SERVICES

on-line information service

a service that extends a computer system to reach vast collections of outside resources

An **on-line information service** extends a computer system to reach vast collections of outside resources. A standard personal computer equipped with a modem and communications software can access enormous databases of information about almost any topic of interest. (See the "Eye on the Web" box for examples of different types of services available on the Web.) Groups of users exchange messages that amount to extended, geographically dispersed conversations on all kinds of topics. The most widely used feature of on-line information services, e-mail, provides a convenient way for customers to communicate among themselves and with users of other services.

Examples of on-line information services include America Online, CompuServe, Prodigy, Dow Jones News/Retrieval, the Microsoft Network, and many other nationwide and local alternatives. Some services base a user's fee on **connect time,** the time spent connected to the provider's computers; others charge fixed monthly fees for unlimited connect time.

connect time
the time spent connected to the provider's computers

Most services provide graphically rich user interfaces that support simple, intuitive navigation through their many functions. A service's menu of choices usually includes news, reports dealing with business and financial management, and travel services, among many others. One current application called PointCast can download information from the Internet and display it as a screensaver. Some of the categories of information are news, companies, weather, sports, industries, and lifestyle. PointCast will download the information and display it on the screensaver for updated news.[2]

News and Features

On-line services distribute detailed, frequently updated accounts of news and feature stories. You can often get information on business, sports, weather, science, the arts, entertainment, and more from the same sources (Associated Press, Reuters, United Press International) that supply reports to more traditional media outlets. Other services get their news from newspaper conglomerates. Many subscribers rely on these services for news from other areas of the country that does not appear in their local media reports. You can even customize some services by selecting from topic lists or conducting searches. On-line services supplement this information with background reports from encyclopedias and other reference sources. You can even review winning lottery numbers from drawings throughout the country.

Business and Finance

Along with business news, on-line services offer a wealth of information on specific companies, industries, securities, and general economic conditions. You can check for news about a specific company and review reports about its finances and securities from respected analysts like Standard & Poor's. Some services provide quotations on stocks, bonds, mutual funds, and other investments, usually within 15 minutes after the transactions take place on national and regional securities exchanges. (To read about a beer company that offers stock on-line, see "Who's Who: Andrew D. Klein/Spring Street Brewing.")

The Wall Street Journal Interactive Edition is one of many available on-line newspapers. (Source: Courtesy of the Wall Street Journal Interactive Edition.)

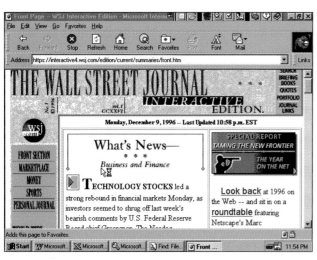

On-line resources allow you to shop a nationwide, perhaps even worldwide, market for financial services like real estate and investment brokers, banks, insurance, credit cards, and loans. You can pay bills and transfer funds between accounts by computer.

Travel

Travel agencies and related services maintain active exchanges on many on-line services. Through these connections, you can browse through a variety of travel options for the most attractive packages and then make instant airline, hotel, car rental, rail, and cruise ship reservations. You can also gather travel-related information like weather reports. (See Figure 6.10.) Travel specialists also share insights and

FIGURE 6.10

Weather Map
Many subscribers to on-line services appreciate their extensive travel-related resources.

information with frequent updates about current discounts and conditions at popular destination sites.

Internet Shopping

Commercial on-line services provide facilities for connecting to the Internet, and through that directly to companies. Customers can read about companies and communicate directly with them via e-mail in boxes.

In addition, several companies are now offering on-line shopping services using "digital cash" (see the "Business Bits" box on cybershopping). Users should be careful to compare the security features of these shopping services to ensure that vital information is protected. But on-line shopping may ultimately save both companies and users time and processing resources.

OTHER PERSONAL COMPUTER APPLICATIONS

Word processing, spreadsheet, database, graphics, and communications programs support people's most common computing needs. These applications do not define all of the functions that computers can perform for individuals and businesses. Specific needs have led to the creation of many powerful PC applications to gather and manage information. Business managers often need help with project management, and all kinds of users find valuable information with the help of reference software. Personal productivity tools make life easier in many ways for PC users.

Project Management

project management program

programs that help users plan, monitor, and control goal-directed sequences of activities

Businesspeople and organizations—and many ambitious individuals—undertake projects to accomplish special goals. Applications software provides tools for planning and managing projects as simple as preparing a large meal or as complex as coordinating a NASA launch. **Project management programs** share a common set of goals: to help users plan, monitor, and control goal-directed sequences of activities.

WHO'S WHO

Andrew D. Klein/Spring Street Brewing

This box isn't about beer; not directly, anyway. It's about a young entrepreneur named Andrew D. Klein who not only formed his own brewing company (Spring Street Beer), but also offered stock to the public—on-line.

Spring Street's mission is to "produce and market in the United States, high-quality, hand-crafted Belgian recipe beers." Its first beer, called Wit, is based on a type of brew that is popular in Belgium and Holland. Wit, a light blond beer, is brewed from wheat and spiced with orange peel and coriander. ("Wit" comes from the old Flemish word "wit," which originally translated to "wheat" but which now translates to "white." Both meanings fit.) The company's Web site address is http://www.witbeer.com.

Enough about the beer. The real flurry surrounding the company is Klein's innovative idea to take the firm public on-line. In the early 1990s, Section A of the Securities Act eased some restrictions on the way private companies could be taken public. So Klein began offering shares for sale on the Internet at $1.85 per share. The minimum purchase was 150 shares. Interested investors could download subscription agreements from the Wit beer Web site, without paying commissions to brokers. Once investors began to buy the shares, Klein realized that, because the company was not listed on any exchange (such as NASDAQ), there wasn't a mechanism for people to trade shares. So Spring Street began to offer a trading system via the Internet, as well. Called Wit-Trade, the system is a bulletin board that buyers and sellers can browse through to find partners (they can also post notices declaring that they want to buy or sell stock). Buyers and sellers do their own negotiating, but Spring Street provides an "Offer and Acceptance" form that users can download, complete, and send to each other to seal a deal.

The Securities and Exchange Commission (SEC) has been keeping a close watch on Spring Street's activities. After studying the company's system, the agency sent Klein a letter that called Wit-Trade "an innovative mechanism that has the potential to provide shareholders with greater liquidity in their investments." But the SEC wanted Spring Street to appoint a bank or escrow agent to handle transaction funds. It also wanted Spring Street to make perfectly clear to investors that the on-line service was still a novelty and that their investment might not be liquid. Finally, the SEC required that Spring Street post a history of trading on the Wit-Trade system.

Even if Wit beer itself falls flat on the tastebuds of consumers, Klein's on-line stock offering will probably change the securities industry forever. In fact, the Internet already holds a tremendous amount of information about financial services, and companies such as E-trade (http://www.etrade.com) offer inexpensive brokerage services for some stock transactions on the Internet. Meanwhile, Spring Street has launched a new beer: Black Wit. Too bad you can't taste it on-line. You have to buy the real thing.

Sources: David Zgodzinski (davidz@cam.org), "Home-Brewed Stock," *Internet World*, July 1996, pp. 89–92; Spring Street Brewing Company home page, http://www.witbeer.com. Photo: Tony Cordoza.

---

activity

a limited, independent unit of work that contributes to the completion of a project

critical path

the sequence of activities with zero slack (i.e., those that will delay the entire project if not completed on time)

project crashing

a function that determines the cheapest investment of additional resources to shorten total project completion time

A project management package helps a user break down a total project into smaller activities. An **activity** is a limited, independent unit of work that contributes to the completion of a project, such as laying the foundation for an office building or completing a wing assembly for an aircraft. The software typically generates time and cost estimates for individual activities based on user input. It then automates common scheduling techniques to specify each activity's earliest start time, earliest finish time, and slack time, which is the amount of delay an activity can tolerate without delaying the entire project. The program then identifies the **critical path**—the sequence of activities with zero slack (i.e., those that will delay the entire project if not completed on time). Any problems with critical-path activities will cause problems for the entire project.

Project management software also sums cost estimates to generate project budgets. Its **project crashing** function determines the cheapest investment of additional resources to shorten total project completion time. Figure 6.11 shows some results of project management software.

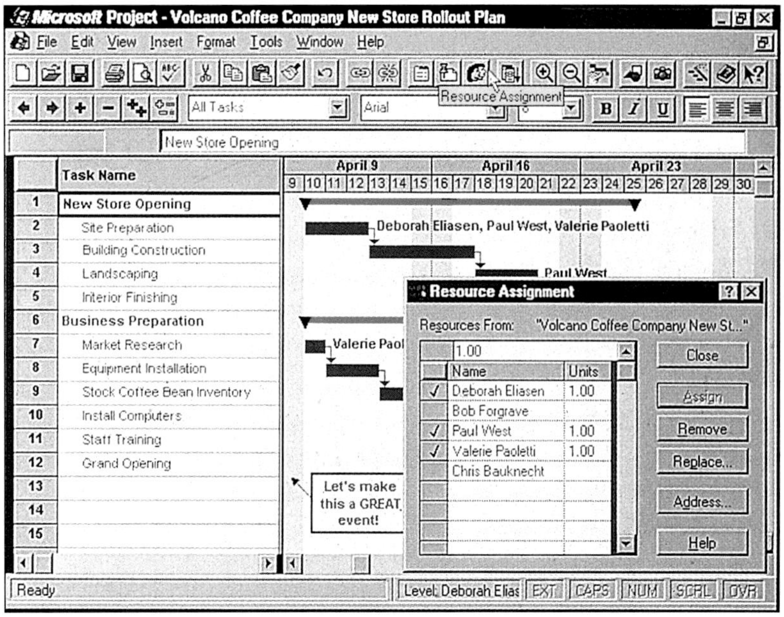

FIGURE 6.11

Project Management Software
Businesspeople rely heavily on applications that aid budgeting and scheduling for projects. (Source: Courtesy of Microsoft Corporation.)

One project management package, PeopleScheduler, integrates employee schedules, vacations, project coverage, and budgets to help managers generate a schedule or multiple schedules.

Reference Software

reference software

software that provides applications tools and database material designed to provide help on a particular topic

Reference software provides applications tools and database material designed to provide help on a particular topic. Like reference books, reference software can provide very valuable information. Unlike reference books, however, reference software often gives outstanding capabilities to search for specific information and print customized summaries. For example, you can search for a specific topic or a general area of interest and then view and print out everything that you find.

American Business Information (ABI), for example, stores a database that covers about 11 million American and Canadian businesses on CD-ROM. Users search the database for a company's address, earnings, sales, and other data. Some reference software products provide realistic reports with animation and sound. Reference materials include CD-based encyclopedias, atlases, and dictionaries, along with more narrowly focused packages on limited topics. The Winn L. Rosch Hardware Bible, for example, contains a vast amount of information on personal computer devices.

Specialized Productivity Software

specialized productivity software

software that handles many kinds of limited processing tasks, such as personal information management, legal assistance, and travel assistance

Individuals include **specialized productivity software** in their computer systems to handle many kinds of limited processing tasks. These packages perform functions as varied as the needs of their users, so this section can only highlight some examples.

Personal Information Management Software. Software can help organize your personal information files, such as calendars, address books, phone numbers, and notepads. Personal planners help keep track of appointments to alert you of upcoming meetings and daily schedules. One such planner is

BUSINESS BITS

Cybershopping with Digital Cash

On-line shopping has been available for a number of years through services like America Online, CompuServe, and Prodigy. But only about 7 percent of Internet users have bought products on-line. The reason? Most consumers are afraid to transmit their credit card numbers through cyberspace.

Some major companies—IBM, Microsoft, MasterCard, and Visa—have recognized the problem and are now supporting a new standard for protecting on-line credit card transactions, called Secure Electronic Transactions (SET). SET is "based on public-key cryptography and electronic certificates" that credit card companies issue to consumers, who in turn send them to merchants to authorize on-line transactions. Microsoft has gone even further, pledging that a new digital-signature technology will be built into Windows. The technology automatically verifies Internet purchases as valid. In general, the on-line infrastucture has now advanced to the point that digital cash can be thought of as virtual currency. The Web now offers a variety of ways in which consumers can shop more safely.

If you want to shop through CyberCash (http://www.cybercash.com), you download Wallet software and establish a CyberCash account. Then you browse through Web pages of participating merchants (CyberCash gets its fees from these merchants, not consumers). If you find something you want to buy, you click the CyberCash "buy" icon, then the credit card icon. The program transmits your CyberCash ID number, which is protected by public-key technology, to CyberCash, which decodes it and sends it to a participating bank for authorization.

First Virtual has one of the widest selections of Web-based stores in its network (http://www.firstvirtual.com). For $2, you establish a First Virtual account and get your VirtualPIN ID. (To do this, you need a MasterCard or Visa account.) To buy something, you transmit your VirtualPIN ID to the merchant, which gets forwarded to the payment server; then you receive an e-mail message for your approval. Once you approve the purchase, the amount is billed to your credit card. First Virtual provides links to sites of merchants who offer both durable goods and intellectual property.

Other on-line shopping opportunities include CheckFree Wallet software (http://www.checkfree.com), an independent application designed to integrate with Web browsers and the Cybertown mall (http://www.cybertown.com), whose stores offer everything from food to art to BMW accessories.

It seems that, as cyberspace shopping becomes more varied, more convenient, and more secure, it will also become more successful. (A recent Forrester Research study predicted that on-line sales could top $6.9 billion by the year 2000.) Still, cybershopping just isn't the same as hanging out at the mall.

1. Have you ever tried on-line shopping? Why or why not? If so, describe the experience. Would you shop on-line again?
2. Access the Internet and browse for companies that offer on-line shopping (or try accessing one of the services listed above) to see whether it appeals to you. Or browse through a few print catalogs to see if any also offer Web sites. Which ones do?
3. Do you think that an increase in on-line shopping could have other consequences for consumers (such as an increase in credit card debt)? If so, what might these consequences be? How might they be counteracted?

Source: Sebastian Rupley, "Digital Bucks? Stop Here," *PC Magazine*, May 28, 1996, pp. 54–60.

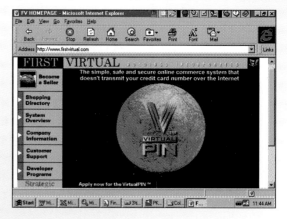

Lotus Organizer, which keeps information organized by sections so that you do not miss important calendar dates or misplace addresses, phone, fax, and e-mail numbers. Contact management software is a specialized information manager sales professionals use to organize their time, track sales calls and account history, and plan future sales activities. One of the well-known contact managers is Symantec's ACT.

FIGURE 6.12

Health and Medical On-line Service
Doctors and patients can get medical information and advice online.

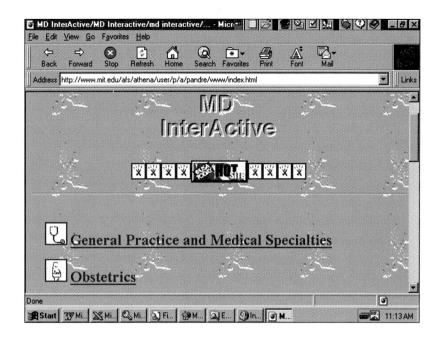

Health and Medical Software. A software program called the Home Medical Advisor accepts user input about symptoms and suggests medical diagnoses. The program covers 450 diseases and can suggest about 800 prescriptions and over-the-counter drugs. The software also suggests when conditions may warrant a visit to the doctor.

Some doctors have also used an on-line database of medical journals called Medline. (See Figure 6.12.) This database catalogs more than 3,700 medical journals and is updated by the National Library of Medicine. Anyone connected to the Internet, however, can access the Medline home page.

Legal Assistance Programs and Related Software. Some software programs explain legal principles to both individuals and business owners. While these applications cannot replace lawyers, they can help people to produce common legal documents and answer routine questions. Win by West Publishing is a legal software research tool that translates English terms into legal terms. Scrivener by Dianoetic Development Corp. generates basic wills, legal contracts, and litigation documents. Similar programs include WillMaker by Nolo Press, It's Legal by Parsons Technology, Personal Law Firm by BLOC Publishing, Quickform Contracts by Invisible Hand Software, and Personal Policy Expert by KnowledgePoint.

Negotiator Pro helps users learn to negotiate effectively with other people and organizations. The software claims to build interpersonal skills, refine structured thinking, and suggest strategy choices.

Travel Assistance Software. When traveling, you may need to access information and programs on your desktop computer at home or the office. PCanywhere and similar programs facilitate exchanges that tie portable computers to remote desktop computers. This type of software package allows you to run applications on your desktop personal computer from anywhere around the world.

Repairs and Home Improvement. Software publishers sell a variety of packages that help people make simple repairs and home improvements. The Home Handyman displays wooden deck designs on the screen and allows you to manipulate the designs to get exactly what you want. The program specifies the support structure and decking and then generates a list of building materials with a cost estimate.

- Files that share a key field form levels in a single, three-dimensional structure of information.

- Use a database program, rather than a word processor or spreadsheet, when your information needs demand large amounts of data, extensive data entry and manipulation, and complex reports.

- If a picture is worth a thousand words, then a moving picture with sound might replace entire volumes of printed information. Incorporating graphics into documents can convey some information such as trends instantly.

- Presentation graphics help users develop pie charts, line drawings, bar charts, organization charts, and so on. They may be used in various forms: printed hard copy, files, on-screen images, and photographic slides.

- An on-line service allows you to shop a nationwide, perhaps even worldwide, market for financial services, travel deals, and all kinds of merchandise, but beware of data thieves.

SUMMARY

1. *Describe principles for organizing and manipulating databases.* A relational database is a collection of related tables with fields that record standard data items for a number of individual records. Users query a database to retrieve records whose field contents match specified criteria. They sort records to define a sequence that meets current information processing needs. Database design begins with processing goals and then determines output requirements to support those goals and input requirements to generate that output. You create a database by naming a new table and then defining fields by name, size, data type, and description; data entry specifies the contents of those fields to create records. You can modify a database design by adding and deleting tables, modifying field structures, and changing data in records. A database report includes selected field contents along with a report header and footer to explain the overall reports and group headers and footers to document the contents of individual report elements.

Databases often provide the central storehouses that supply data to other applications within an integrated information system.

2. *Explain how graphics programs create charts and other illustrations.* Paint programs create bitmapped graphics, while draw programs create vector graphics. Businesspeople often use presentation graphics programs to generate graphs, charts, and other illustrations that communicate essential information. They create graphics by choosing backgrounds and page layouts and then entering data. They can print out graphics, create slides for projection during presentations, display them as on-screen slide shows, or save them as files and import them to other applications.

3. *Describe the resources available through on-line information services.* An on-line service extends a computer system to reach vast collections of outside resources. Through graphically rich user interfaces, these services usually provide menus of choices including news, information for business and financial management, and travel services, among many other features.

4. *List some common special-purpose applications.* Project management packages help business people and others schedule and budget goal-directed sequences of activities. Reference software supplies a searchable database of information about a particular topic. Additional specialized productivity applications meet processing needs as varied as their users.

Key Terms

field 179

record 180

file 180

relational database 180

key field 180

data manipulation language
   (DML) 181

query 181

Find command 181

filter 181

primary sort key 182

secondary sort key 182

cross-tabulation 183

document layout 188

report header 188

report footer 188

contents layout 188

group header/footer 188

detail formatting 188

paint program 193

bitmapped graphic 193

draw program 193

vector graphic 193

snap on grid 193

align objects 193

presentation graphics program 194

clip art 194

Smartmaster 195

slide show 195

speaker note 195

on-line information service 197

connect time 198

project management program 199

activity 200

critical path 200

project crashing 200

reference software 201

specialized productivity software 201

Concept Quiz

Answer each of the following questions briefly.

1. What are presentation graphics?
2. What are the three basic elements of a database?
3. How does a relational database work?
4. In what two ways can a database program perform calculations?

Fill in the blanks to complete each of the following statements.

5. A good database specifies _____ .
6. The goals of the database design should reflect _____ .
7. When building a database, you take the following steps: _____ , _____ , _____ , and _____ .
8. You can make major modifications in your database by _____ .

Choose the best answer for each of the following.

9. All of the following are types of outputs *except*:
   a. form letters with address labels
   b. payroll checks
   c. primary key fields
   d. invoices

10. All of the following are elements of a database report *except*:
    a. document layout
    b. front-end layout
    c. page layout
    d. contents layout
11. When you use a database, you should
    a. review your goals and objectives
    b. practice consistent data input
    c. use tutorials that accompany your application
    d. all of the above

Mark "true" or "false" after each of the following statements.

12. Paint programs produce bitmapped graphics. _____
13. To create a graph, you choose a background and page layout, then enter data in the blank spaces presented by the applications program. _____
14. To develop effective graphics, you should let the graphics program design your image. _____
15. Project management programs help users plan, monitor, and control goal-directed sequences of activities. _____

Discussion Questions

1. In what ways might the clothing buyer for the men's (or women's) department of a department store use a database?
2. In what ways would practicing the fundamentals of good database design help the same clothing buyer in Question 1 get the most out of the information available from the database?
3. How might a marketer for a company that manufactures motorcycles use a graphics package to make a presentation to potential customers overseas?
4. In what ways might Mi Amore Pizza & Pasta (see chapter-opening photo) modify its existing database to offer more options and greater value for its customers?

Team Activity

Divide the class into teams of three or four members each. Each team will begin the process of building a database. First, the team should choose an organization that interests them—for example, a particular company, their university, or a nonprofit organization. Then, using the steps listed in the chapter text, along with the accompanying figures, the team should design a database structure (with design goals, output requirements, and input requirements) for a database that they think would be useful for the organization.

Applying IT

1. Access the Internet to obtain information on two or three different information services such as America Online, CompuServe, Prodigy, Dow Jones News/Retrieval, and the Microsoft Network. Determine which service you would prefer subscribing to for your own needs. (If you already subscribe, determine whether your service is still the best for you.) If you are not yet on-line with your computer, call two or three of these services on the telephone to obtain information about their services. (Most have toll-free numbers.)
2. Using a graphics package or presentation graphics package, generate a simple bar chart or organization chart. Become familiar with the features, and when you have finished, print out the graphic. Then critique it according to the graphics hints from this chapter.

CASE

Corbis Corp.

Doug Rowan's company has an ambitious mission: "to capture the entire human experience throughout history." Rowan is CEO of Corbis Corp., a company funded by Microsoft's Bill Gates. Corbis Corp. acquires the rights to images such as photographs and paintings, then with advanced graphics technology digitizes them and distributes them for a fee to publishers, advertisers, and other customers. For instance, while logged on to the Internet, a photo editor can call a Corbis researcher and describe the type of image he or she is looking for. The Corbis researcher sends photo samples to a Web site for the editor to review while still on the phone. The editor makes his or her choices, and Corbis presses the images onto a CD-ROM, which can be sent directly over the Internet. Although most of Corbis's customers are currently businesses, company executives see the potential for a market of individuals—say, students putting together research reports.

Corbis already has a huge archive of images—the largest acquisition was the Bettmann Archive of 16 million images. Once the images were purchased, technicians set to work digitizing them at a rate of 40,000 per month. In addition, Corbis sends out its own photographers (and freelancers) to capture specifically assigned images, such as the reinterment of the Romanovs in St. Petersburg or certain European battlefields. The company has already produced four CD-ROM titles as compendia of the archive and plans to make these available on-line, with direct links to the entire archive itself.

Corbis (http://www.corbis.com) isn't the only firm with a digital archive, but it is the largest and probably has the highest profile because of Gates's involvement. Picture Network International (http://www.publishersdepot.com) has stock photos, illustrations, clip art, sound effects, and more. PhotoDisc (http://www.pho-todisc.com) offers 15,000 images, for which customers can pay using cybercash. Liaison International (http://www.liasonintl.com) has 4 million photos, 2,400 of which are available on-line. Indeed, although Corbis seems to have cornered a huge chunk of the market, Josh Bernoff, senior analyst with Forrester Research, observes, "Regardless of how much Corbis acquires, they can't compete with the whole rest of the world." But maybe they can, if they do capture the entire human experience throughout history.

Questions

1. How might businesses other than publishers and advertisers use digitized images such as those offered by Corbis?
2. How might you use this type of graphic?
3. Access one of the Web sites mentioned in the case—either Corbis's or one belonging to a competitor—and see what information you can find about the company's offerings.

Source: Katie Hafner, "Picture This," *Newsweek*, June 24, 1996, pp. 88–90.

Answers to Concept Quiz

1. Presentation graphics are applications that are used to generate graphic images, such as pie charts, bar charts, line graphs, organization charts, etc. **2.** Fields, records, and tables **3.** A relational database encompasses a collection of two-dimensional tables of data. When these tables share at least one common field, the database program can link their data into a three-dimensional structure. These links give access to data from several different tables to develop useful information. **4.** It can supply data for calculations by separate applications, or it can carry out the calculations itself based on data in the fields of one or more tables. **5.** A set of tables that record data needed for particular processing tasks **6.** those of the organization **7.** Name the database; create new tables; define fields; enter initial data **8.** adding or deleting tables **9.** c **10.** b **11.** d **12.** True **13.** True **14.** False **15.** True

CHAPTER 7

Business Information Systems

CHAPTER OUTLINE

Transaction Processing Systems
    Batch and On-line Transaction Processing
Management Information Systems
    Inputs to a Management Information System
    Outputs from a Management Information System
Decision Support Systems
    Components of a Decision Support System
    Support for Group Decisions
    Executive Decision Support
Artificial Intelligence
    Components of Artificial Intelligence
Systems Development
    Systems Development Life Cycle
    Computer-aided Software Engineering (CASE)
    Prototyping
    Object-oriented Systems Development

Planning a trip? You'll probably need a reservation. SABRE is one of the world's largest privately-owned real-time computer systems used by travel agencies and individuals worldwide. It offers reservations for more than 350 airlines, 30,000 hotel properties, and 55 car rental companies. SABRE also accesses information and books reservations on railroads, ferries, and cruise lines. The SABRE system operates 24 hours a day, 7 days a week, and handles more than 300 million bookings annually. To keep SABRE up and running, The SABRE Group operates a secure, underground data center in Tulsa, Oklahoma, that can withstand virtually anything—earthquakes, storms, floods, fires, blackouts, even terrorists! (Photo courtesy of American Airlines.)

LEARNING OBJECTIVES

After completing Chapter 7, you will be able to:

1. Demonstrate the contribution of a transaction processing system to a company's overall information system.
2. Describe the reports that managers receive from a management information system.
3. Explain how a decision support system contributes to management effectiveness.
4. Define the term *artificial intelligence* and give examples of its role in business operations.
5. List the steps in the systems development life cycle.

Steven Jobs, cofounder of Apple Computer, is quoted as saying, "If you knew what was going to happen in advance every day, you could do amazing things. . . . Most people don't even know what happened yesterday in their own business. So, a lot of businesses are discovering they can take tremendous competitive advantage simply by finding out what happened yesterday as soon as possible."[1] The accurate collection, storing, and distribution of information in business is one of the most important keys to competitive advantage. To ensure that information is distributed on a timely basis and to the people who need to know, businesses have developed specialized reporting and decision-making systems. These systems are based on getting the right information to the right people at the right time so that a company's operations can be fine tuned and its decision makers can be well informed. Getting critical information to people who need it as soon as possible can help an organization adapt quickly to changes in its environment; providing this information over the long term can give an organization a long-term competitive advantage.

The business information systems discussed in this chapter are key to day-to-day business operations as well as to unique, higher-level decisions. Computer-based information systems (CBISs) can handle a variety of functions that are central to transaction processing: shipping, billing, receiving payments, controlling inventory, ordering supplies, making payroll, and generating reports. Efficient handling of these functions allows businesses to serve customers quickly and correctly, improve product offerings, and improve forecasting and planning. In short, they can increase revenues and reduce costs.

Management information systems distribute the information that a company gathers to help managers and other employees make better decisions. Getting this regular feedback can help employees organize, plan, and control their activities. Decision support systems help managers identify problems and opportunities and formulate alternatives. In other words, decision support systems assist managers in making decisions for the organization. Finally, artificial intelligence has increasingly been applied by businesses through such

technologies as robotics, vision systems, and learning systems. Not only are companies offering products that exploit artificial intelligence, they are beginning to tap its resources to support decision making on a broader scale.

A company can hire internal IS professionals to develop its business information systems, or it can purchase or lease finished systems from an outside company. Either choice follows the same basic process, called *systems development*. All systems development works to ensure that the design and implementation of the CBIS meet the information needs of the organization.

This chapter reviews the elements and functions of business information systems in detail. It further elaborates on this topic by covering the latest CBIS enhancements to emerge from research in artificial intelligence and robotics. Finally, it explains a standard procedure for systems development in which either internal or external IS professionals work with users to fulfill the information demands of effective and efficient business operations.

TRANSACTION PROCESSING SYSTEMS

All business activities focus on transactions—that is, exchanges of value or movements of goods. Common transactions include:

- Selling and shipping products
- Sending bills to customers
- Receiving and depositing incoming payments

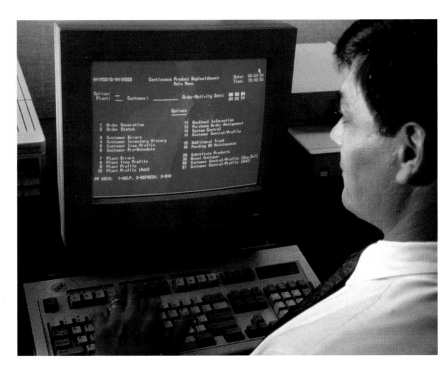

Campbell Soup Company's Continuous Product Replenishment Program is an electronic ordering system that replenishes a retailer's inventory at the same rate as the consumer takes it off the shelf. (Source: Courtesy of Campbell Soup Company.)

batch processing

procedure in which a group (batch) of programs is run on the computer system at one time; ideal for a large number of business transactions that occur regularly and in sequence

on-line transaction processing (OLTP)

real-time processing, in which data are entered as business transactions are completed

- Ordering materials and supplies to replenish inventory
- Paying employees and suppliers
- Filing required reports with state and federal government agencies

An organization's transaction processing system (TPS) must carefully track structured exchanges like these. A TPS function provides essential information that supports routine operations and ongoing evaluation of profitability and other measures of business success.

A TPS usually employs every class of components within a CBIS, including hardware, software (especially databases), people, and procedures. Input hardware like optical scanners, keyboards, and numeric keypads capture transaction data. Processing hardware and software accept this input and complete necessary calculations. Databases store both raw data and calculated results. Processing resources gather selected field contents from databases to produce various business documents and reports.

Batch and On-line Transaction Processing

Early computer-based transaction processing systems accepted and manipulated data only in groups or batches. This so-called **batch processing** required people and procedures to collect data about transactions, often in paper documents, as they occurred and then input each set of data together for periodic processing (see Figure 7.1). For example, sales representatives would collect orders over a period of time and submit them at specified intervals. IS personnel would then input data from paper records for a number of orders, and the computer system would process them all at once. The time between processed batches could vary from under an hour to over a week.

The spread of powerful and inexpensive computer technology has allowed information systems to use instant **on-line transaction processing (OLTP)**, also called *real-time processing*. Today, employees input data as they complete business transactions. The information system then performs appropriate processing and updates database records without delay. When you make an airline reservation to Fort Lauderdale for spring break, the ticketing clerk processes your transaction while you wait. The computer system immediately changes all database files for seat availability, aircraft staffing, meal requirements, and other needs to reflect your purchase. This quick response ensures that everyone in the organization can accurately determine current operating needs.

Immediate processing of transaction data does more than improve efficiency. It redefines effective business processes for organizations like airlines, concert ticket agencies, and hospitals, whose operations generate large amounts of data and whose customers want current information. Many companies have found that OLTP helps them satisfy customers by providing fast, reliable service.

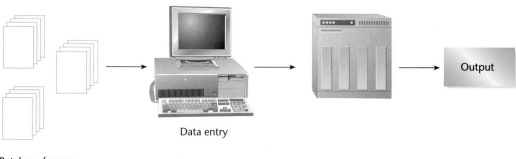

Batches of paper
documents

Data entry

Output

(a) Batch processing

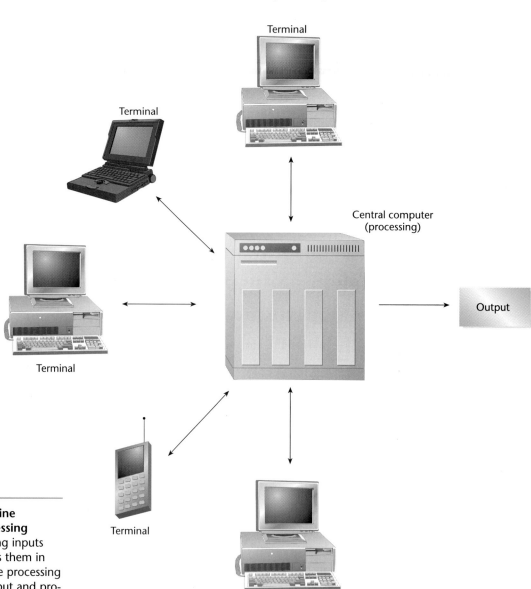

Terminal

Terminal

Terminal

Central computer
(processing)

Output

Terminal

Terminal

(b) On-line processing

FIGURE 7.1

**Batch versus On-line
Transaction Processing**
(a) Batch processing inputs
data and processes them in
groups. (b) On-line processing
completes data input and processing for transactions as they
occur. (On-line entry with
delayed processing combines
aspects of both systems.)

A third type of transaction processing combines on-line data input with delayed processing, creating a compromise between batch and on-line methods. This type of information system continually accepts data for orders and other transactions as they occur, but processing waits until a certain amount of data accumulates or needed resources become available on the computer system. For example, when you call a toll-free number to order a shirt, an operator typically enters data into a computer as you provide it. The information system may not process your order until that evening, when computing workloads fall.

Available technology allows almost any organization to maintain on-line transaction processing for virtually all applications, but other methods persist. In fact, batch processing or on-line entry with delayed processing still provide appropriate, cost-effective solutions for specific information system needs. Companies typically handle payroll transactions and billing in batch processing systems, for example. They would waste time and lose efficiency if an on-line system required workers to feed blank invoice forms or payroll checks into printers each time a customer placed an order or an employee worked a few hours. Different organizations carry out from 20 percent to 40 percent (sometimes more) of their processing in batches. A business's specific goals determine the transaction processing methods that suit the varying needs of its information system.

MANAGEMENT INFORMATION SYSTEMS

A management information system (MIS), sometimes called an *information reporting system,* works primarily to provide feedback about regular company operations to managers and other employees. This output helps them to control, organize, and plan routine business activities. For example, a management information system at a dairy processing plant would provide reports about incoming milk deliveries from farmers, staffing and equipment for production of plastic bottles, filling operations, and sales to grocery stores and other outlets. The plant manager would read these reports to ensure that effective production steps add as much value as possible to raw materials in converting them to finished products. While a TPS most often focuses on supporting organizational efficiency, a management information system supports primarily effectiveness.

The system certainly helps with important suggestions to maintain and improve efficiency. Still, IS professionals (and the managers who rely on their work) must appreciate the important role of these reports in maximizing effectiveness. A management information system provides critical contributions to an organization's fundamental goal of providing *the right information to the right people in the right form at the right time.* IS professionals too often forget this important principle, which should guide all of their efforts. As they work to enhance system efficiencies through integration, IS managers risk overlooking the basic problem-solving needs of functional managers.

summary reports

documents that filter the highly detailed data stored in databases by transaction processing systems

Management information systems usually meet those needs by generating various **summary reports**. These documents filter the highly detailed data stored in databases by transaction processing systems. Careful report formatting helps to present query results in a meaningful way. Managers read summary reports to gather data and information in a form that supports their decision making. Figure 7.2 compares the role of a management information system with those of other sources of management information.

Data sources

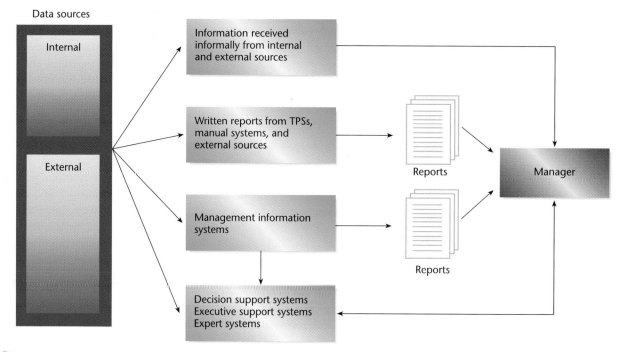

FIGURE 7.2

Sources of Management Information
The MIS is just one of many management information sources.

Inputs to a Management Information System

As technically defined, all data in a management information system come from internal sources. That is, the data enter the information system from the firm's own sources, primarily TPS records. To really understand the system, however, you must evaluate external sources of data as well. (Look again at Figure 7.2.)

The TPS provides data for management reports by capturing and storing records from ongoing business transactions. With every business exchange, various TPS applications update and otherwise modify the organization's database. For example, a point-of-sale (POS) terminal at a grocery store scans a product bar code, displays the correct price and amount due, and records the sale. At the same time, it updates the inventory database by subtracting one unit from that product's total stock on hand. It also increases the store's totals for daily sales and sales tax collected.

Restaurants have also begun to use on-line processing to cut waste and speed service. Boston Markets tracks sales in each restaurant to predict when and how much of an item to cook. Waste has dropped from 5 percent to 1 percent as a result. And Taco Bell

Point of Sale terminals allow companies to track data, analyze sales trends, target marketing, or improve service. (Source: Chuck Keeler/Tony Stone Images.)

Waiters at Taco Bell use a handheld terminal to input orders directly to the kitchen. (Source: Courtesy of PAR Technology Corporation.)

has equipped waiters in a San Francisco restaurant with handheld computers to instantly send orders back to the chefs. The wireless system has saved as much as ten minutes off each meal.[2]

The management information system generates reports from these updated files for the store manager, other members of the organization, and perhaps suppliers. These reports show how much the store has sold, how much it needs to order, and how much it should remit to state tax authorities, among many other pieces of information.

The organization's strategic plan also supplies important internal data. Its details govern the data that managers need to collect and their standards for interpreting that data. Specific functional areas throughout the firm also supply internal data about employee job assignments, hours worked, materials and supplies consumed, and many other topics.

Managers need many kinds of data from external sources as well. Review of competitors' practices may supply essential planning information. Suppliers indicate guidelines for shipments of materials and components. In addition, both customers and suppliers may join in cooperative planning efforts that enhance efficiency and effectiveness for all of the participants. This communication between organizations blurs the distinction between internal and external information sources. It extends the boundaries of each firm's information system to encompass selected resources of other firms.

In addition to competitors and suppliers, financial markets and government agencies also provide valuable data about market and industry conditions.

Outputs from a Management Information System

The management information system does more than simply pass on the raw data from these sources. It collects, processes, and categorizes data to inform managers about important organizational activities. The system distributes its information primarily through predetermined reports.

For example, managers could determine how well their firm's products are selling simply by reviewing a chronological listing of sales orders. Routine sales reports can save much of the time and effort required for this arrangement by accumulating the data into meaningful totals for different products, time periods, sales representatives, regions, and so on. A manager interested in a particular product or sales representative can quickly review relevant information. The same report allows easy comparisons of sales for successive quarters or the same period in the previous year. In addition, each manager need not hunt for the information independently; the reporting system automatically provides it.

Individual information systems gather unique collections of data in their reports, but some typical management needs have defined some standard types. Most companies rely on various kinds of scheduled reports, demand reports, and exception reports.

scheduled reports

documents with standard sets of data about activities for predetermined time intervals delivered on set dates and times

Scheduled Reports. An information system produces **scheduled reports** with standard sets of data about activities for predetermined time intervals delivered on set dates and times. Managers spend much of their time studying daily, weekly, and monthly reports about all kinds of company activities. For example, a weekly summary report might list total payroll expenses and the status of each production job. This information would help a production manager monitor and control labor costs and order delivery schedules. Monthly reports might help managers control customer credit, evaluate the performance of sales representatives, adjust inventory levels, and more.

key-indicator reports

documents that summarize the previous day's critical activities

A special type of scheduled report called a **key-indicator report** summarizes the previous day's critical activities. Managers typically review this report at the beginning of each work day to keep especially close track of activities identified by company strategy as essential to organizational success. These activities vary for different companies and industries. Inventory levels may determine profit growth or loss for a discount retailer. Auto dealers thrive when they achieve high sales volumes and close their doors when volumes fall. The managers of these firms rely on key-indicator reports to identify any need for quick action to correct important imbalances.

demand reports

documents that answer specific questions when requested

Demand Reports. To satisfy less predictable information needs, managers sometimes ask for **demand reports** that answer specific questions when requested. The management information system must then summarize the requested information on demand. Equally important, the report should omit any data not directly relevant to its chosen topic. IS professionals may complete and distribute the reports, or the managers may define the report formats, queries, sorts, and other database manipulations themselves. A sales manager may call for a demand report on a particular sales representative's performance to evaluate that person's prospects for transfer to a new territory. A company president may ask for a report on total annual sales for a product to decide whether to drop it from the product line.

exception reports

documents that are produced in response to unusual circumstances or events that require management action

Exception Reports. A management information system automatically produces **exception reports** in response to unusual circumstances or events that require management action. Managers usually set parameters that call for exception reports. For example, a production manager may direct the information system to generate an inventory report whenever stocks of selected items fall below 50 units. To ensure that overtime costs remain under control, a reporting system may automatically list all employees who work more than 40 hours in a week. An exception report usually helps managers to monitor activities with critical effects on an organization's success. It signals the need for a manager to take some action.

trigger points

parameters in an exception report

The effectiveness of an exception report depends on how managers set its parameters, or **trigger points**. Some decision makers prefer to set trigger points far from critical values to give plenty of warning before a crisis develops. This extreme caution risks generating exception reports when events do not really demand action. On the other hand, trigger points set too close to critical values may not leave enough time to respond.

For example, an extremely nervous construction manager might ask for an exception report any time a $200,000 project exceeds its budget by $500. This low trigger point could result in a report for almost every project. Instead, a trigger point of $5,000 might highlight troubled projects without generating distracting reports about basically routine performance. A trigger point of $25,000 above budget would allow projects to get too far out of control before an exception report would indicate a need for a response.

Effective Use of Information System Reports. Reports of various kinds can help managers to develop better plans, make better decisions, and improve their control over company operations. Many managers base most of their actions on weekly status reports. Special projects almost always call for demand reports about important activities. Exception reports provide security that the information system will catch major problems to allow managers to take corrective action.

This neat division of functions should not hide overlaps between different types of reports. For example, managers often order demand reports about the same information that appears in scheduled reports when they need to make big decisions. The demand reports may organize the data differently, perhaps summarizing for larger groups or longer time periods. Similarly, they often want exception reports with sensitive trigger points for the items listed in daily key-indicator reports. Table 7.1 states some general guidelines for report design and content.

DECISION SUPPORT SYSTEMS

A decision support system (DSS) is the third major element of a business information system. Chapter 1 described it as an organized collection of people, procedures, databases, and devices that helps managers to identify and study alternative solutions to specific problems and then choose from among them. A DSS makes intensive use of databases within the organization's information system. In addition, it often reaches across network connections to access outside resources. A DSS also incorporates elaborate mathematical models in spreadsheets to project the results of alternative decisions based on assumed conditions.

TABLE 7.1

Guidelines for Effective Reports

GUIDELINE	EXPLANATION
Tailor each report to user needs.	Success depends on user involvement and input.
Spend time and effort to produce only needed reports.	Information systems often continue generating reports long after they lose usefulness; avoid filling trash bins with unread reports.
Carefully control report content and layout.	A report's layout should prominently display especially important information, and it should omit unneeded data that would only clutter its pages. It should phrase information in commonly understood language to help managers easily find what they need to know.
Provide effective support for management by exception.	An information system should produce some reports only when events demand urgent responses.
Set careful trigger points.	Excessively sensitive parameters may overload managers with nonessential information; excessively lax parameters risk overlooking key facts.

BUSINESS BITS

The New DSS

If business has entered the information age, then it has also entered the decision age. More and more, as organizations empower both managers and employees to make decisions that affect the course of business, decision support systems are becoming a necessity.

In fact, decision support systems are rapidly becoming more complex. "Decision support is one area where a multitiered architecture is required, never mind desirable," notes Bob Chin, CIO of Healthsource Inc., a $1.2 billion health maintenance organization located in New Hampshire. "The amount of work [in decision support] is so intense that a two tiered platform is almost useless. . . . We're doing so much more that we couldn't conceive of doing before in a more transaction-oriented environment. It's almost priceless."

Tufts Health Plan, another New England–based HMO, uses decision support to get IS personnel out of the report-generation "business"; most Tufts employer groups now generate their own reports, accomplishing this in less than ten minutes. So reports get to customers far more quickly (customers used to have to wait weeks for reports from a backlogged IS staff) and less expensively. The new system has also helped Tufts win two new clients, with a total of 20,000 new members, to the HMO. Tufts CIO Rich Shoup says that efficient reporting and quick access to data were "differentiators" in winning these contracts. "Information is critical to our industry. The ability to get timely access to accurate information is an absolute competitive advantage."

In a completely different type of industry, Cargill Inc., the giant Minneapolis-based commodities trading company, has focused on spreading decision support capabilities to more users with less effort. "As long as all PCs have browsers, we can roll [the technology] without physically touching the PCs," says Chuck Faison, Cargill's data warehouse manager. In other words, Cargill does not need to retrofit or upgrade its existing hardware to offer DSS capabilities to a wide range of users.

In the toy business, Iowa-based Ertl Co., a $200 million manufacturer of toys and model kits, wants to increase the number of users, including executives, who could have reporting and querying power on its system. So it built a three-tiered system. The problem was, it took up to 15 minutes to get a response to a question or request. But with the use of new software, the time

needed for query responses has dropped to one minute. Ertl claims that the system saves the company hundreds of thousands of dollars each year and saves more than 18,000 hours of time the IS staff needs each year to generate reports. That's a 50 percent boost in productivity.

Decision support systems are great if people know how to use them. But it's especially important, in training, not to go overboard, trying to turn every user into an IS professional. "We don't want to make users a bunch of SQL experts," comments Buck Poe, data warehouse administrator at SeaFirst Bankcard Services. "We want to let them focus on the business and not on technology." (With its DSS, SeaFirst, a credit card issuer that handles more than $4 million in transactions each year, has been able to cut query time regarding customers' annual memberships from two days to ten minutes.) But perhaps Teresa Wingfield, a data analyst with Giga Information Group in Massachusetts, sums up the expansion and merging of decision support technologies best: she calls it the new "universal knowledge system."

1. How do you think the expansion of the user base of DSS in business will change the jobs of IS professionals?
2. How do you think training for general users of company decision support systems should (or will) differ from that of IS professionals?
3. Access the Internet and browse for Web sites that provide you with information about new DSS technology. Share your findings with the class.

Source: Emily Kay, "Decisions, Decisions," *Information Week*, June 17, 1996, pp. 73–78; http://www.informationweek.com. Photo courtesy of the Ertl Toy Company.

While a management information system focuses on relatively structured, routine problems, a DSS emphasizes effective decisions about unstructured or semistructured business problems. It helps to guide major, strategic changes controlled by top managers with the potential to substantially raise profits, lower costs, and improve products and services. Of course, operating managers sometimes face relatively unstructured, nonroutine problems themselves, and they also rely on DSS resources (see the "Business Bits" box). Still, managers with broader authority make these kinds of decisions more frequently than their subordinates do, so they rely more heavily on DSSs to help solve problems.

Decision support systems help to clarify management decisions by projecting potential results based on certain assumptions. For example, a newspaper publisher's DSS might predict the effect on profits of an increase in the price of newsprint. The information generated by the decision support system might prompt the newspaper's managing editor and marketing manager to boost revenue by increasing advertising space rather than raising subscription prices.

Although this simple example demonstrates only some characteristics of a DSS, it highlights the essential activity of a decision support system: clarifying the choices that all kinds of managers must make. Its models and output data can only give managers information from which they can determine how those choices will influence progress toward company goals. Machines cannot replace managers; people still must make all decisions.

Components of a Decision Support System

The core components of a DSS—a database, model base, and DSS generator—interact to develop output data that define probable business scenarios. In addition, a user interface allows human control. Connections to external databases and information systems bring in outside resources. Figure 7.3 shows a conceptual model of a DSS.

Dialog Manager. The user interface of a decision support system, called a *dialog manager*, is a "point-and-click" feature that recognizes and reacts to common business terms and phrases to allow easy access to and manipulation of the other components. This component provides much of the power of a DSS, because it frees managers from the complex language of computer applications. The dialog manager helps to adapt the information system to the needs of its users instead of forcing them to adapt their own decision processes to its capabilities.

DSS generator

a DSS component that controls interactions among the database, model base, and external resources to complete the required processing

DSS Generator. The dialog manager translates business language into the code of the **DSS generator**, which then controls interactions among the database, model base, and external resources to complete the required processing. It reports the results to the dialog manager, which translates them for the business user.

Database. The DSS generator selects data relevant to a particular decision problem from appropriate databases, records, and fields. This input ties the calculations of the DSS to the company's actual operations, so the output accurately reflects real-life conditions. The system can also access external databases to gather data about overall economic conditions, industrywide trends, population changes, and many more important inputs. These connections to external databases allow the DSS to supplement the company database with vast stores of information in managing inventory, sales, personnel, production, accounting, and other areas.

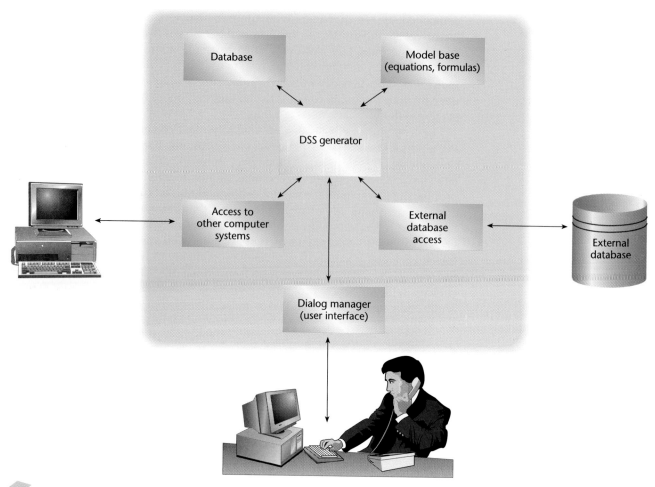

FIGURE 7.3

Conceptual Model of a DSS
The user of a DSS interacts
with the DSS generator
through the dialog manager.
The DSS generator controls
the interactions of the model
base, database, and external
resources.

Model Base. The *model base* includes a variety of equations, formulas, and other processing tools that manipulate input data and produce output to support decision making. These models seek to represent the probable real effects of business processes, assuming that input data accurately reflect beginning conditions. They support decision making by trying to predict the future based on an understanding of the causes that produced past results.

For example, if the user is running financial information to determine whether to lease or buy equipment, the model base would contain financial equations to calculate the cost of the lease and any included maintenance versus the cost of the equipment, interest rates, and so forth. The output will then help the user make the decision.

A DSS model base includes many basic kinds of models designed to represent real-life relationships, including:

- Financial models
- Statistical formulas
- Graphing functions
- Project management tools

Depending on the needs of the decision situation, the DSS generator can call on one or more of these resources to evaluate assumptions in light of input from the database and predict the results of potential decisions.

Financial models analyze data that represent cash flows, interest rates, and other variables to calculate measures of investment success like rates of return. Decision support systems often include spreadsheet programs to provide these kinds of tools. Complex decisions may require even more sophisticated financial planning applications, and some organizations develop customized financial models to handle their own unique situations and problems. As spreadsheet packages continue to increase in power, however, the need for sophisticated financial modeling packages may decrease.

A DSS model base usually includes statistical formulas to compute averages, standard deviations, correlation coefficients, regression analysis, and many more complex statistics. Within a decision support system, these statistics summarize the relationships between quantities, predict trends, test hypotheses, and more. Both PCs and mainframes can run programs like SPSS and SAS to provide these powerful decision-making capabilities. Some programs also produce graphic displays to supplement their statistics with visual illustrations.

As described in Chapter 6, business decision makers often create graphs and charts to visually represent important data. A DSS may integrate software packages dedicated to this function with its other resources. Graphing capabilities can both supplement numerical output and convey meaning in ways that numbers cannot match.

Chapter 6 also mentioned project management software, which helps managers to coordinate large, interrelated sequences of activities. In a DSS, project management tools identify critical individual activities that could determine the success or failure of an entire project. This information tells managers which steps they absolutely must complete on time and within budget. Some of these programs also suggest activities on which to invest extra resources (cash, labor, equipment, etc.) to speed up an entire project while minimizing total costs. Project management models enhance a decision support system with tools for controlling projects of all sizes and types.

One off-the-shelf DSS package currently available is ReloSmart. This decision support package can help employees or small-business owners decide whether moving makes sense. The program contains information about geographic locations and is able to compare current site costs with costs at the new location—from local and state taxes, to real estate costs, to energy costs. It also includes quality-of-life information (e.g., weather, crime rates, average level of education).[3]

```
╔══════════════════════ Analysis ══════════════════════╗
║      Calculation of the Financial Impact of Relocating ║
║ Living in Bergen County, NJ        Moving to San Jose, CA  ║
║ Working in New York, NY            Will work in San Jose, CA ║
║                                                        ║
║ This move will cause the following changes in these expense categories: ║
║          State and Local Income Taxes   (    $2,526)   ║
║          Auto Insurance Expense              $536      ║
║          Housing Costs                        $0       ║
║          Rental Payments                 (  $14,880)   ║
║          Real Estate Taxes                    $0       ║
║          Miscellaneous Expenses             $2,659     ║
║          Sales Tax                       (    $951)    ║
║          Electricity Costs               (    $238)    ║
║ Total change in cash due to relocation:  (  $15,400)   ║
║ Numbers in brackets indicate a loss of cash, numbers without brackets ║
║ indicate gains in cash. All numbers are net of federal income tax ║
║ effect where appropriate. Select HELP for more information ║
║                                                        ║
║ [ Salary ] [ Detail ] [ Quality ] [ Future ] [ Analysis ] [ Restart ] ║
║ [ Print  ]                        [ Previous ] [ Done ] ║
╚════════════════════════════════════════════════════════╝
```

ReloSmart software can assist individuals or companies in their decision to relocate. (Source: Courtesy of Right Choice, Inc. 800-872-2294.)

Support for Group Decisions

Decision support systems have dramatically improved business decisions by individual users at all levels. However, many midlevel and top managers devote much of their time to committee meetings and other group decision-making sessions. A standard DSS accepts input from and sends output to a single user or computer, so its limitations can create frustrating barriers to communication among members of cooperative teams. These decision makers need effective tools for working in cooperation to define and evaluate alternatives and then agree on common positions. A **group decision support system (GDSS),** also called a *computerized collaborative work system,* provides these tools in an integrated collection of hardware, software, people, databases, and procedures that encourages interaction and sharing of data in cooperative decision-making settings.

A typical GDSS configuration (Figure 7.4) includes some basic DSS components—a database, model base, and dialog manager. These components function differently in a GDSS, however. They give simultaneous access to common files and databases by many users, usually through network connections between separate computers. This capability allows group members to work together on a single task despite obstacles like geographic distance.

Dialog Manager and Group Interactions. Within a GDSS, the dialog manager expands its role to help everyone involved with a group decision-making process to communicate with the other components of the GDSS and with each other. This kind of team often includes one or more **group facilitators,** who work specifically to help other group members effectively use the resources of the GDSS. Through their skills in both technological tools and group decision-making techniques, these facilitators can keep group members focused on their joint task while avoiding some common pitfalls of cooperative work. The extent to which the dialog manager and the group facilitator encourage or inhibit user participation often determines the success of the overall GDSS.

Dramatic growth in business use of group decision support systems has propelled annual sales of this software above $1 billion. Further, this total is expected to double every few years.[4] About 40 percent of the businesses that

group decision support system (GDSS)

an integrated collection of hardware, software, people, databases, and procedures that encourages interaction and sharing of data

group facilitator

a person who works specifically to help other group members effectively use the resources of the GDSS

FIGURE 7.4

Configuration of a GDSS
A group decision support system supplements the elements of a basic DSS with groupware, software that facilitates communication among team members.

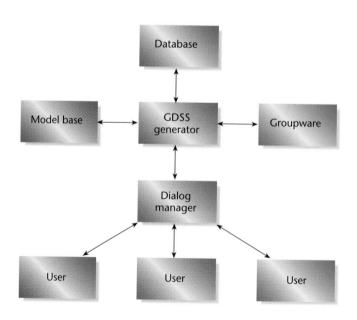

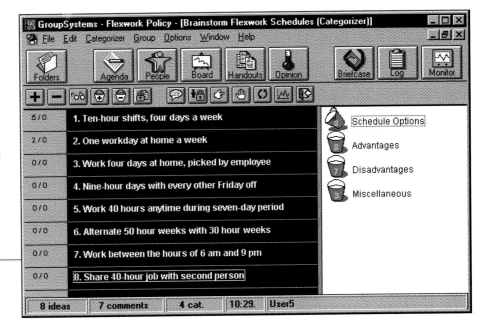

GroupSystems - Flexwork Policy - [Brainstorm Flexwork Schedules (Categorizer)]

File Edit Categorizer Group Options Window Help

5 / 0	1. Ten-hour shifts, four days a week
2 / 0	2. One workday at home a week
0 / 0	3. Work four days at home, picked by employee
0 / 0	4. Nine-hour days with every other Friday off
0 / 0	5. Work 40 hours anytime during seven-day period
0 / 0	6. Alternate 50 hour weeks with 30 hour weeks
0 / 0	7. Work between the hours of 6 am and 9 pm
0 / 0	8. Share 40-hour job with second person

Schedule Options
Advantages
Disadvantages
Miscellaneous

8 ideas   7 comments   4 cat.   10:29.   User5

A GDSS can be a useful tool in the creation of a flexible work policy, allowing several users to share ideas, specify their preferences, and write comments. (Source: Courtesy of Ventana Corporation. Group Systems is registered trademark of Ventana Corporation.)

responded to a recent survey reported either using GDSS software or planning to use it in the near future.[5] Without question, GDSSs are gaining important roles as vital decision-making tools for businesses of all sizes.

Groupware Use in a GDSS. **Groupware** is software that supports group decision making and collaborative work. It can include electronic mail, electronic notes, bulletin boards, and other functions to support people working in groups. Groupware can be an important GDSS software tool to help facilitate group communication.

Price Waterhouse, for example, uses groupware to coordinate diverse contributions to its consulting projects.[6] Through the groupware application, any of the company's 18,000 workers in 22 countries can access over 1,000 bulletin boards devoted to a variety of subjects. Team members routinely post notes for others and read the postings of colleagues. The groupware also gives every employee rapid access to the company's vast collections of information. By keeping all employees up to date on the firm's latest business activities and customer contacts, groupware supports efficient and effective decisions and work processes.

Small businesses also gain substantial benefits from groupware. This application allows cooperation among independent contractors or small firms on a large job that none of them could accomplish alone. A small team of independent artists and advertising copywriters might share messages and sketches to create a joint proposal about a new campaign for a large agency.

Groupware allows team members like these to cooperate in producing compound documents that integrate information from spreadsheet programs, database packages, word processors, and other applications—the document-centric approach that we described in earlier chapters. Compound documents can even include multimedia data like audio and video clips. Unlike traditional integration methods, in which one program imports separate files from other applications, a compound document stores all of this data together in one file. Many groupware programs can bridge gaps between applications from different software publishers to create compound documents.

groupware
software packages that allow two or more persons in a group to work effectively together to use word processing, databases, spreadsheets, and related software packages

intranet

software packages that use Web sites within the company to facilitate the sharing of databases and projects

Corporate Intranets. One of the newest work group applications involves technology similar to the Internet but applied inside a business. These **intranets** allow collaborative work among employees and departments, similar to groupware. For companies that already have Internet software installed, using internal Web sites can allow sharing of information from databases and projects at a relatively inexpensive price. Web browsers are often free, and software is readily available. Since employees have become familiar with browsers, training time is often reduced. The only restriction to running intranets is that the network must run TCP/IP (transmission control protocol/Internet protocol) protocols that define how information is transferred on the Internet.[7] Table 7.2 lists common uses for intranets.

In a recent survey on the use of intranets, 16 percent of the companies already use an intranet, 26 percent plan to install one, 24 percent are evaluating its use, and 34 percent have no plan.[8] Netscape Communications estimates that 70 percent of its sales are used for building intranets.[9]

Intranet use can be expected to grow astronomically in the next few years, as companies make more and more information accessible to their employees. Such free flow of information can help employees and managers make better decisions with more input.

Executive Decision Support

executive support system (ESS)

a specialized DSS that combines hardware and software with data about economic conditions and complex planning models to help top managers develop and evaluate major new organizational initiatives

Top-level executives often require unique resources to support their strategic decisions, which affect a company's entire range of operations. To meet this need, a specialized DSS called an **executive support system (ESS)** combines hardware and software with data about economic conditions and complex planning models to help top managers develop and evaluate major new organizational initiatives. Also called an *executive information system (EIS)*, this collection of IS resources is designed specifically to assist the president and other senior company officers. Even the board of directors may sometimes rely on an ESS in representing the interests of a large company's owners—its stockholders. Figure 7.5 shows these top decision-making levels and their areas of concern.

As a special type of DSS, an ESS shares many of the same components. The two systems differ, however, in important ways. A DSS provides a variety of predefined calculations and analysis tools to help users understand relatively routine problems and the likely effects of potential solutions; that is, a DSS helps managers to answer important questions about company operations. An ESS, in contrast, gathers and presents structured information that indicates

TABLE 7.2

Intranet Uses

- Information sharing
- Group scheduling and calendars
- On-line meetings for questions, comments, brainstorming, and voting
- Videoconferencing
- Employee bulletin boards for information updates, best practice tips, etc.
- Group document handling and review
- Work flow tracking

Source: Adapted from Anne Field, "Group Think," *Inc. Technology*, September 17, 1996, no. 3, pp. 38–44.

FIGURE 7.5

Executive Decision-making Levels

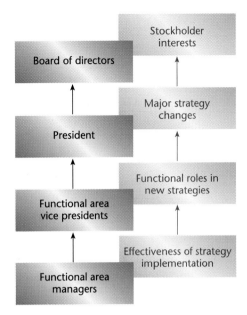

which aspects of company operations have important effects on operating success. In other words, it helps executives to formulate the right questions.

For example, a DSS might help a midlevel manager to decide whether to upgrade old equipment or buy new machines for a particular processing task. An ESS might help the company president evaluate the profitability of that processing activity and decide whether the firm should continue to operate in the same way.

A DSS can usually serve the needs of different users in varying situations. In contrast, the detailed analysis required of an ESS typically demands a system carefully tailored to a particular set of executives and decision situations. This specialization provides powerful support for the overall objective of any information system: to deliver the right information in the right form to the right person at the right time. An ESS is an interactive, hands-on tool with which an executive can focus, filter, and organize data to produce a clear image of an entire company. It then helps to suggest effective measures that will ensure the company's future success.

The Hertz car rental company employs a good example of an executive support system.[10] This ESS allows executives to view data about rental and leasing trends for a particular area simply by touching an on-screen map. The system has made especially profitable contributions to analysis of the company's rate policy. It helps managers to identify firms that generate enough business to justify particular discounts. The ESS then extends this analysis to show executives what aspects of these customers' businesses led them to create such high revenue for Hertz. This information suggests measures for continuing or improving the relationships, and it helps the company to identify other firms with similar business potential.

Getting executives to use computers may be one of the biggest drawbacks to executive support systems. A survey of 245 CEOs, CFOs, and senior vice presidents at large U.S. firms showed that most (84 percent) had a computer on their desk. Approximately half used their computers nearly every day, but 19 percent reported they rarely used it. Younger executives and executives at Fortune 1,000 companies used their computers more often.[11]

ARTIFICIAL INTELLIGENCE

Science fiction novels, movies, and television shows have often featured humans (and other life forms) casually chatting with computer systems. Those fictional systems could answer complex questions and even initiate actions on their own. Real capabilities, like a DSS dialog manager's ability to interpret common business jargon, may seem to give some weight to these entertaining stories. Still, no one should conclude that computer companies will soon create systems capable of replacing human decision makers.

artificial intelligence (AI)

systems that combine sophisticated hardware and software with elaborate databases and knowledge-based processing models to demonstrate characteristics of effective human decision making

Even so, business firms have already begun to implement some direct applications of **artificial intelligence (AI)** systems. These systems combine sophisticated hardware and software with elaborate databases and knowledge-based processing models to demonstrate characteristics of effective human decision making. Practical applications cover a broad range. The most common currently are in the area of expert systems for medical diagnoses, exploration for natural resources, identifying faults with mechanical devices, financial decision making, and even assistance in designing and developing other computer systems. Garry Kasparov recently played a six-game chess match against IBM's Deep Blue computer. He won by adjusting his play to prey on the computer's weakness—lack of adaptability to erratic moves.[12]

AI systems emerge from the work of researchers, scientists, and experts on human thought patterns. These pioneers develop contemporary AI systems, not to duplicate all aspects of human decision making, but to replicate limited problem-solving abilities for certain well-defined situations. These efforts have achieved remarkable success. According to an Ernst & Young survey, more than 70 percent of the 500 largest U.S. companies rely on some form of artificial intelligence.[13]

Components of Artificial Intelligence

Any measure of AI applications must first set limits for the field. A broad definition includes several key components, such as expert systems, robotics, vision systems, natural language processing, learning systems, and neural networks (Figure 7.6). In these interrelated areas of research, advances in one field can lead to comparable or more dramatic progress in others.

Expert Systems. An expert system imitates the problem-solving behavior of a human with extensive knowledge in a particular field. People have developed

The ACM Chess Challenge: Garry Kasparov vs. IBM's Deep Blue Computer. (Source: Courtesy of the Association for Computing Machinery.)

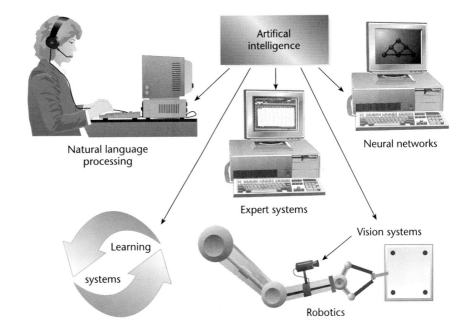

FIGURE 7.6

Conceptual Model of Artificial Intelligence

heuristics

procedures that allow learning along empirical lines using "rules of thumb"

computerized expert systems to diagnose problems, predict future events, and assist in designing new products and systems. Like human experts, computerized expert systems arrive at conclusions or make suggestions based on preprogrammed **heuristics,** or procedures that allow learning along empirical lines using "rules of thumb." The research conducted in AI over the past two decades has produced business expert systems designed to explore new business possibilities, increase overall profitability, reduce costs, and provide superior service to customers and clients.

Expert systems supplement decision support systems and other IS components to help an organization improve the processes by which it creates value for customers. Transaction processing and information reporting systems provide reports about current conditions to support this improvement. Decision support systems facilitate deeper investigation of alternatives and their consequences by human managers. An expert system, however, actually proposes solutions to problems.

Mortgage finance companies, for example, use expert systems to perform credit evaluations on loan applicants. Such a system collects and analyzes various types of data to determine whether each applicant qualifies for credit. This decision speeds the finance company's up-front decision making so it can quickly notify those whose applications the system rejects and complete processing for financially sound borrowers. In this capacity, the expert system acts like a colleague or partner to the user.

robotics

a field involving mechanical, usually computer-controlled, devices to perform tasks that require extreme precision or tedious or hazardous work by people

Robots. Researchers in **robotics** develop mechanical, usually computer-controlled, devices to perform tasks that require extreme precision or tedious or hazardous work by people, like painting cars during manufacturing, making precision welds, and inserting chips in electronic circuit boards. Powerful AI software helps to fully develop the high-precision machine capabilities of robots, often freeing them from direct human control and vastly improving their productivity. Continuing research is testing many new applications for robots and refining existing applications. An initiative of the U.S. Army focused on developing medical robotic systems that would perform surgery in highly dangerous combat

Artificial intelligence dramatically reduces or eliminates the risk to humans in many applications. Dante II, an eight-legged robot, made a week-long trek down into an active volcano. (Source: Courtesy of Carnegie Mellon Robotics Institute.)

vision system

a hardware/software system that permits computers to capture, store, and manipulate visual images

areas under remote-control direction by doctors. This technique would both improve safety for doctors and allow them to oversee several procedures at once, increasing the benefit of their training and experience.[14]

Vision Systems. Some AI systems gather their own sensory input through **vision systems.** These combinations of hardware and software permit computers to capture, store, and manipulate visual images. The U.S. Justice Department implemented vision systems that perform fingerprint analysis almost as precisely as human experts. This system's lightning-speed searches through the agency's huge database of fingerprint images have quickly resolved long-standing mysteries.

Vision systems can work in conjunction with robots to give these machines a kind of sight. Generally, robots with vision systems can recognize black and white and some shades of gray, but they still lack the ability to distinguish colors or evaluate three-dimensional images. Other systems concentrate on only a few key features in an image, ignoring the rest. The most advanced robots and computer systems cannot approach human capabilities to scan full-color images and draw conclusions from what they see.

Natural Language Processing. Recall from Chapter 3 that natural language processing allows the computer to interpret and react to commands and other statements phrased in English or another language. AI systems employ natural language processing to speed up data entry and free people from the limits of more restrictive input methods. The user speaks into a microphone, and the computer converts the electrical impulses generated by the voice input into text files or program commands.

This conversion requires some difficult interpretation. For example, an effective natural language processor must recognize the difference between homonyms (words that sound alike but have different meanings) such as *one* and *won*. To make this judgment, the AI program must evaluate context by comparing a questionable word with other words surrounding it and choosing the spelling that makes the most sense. Eventually, new processing techniques should minimize such drawbacks, making natural language processing an important tool for computer users with physical disabilities and others who prefer to interact verbally with their systems. (See the "Who's Who" box to read about someone who has been working in the area of natural language processing.)

WHO'S WHO

Katherine Hammer/Evolutionary Technologies International

"I am not very good with bosses," admits Katherine Hammer, cofounder of Evolutionary Technologies International, a fast-growing firm that helps large corporations translate databases. She doesn't need to be; she *is* the boss. But she didn't start out at the top; in fact, she didn't start out in computers at all. Hammer was a linguistics professor at Washington State University when, because of a change in her personal life, she decided to pull up stakes and enroll in the University of Texas computer science program.

Hammer quickly realized that rules used to represent linguistic phenomena could be applied to the representation of computer applications, especially the type of formalism used by Noam Chomsky, the linguist who theorized that there is, in fact, a universal grammar. So she put that knowledge to work, through stints at several high-tech firms, including Texas Instruments and Microelectronics & Computer Technology Corp. Impatient by nature, Hammer chafed at corporate constraints and what she perceived as lost opportunities. One day, Hammer and a coworker at MCC, Tina Timmerman, decided to try to write software to automate the transfer of data from one format to another. Ultimately, they wanted users to be able to communicate with their software in plain English. In two years, they had a prototype, and a third interested party: Robin Curle, a new director of strategic marketing at MCC. As she listened to Hammer describe her project, Curle thought, "This is the alchemist's stone."

So Evolutionary Technologies International (ETI) was born. After struggles with bankers and investors, as well as technical challenges, the ETI•EXTRACT Tool Suite came to market, and it is a step toward the ultimate goal. While ETI•EXTRACT does not address the problem of translating a program written in one computer language to a program written in another, it can translate the user's data conversion specification, entered with point-and-click commands and menu-driven interfaces that create English sentences into the one or more programs in one or more programming languages required to carry out the desired conversion. For many businesses, it is a dream come true. In fact, IBM has chosen ETI•EXTRACT for all of its internal data integration projects. Prudential Insurance is using it to transform and move just under 10,000 data elements.

For Hammer and her colleagues, this is just the beginning, even though the company is already bringing in over $17 million a year in revenues. ETI•EXTRACT does have competitors—Prism Solutions and Carleton Corp. But competition doesn't seem to faze Hammer. "Maybe when I finish with this job I'll write a survival guide," Hammer muses. "A survival guide would explain how to position yourself so you are not caught by surprise." With a name like Hammer, survival seems to be inevitable.

Source: Suzanne Oliver, "How Katherine Hammer Reinvented Herself," *Forbes*, August 12, 1996, pp. 98–104. ETI's home page can be accessed at http://www.evtech.com. Photo courtesy of Evolutionary Technologies International.

---

learning system

a system that includes software to track the results of the computer system's actions and then varies system functions in similar situations based on this feedback

Learning Systems. An important artificial intelligence capability comes from **learning systems.** These systems include software that tracks the results of the computer system's actions and then varies system functions in similar situations based on this feedback. For a basic example, a number of computer games record wins and losses and then repeat the moves from winning games under the same conditions while avoiding the moves from losing games.

A learning system must collect feedback at least about whether it encounters desirable results (winning a game) or undesirable ones (losing a game). True artificial intelligence would require more detailed information about the good or bad consequences that have resulted from many combinations of situations and system actions. In any learning system, the software alters its future actions to maximize its chances of desirable outcomes.

neural network

a system that simulates the functions of the human brain

Neural Networks. AI systems extend learning ability through **neural networks,** or systems that simulate the functions of the human brain. Neural computing software uses simulations that mimic the human brain's interconnected structure of neurons, so it can process many pieces of data at once. As it does so, it can learn to recognize patterns and eventually solve related problems on its own. Neural computing works by:

- Retrieving information
- Quickly modifying stored data in response to new input
- Discovering relationships and trends in large databases
- Solving complex problems despite the absence of some relevant information

In particular, neural networks excel at pattern recognition. Banks use them to read bar codes on checks despite smears or poor-quality printing. Stock analysts have created neural networks to recognize patterns in market prices. If the network's evaluation of transaction data reveals a pattern associated with a rising market, it issues a recommendation to buy stocks. If it finds a pattern associated with falling prices, it recommends selling.

IBM has developed a neural network program to detect and eliminate computer viruses. The neural network learns like a human does, from experience. If you tell a child that an elephant is "big" and that a dog is "small" and repeat the process for other things, the child will learn the meaning of "big" and "small" and will be able to conclude that a real truck is big and that a toy car is small. IBM's neural network program can also learn. It can detect new viruses that are similar to or have common characteristics with existing viruses. Every time a new virus type or strain is detected, the program learns. Traditional virus programs can't learn, and thus they must be frequently updated to detect new viruses. According to an employee of US Trust who uses IBM's neural network software, "We had a severe virus problem until 1992. Machines would lock up. Now that we have a good software shield in place, we have less than one machine infected [per incident]."[15]

New technologies are also being developed to use neural networks, database visualization, and other technologies to pull data from large data warehouses to detect credit card fraud, track purchasing trends, and identify other complex patterns. The system will be able to generate three-dimensional graphs of these patterns.[16]

fuzzy logic

a set of rules and techniques that is used in artificial intelligence to represent imprecise, uncertain, or unreliable knowledge

Fuzzy Logic. One of the more recent applications of artificial intelligence involves **fuzzy logic.** Fuzzy logic is a set of rules and techniques that is used in artificial intelligence to represent imprecise, uncertain, or unreliable knowledge. Instead of the usual black and white, yes/no, or true/false conditions of typical computer decisions, fuzzy logic allows for shades of gray, or what are known as "fuzzy sets." The criteria on whether a subject or situation fits into a set are given in percentages or probabilities. For example, a weather forecaster might state that "if it is very hot with high humidity, the likelihood of rain is 75 percent." The imprecise terms of "very hot" and "high humidity" are what fuzzy logic must determine to formulate the chance for rain. Fuzzy logic rules help computers evaluate the imperfect or imprecise conditions they encounter and make "educated guesses" based on the likelihood or probability of the correctness of the decision. This ability to estimate whether a condition fits a situation more closely resembles the judgment a person makes when evaluating situations.

Fuzzy logic is used in embedded computer technology—for example, autofocus cameras, medical equipment that monitors patients' vital signs and makes automatic corrections, and temperature sensors attached to furnace controls.

EYE ON THE WEB

IS personnel can now develop business information systems for use beyond their own organizations. Users may, for example, be located across the city, across the state, or across the nation. Typically, when a new system is installed in an organization, or when an existing system is dramatically modified, training sessions and/or materials are provided to appropriate users. When users include those outside the organization, MIS professionals need to ensure that the system is easy to access, easy to use, and reliable. This is just one of the challenges that face systems developers in the present; these challenges are apt to increase in the future.

As the popularity of the Internet grows, and more and more users discover the wealth of information to be obtained from browsing the Web, more and more organizations will respond to the Web as an opportunity for communicating with their customers, or possibly as a means to attract new customers. As the interactive capabilities of the medium develop, seamless transactions will become a necessity.

On a professional level, the Web presents MIS personnel with the ability to develop networks with other professionals, as well as to monitor more easily some of the events transpiring in the business environment. But developers face new challenges. When designing a transaction processing system, developers will want to ensure that the system adequately conveys the product, the service, or the organization to the customer and expresses exactly the information that is needed for a customer to complete a transaction. Additional security and encryption measures are needed to protect customer information such as credit card transactions.

Systems development efforts do not grind to a halt once the system is installed. Instead, the process is ongoing and extends well beyond installation to include feedback or monitoring and maintenance and modification. Thus, systems developers may wish to incorporate tracking mechanisms within a system to allow an organization to maintain a daily count of "hits" (the number of users who access a Web page). Effective Web page design may enable the firm to broaden its target market for a particular product or service.

Internet systems will undoubtedly lead to more cooperation and partnerships between MIS staff and staff from other functional areas, such as marketing, finance, and accounting.

To take advantage of Web opportunities, companies will need to develop technical network expertise within their MIS staff. For example, the WWW represents an attractive alternative to advertising; perhaps when a new product is under development, budget allocations will be set aside to include funding to launch the product through creation of a new Web page.

In short, the Web presents a means for computers and information systems to step far beyond the common boundaries of processing activities. Rather, systems can be conceived of as a communication method, as a proactive means of identifying customers, as well as a means of helping customers to identify companies offering products and services that match their particular needs and interests.

WEB EXERCISES

1. Locate information on a new automobile in a magazine and on a Web page. How do the two advertisements compare? Does the Web page offer a photograph of the car in addition to text information?
2. Suppose that you are a systems developer in an organization. You have designed a Web page that allows users to input their name and address. What value would such information have for your organization?

SYSTEMS DEVELOPMENT

systems development

a process of defining information needs, designing a system that satisfies users, and effectively implementing that design

Every business requires a unique combination of information system resources for transactions processing, management reporting, decision support, and perhaps artificial intelligence. IS professionals work together with users throughout an organization to complete the **systems development** process by defining information needs, designing a system that satisfies them, and effectively implementing that design. Systems development also includes formal procedures for revising the information system design as necessary to meet users' changing needs. Today, systems development reaches outside an organization's boundaries, as the "Eye on the Web" box illustrates.

Users play critical roles in the systems development process. Managers and employees interact directly with their firms' business information systems. As a result, users of all types participate in development activities; in some cases, they lead the process to ensure that the result meets their information needs.

Different companies and systems require varying development efforts. A retail store manager might ask for opinions from employees before purchasing an inexpensive computer program. On the other hand, a major corporation might form a team with representatives from all departments and regions to design and install a $50 million network of hardware, software, communications systems, databases, and new IS personnel. However, a formal systems development project of any size usually completes a relatively standard set of basic activities known as the *systems development life cycle*.

Systems Development Life Cycle

systems development life cycle (SDLC)

the five stages of developing information system needs: investigation, analysis, design, implementation, and maintenance and review

The store manager might not follow a recognizable procedure for choosing a software package. On the other hand, a large company with complex information needs might define an elaborate, formal process for systems development with extensive printed manuals to document required activities. Despite variation in the specific steps, most decision situations display the five common phases of the **systems development life cycle (SDLC):** investigation, analysis, design, implementation, and maintenance and review. (See Figure 7.7.)

FIGURE 7.7

Phases in the Systems Development Life Cycle
As each set of activities reveals new information, the process may have to reconsider the results of previous phases.

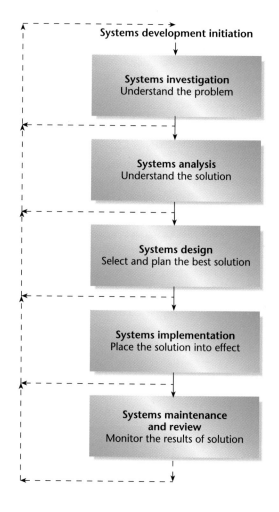

Systems development initiation

Systems investigation
Understand the problem

Systems analysis
Understand the solution

Systems design
Select and plan the best solution

Systems implementation
Place the solution into effect

Systems maintenance and review
Monitor the results of solution

A formal project sets a timeline and deadlines for each phase through final installation and adjustment of the completed system. Maintenance and review activities carry out continuing reevaluation and alteration of IS resources. Periodically, the organization may initiate a new SDLC project to accommodate significant improvement beyond the scope of maintenance, systemwide upgrades to implement a new generation of technology, or a major shift in the company's IS needs.

The words *life cycle* emphasize the ongoing process of completing and reconsidering each decision-making phase. As shown in Figure 7.7, the SDLC activities proceed in sequence, but the results of one phase may affect decisions made in a previous phase. The project may then have to return and correct errors or make adjustments. Thus, the SDLC creates a cycle of activities that continuously rebuild and refine a firm's information system.

Systems Investigation. Creation or modification of a business information system usually begins with **systems investigation.** The SDLC team identifies operating problems and opportunities that affect the information system and then evaluates their causes and scope in light of the company's goals. Sometimes this step begins from scratch, as when a dynamic business environment creates a new problem or opportunity for which the firm has no existing system. More often, the firm already has some system in place. Systems investigation then determines whether the existing system satisfies the goals of the organization.

In either case, systems investigation attempts to answer two questions:

* What problem would the new or modified information system solve?
* Is that problem worth the cost of the solution?

The primary result of this phase is a statement detailing an information system project. This statement should specify the amount of organizational resources committed to the project and outline clear guidelines for systems analysis.

Systems Analysis. The second phase of the SDLC, **systems analysis,** seeks to develop a general understanding of an IS solution that would respond effectively to the problem or opportunity identified during systems investigation. The team carefully studies existing systems (if any) that solve the problem and considers alternative solutions. Analysis continues with an exploration of the feasibility and implications of these solutions. In short, systems analysis attempts to answer the question "What must the information system do to solve the problem?" The primary outcome from systems analysis is a listing of requirements and priorities that guide systems design.

Systems Design. The **systems design** phase focuses on selecting resources and planning a system that fulfills the previously defined requirements for the problem solution. A primary objective of systems design is to modify an existing information system or to create a new one. Typically, the SDLC team creates various *logical design models* of the proposed system's functions that designate activities that it will perform and outputs that it will generate. These logical design models help to verify that the system will in fact produce outputs that meet the company's requirements. After verifying the logical design models, the team begins work on *physical design models*—detailed diagrams and specifications that describe the physical characteristics of the system and its operating environment.

---

systems investigation

the first stage of the SDLC, which involves identifying operating problems and opportunities that affect the information system and evaluating their causes and scope

systems analysis

the second stage of the SDLC, which involves developing a general understanding of an IS solution that would respond effectively to the problem or opportunity identified during systems investigation

systems design

the third stage of the SDLC, which involves selecting resources and planning a system that fulfills the previously defined requirements for the problem solution

Systems design seeks to answer the question "How will the information system complete the activities required for the problem solution?" The primary output of systems design is a set of technical specifications for:

1. System outputs, inputs, and user interfaces
2. Hardware, software, database files, telecommunications, personnel, and procedural components
3. Relationships among these components

systems implementation

the fourth stage of the SDLC, which involves creating or acquiring the components specified in systems design, assembling them, and beginning to operate the new or modified system

Systems Implementation. The **systems implementation** phase of the SDLC involves creating or acquiring the components specified in systems design, assembling them, and beginning to operate the new or modified system. Activities during this phase include:

1. Preparing the site
2. Acquiring and installing hardware
3. Acquiring or programming and installing software
4. Hiring and training personnel
5. Inputting initial data
6. Testing
7. Start-up and initial operations

The primary output of systems implementation is a fully installed, operational information system that realizes the previously defined problem solution.

systems maintenance and review

the fifth stage of the SDLC, which involves reviewing, updating, and modifying the system after implementation to ensure that it continues to perform as designed

Systems Maintenance and Review. The ongoing SDLC activity of **systems maintenance and review** reviews, updates, and modifies the system after implementation to ensure that it continues to perform as designed. Maintenance routinely changes even a successful system simply to sustain its operations and keep it operating as efficiently, reliably, and effectively as possible. The word *review* implies that the company must periodically evaluate the system and any potential adaptations to meet new or evolving organizational goals and system requirements. If this review determines that existing arrangements no longer accomplish important goals, the systems development life cycle process may begin anew.

Computer-aided Software Engineering (CASE)

The success of a systems development project depends substantially on the effectiveness of its software. Applications programs perform the processing tasks identified during systems analysis that solve the problems defined in systems investigation. Small companies often have to rely only upon commercially available programs to perform needed processing, because most of them lack the resources to develop their own applications. Many large organizations also purchase (and perhaps customize) standard software packages, but specialized conditions sometimes justify investments in programming to create unique applications with exactly the right capabilities.

computer-aided software engineering (CASE)

automation of most of the detailed activities required for systems development

Various computerized tools support this process of software development, also called *software engineering*. These **computer-aided software engineering (CASE)** tools automate most of the detailed activities required for systems development. CASE tools can dramatically simplify and accelerate the process of developing transaction processing, management information, and decision support systems.

Some CASE packages focus on activities associated with the early stages of the systems development life cycle. Known as *upper-CASE* tools, these packages automate the rather predictable, standardized requirements for systems investigation, analysis, and design. *Lower-CASE* tools focus on the later implementation stage by generating structured programming code. Since a program requires unique programming steps to solve a particular problem, however, lower-CASE packages have not achieved the popularity of upper-CASE packages.

Some comprehensive packages include lower-CASE capabilities to generate program code from designs developed through upper-CASE tools. Some lower-CASE tools can also use object-oriented programming methods in the process of systems development.[17]

Prototyping

A different technique for systems development uses a phased approach. With this approach, each phase of the SDLC is repeated several times so that requirements and alternative solutions to the problem can be analyzed, solutions can be designed, and some portion of the system can be implemented and subject to a user review.

A prominent example of a phased approach for systems development is prototyping. **Prototyping** typically involves the creation of a preliminary model, a major subsystem, or a scaled-down version of the entire system. For example, a prototype might be developed to show sample report formats and input screens using a graphics program. Once developed and refined, the prototype reports and input screens developed in the graphics program are used as models for the actual system, which may be developed using a programming language such as COBOL, C++, or Visual Basic. In many cases, prototyping continues until the complete system is developed. The first preliminary model is refined to form the second- and third-generation models and so on until the complete system is developed.

prototyping
creating a preliminary model, a major subsystem, or a scaled-down version of an entire system

Object-oriented Systems Development

One of the newest approaches to systems development is object-oriented development. Much the way object-oriented programming reuses components in different combinations, **object-oriented systems development** uses interchangeable software components (objects) to model concepts, places, and behavior in the real world. Designers can develop systems more quickly this way than by starting from scratch. Objects may be reused from previously designed systems that were developed in-house or from purchased products.

Object-oriented systems usually are developed in the phased approach because it is difficult to determine all systems needs from the outset. Also, developers can test and fine-tune the system once they have developed a workable model.

Whatever approach or combination of approaches that is used in systems development, the ultimate goal is a system that meets the organization's and its users' needs.

object-oriented systems development
using interchangeable software components (objects) to model concepts, places, and behavior in the real world

- A particular business's goals determine the transaction processing methods that suit the unique needs of its information system.

- A management information system provides critical contributions to an organization's fundamental goal of providing the right information to the right people in the right form at the right time.

- Formulas in the model base of a DSS support decision making by trying to predict the future based on an understanding of the causes that produced past results.

- Artificial intelligence systems combine hardware and software with elaborate databases and knowledge-based modeling to mimic human decision making. These systems "learn" essentially by trial and error.

- The systems development life cycle involves investigation, analysis, design, implementation, and maintenance and review.

SUMMARY

1. *Demonstrate the contribution of a transaction processing system to a company's overall information system.* An organization's transaction processing system (TPS) must carefully track exchanges during a company's routine operations. These data support essential bookkeeping functions as well as ongoing evaluations of profitability and other measures of business success. A batch processing system collects data about transactions as they occur and then inputs each set of data all together for periodic processing. In an on-line processing system, operating workers input data as they complete business transactions, and the information system then performs appropriate processing and updates database records without delay.

2. *Describe the reports that managers receive from a management information system.* A management information system provides many kinds of summary reports; all of them select, total, and categorize data collected by the transaction processing system and from external sources in ways that reflect the operating priorities of midlevel managers. Scheduled reports provide standard sets of data about activities during predetermined time intervals. Demand reports answer specific questions in response to management requests. Exception reports automatically highlight unusual circumstances or events that require management action.

3. *Explain how a decision support system contributes to management effectiveness.* A DSS helps to clarify nonroutine management decisions by projecting potential results based on certain assumptions. The dialog

manager recognizes and reacts to common business language to help managers interact with the DSS. The DSS generator controls interactions among the database, model base, and external resources based on the user's input through the dialog manager. Complete, accurate databases ensure that the output of a DSS truly reflects real-life conditions. A model base includes a variety of equations, formulas, and other processing tools that manipulate input data and produce output to support decision making. A group decision support system combines these components with a groupware application to encourage interaction and sharing of data among individuals for cooperative decision making. Intranets are an alternative to groupware; they use Internet technology to perform work group and meeting functions. An executive support system combines processing resources with data about economic conditions and complex planning models to help top managers develop and evaluate major new initiatives.

4. *Define the term* artificial intelligence *and give examples of its role in business operations.* An artificial intelligence system combines sophisticated hardware and software with elaborate databases and knowledge-based processing models to demonstrate characteristics of effective human decision making. AI systems employ powerful heuristics to allow relatively independent processing and operations by expert systems, robots, and vision systems. They create exciting possibilities for natural language processing, learning systems, and neural networks among other applications.

5. *List the steps in the systems development life cycle.* Systems development requires procedures for defining information needs, designing a system that satisfies them, and effectively implementing that design. The five-stage systems development life cycle is a formal, recurring process for creating and maintaining effective information systems. During the systems investigation phase, the development team identifies operating problems and then evaluates their causes. During systems analysis, the team formulates an IS solution that responds effectively to that problem by examining the strengths and weaknesses of an existing system, whether manual or computerized. During systems design, the team selects resources and plans a system that fulfills the requirements for the problem solution. A primary objective of systems design is to modify an existing information system or to create a new one. Systems implementation involves creating or acquiring those resources, assembling them, and beginning to operate the system. Systems maintenance and review updates and modifies the system after implementation to ensure that it continues to perform as designed. Based on the outcome of each phase, the process may have to return and reevaluate previous results.

Key Terms

batch processing 211

on-line transaction processing (OLTP) 211

summary report 213

scheduled report 216

key-indicator report 216

demand report 216

exception report 216

trigger point 216

DSS generator 219

group decision support system (GDSS) 222

group facilitator 222

groupware 223

intranets 224

executive support system (ESS) 224

artificial intelligence (AI) 226

heuristics 227

robotics 227

vision system 228

learning system 229

neural network 230

fuzzy logic 230

systems development 231

systems development life cycle (SDLC) 232

systems investigation 233

systems analysis 233

systems design 233

systems implementation 234

systems maintenance and review 234

computer-aided software engineering (CASE) 234

prototyping 235

object-oriented systems development 235

Concept Quiz

Answer each of the following questions briefly.

1. Name three common business transactions that a transaction processing system could expedite.
2. Name two types of transaction processing systems.
3. Where do most data in a management information system come from?
4. A management information system distributes its information primarily through what type of output?
5. Unlike a management information system, what type of problems does a decision support system address?

Fill in the blanks to complete the following statements.

6. The user interface of a decision support system is called a[n] _____ .

7. The model base of a decision support system includes _____ and _____ that manipulate input data and produce output.
8. Groupware allows team members to cooperate in producing _____ that integrate information from spreadsheet programs, database packages, and other applications.
9. A specialized DSS called a[n] _____ helps top managers develop and evaluate major new organizational initiatives.
10. _____ systems combine hardware, software, databases, and knowledge-based processing models to demonstrate characteristics of effective human decision making.

Mark "true" or "false" after each of the following statements.

11. Vision systems in AI can currently "see" in color. _____

12. AI systems extend their learning ability through neural networks, which are systems that simulate the functions of the human brain. _____

13. Most business organizations and systems require the same, standard development efforts by IS professionals. _____

14. Most decision situations display the five common phases of the systems development life cycle: investigation, analysis, design, implementation, and maintenance and review. _____

15. The primary output of systems implementation is a fully installed, operational information system that realizes the previously defined problem solution. _____

Discussion Questions

1. In addition to the common transactions listed in the chapter that transaction processing systems can help expedite, what other business transactions might benefit from the use of a TPS?

2. What should be the guiding principle for all IS efforts? Why is following this principle so important to an organization?

3. What types of information system reports might be useful to the publisher of a widely circulated daily newspaper?

4. In what ways might SABRE operators (chapter-opening photo) use decision support systems?

Team Activity

Divide the class into groups of three or four. Each team should choose one of the following fields:

◆ A travel agency that specializes in outdoor adventure
◆ A manufacturer of camping or climbing gear
◆ A chain of family-style buffet restaurants
◆ A company that sells music CDs on-line
◆ A manufacturer of casual businesswear

Each team should determine the ways its company could use a decision support system. Then it should list the categories of data that its DSS database would include, as well as the basic kinds of models that the DSS model base would include. Finally, it should determine what type of group decision support system would be most beneficial to the company. The team should report its findings either to the class or in writing.

Applying IT

1. How might a corporate intranet benefit a shipping company such as UPS or Federal Express? Write a brief proposal describing what types of information could be shared via the intranet and how the intranet could help the shipping company gain a competitive edge.

2. Does your college or workplace have an intranet? If so, access it and use it either to browse or to gain specific information about something that interests you. Report your findings to the class. If your school or workplace does not have an intranet, interview someone whose company or nonprofit organization does; find out how the intranet benefits the organization. (For instance, your public library might have an intranet; you could interview one of the librarians to learn about the system.) Or, go to the library and look up three articles on intranets. Write a two-page summary of your findings. Report your findings to the class.

CASE

The SET Agreement

Transactions are the basis of all business. Secure transactions may be the basis of all buyer–seller relations. Until recently, commerce on the Internet has been stymied by the lack of security of transactions—consumers have feared (perhaps rightly so) transmitting their credit card numbers through cyberspace. To complicate this situation, once systems for secure transactions became available, Visa and MasterCard chose separate, incompatible formats—setting the stage for an all-out war between the two credit card giants. (Combined, MasterCard and Visa serve about 700 million customers around the world.) Visa allied itself with Microsoft on a system called Secure Transaction Technology (STT). MasterCard chose to work with IBM and Netscape on a protocol called Secure Encryption Payment Protocol (SEPP). Merchants and banks would have to either choose sides between the two or support both systems, neither of which was attractive or beneficial to anyone—banks, credit card companies, merchants, or consumers.

So the two behemoths decided to join forces. They announced that they would both support a single standard for electronic commerce—Secure Electronic Transactions (SET). SET provides security via electronic "certificates" that validate the consumer's identity as well as the merchant's. In addition, SET provides important benefits to the businesses involved. First, it provides confidentiality for all payment and ordering information, through message encryption. Second, it ensures integrity for all transmitted data, making sure that no changes can be made by a third party. Third, it provides authentication (through the "certificates") that a credit card consumer is, in fact, a legitimate user of the account involved in the transaction. Fourth, it provides authentication (again, through the "certificates") that the merchant is part of the system. Fifth, it provides flexibility so that different types of software and network providers can enter into the system.

SET is not a panacea; there are bound to be glitches as general Internet commerce gets under way. In fact, one expert believes that the encryptions are so airtight and complex that they represent overkill. "I think the amount of cryptography used in SET is overkill," asserts Allan Schiffman of Terisa Systems. "It's better than what is used by the military for nuclear launch codes!" But with companies such as Visa, MasterCard, IBM, GTE, Netscape, Microsoft, and others cooperating to open up a huge new market, it's quite likely that electronic credit card transactions will become as commonplace as telephone or ATM transactions are today.

Questions

1. In what ways might electronic transactions benefit a small, start-up company that wants to break in to a specific market?

2. Do you think the new security protocol will stimulate consumer commerce on the Internet? Why or why not?

3. Have you ever tried purchasing an item via the Internet? Why or why not? Would you make such a purchase again? Why or why not? How does the development of SET make a difference in your perception of Internet commerce?

4. Look up MasterCard's and Visa's Web sites at http://www.mastercard.com and http://www.visa.com. Find out the latest on Internet transactions and discuss this with your classmates.

Source: Larry Loeb, "The Stage Is Set," *Internet World*, August 1996, pp. 55–59.

Answers to Concept Quiz

1. Any three of the following: selling products; sending bills to customers; receiving and depositing incoming payments; ordering materials and supplies; paying employees and suppliers; filing required reports with government agencies **2.** Batch processing and on-line transaction processing **3.** Internal sources

4. Predetermined reports **5.** Unstructured or semistructured business problems **6.** dialog manager **7.** equations; formulas **8.** compound documents **9.** executive support system (ESS) **10.** Artificial intelligence (AI) **11.** False **12.** True **13.** False **14.** True **15.** True

CHAPTER 8

Security, Privacy, Environmental, and Ethical Issues

CHAPTER OUTLINE

Computer Waste and Mistakes
    Computer Waste
    Computer Mistakes
    Preventing Computer Waste and Mistakes
Computer Crime
    Computer Systems as Tools for Crime
    Computer Systems as Objects of Crime
    Preventing Computer-related Crime
Privacy
    Impact of Privacy Invasion
    Legal Protections for Privacy Rights
    Business Policies about Privacy Rights
    Privacy and Fair Information Use: General Standards
Work Environment
    Work Force Composition
    Health Concerns
    Avoiding Health Problems
    Effects on the Natural Environment
Ethical Issues in Information Systems
    Four Ethical Issues in Information Systems
    Professional Associations and Ethical Codes of Conduct

It is unlikely that New England Patriots quarterback Drew Bledsoe is a welfare recipient. But that didn't prevent two welfare fraud investigators in Massachusetts from tapping into a state computer system and accessing confidential information on Bledsoe and two other sports figures. Protecting personal privacy in the electronic age has many people concerned. Rumors that confidential financial records are available to any subscriber of the Lexis-Nexis P-trak personal database caused a flurry of phone calls to Lexis-Nexis from worried citizens demanding that their names be removed from the records. The increased awareness of computer security issues has businesses and individuals working to protect their private information from unauthorized access. (Source: <u>The Boston Globe</u>, September 18 and September 19, 1996. Photo: AP/Wide World Photos.)

LEARNING OBJECTIVES

After completing Chapter 8, you will be able to:

1. Describe some typical examples of waste and mistakes in an IS environment, their causes, and possible solutions.
2. Explain the types and effects of computer crime, along with measures for prevention.
3. Discuss the principles and limits of an individual's right to privacy.
4. List the important effects of computers on the work environment.
5. Outline the criteria for ethical use of information systems.

Earlier chapters have detailed the amazing benefits of computer-based information systems in business, including increased profits, superior goods and services, and higher quality of work life. Computers have become such valuable tools that today's businesspeople would have difficulty imagining work without them.

Yet the information age has also brought some potential problems for workers, companies, and society in general:

- Criminals have used computers as powerful tools for mischief.
- Information systems designed to encourage data access may also allow invasions of privacy.

- Computer users may encounter health threats like repetitive-motion injuries and other problems in the work environment.
- Ethical questions cloud many daily choices of computer users.

No business organization, and no business information system, operates in isolation. All are part of society in general and so must observe important social and individual demands for responsible actions. In particular, all managers and workers must follow laws. But obeying laws is not enough—responsible computer users must respect ethical principles and other requirements imposed from outside their organizations. Long-term success depends upon building relationships and trust. Every manager and computer user must carefully consider the potential consequences, both intended and unintended, of IS arrangements and practices.

People who use computers in business need proper education to ensure they are productive and avoid waste. The discussion in this chapter enriches the basic principles of computer use explained earlier in the book by reconsidering some systems design and control issues. It also introduces some topics for future study and reflection to help you anticipate how your choices might affect performance in future information systems.

COMPUTER WASTE AND MISTAKES

computer waste

waste that results from inappropriate uses of computer technology and resources

computer mistakes

human errors, system failures, and other incorrect user actions that reduce the usefulness of IS output or even generate destructive output

Computer waste and mistakes impose high costs for an information system and drag down profits. **Computer waste** results from inappropriate uses of computer technology and resources. **Computer mistakes** are human errors, system failures, and other incorrect user actions that reduce the usefulness of IS output or even generate destructive output. This section explores the potential damage caused by computer waste and mistakes.

Computer Waste

The U.S. government is the largest single user of information systems in the world. Yet it often operates inefficiently by not effectively sharing resources and duplicating efforts, as different agencies collect and store the same data. For example, one newspaper account reported that the U.S. government mails entitlement payments (such as Social Security checks) worth about $5 million every month to recipients who are no longer living.[1] In a similar instance, Florida Health and Rehabilitative Services paid about $173 million to people who should have been removed from Medicaid rolls.[2] More efficient procedures for updating recipient databases would have saved these agencies vast amounts of money, not to mention time.

Critics claim that better systems analysis and design could eliminate much of this waste. By integrating systems to serve multiple agencies and information needs, costs would diminish as performance would improve. These critics claim that federal agencies instead favor bureaucratic, compartmentalized organization structures that prevent a wider perspective on IS needs. Therefore, the government fails to consider all relevant information requirements before designing and implementing new computer systems, leading to unnecessary and wasteful use of resources. Critics also point to inadequate training of IS personnel as a cause of poor overall performance.

Of course, the government is not the only wasteful computer user. Private companies waste and misuse IS resources, as well. Some companies discard old diskettes or other storage media that they could easily reuse. Information from one department may not reach critical decision makers. When firms upgrade their systems, they may scrap complete computer systems that could still perform some processing tasks. Even the new computers could cause waste if the company builds and maintains an overly complex system that requires massive amounts of staff training to operate and maintain.

In a less dramatic example of waste, company employees may spend work time and tie up computer resources playing games, sending unimportant e-mail, and accessing the Internet. A company must guard against paying people to amuse themselves in these ways, especially when increased competition can narrow profits. In addition, as workers use networked computers for these wasteful purposes, they boost traffic volume over communications media. This demand on system resources can interfere with legitimate work and reduce performance across the network.

There are many causes of waste in an information system, including poor analysis of IS needs, insufficient or ineffective user training, and inattentive supervision of processing jobs. A single cause summarizes most of these failures: improper management of IS practices and resources.

Computer Mistakes

Despite many people's distrust, computers themselves rarely make mistakes. They almost always correctly complete the processing steps that software instructions and user input indicate. But even the most sophisticated hardware cannot produce meaningful outputs if users and programmers do not follow proper practices. Thorough analysis of almost all system errors implicates programmers, users, or other people as the cause.

Some mistakes result from inappropriate instructions specified by programmers. In others, users enter erroneous data or give the wrong commands. The speed of computer processing magnifies mistakes like these, because processing routines often spread the incorrect output throughout many interconnected databases and other resources. As information technology becomes faster and systems become more complex, organizations and individuals face greater risk of suffering damage due to computer-related mistakes. News accounts have reported many frightening cases:

- A glitch in the Social Security Administration computer system incorrectly deprived about 500,000 retirees of an average of about $1,000 each in benefits. The victims suffered a total loss of approximately $500 million.[3]
- For three years, a computer system did not call residents of Hartford, Connecticut, for federal jury duty because its records listed all of them as dead.[4]

- A futures trader entered a buy order instead of the intended sell order while executing a securities transaction. The mistake cost the trader's customer (the Chilean government) more than $200 million.[5]
- Inaccurate databases at grocery and retail stores cause point-of-sale terminals to overcharge customers as much as $2.5 billion each year.[6] Shelf tags often list prices lower than those stored in the database that supplies information at the checkout stand.

Types of Mistakes. The variations of mistakes seem many, but the actual types of errors that can occur are relatively few. The major types of errors that have caused millions of dollars to be wasted include those shown in Table 8.1.

Besides simple errors in processing routines and data input, mishandling of IS output can cause problems. An information system must deliver reports and other outputs to decision makers who need them. If it fails to do so, the defect can cause ineffective decisions. Also, failure to control access to IS output might allow competitors and other outsiders to view private information.

Poor systems design causes many kinds of computer system mistakes. If a development team misjudges the number of messages that a communications line must carry, the inadequate capacity can cause delays and breakdowns throughout the system. If they fail to recognize one user's need for access to a particular database, then the system will fail to carry out that person's processing jobs.

Planners must also anticipate common malfunctions in computer systems and take steps to prevent them. All equipment eventually requires repairs, but preventive maintenance often helps to keep hardware functioning as expected. Some systems break down if environmental conditions vary too much—dust, static electricity, high operating temperatures, and humidity can all cause equipment failures.

Rigorous backup procedures can help an information system to recover from many kinds of mistakes, provided that IS personnel protect backup files from damage. Once backups are made, it is critical to store the copies off-site in a safe and secure place. Otherwise, a single fire could destroy both the original files and the backups.

Individuals can also make serious mistakes with their own personal computers. These errors usually have more limited consequences than mistakes in larger systems, because personal computer systems usually do not serve widespread information needs. For the individuals involved, however, even such limited mistakes can have devastating effects. Table 8.2 lists some common mistakes that all PC users should understand and guard against.

TABLE 8.1

Categories of Computer-related Mistakes
Data entry errors
Programming errors that prevent software from generating intended output
Mishandling of computer output
Inadequate systems design
Inadequate planning for and control of equipment malfunctions
Inadequate planning for and control of environmental difficulties (electrical problems, humidity problems, etc.)

Preventing Computer Waste and Mistakes

Any organization that uses computers should implement procedures to prevent common types of waste and mistakes. Efficient and effective information systems require conscious efforts by all employees and managers to avoid or minimize these disruptions.

Basic Precautions. Software packages often include measures to guard against data input errors. For example, a spreadsheet or database application may allow you to specify limits for data input to a particular cell or field. If input falls outside that range, the program displays an error message and instructs you to repeat data entry.

Programmers follow many procedures designed to limit errors. They carefully document processing steps in descriptions and flowcharts. They test preliminary versions of their programs with sample input data and then evaluate the resulting output to ensure that it matches expectations. Programmers often implement new software in limited parts of larger systems, so they can correct any errors before trouble spreads throughout relevant databases and other resources. Some problems may become apparent only after full implementation, however, so programmers expect to spend time fixing and improving existing software. (Applications require maintenance just as hardware does.)

Similarly, systems analysis and design practices fully document sources of input and requirements for output to ensure appropriate and effective data handling. A systems development team usually includes members who will use the output of the new information system. These people must clearly state their needs and make sure that systems designers fully satisfy them.

Systems development projects should also provide for thorough testing of new IS components and connections during systems implementation. This precaution can often catch and correct errors before they cause widespread problems. The project schedule and budget must allow for this activity, however.

TABLE 8.2

Common Mistakes on Personal Computers

- *Making data entry errors.* Someone using a personal finance program might misplace a decimal point while entering an interest rate for a loan. The resulting budget would then dramatically misstate the monthly payment on that loan.
- *Formatting a disk by mistake.* An operating system displays warnings on-screen to remind users that formatting a disk (called *initializing* in the Macintosh operating system) erases all files. Despite this protection, you might easily mistake an important data diskette for an old one and format it. If that diskette had stored the only copy of the document file for a term paper due in a few days, you would have to completely rewrite the paper.
- *Copying an old file over a new one.* In a hurry, you might also copy an older version of a document file over the current version. Operating system messages warn when a copy operation would replace an existing file with the same name, but you could easily become confused about which version is the current one. The old copy would then eliminate important data.
- *Deleting a file by mistake.* You probably delete files often during normal disk maintenance or to free up space on a crowded hard disk. In the process, you can easily delete important files. If you detect this mistake quickly, however, operating system commands or separate utility programs may be able to restore the deleted file. This works because the hard disk does not immediately erase a deleted file from the disk surface; instead, the operating system simply changes disk management records to allow the drive to store later files at that location. You can often recover the incorrectly deleted file if you act before the drive writes another file in its place.

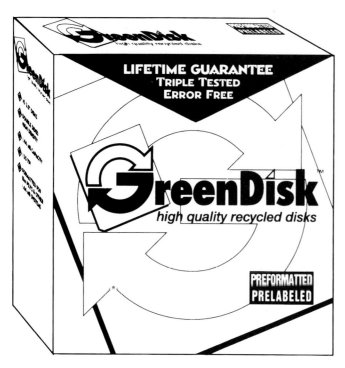

GreenDisk Company earns its revenue by selling recycled diskettes. (Source: Courtesy of GreenDisk, Inc.)

A flexible network can respond to equipment malfunctions by shifting processing jobs away from devices that need repairs or preventive maintenance. An IS facility with especially sensitive equipment must include measures to limit dust, suppress static electricity, and maintain temperature and humidity within acceptable ranges.

Resource Acquisitions. Efficient upgrading policies should guide disposal of unneeded computer equipment and supplies that still function. A company in the state of Washington, for example, earns its revenue by recycling used diskettes, software, and even packaging materials. Another computer salvage operation refurbishes old computer systems for use in developing countries. Some companies donate their used computer systems and devices to schools or charitable organizations, often gaining valuable tax deductions in the process. These thoughtful measures benefit the environment and society as well as the companies themselves.

Companywide policies should govern acquisition of new IS resources. Individuals and work groups continually request access to information systems to meet their legitimate processing needs. Still, some may want new equipment simply because it brings flashy capabilities, whether or not those functions support real information needs. Unnecessary purchases waste a company's resources.

Responsible managers have developed strict guidelines that allow purchases of new IS resources only for important needs that existing systems cannot meet. Any purchase request typically must include a formal statement justifying the investment. This written document must describe the intended uses of the new system and the expected benefits to the organization that would justify its cost.

User Practices. Efforts to prevent waste and mistakes must also extend to the routine activities of users. In particular, users often develop their own spreadsheets, databases, and other tools to meet their individual processing needs. Many organizations prefer to give users as much freedom as possible to develop their own systems. This policy encourages creativity, speeds processing, and targets IS resources at specific needs.

Unfortunately, many users lack the knowledge and skills they need to develop and implement these tools. Poor designs can waste processing capabilities and yield confusing or even incorrect results. Also, disjointed processing activities often sacrifice important gains in efficiency, since integrated systems could share existing databases and other resources.

IS professionals can help create more consistent, effective processing tools, because they bring more skills and a broader, companywide perspective to these jobs. Still, users may resent giving up control to specialists. They may fear that the resulting processing systems will ignore or compromise their information needs so that no one gets the information he or she wants. In addition, IS professionals may not have taken the time to understand users' problems fully so that good solutions can be found. Organizations must balance these conflicting priorities to avoid stifling user creativity and demands while eliminating potential waste and mistakes from untested tools.

Several policies help to prevent problems by creating partnerships between IS staff and other employees:

- Training programs for individuals and work groups help to ensure that all processing functions implement standard methods and generate accurate data.
- Manuals and documents detail approved procedures.
- IS professionals may review and approve certain systems and processing tools before users implement them.
- Individuals may be required to submit documentation and descriptions of certain processing tools to a central office; this repository would store all cell formulas for spreadsheets and descriptions of all data elements and relationships in database systems.

Organizations set policies like these because managers realize that good IS practices can prevent waste and mistakes worth thousands or even millions of dollars. These improvements in IS effectiveness and efficiency directly affect overall company performance. Of course, the costs of control measures increase as IS tools and procedures become more complex. Managers must always balance the expected savings from reductions in computer waste and mistakes against the cost of achieving those gains.

Outside Causes of Waste. Waste in information systems can also come from outside the organization. Some outside marketers and advertisers have misused e-mail and fax resources by sending unwanted advertisements and messages. For example, companies continue to send unsolicited advertising over fax machines despite a ban on this practice in the Telephone Consumer Protection Act of 1991.[7] These faxed advertisements waste supplies and tie up phone lines, not to mention the individual user time it takes to read and discard unwanted transmissions.

To help stop this waste, a group of Texas businesses has filed a class action suit against the companies that send the ads. If the suit succeeds, other companies and individuals may file similar suits. IS professionals need to be aware of the potential misuse of resources. Legal protections combined with private security measures help companies prevent a particularly dangerous kind of waste: computer-based crime.

COMPUTER CRIME

Even good IS policies and careful management may fail to predict or prevent computer crime. A computer's ability to process millions of pieces of data in less than a second can help a thief to steal data worth thousands or millions of dollars as easily as it supports any other task. Computer criminals can steal large amounts of money without facing the dangers of pulling a gun to rob a bank or retail store. Instead, someone with the right equipment and know-how can commit many offenses without even leaving home. Computer crime often defies detection, and its nonviolent image has kept penalties low compared with those for other offenses.

Scarce statistics obscure the costs of computer crime. Many companies even hide such crimes, fearing that reporting their losses would damage customer confidence. Also, it is hard to place accurate values on assets like data files that criminals steal or destroy. Despite these limitations, estimates suggest that computer crime may cost U.S. businesses close to $5 billion each year.

Of course, computer crime is hardly new, but the nature of the crimes has significantly changed. In September 1991, the U.S. Department of Justice established a computer crime unit primarily to detect and arrest fraud artists and others who gained illegal access to information systems. Today, bolder, more creative criminals have sprung up. In the words of a criminology professor at Northern Illinois University, computer crimes "aren't simply the esoteric type they were 5 years ago." New crimes are *computer* crimes "only in the sense that a bank robbery with a getaway car is an 'automobile crime.'"[8]

Unfortunately, today's vast, interconnected information systems provide relatively easy access and escape for criminals. While law enforcement officials have hurried in pursuit, modern computer criminals have seemed to remain one step ahead of the police. But officials are learning new methods of detection, and tougher penalties await convicted violators.

The dual nature of computer crime has complicated enforcement efforts. Computer systems are both tools for people to commit crimes and the objects of those crimes.

Computer Systems as Tools for Crime

Just as a burglar can use dynamite to open a safe, a thief can use a computer to open valuable data files. The data may represent company secrets or money to be transferred illegally to another account. Just as the burglar can break into a residence or store through many doors or windows, a computer criminal can breach a system's security in many ways.

In general, a criminal must know how to do two things to commit most computer crimes: gain access to the computer system and manipulate the system to produce the desired result. Security measures often require users to enter identification numbers or passwords to gain access. To gain access, the criminal must either discover existing codes or learn how to generate new ones. Company employees and other authorized system users can meet these requirements more easily than outsiders can. Sometimes, the potential gains entice insiders to abuse their privileges as users.

In one instance, a U.S. Defense Department employee introduced fraudulent payment vouchers for items never delivered and walked off with $100,000. In another case, a warehouse employee manipulated an inventory control system to cover up thefts valued at more than $200,000. The spread of sophisticated desktop publishing software along with high-quality scanners and printers has accelerated crimes involving counterfeit money, bank checks, traveler's checks, and stock and bond certificates.[9]

The rapid growth of telecommunications technology has also brought new types of crime. Experts estimate that communications and telephone fraud cost consumers and companies from $2 billion to $4 billion each year.[10] One electronics company, for instance, received a bill for almost $17,000 in fraudulent long-distance calls. The same media and devices that improve communications among businesses and managers also create opportunities for criminals. Law enforcement officials are particularly concerned about the use of cellular phones in fraud and illegal trafficking schemes.

Computer Systems as Objects of Crime

A computer can also be the object of a crime, rather than a tool for committing the crime. In the most common case, employees and authorized users steal computer time and resources worth millions of dollars every year. Each time someone obtains access to a computer system without permission, steals or destroys data or equipment, or illegally copies software, a computer becomes the object of a crime. These crimes fall into several categories:

- Illegal access to and use of computer systems
- Destruction of data and programs by viruses and worms
- Theft of data, equipment, and software
- International computer crime

Illegal Access and Use. Crimes involving illegal access to and use of computer services concern both government agencies and businesses. Computers in federal, state, and local government offices sometimes sit unattended over weekends without proper security. Students and others often use university computers for commercial purposes under the pretense of research or other legitimate academic work. Criminals sometimes gain illegal access to systems from other computers.

hacker
a computer enthusiast who enjoys manipulating the capabilities of computer systems as a personal challenge

criminal hacker
a computer-savvy but ethically weak person who attempts to gain unauthorized or illegal access to other computer systems

A **hacker** is a computer enthusiast who enjoys manipulating the capabilities of computer systems as a personal challenge. A **criminal hacker** is a computer-savvy but ethically weak person who attempts to gain unauthorized or illegal access to other computer systems. Many criminal hackers commit their crimes in pursuit of fun and excitement—to beat the system—but their actions still violate the law.

Police agencies face a difficult challenge catching and convicting criminal hackers. Their methods of gaining access remain mysterious, even after security measures detect the invasions. For example, one criminal-hacking attack shut down the computers of an on-line service by deluging those systems with requests for connections. The assault blocked legitimate traffic at that network site, and system managers could not even trace the sources of the offending contacts.[11] (The "Eye on the Web" box discusses some changes in transaction security procedures to protect expanding commerce over the Internet.) Even if investigators can determine the method behind the crime, sometimes the criminals can elude capture. The FBI spent years tracking one hacker who allegedly intercepted almost 20,000 credit card numbers that had been sent over the Internet.[12]

Data Alteration and Destruction. Like computer hardware and software, data and information represent valuable assets. Some computer crimes involve intentional creation and distribution of destructive programs. These illegal acts amount to vandalism as serious as destruction of more tangible goods.

EYE ON THE WEB

When you've bought something with a credit card, you may have noticed that the cashier took a moment to compare the signature on the sales receipt with the signature on the back of the credit card. Such comparisons provide both consumers and merchants with a simple means of detecting and preventing fraudulent card usage. However, when electronic transactions become the norm, this simple comparison will no longer be available. While the Internet presents opportunities for customers and organizations, it poses security challenges as well.

Although many of those who browse the Web are legitimate, honest users, electronic information storage, access, and transactions raise issues of security and ethics. For example, a company may request verification information (such as billing address and the like) when a customer uses a credit card for a telephone purchase. As the Internet becomes accessible to more and more customers and organizations, both parties will require that protective measures be taken to ensure that information concerning purchases, as well as other personal or corporate information, be recorded accurately and reliably and be safeguarded against illegal access and usage. (In fact, when accessing certain transaction sites on the Web, users may notice the appearance of a cautionary warning, noting that information input in completing a transaction may not be totally private or secure.)

Internet information access has raised ethical issues in addition to security issues. For example, one well-known northeastern university recently attracted attention when it proposed limiting student access to pornographic materials housed on the Internet. The university believed that having its resources used for such access constituted misuse of university facilities. The students, however, countered that the university's actions violated their rights of information access. Restricting access in one area, however dubious the area, opened the door for possible future restrictions by the university, restrictions that the student body might consider as arbitrary, as restrictions resulting from disagreements, disputes, or differences in philosophic outlooks between the students and the university. The university sought to restrict use for what it considered legitimate purposes; the students viewed the incident as an infringement.

Corporations may face disputes that, although different in content, are no less intense. For example, the Internet is an uncontrolled resource. As such, it is not monitored by any agency or group. Anyone with access may use the information housed on the Internet; likewise, posting new information is an easy task. Hackers have these same privileges. While the information stored on the Web is a great resource, this information may be misleading or inaccurate.

In part, then, one issue facing organizations is to protect the reliability, accuracy, and (possibly) the confidentiality of transactions conducted electronically. These organizations will want to install safeguards to prevent illegal users from gaining unlawful access to proprietary information housed on organizational systems. Such information may harm a firm's competitive posture. On the other hand, these organizations have an obligation to their customers to use ethically the information that they gather from these transactions.

Any information resource may be used to advantage, or misused. Several business issues have arisen along with commercial use of the Web. Protecting the interests of the players—while promoting fun, entertainment, and legitimate commercial transactions—will likely remain high on the list of Internet priorities.

WEB EXERCISES

1. Why might the use of an encryption method (i.e., changing the information into a kind of code) be insufficient in guarding against fraud?
2. Begin the process of making an on-line purchase. When you indicate that you wish to make a purchase at the particular Web site, do you receive a cautionary warning that the information you enter might not be protected? How is the warning worded?

---

virus

a program that enters a computer system without the user's knowledge disguised within the program files of another application

worm

a program that replicates its own files until it destroys other programs or interrupts IS operations

Destructive programs called *viruses* and *worms* disrupt processing or cause errors when loaded into a computer system. A **virus** is a program that enters a computer system without the user's knowledge disguised within the program files of another application. Once viruses enter and infect target computer systems, they cause varying kinds of damage and destruction; some overwrite document files, destroying the data in them, while others display annoying screen messages or even damage hardware components (see Figure 8.1). A **worm** functions as an independent program, replicating its own program files until it destroys other programs or interrupts IS operations.

FIGURE 8.1

How a Virus Can Be Spread

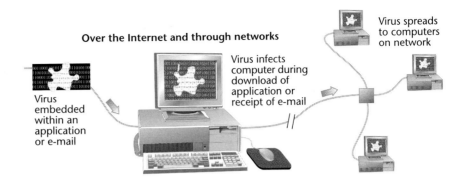

Over the Internet and through networks

Virus embedded within an application or e-mail

Virus infects computer during download of application or receipt of e-mail

Virus spreads to computers on network

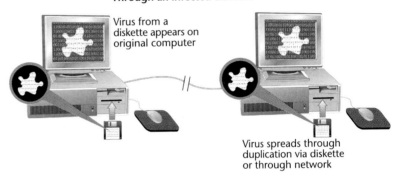

Through an infected diskette

Virus from a diskette appears on original computer

Virus spreads through duplication via diskette or through network

A virus or a worm can sometimes completely halt the operation of a computer system or an entire network for weeks or even longer. In perhaps the most famous attack, Robert Morris inserted a worm into the ARPAnet that infected more than 6,000 computers on that network. (ARPAnet—Advanced Research Projects Administration Network—was the ancestor to the Internet. It was a communications network started by the Department of Defense in 1969 to link the military with military research contractors, including many universities.) Networks usually suffer more severe damage than isolated systems, because links between systems allow the destruction to spread. In either case, the infected systems function poorly or not at all until someone finds the offending program, removes it, and corrects its effects.

Data Destruction: Protection against Damage. Fortunately, computer users can install and run **virus scanning software,** which detects and eliminates known viruses in a system. Cures may not always come in time, though. Spectre, a virus from China, can even destroy virus scanning software, making it very difficult to detect and eliminate. Even when scanning programs work perfectly, they can detect only the viruses known at the time of their creation; later viruses may slip past the scans and continue their destructive work. However, as discussed in Chapter 7, IBM has developed a neural network program that can learn to detect and eliminate viruses. This type of application shows great promise, allowing virus protection to evolve as new viruses are created.

Clearly, prevention provides the best chance of avoiding damage. Beginning with installation of scanning software, all systems and networks should implement some basic steps for virus prevention and detection:

virus scanning software

software that detects and eliminates known viruses in a system

1. *Install a virus scanner and run it often.* Many of these programs automatically check for viruses each time you boot up your computer or insert a diskette, and some even monitor all transmissions and copying operations. Effective shareware programs provide this protection at low cost, and some universities and colleges provide this software to students free of charge.
2. *Update the virus scanner often.* Old programs may fail to detect new viruses.
3. *Scan all diskettes before copying or running programs from them.* Hiding on diskettes, viruses often move between systems. If you carry document or program files on diskettes between computers at school or work and your home system, always scan them. Networks at school or work may very well harbor viruses.
4. *Install software only from a sealed package produced by a known software company.* Even software publishers can unknowingly distribute viruses on their program diskettes. Most scan their own systems, but viruses may still remain.
5. *Follow careful downloading practices.* If you download software from the Internet or a bulletin board, check your computer for viruses immediately after completing the transmission.
6. *If you detect a virus, take immediate action.* Early detection often allows you to remove a virus before it does any serious damage. After activating your scanning software to clean viruses from your hard disk and other components, scan your diskettes as well, since they may have picked up the virus (or perhaps introduced it in the first place). If you copy from an infected diskette, you may allow the virus back into your system.

Despite careful precautions, viruses can still cause problems. They can elude virus scanning software by lurking almost anywhere in a system.

application virus

a virus that infects executable program files for such applications as word processing programs and spreadsheet packages

Data Destruction: Types of Viruses. The two most common kinds of viruses are application viruses and system viruses. **Application viruses** infect executable program files for such applications as word processing programs and spreadsheet packages (in MS-DOS, file names with extensions .EXE and .COM). When the user launches the infected application, the virus begins to execute and establishes its own program files in the computer system. Virus scanning software can often detect these programs by checking the length or size of program files before installation. A file larger than the standard size for that program may be carrying a virus.

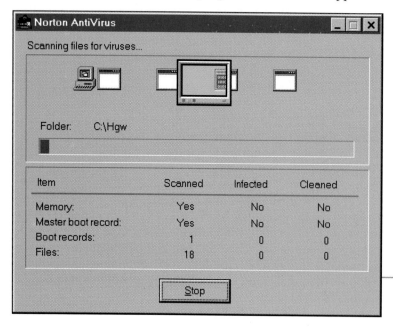

Virus scanning software can protect your computer from destructive computer viruses. (Source: Courtesy of Symantec Corporation.)

system virus

a virus that infects operating system programs or other system files, usually as soon as the user boots up the computer

logic bomb

an application or system virus designed to execute at a specified time and date and do explosive damage to the infected system

Trojan horse

apparently useful programs that actually mask destructive programs

document virus

a virus that attaches itself to a document file rather than a system file or an application's program file

A **system virus** typically infects operating system programs or other system files, usually as soon as the user boots up the computer. A **logic bomb** is an application or system virus designed to execute at a specified time and date and do explosive damage to the infected system. In one example, the well-publicized Michelangelo virus first appeared on March 6, 1992. This system virus activates every year on that date (the anniversary of Michelangelo's birth), overwriting infected hard disks without warning and erasing vast collections of data. Logic bombs are often disguised by **Trojan horses,** apparently useful programs that actually mask the destructive programs. These bombs may lie inert as nonfunctioning processing instructions until they detect certain codes. They then explode in destructive system actions, perhaps months or even years after being planted.

Another type of virus, called a **document virus,** attaches itself to a document file rather than a system file or an application's program file. A letter created using a word processing application or a graphic developed for a presentation could harbor such a virus. Some document viruses conceal themselves in macros or other hidden storage areas related to document files. WW6macro, for example, attaches itself to Microsoft Word for Windows documents.[13] Although document viruses can sometimes effectively hide in document files, special scanning programs can find and remove specific examples.

While some information systems never suffer viral attacks, the debilitating effects of these incidents justify rigorous prevention and detection measures. If the destructive program escapes detection and damages important document and program files, the system administrator must reinstall the files from backup copies. Without adequate backups, the data and programs may never become fully functional again. Table 8.3 lists some common computer viruses and their effects.

TABLE 8.3

Common Computer Viruses and Their Effects

VIRUS NAME	EFFECT ON COMPUTER
Cascade	Makes characters on-screen detach and fall into a heap at the bottom of the screen.
Dark Avenger	Adds 1,800 bytes to the length of files. When an infected program is run, there is a 1 in 16 chance the virus will trash a random disk sector.
Disk-killer	Instructs the screen to display the following warning: "Disk-killer—version 1.00 by Computer Ogre 04/01/1989. Warning! Don't turn off the power or remove the diskette while Disk-killer is Processing! PROCESSING." Encrypts all data on the hard drive; after it is finished, it says, "Now you can turn off the power. I wish you luck!"
Fro-Do	Stealth virus that activates on September 22. May attempt to place a Trojan horse on boot sector; if so, it displays "FRO-DO LIVES," surrounded by a moving pattern.
Green Caterpillar	Places a crawling green caterpillar on-screen.
Jerusalem	Activates on Friday the 13th and deletes programs run on that day.
Michelangelo	Activates March 6; formats the hard drive.
Monkey	Infects the boot program on the hard disk and DOS boot programs on diskettes. Moves master boot files to the third sector of hard drive and replaces them with its own code; the hard drive becomes inaccessible, and an error message appears: "invalid drive specification."
Ping-Pong	When activated, inserts a small bouncing ball on-screen. In most cases, no serious damage occurs.
Yankee Doodle	Increases file size by 1,961 bytes; searches for a noninfected file and upon finding one, infects it while playing "Yankee Doodle."

Theft of Computing Resources. Some criminals intend to steal valuable data rather than to destroy them. This category of violations overlaps with illegal access, since many system invaders intend to steal. While data theft by crooks outside an organization receives wide publicity, insiders more often commit this kind of crime, since they know how to locate and retrieve the right data. For example, two departing employees printed out all of the customer account information for one Connecticut firm and relayed it to a competitor. Soon after, the company installed a security system that limited access so employees could view only the information they needed for their jobs.[14] Small, high-density diskettes make theft of software and data even easier for disgruntled workers. An employee bent on revenge can carry gigabytes of software and data—perhaps the core assets of an information-oriented company—in a lunch bag or briefcase!

Theft of IS Resources: Equipment. Computers themselves have disappeared from inadequately secured offices. Equipment theft became a major problem as relatively portable PCs began to take over processing jobs from large mainframe installations. It became even easier as smaller computers like laptops gained popularity. Without adequate protection, a thief can easily walk away with an expensive, portable computer and the even more valuable data it stores.

In fact, there have been increasing reports of stolen notebook computers as businesspeople go through security checks at airports. Once the computer is out of the owner's hands, it can be picked up by thiefs who team up to lift the computer while blocking the owner, who is in line.

intellectual property
creative works of someone's imagination

software piracy
illegal duplication of program files

Theft of IS Resources: Software. Perhaps the most common thefts of computing resources result from violations of intellectual property rights. Copyright laws confer rights to own and control **intellectual property,** creative works of someone's imagination, to the creator of that property. Each time you use a word processing program or another software product, you benefit from someone else's intellectual property, just as you do when you read a book or watch a movie. People who would never think of plagiarizing another author's written work often copy and use software without paying for it. Such illegal duplication of program files is called **software piracy.**

Technically, software buyers pay for licenses to use the programs under certain conditions; they never really own the software. These conditions usually include restrictions on copying. A licensed user may generally make only one

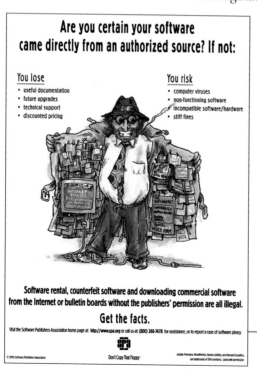

The Software Publishers Association is an organization that, among other activities, works to protect software copyrights. Its anti-piracy campaign includes an 800 toll-free hotline and Web site (WWW.spa.org). (Source: Courtesy of Software Publishers Association.)

backup copy of a package's program files to guard against loss of the originals. Federal law punishes any further copying by damages of up to $100,000 per violation.

The Software Publishers Association (SPA), an industry group, estimates that pirates illegally copy more than $13.1 billion worth of software every year. That translates to about one of every two applications being illegal. The SPA has initiated over 1,300 cases against violators since 1990. If software publishers could monitor this activity, their concern with public relations probably would restrain them from bringing lawsuits against individual customers.

Still, the slim chances of legal sanctions do not represent permission to violate the law. Further, many computer users encounter software piracy in the workplace, where chances for detection and punishment increase.

International Computer Crime. Computer crime becomes more complicated when it crosses international borders. Estimates on global software piracy indicate that pirated copies account for more than 90 percent of the software in use in Uruguay, Costa Rica, Greece, Spain, and some other countries.[15] Piracy is not limited to software, though: In May 1994, knife-wielding, masked criminals stole a shipment of microchips in Scotland worth nearly $4 million.[16] Companies sometimes produce their own versions of popular products and sell them across international borders to escape prosecution. One company made fake Apple computers with the name *Lemon*. A producer of Apple duplicates even had the audacity to file for bankruptcy protection in the United States! Instead of receiving protection from creditors, however, company officers faced charges of illegally using Apple software and systems.

U.S. government restrictions on international technology transfers affect otherwise legitimate sales of computers. Some companies try to escape these limitations by selling restricted technologies to legally acceptable countries with less stringent laws and then reselling them to restricted buyers. For instance, the U.S. Department of Commerce fined a U.S. computer manufacturer $1.5 million for letting a German subsidiary sell restricted information technology to other countries. In a more direct violation, a European country's intelligence agency stole computer chip designs from a U.S. company and passed them to a European manufacturer.[17] To avoid complex legal entanglements, many countries require buyers of computer equipment and software to register the products with appropriate authorities before bringing them across any borders.

Preventing Computer-related Crime

More than 45 American states have passed laws against computer crime, but some critics doubt their effectiveness for three reasons:

* Companies do not always actively pursue computer crime.
* Inadequate security leaves opportunities for criminals in all kinds of systems.
* Convicted criminals often escape serious punishment.

As computer use has increased in recent years, so has the emphasis on the prevention and detection of computer crime. All over the United States, private users, companies, employees, and public officials are working individually and jointly to curb illegal activities, and their efforts are achieving some success.

Law Enforcement Responses. State and federal government agencies have begun aggressive attacks on computer criminals, including criminal hackers of all ages. In 1986, Congress enacted the Computer Fraud and Abuse Act, which mandates punishment based on the victim's dollar loss. More legislation should follow in answer to recent concerns about the use of telecommunications and the Internet. Also, the Department of Defense has supported the Computer Emergency Response Team (CERT). This research center at Carnegie Mellon University responds to network security breaches and monitors systems for emerging threats. Recent court cases and police reports involving computer crime seem to have spurred lawmakers nationwide to introduce new, tougher computer crime legislation.

Successful enforcement initiatives include Operation Sundevil. In this federal effort to crack down on computer crime, the government successfully prosecuted a criminal who had gained unauthorized possession of 15 or more computer system access codes.[18] In another case, FBI agents raided the Davy Jones Locker Service, a computer bulletin board, for allegedly distributing illegally copied program files for 200 software packages.[19] The New York City School Construction Authority has set up a vast network to help investigators recognize and stop illegal use of taxpayer funds.[20] The system's networked PCs allow law enforcement officials to conduct complex searches of various databases to uncover racketeering, fraudulent schemes, and other crimes.

Company Responses. Businesses are also seriously fighting crime. Many businesses have implemented procedures and installed new protections for their data and systems. Specialized hardware and software allow encryption of stored and transmitted data to render data useless and eliminate the motivation for unauthorized access. Another security device, the Sentinel, plugs into the parallel port of a personal computer to prevent piracy and theft of software. Accompanying software checks for the presence of certain formulas supplied by the Sentinel before allowing an applications program to function. If the check finds the formula, the program runs as usual; if not, it immediately shuts down. One major software company uses the device to protect software sold overseas, where organized, large-scale piracy causes serious problems.[21]

In addition to specialized hardware and software, effective procedures can help to deter crime. In one simple precaution, a firm divides data processing tasks into separate activities and spreads them among a number of workers. Those people would then have to cooperate to commit any illegal act, so each one checks any tendencies toward dishonesty in others.

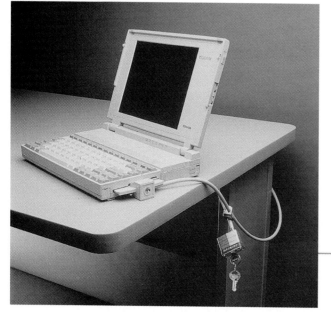

To fight computer crime, many companies use devices such as BookLock™ (shown here) which disables the disk drive and locks the computer to the desk. (Source: Courtesy of Secure-It, Inc.)

TABLE 8.4

Basic Methods of Computer Crime
The ingenuity of criminals guarantees limitless variations on some basic types of computer crime.

METHOD	EXAMPLE
Add, delete, or change inputs to a computer system	Delete records of absences from class in a student's school records
Modify or develop a computer program that carries out illegal acts	Change a bank's program for calculating interest to make it deposit rounded amounts in the criminal's account
Alter data in document files	Change a student's grade from C to A
Operate a computer in an illegal way	Access a restricted government computer system
Divert or misuse valid output from a computer system	Steal discarded printouts of customer records out of a company trash bin

Whatever the specific method, any information system needs some kind of active measures to prevent and detect crimes. The most effective security measures form part of an information system's initial design. Before beginning to design and implement controls, however, an organization must evaluate several things: the types of computer-related crime likely to occur within that system, the consequences of these crimes, and the cost and complexity of needed controls. Most organizations conclude that reductions in crime justify the additional cost and complexity of better system controls. Table 8.4 lists some general types of illegal activities along with examples that show how criminals might adapt them to specific systems.

PRIVACY

Not all invasive, unethical uses of data result from unauthorized access by criminals. Government agencies and business organizations operate many giant information systems primarily to collect and store data on private individuals. Data begin to accumulate when a baby is born. Databases grow as he or she receives immunization shots, takes certain high school exams, starts working, enrolls in a college course, applies for a driver's license, buys a car, serves in the military, gets married, buys insurance, gets a library card, applies for a charge card or loan, and buys a house. Even the simple, daily act of buying some product adds another fact to a database stored somewhere in a computer file.

Information systems often exchange these facts—and even more sensitive personal information—over easily accessed networks and without the knowledge or consent of the people profiled in the databases. Much of this activity serves innocent purposes of normal business transactions and government operations. Some of it, however, targets people for unwanted, annoying marketing appeals and perhaps more disturbing kinds of attention. If given the opportunity, many people might object to indiscriminate data collection for some purposes, and almost all would appreciate tight control over access to the data.

Impact of Privacy Invasion

Although most companies use data files for legitimate, justifiable purposes, opportunities for misuse abound. In one case, a computer-dating service sold a list of its female customers to another company, which published the information in a book entitled *Girls Who Want Dates*. These women endured embarrassment, and they faced the potential danger that someone would use the information to target crime victims. Another book, *E-mail Addresses of the Rich and Famous*, has led to on-line harassment of some celebrities. These examples show the potential for unforeseen and unwanted uses of easily available information freely given in the normal course of a person's life.

In practice, invasive uses of information create more nuisances than real threats to individual safety or privacy. Companies often exchange customer databases with information for junk mail and telemarketing campaigns. Junk e-mail and faxes now clutter people's lives, as well. This junk correspondence offers credit cards, subscriptions to magazines, memberships in book and record clubs, life insurance, even vacuum cleaners and discount clothing. People who do not want these products must continually fend off urgent appeals simply because their information appears in certain computer files.

Advances in telecommunications technology have fueled rapid growth of junk electronic mail and faxes, but technical progress has also provided some defensive weapons. Automatic call-back services and caller identification devices allow people to identify the sources of unwanted phone calls and stop them.

kill file

file of addresses from which users do not want to accept e-mail messages

Unix-based e-mail systems often allow users to create **kill files** of addresses from which they do not want to accept messages. Popular commercial services have also weighed options for protecting subscribers from wasting connect time, for which they must pay, to handle unwanted messages. Some critics compare this correspondence to junk mail that arrives postage due, and their complaints have led to new methods for dropping messages and even blocking them before delivery.[22] The mailers have responded with charges that these methods effectively censor information exchanges; they have even filed federal lawsuits seeking their own protection under the constitutional principle of freedom of speech.[23] (To read about someone who believes direct marketing on the Web is not junk, see "Who's Who: Chris Peterson/Times Direct Marketing.")

Legal Protections for Privacy Rights

Computer-based information systems pose an especially serious challenge to an individual's right to privacy. Organizations produce and use more data and information today than ever before. No one has yet provided a comprehensive answer to the difficult question "Who owns this information and knowledge?" If a public or private organization spends time and resources to gather data about you, does the organization own the data? Can it use the data in any way it desires?

Federal laws provide answers that limit the activities of government agencies to some extent. These laws provide important protections for citizens, because the federal government may collect more data than any other single organization. About 100 federal agencies store close to 4 billion records on individuals, including:

- Bureau of Alcohol, Tobacco, and Firearms
- Department of Defense
- Department of Housing and Urban Development
- Department of Education
- Department of Labor
- Department of Health and Human Services
- Federal Bureau of Investigation
- Federal Communications Commission

WHO'S WHO

Chris Peterson/Times Direct Marketing

Everyone has a different definition of "junk mail"; one person's junk is another person's mail. Chris Peterson, founder of Times Direct Marketing (http://www.tdmi.com), believes that direct marketing on the Web is not junk; in fact, he believes that it's the next major wave in marketing.

When Peterson first founded Times Direct, he managed to stay in business by maintaining accounts for a few dozen credit card companies. Then he learned that Union Bank of California wanted to hire someone to handle a new credit card sales campaign; he figured he was perfect for the job. He proposed using the envelope itself to describe the offer, instead of using written copy inside the envelope to coax the recipient into considering the offer. He got the job, and the sales campaign was a huge success.

Next, Peterson set his sights on Silicon Valley. After handling a few campaigns for companies there, the idea hit him: the Internet held the future of direct marketing. At first he thought he'd just supplement direct-mail campaigns by giving recipients of mass mailings the opportunity to access a Web site for free offerings. Phone and postage costs would plummet, he figured. But no one was interested. The Web was still uncharted territory—no one had launched a massive effort to use it for direct mail, and no one wanted to risk failure. "I was frustrated," Peterson recalls. He finally convinced NCD, a manufacturer of networking terminals, to give the idea a try. Peterson created a Web page as part of NCD's larger direct-mail campaign. He got a workstation as payment.

Twenty percent of people who responded to NCD's ad did so through the Web. Later, Peterson got the same result with a new campaign for Union Bank. In the meantime, advertisers had begun to purchase space on Web sites, but all they did was tout products as they did on television or in newspapers. Peterson wanted to use the Web as a direct-mail medium. He wanted to be able to write ads that said, "Click here for a free CD!" Still, he felt as though he was beating his head against a wall.

Finally, Peterson contacted Bay Networks, asking them to buy some banner ads promoting a free offer. If they did that, he said, he would create and manage the program free of charge. They accepted. Then he agreed to do a similar thing for Perkin Elmer, a pharmaceutical company. "When we have the statistics, we may be able to justify adding more money to the budget," says Debbie Perry, a marketing executive with Perkin Elmer. Peterson himself shrugs off the issue of money. "It's a chance to help build an entirely new medium," he explains. "How often does that happen?"

Eventually, Peterson may become a marketing hero. Or he may become a villain to users who don't want to receive marketing mail in their e-mail boxes. Either way, he's something of a cyber-revolutionary.

Source: Thomas Petzinger, "Chris Peterson Wants to Toss Out Junk Mail and Deliver the Web," *Wall Street Journal*, August 16, 1996, p. B1. Photo courtesy of Times Direct Marketing.

- Justice Department
- Securities and Exchange Commission
- Small Business Administration
- Social Security Administration
- State Department
- Treasury Department
- Veterans Administration

State and local governments also maintain their own records for property ownership, sales tax payments, auto license plates, and so on.

Privacy Act of 1974
the law that serves as a nationwide moral guideline for privacy rights and activities by private organizations that affect those rights

Federal Privacy Laws and Regulations. Federal laws provide significant protection for an individual's right to privacy as well as business privacy rights and standards for fair use of data and information. Congress enacted the most important of these laws, the **Privacy Act of 1974**, during Gerald Ford's presidency. Although the act applies only to certain federal agencies, it serves as a nationwide moral guideline for privacy rights and activities by private organizations that affect those rights. With text only about 15 pages long, the Privacy Act establishes straightforward and easily understandable requirements for all federal agencies except the CIA and law enforcement agencies (except as otherwise provided by law):

1. Individuals may determine what information about them appears in records an agency collects, maintains, uses, or disseminates.
2. If an agency creates records pertaining to individuals for specific purposes, those people can prevent the use or distribution of those records for other purposes without their consent.
3. Individuals may gain access to information about them in federal agency records, obtain copies of that information, and correct errors.
4. Agencies must collect, maintain, use, and disseminate all identifiable personal information only for necessary and lawful purposes. They must keep the information current and accurate for its intended use and provide adequate safeguards to prevent misuse.
5. Agencies may violate the requirements of the act only through an exemption justified by an important public need.
6. Individuals may bring civil suits for any damages they suffer as a result of willful or intentional violations of these rights.

Beyond these protections, the Privacy Act established a Privacy Study Commission to evaluate the functions of existing data banks and recommend legislation for consideration by Congress. It also requires training for any federal employee who interacts with a "system of records" as defined under the act. The Civil Service Commission and the Department of Defense conduct most of this training.

Various additional federal laws affect citizens' privacy rights (see Table 8.5). A 1992 law bans unsolicited advertisements over fax machines. In a 1995 ruling, the Ninth U.S. Circuit Court of Appeals upheld this law, concluding that it provides a reasonable way to prevent advertisers from shifting their costs to customers.

Not all new laws in this area seek to expand privacy rights. Each year, some legislative proposals include steps that would reduce privacy protection. For example, the FBI Counterintelligence Act of 1995 would allow easier access to credit reports. The Criminal Alien Deportation Act of 1995 would authorize wiretaps for immigration investigations. The 1995 Conference on Computers, Freedom, and Privacy, held in California, and other national meetings focus on privacy issues and future legislative proposals.

State Privacy Laws and Regulations. Some states have either enacted or proposed their own privacy laws. Many people advocate stronger state laws to reduce the control of the federal government. More comprehensive provisions cover uses of Social Security numbers, criminal files, and medical records. Additional restrictions limit disclosure of unlisted telephone numbers, credit reports, and information held by banks and other financial institutions. Furthermore, many of these laws extend their requirements to both public and private organizations.

Business Policies about Privacy Rights

Even though privacy laws impose few restrictions on private organizations, most of them treat privacy issues with extreme sensitivity and fairness. They

TABLE 8.5

Federal Privacy Laws and Their Provisions

LAW	PROVISIONS
Fair Credit Reporting Act of 1970 (FRCA)	Regulates operations of credit-reporting bureaus, including how they collect, store, and use credit information
Tax Reform Act of 1976	Restricts collection and use of certain information by the Internal Revenue Service
Electronic Funds Transfer Act of 1979	Outlines the responsibilities of companies that use electronic funds transfer systems, including consumer rights and liability for bank debit cards
Right to Financial Privacy Act of 1978	Restricts government access to certain records held by financial institutions
Freedom of Information Act of 1970	Guarantees access for individuals to personal data collected about them and about government activities in federal agency files
Education Privacy Act	Restricts collection and use of data by federally funded educational institutions, including specifications for the type of data collected, access by parents and students to the data, and limitations on disclosure
Computer Matching and Privacy Act of 1988	Regulates cross-references between federal agencies' computer files (e.g., to verify eligibility for federal programs)
Video Privacy Act of 1988	Prevents retail stores from disclosing video rental records without a court order
Telephone Consumer Protection Act of 1991	Limits telemarketers' practices
Cable Act of 1992	Regulates companies and organizations that provide wireless communications services, including cellular phones
Computer Abuse Amendments Act of 1994	Prohibits transmissions of harmful computer programs and code, including viruses

realize that weak protections for privacy can alienate employees and suppliers, turn away customers, and dramatically reduce revenues and profits. For example, a major credit card company would face a potentially disastrous public relations problem if news leaked that it sold confidential financial information on customers. In a matter of days, customer reaction could cause a dramatic drop in business and revenues. Similarly, if a company indiscriminately shared information about employees' health insurance claims, it might have trouble recruiting and retaining good workers. Suppliers might refuse to sell to a company that declined to protect the privacy of their product specifications.

Thus, most organizations maintain privacy policies for information about employees, customers, and suppliers more strict than the law requires. A business's privacy policy should provide specific guidelines for informing a customer of data that the firm records, its uses of that data, and its controls on access. The policy should require notice to the customer of any intention to distribute that data and ask for consent. Finally, it should block that distribution at the customer's request.

Some database management systems provide reliable tools for implementing these restrictions and controls. Work procedures also help to establish limits on data access and use. These limitations may raise the cost of designing and administering the company's information system. They may also increase the system's complexity. Still, careful precautions usually provide benefits that justify the investments of resources. If an organization allows an invasion of someone's privacy, it may face far more serious consequences (like loss of public confidence and employee morale) than spending time and money to protect data.

Customers' Privacy Rights. Car dealers and other retailers of expensive products collect extensive financial and personal information on customers. People usually understand the need for this data to approve credit sales, but some fail to realize that grocery stores and small retailers do the same thing. A retailer's information system gathers personal information when someone pays with a credit or debit card; it gathers product information as the point-of-sale terminal scans bar codes of purchases. By combining these sets of information, the system can provide the company with up-to-date customer/product profiles. Some companies create sophisticated databases in this way with names and addresses of potential customers along with detailed product preferences.

At what point does this practice infringe on privacy rights? Some customers might appreciate offers of discount coupons on their favorite products, as determined by their accumulated purchase records. They may also welcome marketing appeals targeted at their needs and interests, which the retailer creates by grouping customers with similar purchase patterns. Would they also welcome sales calls from other companies that bought the retailer's customer lists? Would customers who bought beer object to the sale of their names to a local citizen's group eager to protest against alcohol consumption in the community? In this and similar cases, abuses of privacy rights tend to begin when companies and individuals divert data collected for one use to new purposes that customers did not anticipate when they supplied the data. The retailer must resolve these and other details and then ensure fair treatment for all by specifying them in a uniform policy.

More obvious infringements of privacy rights demonstrate the need for vigorous protection. One information service scanned the hard disks of people who logged on via modem to collect personal information about users.[24] Information like this might help a company to understand its customers and supply services that please them. The incident created fear among many customers of on-line services, however, that other systems could access important personal and financial data without their knowledge or consent.

Employees' Privacy Rights. Along with customers, employees usually expect some right to privacy at work. This desire sometimes conflicts with companies' determination to know as much as possible about their employees, and some experts foresee a growing conflict. Recent advances in technology have allowed companies to monitor their employees' activities closely enough to raise serious concerns about privacy. For example, computer monitoring systems can tie directly into individual workstations to keep track of every keystroke a user makes. A supervisor can literally determine exactly what workers are doing every second of the day. The system might benefit both company and worker by determining how a person does his or her job and suggesting needs for additional training. It can also compute work speed, record any mistakes, and gauge how often and for how long a worker pauses. But many workers feel alienated and dehumanized by such intense supervision.

Company e-mail accounts also raise some interesting issues about privacy. About ten million business professionals send e-mail messages each day. Some employees want guarantees of privacy in their electronic communications. On the other hand, some employers argue that they maintain e-mail systems only for company purposes, so authorized personnel can freely monitor all messages to guard against dissemination of restricted information and nonbusiness use of the systems. Federal law supports the employers, but employees still have objected when managers and other overseers have read messages without their knowledge or consent.[25]

E-mail messages can even spark disputes in lawsuits. The legal rules of discovery demand that companies produce all business documents relevant to a suit. This requirement can include e-mail messages, including deleted messages retrieved before they are overwritten.[26]

"Open meeting" laws add even more restrictions on the privacy of e-mail. These laws demand that many local, state, and federal officials conduct meetings in public. Members of the Garland, Texas, city council faced sanctions for violating such a law when they exchanged e-mail messages about a public proposal.[27] In effect, the law prohibited privacy in communications between these municipal employees. Complex and paradoxical privacy concerns like these will challenge all businesspeople in coming years.

Privacy and Fair Information Use: General Standards

Comprehensive information can bring valuable benefits. It can help a company target its products to the demands of customers and focus employee training programs on needed skills. A company can even sell information it gathers in processing transactions; in fact, some companies process and distribute information as their primary products.

The value of information as a business resource seems likely to continue to attract companies that collect, store, and sell data about customers, employees, and others. Federal law imposes some restrictions that everyone must observe. Beyond those basic requirements, however, some additional principles help to guide fair treatment for the individuals profiled in company databases: knowledge, control, notice, and consent (see Table 8.6). These guidelines cover people's right to know and make some decisions about data collection and storage that affect them.

Knowledge. Individuals should know who maintains data files about them and what those data files contain. Some information providers routinely inform individuals that data files contain information on them. Others gather and store extremely personal information without alerting the subjects of their research.

Control. Individuals need not govern every decision about a database that includes them, but they should have the ability to correct errors. Most information providers observe this standard for one reason: because they do not want to base business decisions on inaccurate data. Corrections that affect many separate data files can require major efforts, though.

Notice. Before using personal data for any purpose other than one for which people agreed to provide the data, an information service should notify the subjects of the data file in advance. For example, if a mail-order retailer or grocery store wants to sell information collected from customers to another company, it should inform those individuals in advance of the transaction.

TABLE 8.6

Principles of Fair Information Use		
FAIRNESS ISSUE	PRINCIPLE FOR DATABASE STORAGE	PRINCIPLE FOR DATABASE USAGE
Right to know	Knowledge	Notice
Ability to decide	Control	Consent

Consent. An information provider should ask for the approval of subjects of a data file before using it for purposes other than those for which they provided the data. Many companies ignore this principle and deny individuals the ability to decide whether they want data about them sold or used for other purposes. Some mail-order retailers and magazine publishers openly warn customers that they will sell mailing lists, however, and most of these firms allow individual customers to prevent the distribution of their information.

WORK ENVIRONMENT

Some people worry less about computer crime and privacy issues than about the threat that computers will completely transform the work environment. Computers impose new demands for problem-solving skills and systems thinking. They do not eliminate physical work, of course, but they change daily tasks in ways that challenge people's abilities to adapt. They even threaten to take over some jobs completely, displacing workers.

Work Force Composition

No one can deny that computer-based information systems have changed the makeup of the work force. Increasing numbers of jobs now require IS literacy. Computers, robots, and other sophisticated equipment have even eliminated many less-skilled positions.

Yet that same growth in IS technology has opened up new opportunities for both professionals and nonprofessionals. Enhanced telecommunications options have spawned entirely new types of businesses. The explosive growth of cable television companies, for example, has created jobs across an enormous skill range, from Ph.D. satellite designers to high-school-educated installers. Even small, local firms can now reach global markets in many industries, allowing employees, suppliers, and customers to interact in new ways.

Computers have increased the productivity and enriched the activities of even the simplest jobs. Retail clerks no longer merely collect money and return change. Now they operate complex, integrated networks of IS resources to speed transaction processing, maintain accurate company records, and often send daily operating data to distant headquarters via telecommunications systems. While IS equipment and software automate much of this activity, users must understand it well enough to operate it correctly and handle inevitable problems.

Devices such as dictation software enable hands-free computer use. (Source: Courtesy of Dragon Systems, Inc.)

Technology has expanded job opportunities in another way by helping disabled workers to participate more actively in the work force. Computers and related devices allow these people to accomplish tasks that they could not manage on their own.

As computers and other IS components become cheaper and easier to use, even more workers will benefit from the increases in productivity and efficiency that technology allows. To fulfill this promise, people will have to learn how to work effectively with these tools.

Health Concerns

Effective work in today's environment requires thoughtful responses to a number of health concerns. First, computers seem to affect workers' emotional health by increasing occupational stress. Workers' anxieties about job security, loss of control, incompetence, and demotion show an apparent association with computer tasks.

This stress could become so serious, according to some experts, that threatened workers may react by sabotaging computer systems and equipment. A business needs monitoring programs and alert managers to spot employees who are suffering unusual stress. Training and counseling can often help these workers to relate more effectively to information systems and avoid potential problems.

Computer work affects physical health, as well, and the benefits of computers decline as unexpected hazards interfere with workers' activities. Long-term work with computer keyboards and similar equipment sometimes produces **repetitive stress injury (RSI)**, also called *repetitive motion disorder*. These injuries show up as tendinitis, tennis elbow, weakness in the hands and forearms, and sharp pain in the fingers. A common repetitive stress injury, **carpal tunnel syndrome (CTS)**, occurs when prolonged, repetitive motion of the hands (such as typing) irritates and inflames the nerve pathway through the wrist (the carpal tunnel). CTS sufferers experience wrist pain, feelings of tingling and numbness, and difficulty in grasping and holding objects. Stress and lack of exercise may contribute to this ailment.

Over 40 million people—more than 40 percent of the nation's work force—now type at computer keyboards. Of these 40 million, about 300,000 report problems with RSI each year. This number has risen no doubt because awareness of the problem has increased. Still, the trend toward more computer-centered work has also caused many new cases.

Emissions from improperly maintained and operated equipment may also cause work-related health hazards. Some studies show that poorly maintained laser printers may release ozone into the air; others dispute the claim.

Numerous studies have evaluated the impact of electromagnetic field (EMF) emissions from display screens, also with conflicting results. Although some medical authorities believe that long-term exposure to these emissions can cause cancer, no conclusive studies have yet confirmed or refuted the claim.[28] Many organizations respond to this uncertainty by developing conservative and cautious policies. Most computer manufacturers publish technical information on EMF emissions from their screens, and many users pay close attention.

repetitive stress injury (RSI)

injury produced by long-term work with computer keyboards and similar equipment

carpal tunnel syndrome (CTS)

a repetitive stress injury that occurs when prolonged, repetitive motion of the hands irritates and inflames the nerve pathway through the wrist

Avoiding Health Problems

Companies often try to slow the spread of computer-related health problems by maintaining awareness and training programs that teach proper work techniques. Simply by learning to keep their wrists straight, typists can avoid or reduce the severity of repetitive stress injuries. Training cannot remove irritating conditions caused by poor design of the work environment, though.

Employees should not have to tolerate continuing discomfort, and even disabling injuries, that the company could prevent through better design. The hazards associated with unfavorable environment design are collectively called *work stressors*. The science of **ergonomics** studies the effects of work tool designs to identify and reduce continued stressors like repetitive motion, awkward posture, and eye strain. Employees benefit from this investigation by avoiding discomfort and even disabling injuries. The employer also benefits by reducing limits on productivity and performance caused by these problems.[29]

Ergonomic initiatives might include changes in lighting to eliminate problems of glare and poor contrast so that workers need not strain to read computer screens. These studies might lead to appropriate designs for desks and chairs to provide relief from uncomfortable working positions. Similar investigations highlight the importance of moveable keyboard and screen positions.

In particular, new, ergonomic keyboard designs help to alleviate repetitive strain from extended typing. Wrist supports maintain the hands and arms in appropriate positions. Keyboards that pivot in the middle allow users to adjust the angles of the two halves until their hands rest at comfortable angles. This design change prevents problems caused when standard keyboards force the hands together near the center of the body.

The ergonomic principle of flexibility underlies many important design features of computer devices. People of different sizes and varying preferences need equipment that allows them to change positioning. Tall people usually want screens higher than short people find comfortable. Some typists want to hold keyboards in their laps; others prefer to place them on solid tables. Ergonomically aware computer designers work continuously to develop new systems and refine old ones to allow flexible positioning.

ergonomics

the science that studies the effects of work tool designs to identify and reduce continued stressors like repetitive motion, awkward posture, and eye strain

Management awareness of ergonomics has helped many companies create and maintain safe and successful work environments. Both large organizations, like microchip maker Intel, and smaller firms, like mail-order retailer L. L. Bean, have implemented ergonomics programs. Besides new equipment and other design changes, these programs include training sessions.

Ergonomic keyboard. (Source: Courtesy of Microsoft Corporation.)

Employees learn how to reduce workplace health risks by adjusting chairs and monitors and taking regular breaks. As a result, Intel reduced the number of lost or restricted work days for RSI sufferers by 30 percent from one year to the next. L. L. Bean cut its time lost to RSI by 50 percent. These ergonomic initiatives show vividly the value of voluntary preventive programs as medicine for work-related injuries.[30]

Effects on the Natural Environment

Company actions affect the health of the natural environment as well as the internal work environment. Like other industries, computer companies are investigating ways to operate with minimal damage to the natural environment that everyone must share. For example, AT&T Bell Laboratories has developed a nontoxic solvent derived from orange peel and cantaloupe to clean computer chips during the manufacturing process. Companies in all industries cut both costs and trash discharges by recycling printer ribbons, laser ink cartridges, and rechargeable batteries for laptop computers.[31]

Important advancements in computer design now allow PCs to consume less power. The EPA estimates that PCs, printers, and related equipment waste about $2 billion of electricity each year. To reduce this waste, the EPA's Energy Star program encourages design features that allow a personal computer to use no more than 60 watts of electricity while sitting idle. IBM and other companies are developing systems that meet this standard.

ETHICAL ISSUES IN INFORMATION SYSTEMS

Ethical principles span many of the issues discussed so far in this chapter. For example, ethical computer users define acceptable practices more strictly than just refraining from committing crimes; instead, they consider the effects of their IS activities on other people and organizations. Ethical standards encourage privacy limits for computer data far more protective than those required by law. Further, an ethical company identifies a healthy work environment as a key organizational goal without waiting for government agencies to impose requirements for safe conditions.

ethics

standards that determine generally accepted and discouraged activities within a company and society

In these and other cases, **ethics** determine generally accepted and discouraged activities within a company and the larger society. IS professionals encounter many opportunities for unethical behavior, and they must observe some general guidelines to promote good decisions in actual situations. Top-level managers can help to discourage unethical behavior by developing, discussing, and enforcing companywide codes of ethics. IS professionals and other employees often feel more satisfied with their jobs when they can rely on top management support for ethical behavior.

BUSINESS BITS

The Telecommunications Act

With new ways of communicating emerging as fast as they are, new regulations governing their use are trying to keep up. The newly passed Telecommunications Act of 1996 addresses a number of issues, including restricting the posting of "indecent" material on the Internet and the deregulation of phone and cable rates.

For instance, under the new law, vendors can "merge, invade each other's territories, and offer one-stop shopping for phone, TV, and Internet service," says one writer. It means that Regional Bell operating companies can sell long-distance service outside their own areas (this will probably mean lower rates). Long-distance carriers and cable companies can now offer local phone service (rates may rise in the short run). There will be fewer restrictions on how many television and radio stations a single company can own. Television manufacturers will be required to install a "V chip" that parents can activate to block violent or sexually explicit programming from children. (This provision also prevents on-line services and users from posting "indecent" material that children could access.) This provision is already in court, as plaintiffs challenge it as a form of unconstitutional censorship.

Experts have made a variety of predictions about the effects of the Telecommunications Act on consumers. "More people are going to have access to high bandwith [networks] than ever before," predicts Marc Andreessen, vice president and cofounder of Netscape Communications. True enough. But James Love, director of the Consumer Project on Technology, notes that phone and cable companies, which spent millions of dollars lobbying for the new law, didn't do it out of altruism. "They didn't hire an army of lobbyists to make rates go down," he observes. Other experts are concerned about the aspect of the law that relinquishes the requirement that telecom providers be "common carriers," whose wires transmit any content. In essence, "The cable company would effectively be the Internet service provider, and they will want to control content,"

explains Bradley Stillman, telecom policy director for the Consumer Federation of America.

The issues addressed by the new law, as well as new issues raised by the law itself, are complicated and numerous; they won't be resolved quickly. "You can expect to see some of the unresolved issues back on the table," says Rep. Rick Boucher (D-Va.). [For example, the indecency provision has been overturned.] Stillman encourages consumers to access the Web site for Telecom Information Resources (http://www.spp.umich.edu/telecom-info.html) for more information about the telecommunications bill. "After all," he remarks, "you're a taxpayer so you should be involved in the decision."

1. If possible, access Telecom Information Resources on the Internet at the address above to learn more about the telecommunications bill. Share your findings with the class.
2. In addition to the issues mentioned above, what others do you think the new regulations might raise?
3. Do you think the Telecommunications Act is necessary? Why or why not?

Source: Laurianne McLaughlin, "Telecom Reform: Next Steps," *PC World*, May 1996, pp. 58–60. Photo courtesy of Congressman Edward J. Markey.

Despite a promising trend toward emphasis on ethical behavior, however, some businesspeople continue to commit unethical and even illegal acts. For example, a senior vice president of a large charge card company allegedly used his position to generate business for a separate company that he ran. In an unrelated case, a company was charged with using its human resource information system to identify employees approaching eligibility for pensions; these people allegedly became targets for layoff and dismissal to reduce the company's pension costs.[32]

The new importance of ethics in business has caused some conflicts with older standards. Early capitalists acknowledged responsibility only to the owners of their firms. They willingly pursued any legal action that increased the returns to company stockholders or other owners. Today's businesses generally acknowledge a social contract with employees, customers, and suppliers, however. As part of this bond, they accept responsibility for the effects of their actions on both owners and other members of society.

The "Business Bits" box discusses the interplay of legal and ethical issues as they relate to telecommunications—in particular, the new Telecommunications Act of 1996.

Four Ethical Issues in Information Systems

Information systems have experienced strong influence as part of the larger drive for ethical practices in business. Ethical standards normally affect the uses of these systems in four areas: privacy, accuracy, property, and access (summarized by the acronym *PAPA*).[33]

Privacy. Ethical IS practices demand answers to several questions about privacy:

- What information should a business reveal about individuals profiled in its databases?
- What safeguards should protect against revealing additional information?
- What information should the system omit so that people can preserve the privacy and confidentiality of certain facts?

Furthermore, people may prefer to keep some kinds of data private, such as data on treatments for medical problems or past bankruptcy filings. IS users must make some difficult ethical choices about how much data to gather about people.

Accuracy. Ethical practices require thorough, effective actions to keep accurate data in a computer-based information system. Inaccuracies in data files have caused problems with legitimate information use. Errors in credit bureau files have prevented loan approval for people with excellent payment histories. Hiring decisions often hinge on the accuracy of data files maintained by firms that perform background checks. Inaccurate high school records could prevent a good student from gaining admission to college or consideration for employment.

A company's information system must resolve some critical questions to ensure accuracy:

- Who in the organization bears responsibility for storing and disseminating inaccurate information?
- What procedural safeguards does the firm need to ensure accuracy?
- How does the information system allow individuals to review stored information and confirm its accuracy or correct it?

Property. Software piracy violates important intellectual property rights concerning the ownership and use of information, as an earlier section explained. Unauthorized, illegal, and unethical copying of program files costs software manufacturers an estimated $18 billion annually in U.S. sales and $25 billion in foreign sales.[34]

Expert systems raise less common concerns about property rights. By definition, knowledgeable people must contribute information for an expert system. For example, an oil company would need input from an expert in the field of oil exploration to create an expert system that guides its drilling operations. But who owns the information in the resulting expert system? Does the subject matter expert retain property rights? Does the company that develops the system gain all rights? Do the expert and company share joint ownership?

These and other situations raise ethical questions about property rights to information:

- Who owns specific pieces of information?
- Who has the right to buy or otherwise acquire the information?
- How should an information system regulate access to intellectual property?
- Who determines the value of specific intellectual property?

The right to buy and sell sensitive information causes particularly troubling ethical disputes. For years, companies have sold or exchanged information from their databases. In a recent settlement with the New York attorney general, a charge card company agreed to inform its 25 million cardholders that it had been sorting records about them according to spending patterns and selling names and addresses to companies interested in specific markets such as retail stores and insurance companies.[35] Once someone sells information about you to another company, others can use it in almost any way, including reselling it again and again, without your awareness or consent.

Federal government data files have suffered the same breaches of privacy ethics and laws. After an 18-month federal investigation of a nationwide ring of information brokers, the FBI and the Department of Health and Human Services indicted 18 individuals, including employees of the Social Security Administration and even law enforcement officers, for peddling revealing personal information from federal databases in exchange for bribes.[36]

Today, ethical companies realize that this kind of activity damages both their customers and themselves. They agree that all should maintain customer privacy, if for no other reason than to build customer loyalty and a responsible company image.

Access. Critical ethical standards govern the ability of individuals to gain access to IS files. All information systems should set practices based on answers to some specific questions:

- To what information should a person have access?
- What information should a person be able to protect from access by others?
- What safeguards limit access to appropriate people?

Many people believe, for example, that an individual should always enjoy the right to review and correct information about himself or herself stored in public and private databases. Many companies maintain information about payment histories in their customer databases. Should these companies allow all customers to see and correct this kind of information about themselves? Federal laws described earlier ensure this right of access to government databases, but no comprehensive law imposes the same requirements on private companies.

In addition to legal and appropriate procedures, ethical standards for access must also address differences in literacy and economic status. Some individuals without IS training or skills may encounter practical barriers to access. In addition, some people cannot afford the equipment and software necessary to gain access to databases. These individuals also face denial of access to certain information. IS professionals and others must decide how to ensure fair access and preserve important rights.

Professional Associations and Ethical Codes of Conduct

IS professionals often join organizations and associations devoted to sharing insights and promoting high standards of practice. Examples include:

- Computer Professionals for Social Responsibility (CPSR)
- Data Processing Management Association (DPMA)
- Association for Computing Machinery (ACM)
- Institute of Electrical and Electronics Engineers (IEEE)
- British Computer Society (BCS)

Many of these groups have defined ethical standards that guide members' practices.

DPMA Code of Ethics. Figure 8.2 summarizes the DPMA code of ethics, which gives broad responsibilities to the association's members. This statement outlines obligations of every DPMA member to management, to fellow DPMA members, to society in general, and to his or her employer.

For each obligation, standards of conduct describe the specific duties and responsibilities of DPMA members. In addition, enforcement procedures help to ensure compliance. Any DPMA member in good standing may initiate a complaint against another member through a detailed and rigorous procedure.

ACM Code of Professional Conduct. The ACM code details a number of general principles that it calls **canons of professional conduct.** Each canon summarizes a number of ethical standards and disciplinary rules:

- An ACM member shall act at all times with integrity.
- An ACM member should strive to increase his competence and the competence and prestige of the profession.
- An ACM member shall accept responsibility for his work.
- An ACM member shall act with professional responsibility.
- An ACM member should use his special knowledge and skills for the advancement of human welfare.

canons of professional conduct

principles of conduct that specify ethical standards and disciplinary rules

FIGURE 8.2

DPMA Code of Ethics
Source: Copyright Association of Information Technology Professionals (formerly Data Processing Management Association).

CODE OF ETHICS

I acknowledge:

That I have an obligation to management, therefore, I shall promote the understanding of information processing methods and procedures to management using every resource at my command.

That I have an obligation to my fellow members, therefore, I shall uphold the high ideals of DPMA as outlined in its International Bylaws. Further, I shall cooperate with my fellow members and treat them with honesty and respect at all times.

That I have an obligation to society and will participate to the best of my ability in the dissemination of knowledge pertaining to the general development and understanding of information processing. Further, I shall not use knowledge of a confidential nature to further my personal interest, nor shall I violate the privacy and confidentiality of information entrusted to me or to which I may gain access.

That I have an obligation to my employer whose trust I hold, therefore, I shall endeavor to discharge this obligation to the best of my ability, to guard my employer's interests, and to advise him or her wisely and honestly.

That I have an obligation as a personal representative and as a member of this association. I shall actively discharge these obligations and I dedicate myself to that end.

A company can easily suffer devastating consequences if it mishandles ethical situations. Similarly, IS professionals and other organization members must guard carefully against waste and mistakes, crime, invasions of privacy, and damage to workers' health. Problems in these areas often plague poorly managed companies and inhibit the effectiveness of critical IS assets.

Ultimately, individuals must accept and fulfill these important responsibilities, because no system of technical and procedural safeguards can guarantee appropriate behavior and decision making. This role ensures that people always remain the most important components of any computer-based information system.

- Thorough analysis of almost any computer system mistake will implicate programmers, users, or other people as the cause.

- Company employees and other authorized system users can commit computer crimes more easily than outsiders can; sometimes, the potential gains of crime entice these people to abuse their privileges as users.

- Exchanges of information between companies help to encourage annoying junk e-mail and faxes along with other invasions of privacy.

- The ergonomic principle of flexibility underlies many important design features of computer devices.

- Ethics define generally accepted and discouraged activities. In IS, they consider the effects of IS activities on other people and organizations.

SUMMARY

1. *Describe some typical examples of waste and mistakes in an IS environment, their causes, and possible solutions.* Computer waste and mistakes impose unnecessarily high costs for an information system and drag down profits. Waste often results from poor integration of IS components leading to duplication of efforts and overcapacity. Inefficient procedures also waste IS resources, as do thoughtless disposal of useful resources and misuse of computer time for games and personal processing jobs. Inappropriate processing instructions, inaccurate data entry, mishandling of IS output, and poor systems design all cause computer mistakes. Careful programming practices, thorough testing, flexible network interconnections, and rigorous backup procedures can help an information system to prevent and recover from many kinds of mistakes. Company policies should specify criteria for new resource purchases and user-developed processing tools (like spreadsheet templates) to help guard against waste and mistakes.

2. *Explain the types and effects of computer crime along with measures for prevention.* Some crimes use computers as tools (e.g., to manipulate records,

counterfeit money and documents, commit fraud via telecommunications links, and make unauthorized electronic transfers of money). Other crimes target computer systems, including illegal access to computer systems by criminal hackers, destruction of data and programs by viruses, and simple theft of computer resources. Software piracy may represent the most common computer crime. Security measures like using passwords, identification numbers, and data encryption help to guard against illegal access, especially when supported by effective control procedures. Virus scanning software identifies and removes damaging computer programs. Law enforcement agencies armed with new legal tools enacted by Congress now actively pursue computer criminals.

3. *Discuss the principles and limits of an individual's right to privacy.* Although most companies use data files for legitimate, justifiable purposes, opportunities for invasions of privacy abound. The Privacy Act of 1974, with the support of other federal laws, establishes straightforward and easily understandable requirements for data collection, use, and

distribution by federal agencies; federal law also serves as a nationwide moral guideline for privacy rights and activities by private organizations. Some states supplement federal protections and limit activities within their jurisdictions by private organizations. A business should develop a clear and thorough policy about privacy rights for customers, including database access. That policy should also address the rights of employees, including electronic monitoring systems and e-mail. General standards for privacy rights emphasize knowledge, control, notice, and consent for people profiled in databases.

4. *List the important effects of computers on the work environment.* Computers have changed the makeup of the work force and even eliminated some jobs, but they have also expanded and enriched employment opportunities in many ways. Computers and related devices seem to affect employees' emotional and physical health, especially by promoting repetitive stress injuries. Some critics blame computer systems for emissions of ozone and electromagnetic radiation. Ergonomic design principles help reduce harmful effects and increase the efficiency of an information system.

5. *Outline the criteria for ethical use of information systems.* Ethics determine generally accepted and discouraged activities within a company and society. Ethical computer users define acceptable practices more strictly than just refraining from committing crimes; instead, they consider the effects of their IS activities on other people and organizations. Ethical standards normally affect the uses of computer systems in four areas: privacy, accuracy, property, and access. Many IS professionals join computer-related associations and agree to abide by detailed ethical codes.

 ## Key Terms

computer waste 242
computer mistakes 242
hacker 249
criminal hacker 249
virus 250
worm 250
virus scanning software 251

application virus 252
system virus 253
logic bomb 253
Trojan horse 253
document virus 253
intellectual property 254
software piracy 254

kill file 258
Privacy Act of 1974 259
repetitive stress injury (RSI) 265
carpal tunnel syndrome (CTS) 265
ergonomics 266
ethics 267
canons of professional conduct 271

 ## Concept Quiz

Choose the best answer for each of the following.

1. While the information age has benefitted workers in many ways, it has also caused some problems. Which of the following is a computer-related problem?
   a. a decrease in computer crime
   b. new health hazards in the workplace
   c. an increase in manufacturing jobs
   d. fewer opportunities for invasion of privacy

2. *Computer waste* can be defined as
   a. system errors that destroy data.
   b. inappropriate uses of computer technology and resources.
   c. programmer errors.
   d. data entry mistakes.

3. All of the following are common causes of computer mistakes *except*:
   a. inappropriate instructions specified by programmers
   b. poor systems design
   c. errors in processing routines and data input
   d. hardware malfunctions

4. All of the following are steps IS staff can take to prevent computer waste and mistakes *except*:
   a. fully document sources of input and requirements for output
   b. provide for thorough testing of new IS components and connections
   c. discard hardware or software as soon as there is a mistake
   d. include output users on the systems development team

Answer the following questions briefly.

5. To commit a computer crime, what two things must a criminal know how to do?
6. Name the four general categories of computer crime.
7. Name and describe briefly the three most common kinds of viruses.
8. What are the three reasons that critics cite to doubt the effectiveness of laws passed against computer crime?

Mark "true" or "false" after each of the following statements.

9. The same media and devices that improve communications among businesses and managers also create opportunities for criminals. _____
10. A hacker is automatically considered a criminal. _____
11. The most common thefts of computing resources result from violations of intellectual property rights. _____

12. The Privacy Act of 1974 allows that individuals may determine what information about them appears in records a federal agency collects, maintains, uses, or disseminates. _____
13. Some database management systems provide reliable tools for implementing restrictions and controls on users' access to information about individuals. _____
14. A company does not need to ask for the approval of subjects of a data file before using it for purposes other than the original purposes. _____
15. A good system of technical and procedural safeguards in an information system guarantees appropriate ethical behavior by employees. _____

Discussion Questions

1. If your computer is connected to an e-mail system (or if you have access to one), you've probably received "junk e-mail." What is your response to such mail—do you like receiving it, or would you prefer not to? In what ways do you think it should be controlled? Do you think users should have to pay to have such messages blocked? Why or why not?
2. What is your response to the question raised in the text "Who owns the information and knowledge gathered about you?" If a public or private organization spends its time and resources to gather data about you, do you think the organization should "own" the data? Should the organization be able to use the data in any way it desires? Why or why not? If not, what kinds of restrictions should there be?
3. Do you think that employers should be able to monitor their employees' electronic communications? Why or why not?
4. Do you think that database information on a public sports figure like Drew Bledsoe (chapter-opening photo), a political candidate, or an entertainer should be protected by the same level of security as information on the average private citizen? Why or why not?

Team Activity

Divide the class into teams of three or four. Each team then designs what they believe to be an ergonomic office or workplace. If the team has access to a graphics program on a computer, they can use a computer to design the office, or they can create a design on paper. The team should address the ergonomics of equipment, lighting, seating, and anything else that creates a favorable work environment. A written explanation should accompany the design.

Applying IT

1. If you have access to the Internet, access one or two of the federal agencies listed in the chapter that stores records on individuals (such as the Department of Labor) to find out what *types* of information are available to the public. If you do not have access to the Internet, call one or two of the agencies on the phone to obtain the same information. Share your findings with the class.

2. In your own workplace, observe as many examples as you can of ways that IS technology has changed the types of jobs available, changed the way the company does business, changed the way it interacts with customers, and so forth. Then determine ways these changes have actually changed the work force composition at the company. (If you do not currently have a job, make the same observations about your college or university or about a company with which you are familiar.)

CASE

Raptor Systems

They named their company after a predatory reptile made famous by Hollywood; their mission was to hunt down and capture criminal hackers. Robert A. Steinkrauss, president and chief executive; Shaun McConnon, executive vice president; and creator David Pensak are on the prowl. Their company, Raptor Systems, designs and manufactures software "firewalls," which block unauthorized access and theft of data from business and other organizations.

Surprisingly, even after David Pensak created his first firewall, it took years for the idea to take hold in the market. The Internet was not yet widely used, and companies didn't see the need to spend the money for security. But then computer break-ins began to proliferate. Software thefts were reported by Harvard University, the White House, and the Pentagon. Thousands of credit card numbers were stolen by a single computer hacker. Citibank reported a loss of $400,000 due to electronic theft. An *Information Week*/Ernst & Young survey revealed that 600 of the 1,200 respondents said their companies had suffered financial losses because of computer theft, and 20 said their losses exceeded $1 million. Raptor's time had come. "It was story after story . . . it went on and on. We couldn't write any better publicity for the company," recalls McConnon.

Raptor does have competitors—some of them huge, like Digital Equipment Corp. and Checkpoint Software. But Raptor claims technical superiority over the products offered by its competition. Raptor was the first company to provide a graphical user interface for its firewalls; the first to offer detailed monitoring and instant notification of unusual activity (much like a home security system); the first to offer security for remote access activities; and the first to offer security for networks that run on Windows. The company is now developing three-dimensional graphics that display network activity so that users can get the picture at a glance rather than scrolling through text. "Raptor is a leading developer of firewall software in terms of the technology and their marketing approach," notes David Readerman of Montgomery Securities in San Francisco. Readerman goes on to observe that the company is also well managed. Still, the security market is not a sure thing. If hardware manufacturers begin to build security into the systems they make, firewalls could quickly become obsolete. On the other hand, new technology for different types of security may become necessary, as hackers try to outsmart computer manufacturers. Whatever direction security software takes, Raptor is bound to be there. Its founders have no intention of becoming extinct.

Questions

1. Do you think it will be possible for businesses and software manufacturers to stay ahead of computer crime? Why or why not?
2. Depending on your answer to question 1, what do you think the future holds for Raptor Systems? What strategies might the company use to stay in business?
3. Access the Web site for Raptor Systems (http://www.raptor.com) to learn what you can about the company and its products.

Source: Robert Keough, "Raptor Running Wild," *The Boston Globe*, April 10, 1996, pp. 33, 45.

Answers to Concept Quiz

1. b **2.** b **3.** d **4.** c **5.** Gain access to the system; manipulate the system to get the desired result **6.** Illegal access to and use of computer systems; destruction of data and programs by viruses and worms; theft of data, software, and equipment; international computer crime
7. Applications viruses infect executable program files for applications; system viruses infect operating system programs or other system files as soon as the user boots up the computer; document viruses spread when a document is opened on a computer. **8.** Companies do not always pursue computer crime; security is inadequate; convicted criminals do not receive harsh punishments.
9. True **10.** False **11.** True **12.** True **13.** True **14.** False **15.** False

CHAPTER 9

Issues and Trends: The Impact of Computers at School, Home, and Work

CHAPTER OUTLINE

Issues and Trends at School and Home
>   Computerized Schools: Computer-assisted Instruction
>   Computerized Houses and Apartments
The Impact of Telecommunications
>   Telecommunications at Home and School
>   Telecommunications in Business
Business Trends and Information System Effects
>   Process Reengineering and Continuous Improvement
>   Emphasis on Quality
>   Emphasis on Speed
>   Embedded IS Technology
>   Global Business Environment
>   Effective Business Information Systems in Action

Grocery shopping from home is now a reality. With Peapod, you can shop with a computer and modem at home in just minutes. You'll have over 20,000 items at your fingertips—including fresh produce, deli, bakery, meat and frozen products, and drugstore merchandise like batteries and cosmetics. Before you purchase an item, you can display a picture of it and view nutritional labels as well. You can give specific instructions to the Peapod shopper such as "slice turkey extra-thin." Peapod shoppers will even pick up your processed film and prescriptions. Everything will be delivered right to your door. Photo courtesy of Peapod.

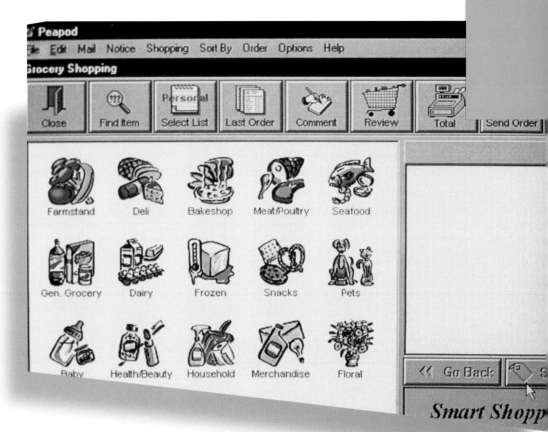

LEARNING OBJECTIVES

After completing Chapter 9, you will be able to:

1. Describe the expanding roles that computers will play in technologically advanced homes and schools.
2. Explain the impact of telecommunications on future applications of IS technology at home and in school.
3. List the newest business applications of telecommunications technology.
4. Outline the effects of information systems trends on business.

The preceding chapters have explained different parts of the current and emerging roles that computer-based information systems play in people's everyday lives at school, home, and work. Together, this discussion describes a set of dynamic IS resources devoted to personal and business success. Computer hardware and software have become familiar tools that help both individuals and organizations to achieve their goals.

New tools and functions will continue to accelerate acceptance of and reliance on computers. Consider just a few of the most recent announcements in the press:

- A new imaging technology that allows a computerized image to be projected directly into the eye instead of on a screen. Microvision Inc. in Seattle is developing the ability to create "virtual retinal displays" on the human eye. The displays would allow viewers to see information on what appears to be a computer screen hanging a few feet in front of them. The technology would allow soldiers facing a minefield to see the buried mines, surgeons to see "inside" a patient, and mechanics to see the workings of an engine.
- A tiny computer so small that you could put it in your pocket, or even swallow it. The army already has developed a pill-sized computer that could be swallowed to track soldiers' body temper-

atures while they are in the field.
- Wearable PCs, in which the components are attached to the users. The CPU can hang from a belt, the output screen is suspended in front of one eye, and a keyboard is attached to the wrist. Xybernaut has developed such a computer.
- A scanner that maps the human body. It is used for designing artificial limbs, aircraft helmets, and garments that surround burn victims to reduce scarring. Cyberware and the air force have cooperated to develop this technology.
- A smart card that carries your medical history on a credit-card-sized card. Patients carry the card with them so it is available during emergencies. This technology is already in use in Europe.

Today's dizzying parade of new developments will soon become commonly accepted. Technical progress will integrate exciting IS capabilities so completely into all aspects of life that users will scarcely notice the tools themselves.

Instead, people will focus on their information needs and the creative processing tasks required to meet those needs.

This chapter investigates computer-based information systems of today and tomorrow. It begins with some changes coming to schools and the home. Many of these issues reflect the explosive growth of telecommunications, and the chapter explores some results of this revolution in human and organizational interactions. It focuses in particular on new business relationships that emerge from telecommunications links. The chapter then expands the discussion of business applications by considering how information systems will adapt to new strategic trends like process reengineering, quality and speed initiatives, and global operations. It concludes with several real-world examples of IS solutions developed by businesses around the world. These companies are pioneering creative applications of IS technology to specific problems and showing all businesses, large and small, how computers can fulfill their exciting potential.

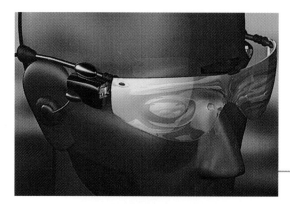

Microvision has developed a headmounted display that will project a computerized image directly onto the eye.
Photo courtesy of Microvision, Inc.

ISSUES AND TRENDS AT SCHOOL AND HOME

As more and more people recognized the value of computers, they moved from business use, to school, to home. The capabilities of computers have also changed as they have been applied to new problems and situations. Decreasing prices and increasing capabilities have drawn personal computers into almost all schools and many homes. In fact, sales of PCs for home and school use may soon exceed sales for business use.

Educators rely on computers for many basic functions:

* Recordkeeping, including grades and attendance
* Student work, including reports prepared in word processing software and other applications
* Class presentations, based on interconnected multimedia resources such as text files, graphics, and images and sounds stored on disk, all under central computer control

IS technology also advances beyond the supporting role of enhancing the teacher's instruction by actually delivering instruction itself.

Computerized Schools: Computer-assisted Instruction

computer-assisted instruction (CAI)

instruction in which the computer presents self-paced sequences of text, graphics, and sound

Computers create entirely new kinds of education through **computer-assisted instruction (CAI),** in which the computer presents self-paced sequences of text, graphics, and sound. Students usually control the speed and even the sequence of materials, so they can study at their own pace, repeat information when needed, and follow ideas that interest them and apply these ideas to their current problems. By including video clips and animation, these systems can vividly illustrate concepts and demonstrate trends or processes. Music, vocal narration, and sound effects sustain attention and reinforce learning.

Classroom use of these resources offers new ways to reach students who may not respond to traditional methods of instruction. It can also provide flexibility by allowing some students to explore additional material while the teacher works closely with small groups or individual students. CAI systems have provided cost-effective resources that dramatically enhance education for many learners.

tutorial

on-screen presentations that incorporate examples to guide new users through actual commands and menu choices to accomplish important program tasks

Software publishers have implemented many principles of CAI by including **tutorials** with their packages. (See Figure 9.1.) For example, tutorials that accompany spreadsheet programs teach the basics of spreadsheet use along with specific commands for functions. These on-screen presentations incorporate examples that guide new users through actual commands and menu choices to accomplish important program tasks. Users quickly learn enough to start productive work with a program through these realistic and practical instructional tools.

The programs themselves may also help new users to learn how to perform essential tasks, especially when those users already understand another program with similar functions. For example, Microsoft Word will recognize and respond to commands and procedures of WordPerfect, another popular word processing application. This helpful capability provides a bridge to speed and softens a user's transition from another program, reducing the time spent learning new tools and increasing the time spent performing valuable work.

FIGURE 9.1

Computer-assisted Instruction Product
Interactive tutorials, such as the Windows 95 CD from Course Technology, can speed a new user's learning of a software package. Some people treat these professionally produced programs as computer games.

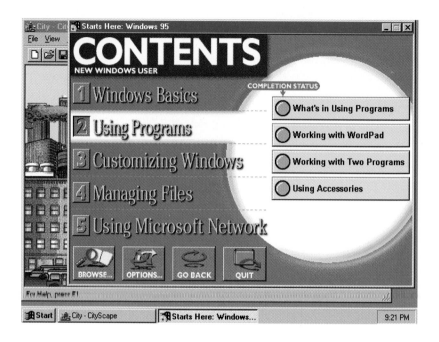

Consider a newer technology that could affect your learning—a book that is a computer. An instructor at MIT is developing a computer that is shaped like a book, including pages. The electronic book will have about 200 very thin and flexible display panels. What is shown on these "pages" is controlled by a driver in the book's spine. Software could be changed to allow different subjects, and the size of the text could be changed to accommodate visual handicaps.[1]

Also, many technologies are now available to assist students with disabilities: students who cannot control their arms can write assignments by using a light pen attached to their head, and blind students can use voice-activated computers to carry out their commands. Oversized keyboards allow easier input. Some input devices are controlled by air puffs in a strawlike device. And currently under development is a wheelchair equipped with a modem to allow the manufacturer to diagnose malfunctions; this innovation should reduce down time for repairs. Such technologies allow students with disabilities to participate more actively in life. It could even be possible for them to use intelligent robots in their school and daily activities in the near future (see the "Who's Who" box).

Computerized Houses and Apartments

Many computer users want the advantages of IS technology at home once they experience its benefits at school and work. Home-based computers have long provided entertaining games and tools for many hobbies. In addition, general-purpose spreadsheet applications and dedicated budgeting programs help people to track personal finances. A database program can handle names for a Christmas card list, and a word processing program can help to create personalized holiday greetings.

Besides these activities, many people use processing hardware without knowing it. All kinds of consumer electronics products include embedded computers and software that allow elaborate control of their operations. Microprocessors control timing, heat settings, and other operating characteristics for microwave ovens, stoves, dishwashers, and even coffeemakers and irons. Expansion of computer

WHO'S WHO

Douglas Lenat and Rodney Brooks

They are fierce rivals. Each believes passionately that his route toward the perfection of artificial intelligence is the right one. Each snubs the other heartlessly. They both sound like Hal, the computer star of the science fiction classic film *2001*. But they are both men. Douglas Lenat and Rodney Brooks are engaged in a race to produce the first truly intelligent computer.

Lenat, a researcher sponsored by a high-tech consortium in Texas called MCC (http://www.mcc.com), believes that he can teach a computer common sense. He believes that the human capacity for mental gymnastics comes from symbolic knowledge, or language. Thus, he has headed the development of a huge digital base of common knowledge; he calls his system Cyc (as in *psych*). He hopes that, eventually, Cyc will be able to actually expand its own knowledge base by combining different texts automatically. If this becomes possible, "AI [artificial intelligence] would be a change probably as fundamental for our species as the development of language."

Rodney Brooks has a completely different view of the challenge of creating artificial intelligence. Working out of MIT with a group called IS Robotics (http://www.isr.com), Brooks has been trying to build a humanoid robot that learns by interacting with people (much the way babies do). Called Cog, Brooks's robot will start its "life" with little knowledge but will acquire it through sensory experience. "Intelligence cannot be separated from the subjective experience of a body," explain Brooks and his colleague Lynn Andre Stein in a published paper. Cog's "intelligence will be grounded in computation on sensory information."

Both projects (and their leaders) are ambitious. How close have they come to their goal? Not very. But the journey itself has been impressive. As each project makes progress, it encounters deeper and deeper questions. For instance, as Cyc's knowledge base grows, the system needs to have a mechanism for choosing information that is relevant to a problem and discarding the rest. Currently, Cyc's knowledge is organized by context, or groups of rules—say, Western medicine practices or behavior in the workplace. Cyc can make inferences by consulting nearly half a million bits of common knowledge and retrieving those that apply to a problem. Cog, on the other hand, relies on specialized program applications called "behaviors" (because they mimic human behaviors) that run simultaneously to create an entire function.

Recently, money for the two projects has begun to dry up, and both pioneers have been forced to research practical applications for their systems, although they don't like to talk about it. Cyc's first real-world application will help managers find answers to "what-if" questions. Nick Siegel, a member of the Cyc team, rationalizes, "We're not abandoning the grander scheme, but our approach right now is ruthlessly practical." Cog is not publicizing any commercial applications at the moment. "There will be spinoffs, but I can't give you a commercialization plan," demurs Brooks. "That would narrow the thinking too much." Which might be a sad day for two true believers, however diametrically opposed they might be.

Source: David Stipp, "2001 Is Just Around the Corner. Where's Hal?," *Fortune*, November 13, 1995, pp. 215–228. Photo © Sam Ogden.

control to new products will continue to improve convenience and provide new functions. Also, since owners can now operate these products only when needed (e.g., motion detectors on lights and thermostat controls for furnaces), enhanced control improves energy efficiency as well.

Once-amazing functions have become typical requirements. Further, today's developments are continuing the trend by fully integrating IS technology into existing electrical and telephone wiring to accommodate computer control of all kinds of household activities. The Electronics Industries Association developed the Consumer Electronics Bus (CEBus) wiring standard to unify the operating routines and functions of information systems for homes and apartments. CEBus systems give both new and existing homes and apartments elaborate capabilities, including security management, lighting and appliance control, and even lawn and garden care.

Security. As concerns about crime increase, many people are equipping their homes and apartments with security systems. A relatively simple burglar alarm triggers a siren when someone disturbs electromagnetic sensors on doors and windows. Today's more sophisticated security systems monitor all kinds of activity within and around a residence:

- Motion detectors inside and outside turn on lights and perhaps sound a siren in response to movements in front of them.
- Sound detectors trigger the security system when they sense noises.
- Smoke detectors and carbon monoxide detectors sound an alert if they sense the smoke or heat of a fire or chemical ranges higher than normal for carbon monoxide.

In addition to audible alarms, today's security systems can automatically route recorded calls for help over existing household phone lines to monitoring offices or police departments. (See Figure 9.2.)

Lighting and Appliance Control. Beyond security protection, home automation systems can also control lighting and appliances. Some allow owners to activate selected devices remotely by phone. From the office phone or a cell phone while commuting home, you can turn on lights or the air conditioner and start the microwave. At the end of the commute, a well-lit house or apartment waits with a comfortable temperature and dinner ready for the table.

Lawn and Garden Care. Computers can also automate many aspects of lawn and garden care. Specialized programs can help with an effective landscape plan, including locations for trees, grass, shrubs, fences, and other design elements. These tools apply professional design principles to make a home attractive and increase its value while reducing energy costs by shading summer sun and buffering winter wind. Computer programs help gardeners to plan flower and vegetable beds to take advantage of seasonal changes and other growing conditions. Computer-controlled sprinklers can save maintenance work and water.

FIGURE 9.2

Home Security System
Home security systems are common today. Burglars and other criminals can be discouraged from breaking into houses and apartments equipped with home security systems. Central processing equipment monitors door and window sensors, motion detectors, sound detectors, and smoke detectors. You can also include video monitors to view specific areas (e.g., the front or back door). If the system identifies a problem, it issues a call to a security office or the police department. (Source: Courtesy of ADT Security Systems.)

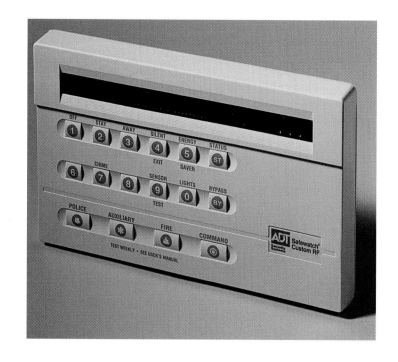

In the future, most of your computer devices will be connected, and they'll be able to share information. Perhaps your home of the future will be able to adjust the temperature controls and lighting as you move from room to room. If you are reading, lamps could be brightened. Companies such as Texas Instruments are already exploring such possibilities.[2]

Entertainment, Sports, Art, and Leisure. Nowhere is the computer revolution so evident as in home entertainment. (See "Business Bits: Digital Video Disks.") Early computers provided such adaptable tools that companies quickly saw their potential for playing games. But we have come a long way from the flat, repetitive routines of Pac Man. Enhancements in sharp color graphics have led to lifelike, exciting games of all kinds. The newest inventions for video game playing use 32-bit and 64-bit processors to produce three-dimensional games. The Sega Saturn and new Nintendo provide more lifelike games, where you can explore the virtual environment, return to scenes you've already passed, and zoom in or out to get different perspectives. The 64-bit Super Mario game, for example, let's you get a bird's-eye view of the castle and its grounds or swoop in to see things the way Mario does. And Mario can jump, slide, do handstands, climb trees, and even swim in the castle's moat—all with sound effects.

The entertainment role of IS technology has also expanded to encompass video and audio production, sports, and other leisure pastimes. Personal computers can give amateur athletes and outdoor enthusiasts the same advantages that professionals enjoy. Personal computers help people to develop personal exercise programs, track workouts, plan nutrition programs, organize outdoor adventures, and so on. The Polar Heart Rate Monitor provides an example of this application of IS technology. It can accurately record your heart rate every 5 seconds during exercise, helping you to optimize training just as professional athletes and Olympic teams do. (See Figure 9.3.) An infrared transmission then uploads the recorded results to a personal computer with software for analyzing one or more training sessions and tracking a complete season of exercise or competition.

FIGURE 9.3

Polar Heart Rate Watch
This personal application of IS technology allows an amateur athlete to monitor a workout or exercise program and upload the results to a personal computer for analysis.
(Source: Courtesy of Polar Electro, Inc.)

BUSINESS BITS

Digital Video Disks

Just when you think you have your house wired with the hottest in electronic entertainment technology, someone launches a new product that does everything better and faster. In this case, it's the DVD—Digital Video Disk. The DVD is a standard for high-capacity optical disks that can store data, CD audio, and digital video. Toshiba is already offering one for about $600. The device connects to your television and can play a feature-length movie from a platter the size of a conventional CD. Soon, Toshiba will ship to market a $500 DVD-ROM drive that can read current CD-ROMs along with new ones that store many times more data.

So what, you ask? The high capacity of DVDs gives you audio and video quality that are orders of magnitude greater than those of CD-ROMs, VHS tapes, and even laser disks. DVD technology can handle six channels of audio and eight different foreign languages, and it offers three types of theater-quality sound. In addition, a DVD is nearly as fast as a hard drive (important for retrieving data quickly).

For most people (other than hard-core electronic entertainment buffs) the DVD isn't practical yet. For one thing, there's the high price tag. For another, current PC users who want to use DVDs will have to buy a sound-and-video card to upgrade their computers to accept the DVD. The hardware is not yet available, but when it is, it will cost around $200 (in addition to the DVD device itself). Right now, DVD's focused lasers have difficulty reading the more loosely packed data on today's

CDs. Finally, the current DVD devices are not able to record (eventually, they will; but it will take a few years).

But DVDs do seem to be the wave of the future for home entertainment. The film industry has been intensely involved in the development of DVDs, because the new disks will be cheaper and more durable than videotape; DVD movies are already being prepared for shipment, and DVD-ROM titles should follow in the next two years. Still, you don't need to put your old entertainment equipment in a yard sale yet.

1. As a consumer, would you have any interest in purchasing the new DVD devices? Why or why not?
2. If possible, access Toshiba's Web site at http://www.toshiba.com to learn more about its DVD products.
3. In addition to home entertainment, what kinds of uses could you imagine for DVD technology?

Source: Photo courtesy of Toshiba America Information Systems, Inc.

Soon, technology may also help us *perform* in sports. A NASA physicist is a co-inventor of a walking device that could allow us to run at 30 miles per hour in the future. The early prototype straps to the back of the person and provides mechanical legs below.[3]

Today, comparatively inexpensive IS technology can create an integrated home entertainment center with astounding potential. Wide-screen TVs with full-stereo surround sound combine with VCRs and disk players to show movies and video programs that rival viewers' experiences at movie theaters. Gateway 2000 has introduced a PC that looks like a big-screen TV. It has a 31-inch screen, remote keyboard, and mouse that can be operated from a distance of 15 feet. The system can also be used for business presentations or at home for video games, Internet connections, or just TV viewing.[4]

PCs and software available to home users because of lower prices allow you to edit video and audio tapes and create customized output comparable to that of a professional editing studio. You can incorporate titles, music, still pictures, graphics, and special effects like fades and morphs (which smoothly transform one image into another). Amateur producers and directors can make films and music videos for their own amusement; talented and creative individuals can even use the same tools to launch careers without the need for access to costly dedicated editing equipment.

Artistically inclined users take advantage of similar capabilities to create elaborate still and animated images with stunning effects. In fact, artists have worked with PCs and software for years, just as others work in paint, marble, and more traditional media. Three-dimensional images, special effects that simulate water color painting, and other effects are possible to create stunning images. Specialized applications provide powerful tools that help even the most casual artists produce attractive graphics, either from scratch or by modifying and combining clip art files. More and more multimedia and graphics packages are becoming available to the budding artist.

Developments in specialized input hardware help artists to create and capture images in new ways. A **graphics tablet** translates movements of a stylus across its surface into an image on the screen (see Figure 9.4). As described in Chapter 2, digital cameras work much like normal cameras to record images, but they store the pictures as electronic data rather than patterns of light on film. After uploading this data to a personal computer, the artist can edit it extensively to manipulate the images. Color laser printers, and even inexpensive color ink jet printers such as Hewlett-Packard's Model 870, can produce hard copies, perhaps to enhance holiday greeting cards, letters to friends, club newsletters, and other documents.

Expanding capabilities for generating and handling graphics have accompanied explosive developments in telecommunications also. Together, these changes have spurred the growth of valuable new business, educational, and personal resources on the Internet (especially the World Wide Web) that are quickly becoming essential parts of many people's daily lives.

graphics tablet

a specialized input device that translates movements of a stylus across its surface into an image on the screen

FIGURE 9.4

Graphics Tablet
Source: Photo ©1996 Wacom Technology Corp.

THE IMPACT OF TELECOMMUNICATIONS

Telecommunications Act of 1996

legislation that removed regulatory barriers to competition among traditional telephone, computer, and cable TV companies

On February 8, 1996, as the promise of the Internet had only begun to unfold, President Clinton transformed the entire spectrum of IS resources by signing the **Telecommunications Act of 1996.** This far-reaching legislation removed regulatory barriers to competition among traditional telephone, computer, and cable TV companies. In the process, it guaranteed exciting and unpredictable new combinations of phone, TV, and computer-related services. Individuals, schools, and businesses will integrate these emerging services into their most essential activities within a few years. The bill also contains provisions to limit posting of indecent materials on the Internet and to allow for a "V-chip" in televisions so that parents may block violent or sexually explicit shows from their sets. Controversy surrounds these provisions, and modifications will be made.

At home, people will expand their use of the Internet for entertainment, shopping and other commercial transactions, and personal interrelationships. Schools will spread out across the Internet in search of information, and they will increasingly present courses and special programs there for a worldwide audience. In the process, schools will redefine the institution of education through distance learning and other innovative joint programs with businesses and telecommunications providers.

Business organizations will integrate new telecommunications services in even more dramatic ways. Telecommuting, teleconferencing, and virtual work groups have changed relationships between company and employee and among colleagues. Expansion of important networks, including electronic data interchange, will blur the boundaries of many organizations. Eventually, joint government and business development of a National Information Infrastructure should reinforce and renew the ongoing transformation of all these activities.

Telecommunications at Home and School

Telecommunications technologies have already extended people's reach across the globe. As television spread in the early 1960s, people became accustomed to viewing live pictures of distant events that would have amazed earlier generations. In the same way, the spread of telecommunications will routinely bridge vast distances between people and institutions and enrich their lives.

Internet and On-line Services. Just within the last few years, an entirely new industry—on-line services—has sprung up and continued its explosive growth. America Online, CompuServe, Prodigy, and MSN give individuals access to important new sources of information, ideas, and relationships via their modems and telephone lines. The World Wide Web's inviting, easy-to-use graphical interface will develop into a global bazaar of commercial and personal exchanges between subscribers. When security measures become reliable (and they are becoming so), subscribers will shop the entire world for merchandise while sitting comfortably at home. On-line job searches are now possible. Increasingly, comprehensive databases of employment opportunities will allow people to conduct worldwide job hunts; at the same time, organizations will benefit by recruiting from the widest possible pool of talent. Individuals will regularly exchange information and opinions with others who share their interests in on-line forums. These on-line conversations will forge rich relationships between like-minded people that would be rare or impossible without telecommunications.

EYE ON THE WEB

In a short period of time, interest in the Internet's resources has exploded. Commercial service providers, such as America Online, CompuServe, MSN (Microsoft Network), and Prodigy have seen fantastic subscriber increases (America Online, for example, announced that it had surpassed the two million subscriber milestone).

Access used to be restricted to textual searching, but now graphic browsers such as Netscape broaden the capabilities of on-line information storage and retrieval. A few years ago, students in MIS courses may have read descriptions of image databases, hypertext, and hypermedia but believed these to be no more than experimental technologies, or technologies beyond the purview of common usage. However, as you browse through various Web pages, you are taking advantage of these very technologies and capabilities.

All indications are that the Web has already crossed the line beyond mere entertainment and fun into corporate necessity. One consulting service, for example, notes that it is becoming essential for successful companies to maintain a Web presence. A Web presence can present business opportunities to companies. Designing a Web page may be a means of attracting a wider target market or alerting consumers to the latest product advances and developments. Alternately, the Web is creating new business opportunities for those who, much like the consultant just mentioned, stand ready to assist firms in achieving effective Internet utilization.

In the academic domain, students and researchers stand to reap enormous benefits from the World Wide Web. Students can undertake research and information searches from their dorm rooms, rather than needing to schedule library hours. Scholars can keep abreast of their fields, often accessing current information on a particular area of interest. Corporate users can monitor stock activities, business trends, and even regulatory issues of concern to their organization.

Considering that the Web represents an aspect of the Internet that is still relatively in its infancy, its growth has been no less than phenomenal. Specifically, graphical browsers have transformed usage beyond that of research and communication, into an information treasure chest. The Web now houses information pertaining to all interests. Learning to find the information translates into fun and entertainment. As more and more users learn to access the Web and undertake information searches, its use and popularity are expected to grow tremendously.

WEB EXERCISES

1. Have you streamlined your ability to obtain information as a result of using the Web, or have you discovered that the ease of obtaining information has caused you to undertake more ambitious information searches? In what ways have your abilities to access information helped you through your courses this year?

2. How many times during this year have you found yourself browsing the Web as a means of exploring new information, rather than strictly as part of an assignment for this course?

Internet phone service is already becoming a reality. One of the biggest appeals to this service is the lower cost from traditional long-distance service. Another is the Net's ability to handle text and graphics, in addition to sound. A new technology called computer-telephone integration (CTI) is working to merge telephone and computer use. Imagine being able to correct numbers before they are dialed so that you would not be charged for wrong numbers or accessing both faxes and voice mail from one mailbox on your PC.[5] That may be coming sooner than you think.

Growing numbers of users are regularly sharing parts of their lives and knowledge with others by developing their own **home pages** on the Web. These documents often include pictures of the page authors and describe people's personal and professional activities, usually supplemented with links to related Web pages. This electronic presence invites contact from others with their own diverse perspectives. (The "Eye on the Web" box discusses the importance of a business firm's electronic identity.)

home page

a document on the World Wide Web that includes pictures of the page authors and describes the authors' personal and professional activities, usually supplemented with links to related Web pages

Advances in hardware will expand access to the Web and related resources. Computer makers are developing inexpensive PCs, costing about as much as a color TV, designed specifically to access on-line services and the Internet. They are called NCs, for network computers. An on-line service supplies some of the processing power and software capabilities, including basic capabilities such as game playing and word processing in addition to Internet access. This innovation replaces or reduces individuals' needs for more expensive PCs with large hard disks and fast processors.

Schools use the Internet for the same purposes as individual on-line subscribers, and students will make up a larger proportion of its so-called *netizens* as time passes. Schools are using the Net for many purposes—some boost students' pride in their work by posting it for all to see on the school's Web page.

In addition, schools will increasingly reach across telecommunications links to bring their students into contact with experts in many fields. For example, the JASON Project brought satellite broadcasts of undersea exploration directly into schools. Scientists answer students' questions live on the television screen and even guide underwater equipment as directed by students.[6] The expansion of initiatives like this one will take students to the cutting edge of research, where they can learn firsthand in ways that traditional instruction cannot match. Telecommunications systems will also increasingly help college and university systems to share resources.

Distance Learning. The most common method of remote instruction, **distance learning,** connects classrooms at different locations via computers and telecommunications. An instructor can deliver lectures, demonstrations, and other educational materials simultaneously to hundreds or even thousands of people on computer monitors or TV screens. Microphones and cameras in students' classrooms often carry their questions and feedback to the distant instructor. This method brings the benefits of expertise and materials from distant institutions to locations convenient to students.

Some educators, especially those in rural areas, believe that these links can provide high-quality instruction that students could not experience in any other practical way. A rural high school may not be able to justify hiring someone to teach Japanese to a few interested students, but those students could receive instruction via distance learning.

Critics cite some potential disadvantages, however. The initial investment to establish such a system requires potentially high costs to acquire the computers, telecommunications devices and services, and related equipment. The rural high school, for example, might have to rent expensive time on a satellite channel to carry broadcasts of the

distance learning

a method of remote instruction that connects classrooms at different locations via computers and telecommunications

The JASON Project allows students to take an electronic field trip to explore the ocean floor. (Source: Photo courtesy of The JASON Foundation for Education and TRICOM Associates.)

Japanese lessons. In a more serious criticism, many instructors and students doubt the effectiveness of distance learning. They dislike the loss of rewarding and effective interactions between individual teachers and small numbers of students.

Despite its limitations, this method has proved effective for standardized instruction on certain topics. The state of Florida, for example, has developed the Corrections Distance Learning Network (CDLN) to teach AIDS prevention and awareness via satellite to hundreds of employees and inmates at prisons throughout the state. CDLN was one of the first and largest distance learning systems in the state of Florida. Further, cable TV's Mind Extension University carries college classes from institutions nationwide into people's homes. Any interested subscriber can view these presentations and share in the learning.

Telecommunications in Business

As much as individuals at home and at school have gained from telecommunications technology, businesses have developed even more profound applications. New technological arrangements are completely redefining the relationships organizations have built with other companies and with their own workers. For example, after recruiting new employees from Web surfers worldwide, companies also put them to work directly from their homes.

telecommuting

a way of working that involves employees working some or all of the time at home PCs, accessing input from company computers and returning output via modem

Telecommuting. Relatively simple technology created **telecommuting,** in which employees work some or all of the time at home PCs, accessing input from company computers and returning output via modem. People have been telecommuting for nearly a decade. Telecommuters can connect to central systems almost as easily as employees in the same building to access needed information like daily sales reports and customer databases. Some jobs may require employees to visit the office only rarely—for example, sales professionals spend most of their time in the field dealing with customers or suppliers, and they send and retrieve information from a central system. Most telecommuters, however, spend some time at home handling routine information processing and some time at the central office meeting with colleagues.

Telecommuting has had a profound effect on the productivity of some businesses. A recent study estimated that employees who work at home can accomplish 10 to 20 percent more than when they are in the office. The looser work schedules that allow them to work at their peak productive times is cited as the reason. In 1993, 8.4 million workers telecommuted at least eight hours per week. This number is expected to top 30 million by the year 2000.[7] Companies need to ensure that employees are trained and ready to work without supervision, however. Successful telecommuters are usually familiar with their job, self-motivated and self-disciplined, adaptable, and knowledgeable about organizational rules and procedures.

Telecommuting also helps independent entrepreneurs to serve distant customers. For example, one Colorado resident works from his farm as a health care consultant.[8]

virtual office

a way of working that involves employees sharing resources but not physical facilities

Telecommuting creates a **virtual office,** where workers share resources but not physical facilities. In a newer twist on telecommuting, called *hoteling,* an organization maintains office space that its employees share. Employees make "reservations" to use the space and its hardware and software. The space may be used by many different employees, but not at the same time. Employees may also work from *telework centers,* which are smaller office environments located closer to residential neighborhoods.[9]

Telecommuters often report high satisfaction with their jobs, while companies gain flexibility in their labor resources and office facilities. Both sides must resolve important issues of employee supervision, support, and training, however.

Teleconferencing and Videoconferencing. Advancements in hardware and software will continue to expand and enrich the possibilities for virtual interactions between colleagues. Telephone technology has long allowed **teleconferencing,** in which many people using separate phones confer together in a single voice call. **Videoconferencing** extends this idea by combining voice, video, and data transmissions from several sites and sending them over phone lines or a satellite to display all participants' input together on a single monitor at each site. (See Figure 9.5.) The video component usually displays the participants' faces; the audio component carries their voices (and perhaps other sound input); the data component allows them to view the same documents and swap notes and drawings. Some systems already allow participants to make changes to shared documents in real time.

As discussed in Chapter 4, the substantial costs of high-speed phone lines inhibit the growth of videoconferencing. Other equipment also drives up costs, as do essential training and support. Yet, rapid changes in technology will help solve these problems, and videoconferences create new opportunities for profitable, cost-effective deployment of personnel. They also help to reduce the time and expense of business travel.

The lack of standards for videoconferencing technology had limited its spread, because potential users could not count on compatibility, especially between currently installed systems and future ones.[10] Technical advances are removing this obstacle, and costs will fall, as well, making videoconferencing an important and more routine business tool.

Another new technology involves linking employees with their computers and other equipment at the business site. Employees at Olivetti Research Laboratory wear tiny badges when they arrive at work. These badges allow their computers to follow their movements so that workers can pull up their

teleconferencing

technology by which many people using separate phones confer together in a single voice call

videoconferencing

technology that combines voice, video, and data transmissions from several sites and sends them over phone lines to display all participants' input together on a single monitor at each site

FIGURE 9.5

Videoconferencing
Videoconferencing technology allows distant participants to conduct face-to-face meetings and work cooperatively without costly travel. (Source: Photo courtesy of PictureTel.)

files on whatever computer is in front of them. In addition, the system forwards phone calls to voice mail whenever it detects three or more badges in one room; the program assumes that such employees are in a meeting and should not be disturbed. Phone calls can also be automatically forwarded to other offices by following the badges to ensure employees get their calls. Work is also under way on a built-in compass to dim computer screens when employees are turned away from their screens. This would allow the company to conserve energy.[11]

Software for Work Groups. While videoconferencing supports occasional meetings and other periodic events, work teams also need tools for routine exchanges of data and ideas within the office or around the world. We have already discussed the importance of groupware and intranet applications for this capability. They will become more important with the growing trend of combining team members from diverse locations and even organizations.

In addition to basic housekeeping functions like sending messages, more creative applications can stimulate the development of new ideas. For example, a team of independent copywriters, graphic artists, and media producers might hold brainstorming sessions via a groupware application to generate ideas for a bid on a prospective advertising campaign. Domecq Importers, a liqueur importer in Connecticut, generates ideas for promotions in just such a format.[12] In larger organizations, exchanges over the in-house network allow workers to propose their own initiatives and receive feedback from many people. The organizations can also post news, recommendations, and policy statements. Some human resource departments also use intranets to disseminate benefits information.

This support for information and original and innovative projects can provide a critical strategic tool for firms that must continually struggle to keep up with vigorous competition. Unfortunately, the characteristics that promote communication and creativity also bring potential disadvantages. Interactions in networked work groups may lack a human feel. Impersonal exchanges via electronic messages may fail to build strong bonds between co-workers. Also, misunderstandings may result from the lack of nonverbal communication cues like gestures and smiles.

Networking. Continuing the trend of increasing links within and among organizations is networked systems. We discussed client/server systems briefly when we described local-area networks. Today's integrated information systems demand flexible and powerful hardware configurations. Client/server systems create networks that connect users' computers (called *clients*) to one or more host computers (called *servers*). Personal computers often act as clients, and computers of all sizes act as servers, depending on particular network needs. A powerful PC or workstation might provide this function in a small network; many client/server systems include minicomputers, and the largest need mainframes. Chapter 4 introduced the first type of server, a file server, which distributes program files and document files to the network clients at their request; the clients then complete needed processing. A more centralized client/server network might require an **application server,** which stores program and document files for a particular application, such as an inventory database. A network client requests output data, and the application server responds by completing the necessary processing and returning only the needed results—not the application and input files. The server performs most processing, although the client can further process the results it receives.

application server

a server that stores program and document files for a particular application

middleware

systems software that controls interactions between clients and servers

peer-to-peer network

a network that allows a small business to connect personal computers to share files, printers, and other resources

electronic data interchange (EDI)

technology by which common network resources, standards, and procedures allow one system to pass its output directly to other systems as input

Middleware controls interactions between clients and servers. The layers of systems software that make up a network's middleware help to link diverse computing resources by translating all requests from client computers so they conform to network protocols and standards. Middleware also allows flexible access to all system resources by keeping track of what data and programs are stored on which servers.

Client/server systems have propelled a movement away from mainframes to smaller computer systems. Smaller, distributed networks often achieve lower long-term costs than larger, centralized networks. In addition, users enjoy more desktop control, enhanced flexibility, and responsive tools that adapt to business changes.

A small business can connect personal computers in a **peer-to-peer network** to share files, printers, and other resources. Each computer functions independently, but it can also access specific files on the hard drives of other computers or share printers connected to those machines. No server performs central coordination in this type of network. Instead, each computer connects to adjacent machines through cables and a network interface card. A special network operating system handles communications between nodes along with other file management and operating system tasks. Microsoft's Windows for Workgroups and Windows 95 operating systems can control peer-to-peer networks, as can Apple's Local Talk, Artisoft's LANtastic, and some less popular packages.

The computers in a peer-to-peer network usually complete processing tasks more slowly than comparable machines with internal access to all the necessary resources. On the other hand, the gain in flexibility from access to diverse resources usually compensates for the lost speed. Peer-to-peer networks often provide beginning systems from which small businesses can grow. They require only minimal costs for software and network interface cards, and some resources can become part of an enlarged system as the need arises.

Electronic Data Interchange. Businesses that establish connections between their computers quickly see benefits in expanding their networks to reach those of other organizations. This natural growth creates a system of **electronic data interchange (EDI)**, in which common network resources, standards, and procedures allow one system to pass its output directly to other systems as input. EDI links a company's computers with those of customers and vendors (Figure 9.6). This technology eliminates the need for many paper documents and substantially cuts down on costly data input errors. Customers can enter orders and inquire about delivery dates from their own computers rather than calling a sales rep and asking him or her to access the system. The producing company can then order its own materials and supplies directly in its supplier's computers.

EDI is a functional necessity for many firms. The largest companies, including General Motors and Dow Chemical, now draw most of the input to their computer systems not from their own transaction processing systems but from the computer systems of other companies. Smaller companies that want to do business with these companies must agree to implement compatible systems themselves. When they do, they gain important savings in data input costs as well as a deeper pool of data to support decision making. In addition, EDI helps separate companies to coordinate their activities so closely that they can operate with efficiency approaching that of a single company.

FIGURE 9.6

Two Methods of Electronic Data Interchange
EDI systems connect the computers of vendors and customers either (a) directly or (b) indirectly through the services of a third-party clearinghouse, which provides bookkeeping services for all participants. Many organizations now deal only with suppliers that operate their own EDI systems.

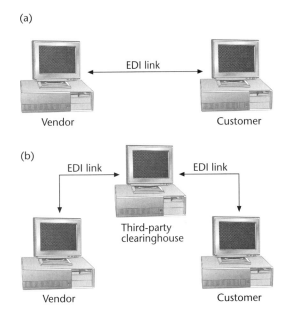

National Information Infrastructure (NII). Business networks will still continue expanding beyond the thorough integration of EDI. To accommodate this growth, a proposed National Information Infrastructure (NII) will combine fiber-optic cables, advanced switching equipment, and wide-ranging protocols to carry high-speed, digital information into businesses, schools, and even homes. The infrastructure will transport text, graphics, audio, and video data efficiently and effectively between almost any group of sites in the country.

The NII could cost hundreds of billions of dollars to construct, but it will bring incalculable benefits that will propel the United States to a new technological level. In addition, the lucrative contracts to construct its advanced facilities will nurture many successful companies and help to fuel nationwide economic growth.

The sources of funding for this massive undertaking remain uncertain, however. The U.S. Congress has already approved funding for the National Research and Education Network (NREN) to connect computers at U.S. universities. Proponents of the National Information Infrastructure hope that the NREN project will become a positive step toward full implementation.

BUSINESS TRENDS AND INFORMATION SYSTEM EFFECTS

Electronic data interchange and the National Information Infrastructure illustrate the IS effects of dramatic changes in customer expectations and companies' strategic responses. Some businesses have launched companywide process reengineering programs to completely redesign their basic activities and functions. In particular, quality and speed must increase to meet new customer expectations and competitive conditions. Businesses are also finding new ways to improve their products by embedding IS technology into the goods and services they sell. Firms of all sizes must respond to threats from global rivals and exploit opportunities for new relationships with global customers and suppliers. As leading business organizations have recognized and taken advantage of these trends, they have also reduced costs, increased profits, and improved customer satisfaction.

Process Reengineering and Continuous Improvement

Organizations in many industries can no longer stay competitive simply by maintaining practices that have produced past success. Most firms must regularly reevaluate and refine their business activities to keep pleasing customers and ward off competitors. In other words, they must abandon old processes and implement new ones to continue to prosper—or even to survive. This ongoing effort for **process reengineering**, also called *process redesign*, creates a need for simultaneous changes in the company information system to ensure that it effectively supports new tasks and activities. Reengineering effectively promotes important new business goals: to reduce delivery time, increase quality, enhance customer satisfaction, and boost revenues and profits.[13]

Hertz reengineered its information system to allow customers to enter their destinations into computer terminals and receive printouts containing maps and directions. Reengineering allowed it to add value for customers by integrating IS components into essential activities.

The new processes cannot guarantee continued success, however. Reengineering usually forms part of a drive for continuous improvement. The business ethic of **continuous improvement** requires all personnel to probe constantly for improvements in existing processes that will boost the value of the company's products to customers. In turn, the resulting increase in customer satisfaction and loyalty helps to frustrate competitors and ensure long-term profitability. IS resources have become such effective strategic tools that IS professionals sometimes lead reengineering initiatives.

Emphasis on Quality

Continuous improvement programs often target quality as a critical product characteristic. Many companies have found that quality enhancements provide valuable, long-term competitive advantages that other firms must struggle to match. As these firms pitch their well-made products, customers' expectations rise, and competitors must meet the new requirements or risk losing sales.

process reengineering

process that involves investigating and changing the tasks and activities performed by the organization and the technology used to support these tasks and activities

continuous improvement

a corporate goal of which the idea is to constantly seek ways to improve the business processes or tasks to add increased value to products and services in order to remain competitive and keep a strong customer base

Some car rental agencies are able to obtain a competitive advantage by offering on-the-spot printouts of directions to the customer's destinations. (Source: ©1996 Hertz System, Inc. Hertz is a registered service mark and trademark of Hertz System, Inc.)

```
                    H E R T Z
         COMPUTERIZED DRIVING DIRECTIONS
                 NEWARK AIRPORT:

EMBASSY SUITES HOTEL PARSIPPANY         APPROXIMATELY
909 PARSIPPANY BLVD.                      23.5 MILES
PARSIPPANY, NEW JERSEY                    0 :46 TIME
201 - 334 - 1440
- - - - - - - - - - - - - - - - - - - - - - - - - - - - - -

***ATTENTION***

These directions assume a departure from the Hertz Lot.  If you are
leaving from the terminal, please ask a Hertz representative for
directions.
-----------------------------------------------------------
TO EXIT: Follow arrows to main gate; show HERTZ rental envelope
         to guard.  Turn right, proceed to STOP sign, turn left,
         continue to airport exit signs.
-----------------------------------------------------------

  2.0 MI  NORTH  TO    I-78 WEST enter LEFT
  8.0 MI  WEST   TO    EXIT 48/RTE 24 WEST bear RIGHT
  9.0 MI  WEST   TO    I 287 NORTH        continue
  4.5 MI  NORTH  TO    EXIT 41A/RTE46WEST continue
                       LIGHT           turn LEFT continue
                       SIGNS FOR RTE 46 W  continue
                       PARSIPPANY BLVD     turn RIGHT
                       EMBASSY SUITES on your RIGHT
-----------------------------------------------------------
```

In fact, international buyers often demand formal certification of quality. Sellers must show evidence of conformance to recognized quality standards, such as those developed by the International Standards Organization (ISO) in Geneva, Switzerland, before these customers will consider any purchase. Developed in 1987, the ISO 9000 standards require certification of a seller's processes by an independent inspector. The ISO 9000 standards include requirements for issues such as establishing quality standards and documenting work processes. Standards cover product or service design, manufacturing, installation, and customer service. European companies, in particular, have widely adopted ISO 9000 standards, and many will place orders only with certified vendors.

The certification process requires substantial support from a candidate's information system. IS resources help decision makers to plan for quality improvement by compiling statistics that indicate current conditions and identify the sources of problems. IS resources also help to develop standards and procedures, monitor continuing gains in quality, and generate reports for managers and documentation for the independent inspector.

Several institutes and organizations help to maintain quality in IS processes themselves. The Software Engineering Institute (SEI) sets standards and guidelines for developing software. The Institute for Certification of Computer Professionals (ICCP) defines requirements that formally verify and recognize the skills of programmers, network managers, and IS managers.

Emphasis on Speed

Among sellers that meet customers' expectations for quality, speed in delivery of products and services can often be the determining factor for competitiveness. Fast suppliers allow a firm to maintain low inventories of components and to react quickly to changes in the requirements of its own customers. This has helped to accelerate all kinds of business activities and processes.

Computers can dramatically shorten time to market, the period during which a company introduces a newly designed product to the marketplace. Time to market begins with the period required for product design, including basic research, constructing and testing prototypes, and developing final specifications. **Computer-assisted design (CAD)** accelerates these activities by allowing repeated changes to a single product design, instead of completely redrawing each new version. In addition, product designers can quickly gather information from company databases and on-line resources, speeding research.

computer-assisted design (CAD)

technology that allows repeated changes to a single product design

In later stages of the design process, computer models simulate the results of physical tests without actually building prototypes and testing facilities. They may not replace all physical design evaluation, but they help to refine early versions so the characteristics of a prototype can closely resemble those of the final product. And in a new twist to CAD, companies are actually generating prototype parts in a few hours. CAD drawings are fed into a machine that creates a plastic prototype part. Tupperware is one company that is using this technology to speed product design and development.

In consumer testing of design proposals, computers quickly process survey responses and other types of customer feedback. Throughout all phases of this process, groupware helps members of the design team to share information and ideas. IS resources have contributed important support for an industrywide drive to cut time to market for new car designs from about five years to under three years.

computer-assisted manufacturing (CAM)

technology that allows central, electronic control of shop-floor activities

numerically controlled (NC) machines

machines that can process materials and complete production tasks in response to instructions from computer systems

In routine operations, computers reduce cycle time, also called *time to product,* the length of time a firm needs to make units of an existing product design. **Computer-assisted manufacturing (CAM)** cuts this time through central, electronic control of shop-floor activities. Robots and other **numerically controlled (NC) machines** can process materials and complete production tasks like welding and painting in response to instructions from computer systems. The main role of workers in such a system centers on programming, monitoring, and servicing these machines. Using systems like these, some automobile manufacturers have reduced the time a single car spends in production from about 15 days to about 3 days.

Embedded IS Technology

Besides using IS technology to support manufacturing and other business processes, increasing numbers of companies are building hardware and software into the products themselves. Chapter 2 described the functions of embedded microprocessors that control devices like microwave ovens. Extremely complex electronic control systems in today's cars sense operating conditions and automatically adjust air intake, spark duration, braking, and other functional variables.

Service providers also embed IS technology in the products that they offer to customers. FedEx, for example, relies on innovative information management processes to control the flow of overnight packages. As part of its service, FedEx provides software that helps shippers use the Internet (http://www.fedex.com) to schedule pickups by sending electronic messages to the company's dispatching centers. The software also allows customers to track letters and packages through every step on the way to their final destinations. By embedding software into its courier services, FedEx promotes customer satisfaction through prompt responses and open sharing of information. In addition, the software saves staffing expenses, since customers can answer their own queries instead of occupying the time of FedEx employees.

global positioning system (GPS)

technology that can indicate an individual car's location within 100 feet anywhere on the face of the earth based on data broadcast by satellite

Future trends promise still more elaborate IS components embedded into products. The Lincoln Continental automobile includes electronics to control braking and engine functions that have become standard inputs to most cars. In addition, the car's IS technology informs the driver of current driving conditions, including direction of travel, outside temperature, and much more. Still more innovative capabilities include a **global positioning system (GPS)**, which can indicate a position, such

Using computer-assisted design software, users can easily make changes to drawings and gather information from other sources. (Source: Image reprinted courtesy of Autodesk, Inc.)

as an individual car's location, within 100 feet anywhere on the face of the earth based on data broadcast by satellite. Lincoln's RESCU service accesses data from this GPS system through the car's cellular phone to speed emergency response when the driver requests help by pushing a button.

Another innovative automobile technology involves the sound system. Noise Cancellation Technologies has developed a way to use the lining of the car's roof as a "surround-sound" speaker. This eliminates the need for speakers in the dashboard and rear of the car.[14]

Global Business Environment

GPS technology represents only one result of the increasingly global business environment. Companies no longer buy materials and components only from suppliers in their own regions, and they need not deliver their own products only to local customers. IS technology plays a prominent role in global exchanges between customers, facilities, and suppliers. Advanced telecommunications systems allow Honda and BMW to integrate U.S. plants with their other worldwide facilities. McDonald's restaurants around the globe maintain close contact with the home office near Chicago. Even a two-employee bookstore can post its inventory of rare volumes on the World Wide Web and sell to collectors anywhere on the globe.

Business information systems support global operations by handling foreign languages, currency exchange rates, and varying rules and regulations. American Express runs a processing center near London that converts purchase data between many European currencies, including the British pound, the German mark, and others. A German citizen might charge purchases while traveling through Spain, Greece, Italy, and Britain. The American Express system restates these amounts in deutschemarks on a monthly statement printed in German.

value chain

an element that links an entire sequence of suppliers and customers to control production and distribution at every stage from raw materials to the final consumer

IS technology can link an entire sequence of suppliers and customers into a **value chain** that controls production and distribution at every stage from raw materials to the final consumer. Equally important, IS technology carries rapid feedback up the value chain to inform all participants how well their efforts have satisfied people who depend on them. Groupware and telecommunications systems allow global customers to join a company's product design and development teams, helping to ensure that those products provide needed features and capabilities.

global strategic alliance

a partnership formed by two or more companies from different countries to cooperate in joint production and distribution of goods and services

Applications of this technology can create new operating possibilities, and even new companies, that consolidate elements of formerly separate organizations. Two or more companies from different countries form a **global strategic alliance,** also called a *global strategic partnership,* when they agree to cooperate in joint production and distribution of goods and services. Chrysler and Mitsubishi developed such an alliance to jointly produce and distribute automobiles. Each company marketed identical car models produced on the same assembly line with its own names and some differences in equipment. A global strategic alliance demands careful coordination between the partners' information systems and technologies. Hardware, software, and procedures must compensate for differences in languages, currencies, cultures, electrical power systems, and government regulations.

Effective Business Information Systems in Action

Every year, *Computerworld* magazine publishes a list of the top 100 users of computers and information systems. The list, called the Computerworld *Premier 100,* cites businesses in almost every major industry that gain competitive advantages through their use of IS technology. In recognition of the importance of global business, *Computerworld* has recently begun to track the *Global 100*—the 100 most outstanding IS users around the world—as well.[15] Although this chapter cannot list and discuss the IS programs of all 100 firms, you can glimpse some general implementation issues by looking briefly at three industry leaders: one from Asia, one from Europe, and one from North America. Like most successful IS users, these three companies focused on a few critical factors that would determine the effectiveness of their information systems.[16]

Toyota. Toyota is Japan's biggest automobile exporter, with revenues of $94.6 billion a year. The company operates facilities in more than 20 countries, and it buys components from over 450 suppliers in the United States alone. It spends over $35 million annually to implement and maintain information systems in support of its auto production.

Toyota also provides an outstanding example of the contribution of information systems. The company uses IS technology extensively to integrate business processes and take maximum advantage of market opportunities. For one example, Toyota personnel developed the company's own computer-assisted design system through which engineers coordinate design work. The company's Lexus customer database also allows dealers for that luxury car division to obtain satellite transmissions of comprehensive customer service records on individual cars from a central database.

Toyota's most recent IS efforts center on implementation of a vast global network. Pressure from trading partners and a high value of the yen force the company to consider extensive component purchases from other countries. It has responded by linking widespread operations into one interconnected network to carry data and messages between headquarters in Japan and suppliers worldwide. The network helps Toyota to gather sales data, project production requirements, and communicate with suppliers via electronic data interchange. Toyota views the construction and refinement of this telecommunications system as an extremely important project. In the words of Kensuke Nagame, general manager of systems planning, "Our number one task is enhancing our global network." Toyota plans to continue upgrading the network to incorporate multimedia capabilities and Internet connections throughout Asia.[17] The primary keys to Toyota's IS success include:

- Telecommunications links that integrate worldwide operations and provide superior customer service
- Careful deployment of new technology where it provides the most powerful benefits for the company and best promotes the overall business strategy
- Emphasis on continuous improvement, which drives perpetual enhancements to its information systems

Asea Brown Boveri (ABB). Asea Brown Boveri, one of the world's largest engineering firms, specializes in designing robots and power plants. Born out of a merger with smaller companies from separate countries, the $28 billion firm maintains a paradoxical mission of a global company with a local vision

—"large overall, but individually small, with 5,000 profit centers; decentralized but with centralized reporting."[18] Since its inception, ABB has spent about $700 million annually on IS resources. It employs 5,000 IS personnel to coordinate its vast information resources.

After the merger, the company's first IS task centered on building an integrated information system from an initial patchwork of hardware and software. Within months, IS personnel had created a centralized financial reporting application linking the company's operations in 140 countries to headquarters in Zurich. IS manager Bengt Skantze noted some daunting challenges in building the telecommunications system to support the reporting application; poor telephone networks in some countries forced ABB to transmit data from many locations over satellite links.

Within financial controls from headquarters, ABB maintains a strong commitment to decentralization. Each business unit typically chooses its own applications for local processing tasks. Separate operations share only two standardized applications: the financial reporting system and a groupware system that facilitates interactive work among 13,000 users worldwide.

IS resources provide important capabilities that help ABB to improve the business. CEO Percy Barnevik has stated that "any company that doesn't consider itself an [IS] company is doomed."[19] Information systems contribute to ABB's competitive advantage in several ways. They reduce cycle times in engineering, manufacturing, and field work through computer simulation, robotics technology, and the integrated links with suppliers. IS resources also boost sales by showing customized products on-screen to help prospective customers visualize ABB's products. During sales calls, the firm's IS tools perform what-if analysis of price projections on-site. If necessary, sales reps can immediately connect to specialists via telecommunications links.[20]

Major keys to ABB's success include:

- A T – 50 program (named for the phrase "time minus 50 percent") designed to improve customer service and cut lead time in half
- A continuing commitment to decentralization that allows each unit to choose the best IS solution for its operations, while maintaining efficient, centralized activities for certain tasks
- Continually sharing information about "best practices" and successful routines and ideas through global circulation of assignments for outstanding managers

United Parcel Service (UPS). UPS provides international shipping service to customers in 200 countries and territories, delivering some three billion packages each year. The company intends to maintain its position among the most effective IS users today by creating a new competitive edge based on those capabilities.

UPS became an IS leader by launching a five-year, $2 billion plan in 1985 to introduce information technology that would provide an advantage over rivals Federal Express and Roadway Services. The plan has since grown into a ten-year, $3 billion comprehensive strategy for information systems.

In the course of this initiative, the company's information systems group has grown by 3,800 people, and the budget has expanded by $160 million. Chief Information Officer Frank Erbrick and his IS team have become technology champions, linking 70 commercial carriers in the first nationwide mobile data service. The team also invested $180 million to equip all 53,000 delivery vehicles with handheld computers. In 1994, UPS began taking customer orders via on-line services like CompuServe and Prodigy. It now offers various services on its World Wide Web page (http://www.ups.com): on-line supply ordering, a locator for drop-offs, pickup service notification, and quick cost calculation, as well as package tracking and estimations of ground transit time—all in both IBM and Apple formats.

Information systems have created undeniable advantages for United Parcel Service. Sales have risen $11.8 billion, and income is up $332 million during the strategic IS initiative. UPS will continue its successful plan by building a global customer automation system and installing handheld units in all new company vehicles. By 1996, UPS revamped its package tracking systems, providing on-line data on the status of over two million packages.[21]

Some of the company's primary keys for success include:

- Aggressive, intimately linked strategies for the business and its information systems, with clear goals and strong investments
- Meticulous implementation of new technology and information systems to coordinate business processes
- Adding value for customers and suppliers by making the company more accessible via computers

Such uses of technology will be surpassed by the time this book is in print. But gaining knowledge of computers and information systems can help you maintain your competitive advantage in business, whether you plan to operate your own small business or become part of a larger organization.

This book has presented the basics of information systems to show how you can use IS in your daily life. But it is up to you to continue your education by reading news articles, subscribing to computer and professional journals, and being aware of the technology around you. Staying current can give you the best career boost and help you take advantage of innovations to enrich your life.

- Today's software helps busy people to reduce the time they spend learning new tools and increase the time they spend performing valuable work.

- Telecommunications-based initiatives like the JASON Project will take students to the cutting edge of research, where they can learn in direct ways that traditional instruction cannot match.

- Middleware links together diverse computing resources in a client/server system by translating all client requests so they conform to network protocols and standards; it also tracks the locations of specific resources within the system.

- Information systems have become such effective strategic tools that IS professionals sometimes lead companywide process reengineering initiatives.

SUMMARY

1. *Describe the expanding roles that computers will play in technologically advanced homes and schools.* Computer-assisted instruction methods, including software tutorials, rely on IS technology to present self-paced sequences of text, graphics, and sounds that convey information. At home, many people use processing hardware built into consumer products without knowing it. Sophisticated new systems based on the Consumer Electronics Bus (CEBus) standard use IS resources to support many more visible domestic tasks, as well, including security, lighting and appliance control, and even lawn care. Computers support many leisure activities through games and other entertainment software, sports training hardware and software, and artists' tools.

2. *Explain the impact of telecommunications on future applications of IS technology at home and in school.* The Internet leads the list of telecommunications applications at home and in school. Students and home users can share their work and interests with others by creating their own home pages on the World Wide Web. Future developments will bring shopping, conversation, and unforeseen kinds of interactions to home computer screens. Despite limitations created by impersonal interactions, schools implement cost-effective distance learning programs to bring remote expertise and materials to locations convenient to students.

3. *List the newest business applications of telecommunications technology.* Companies have begun to transform traditional relationships with employees, customers, and suppliers through telecommunications links. Telecommuters work some or all of the time at home PCs, accessing input from company computers and returning output via modem. Videoconferencing and groupware already allow team members at separate locations to work effectively together on shared projects. Client/server systems and peer-to-peer networks are replacing centralized networks with flexible, decentralized information systems that place processing capabilities where users need them. Customers and suppliers often coordinate network resources, standards, and procedures to create electronic data interchange (EDI) systems in which one information system passes its output directly to other systems as input. The National Information Infrastructure (NII) will promote even more integration of separate IS resources.

4. *Outline the effects of information systems trends on business.* Information systems have become essential competitive tools for process reengineering driven by a widely recognized need for continuous improvement. IS resources support strategic efforts to speed production or improve quality by compiling statistics and other documentation required for certification programs like ISO 9000. In addition, several institutes and organizations set standards for quality in IS processes themselves. IS technology like computer-assisted design (CAD) and groupware promotes strategic improvements in speed by cutting the time needed for product design and other elements of time to market. Computer-assisted manufacturing (CAM) increases speed by accelerating production schedules and other components of cycle time. IS resources embedded in products (like FedEx's tracking software and Lincoln's global positioning system) add new capabilities that enhance customer satisfaction. As business exchanges demand more global partnerships, organizations expand electronic data interchange and other IS arrangements in ways that blur the boundaries between them. Toyota, Asea Brown Boveri, and United Parcel Service provide valuable examples of IS resources implemented to meet specific organizational and operating needs.

 ## Key Terms

computer-assisted instruction
  (CAI) 279
tutorial 279
graphics tablet 285
Telecommunications Act of 1996 286
home page 287
distance learning 288
telecommuting 289
virtual office 289

teleconferencing 290
videoconferencing 290
application server 291
middleware 292
peer-to-peer network 292
electronic data interchange (EDI) 292
process reengineering 294
continuous improvement 294
computer-assisted design (CAD) 295

computer-assisted manufacturing
  (CAM) 296
numerically controlled (NC)
  machines 296
global positioning system (GPS) 296
value chain 297
global strategic alliance 297

 ## Concept Quiz

Answer the following questions briefly.

1. Name three ways educators use computers for basic functions.
2. What is computer-assisted instruction?
3. Name three general areas in which computers are used to help households function.
4. How does a graphics tablet work?
5. What legislative act has removed barriers to competition among telephone, computer, and cable TV companies?

Fill in the blanks to complete the following statements.

6. Individuals can share knowledge as well as personal histories by developing their own _____ on the World Wide Web.

7. The most common method of remote instruction, _____, connects classrooms at different locations via computers and telecommunications.

8. _____ allows employees to work at home on PCs, accessing input from company computers and returning output via modem.

9. _____ create networks that connect users' computers to one or more host computers.

10. A small business can connect personal computers in a _____ to share files, printers, and other resources.

Mark "true" or "false" after each of the following statements.

11. Quality and speed of information systems will have to continually increase to meet new customer expectations and competitive conditions in the business environment. _____

12. Computer-assisted design can help a company shorten the length of time it takes to get a product to market. _____

13. In computer-assisted manufacturing, many people are needed on the assembly line. _____

14. IS technology can now link an entire sequence of suppliers and customers into a value chain that controls production and distribution at every stage from raw materials to the final customer. _____

15. Global strategic alliances rarely function well because of such a vast difference between countries in information systems and technologies. _____

Discussion Questions

1. During your entire school career, what kinds of changes have you observed or experienced in the process of education due to computers?

2. In what ways does your household (dorm, apartment, family, etc.) depend on computers to function?

3. Do you think that expanded use of telecommunications (in particular, the Internet) will increase or decrease individuals' isolation from one another? Explain your answer.

4. Think of the chapter-opening photo on the Peapod Grocery Service. Do you look forward to grocery shopping from home? Why or why not?

Team Activity

Divide the class into teams of three or four. Each team should choose a topic—a particular company or industry that interests them—and design a distance-learning session on the topic. The team does not have to conduct extensive research on the company or industry itself but should concentrate on the components of the distance-learning situation. What media will they use? What equipment will they need? Will they use a lecture or demonstration? Will they need graphics? Applications software? Where will they obtain the components they need? The team should write a brief description of its plans.

Applying IT

1. If possible, access the Internet and browse for any information you can find on the Telecommunications Act of 1996. Look for information that refers to ways that communications will change and expand as a result of the act. Think about how the legislation may change your own life. If you do not have access to the Internet, go to the library to find out what you can about the Telecommunications Act.

2. Go to the library to obtain *Computerworld's* list of Premier 100 and/or Global 100 companies. Choose a company from the list (not the ones discussed in the chapter) and, through the Internet, see what you can learn about the company's IS programs. If you do not have access to the Internet, try to obtain your information about the company from the library. Write a short report for the class and be prepared to discuss it.

CASE

Smart Cars

Cars are getting smart, and if firms like Delco Electronics, TRW, Eaton, and Leica have anything to say about it, they'll be getting even smarter. What these firms have in common is the goal of equipping your car with computer-driven devices that can navigate, offer "intelligent" cruise control, and give you night vision. In some cases, these products are already available—on some cars, and for a fairly high price. The goal is to get them into every car, at an affordable price.

Navigation products using global positioning systems (GPSs) are already on the market. These work via a computer built into the car that communicates with a satellite to determine your location. General Motors (http://www.gm.com) offers these on its new Cadillacs. Called OnStar, the computer program uses the GPS to find your location and then gives you directions via a cellular telephone. OnStar also works as an emergency service system. If your car breaks down, to obtain help you can push a button on your cell phone and you are connected to an advisor who can pinpoint your location and send help. If your car is in a collision, OnStar automatically sends a signal to the control center. The cost of OnStar is $1,000. Japanese car companies offer a similar product that uses electronic maps instead of the cell phone to tell you where you are; the price tag is around $2,000.

Delco (http://www.delco.com), TRW, Eaton, and Leica are all working on intelligent cruise control products, ones that automatically slow down your car when they detect another vehicle close by. Texas Instruments (http://www.ti.com) has developed a night vision camera that can be set into a car's front grille. The camera, like those used by the military, sees objects in terms of their temperature rather than their light, producing a picture that looks like a photographic negative. The display device sits on top of the dashboard. Night vision capability would allow a driver to see a pedestrian walking off the side of the road (outside the range of headlights) at night. But the price tag is hefty (it costs the military about $20,000 to equip just one vehicle with night vision), and Texas Instruments is working on getting it down to about $2,500.

One major concern about these products—other than malfunctions and the possibility of false signals—is distraction to drivers. "The concern is, are these products going to cause more accidents than they help you avoid?" notes John Ference, an electronics engineer in the Office of Crash Avoidance Research. "We can't expect drivers to become fighter pilots." But most likely, drivers will learn to adapt—in fact, eventually they will probably insist on all the extra bells and whistles.

Questions

1. How do you think these new products will affect manufacturing standards in the auto industry?
2. Would you find these products distracting as a driver? Why or why not? Do you think they represent a new wave of technology for consumers? Why or why not?
3. If possible, access the Web sites for Delco and Texas Instruments to see what you can learn about their products. Then access the site for General Motors to see how it presents OnStar.

Source: Edward A. Robinson, "Soon Your Dashboard Will Do Everything," *Fortune*, July 22, 1996, pp. 76–78.

Answers to Concept Quiz

1. For recordkeeping; for student work (such as reports); for class presentations 2. Instruction in which the computer presents self-paced sequences of text, graphics, and sound 3. Any three of the following: security; lighting and appliance control; lawn and garden care; entertainment and leisure 4. It translates movements of a stylus across its surface into an image on the screen.
5. Telecommunications Act of 1996 6. home pages
7. distance learning 8. Telecommuting 9. Client/server systems 10. peer-to-peer network 11. True 12. True
13. False 14. True 15. False

APPENDIX A

Buying, Using, and Upgrading a Personal Computer

CHAPTER OUTLINE

Before Buying a Personal Computer System
    Do You Need a Computer?
    What Is Your Budget?
    Study New Computer Developments and Prices
Buying a Personal Computer System
    Buying Software
    Finally, the Hardware
    Peripheral Components, Supplies, and Services
Using a Personal Computer System
    Using Hardware
    Using Software: General Principles
    Using Software: User Interfaces
When Something Goes Wrong
    General Strategy for Solving Problems
Upgrading an Existing Computer System

Businesses rely on their computer systems for daily operations. What if something goes wrong or the equipment or software needs to be upgraded? Many companies do not have an in-house computer expert to assist them with their computer problems. ComputerNerds to the rescue? ComputerNerds specializes in providing businesses with highly trained, tested, and certified computer technicians. Their experienced computer professionals can step in at a moments notice and satisfy a business's computer system demands, whether the job is adding servers and workstations or upgrading software, ComputerNerds can send the right technician for the job, right away. Photo courtesy of ComputerNerds (954) IM A NERD.

OBJECTIVES

This appendix contains tips that will help you to:

1. Prepare before shopping for a personal computer system.
2. Buy software and then hardware appropriate for your personal information system.
3. Use hardware and software effectively.
4. Formulate a constructive response when something goes wrong with your system.
5. Decide when and how to upgrade a personal computer system to maintain or improve its performance.

New computer systems line the shelves of retailers, each one promising amazing technical wonders. Their exciting demonstration displays fill the aisles with flashing colors and dazzling sound effects. Bright color ads crowd the pages of newspapers and computer magazines with desirable product features and appealing claims.

So many intriguing options make computer shopping a challenge, even for long-time PC users. Someone who has never purchased or used a personal computer could feel completely lost in this complex and dynamic market.

Almost everyone will likely buy many personal computers in the future, either for their own use at home, for their business, or through their employers' purchasing functions. Computer users need clear guidelines for making important decisions about buying new hardware and software. This appendix presents some guidelines, suggestions, and hints to help you understand when, what, and how to purchase. It also refers to installation procedures and covers priorities in upgrading existing systems.

BEFORE BUYING A PERSONAL COMPUTER SYSTEM

The purchase decision requires some preliminary thinking before you start shopping for features and prices, as Figure A.1 illustrates. Do not buy anything until you have determined whether you really need a personal computer of your own. Systems at your workplace or school may allow you to complete essential computing tasks. If you do not need a system for after-hours work or for your own purposes, you may decide not to buy one.

As computers gain new and exciting capabilities, growing numbers of people decide to invest in their own systems. If you are among them, continue the decision process by evaluating your total budget, studying new developments in personal computer technology, and gathering general information about prices.

Do You Need a Computer?

People use personal computers for many purposes. Students and workers use computers at home, in school-based labs, and on the job to conduct research,

FIGURE A.1

The Purchase Decision Process
After resolving initial questions of need and budget and researching the market, choose applications software. Then choose an operating system and hardware that will run the desired applications.

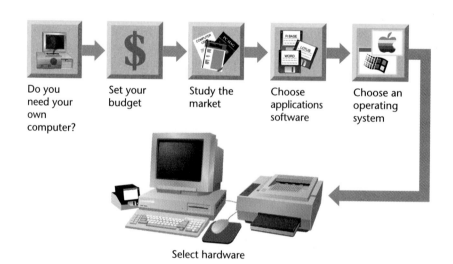

Do you need your own computer? Set your budget Study the market Choose applications software Choose an operating system

Select hardware

TABLE A.1

Checklist for Buying a Personal Computer
For each computing task, mark a priority from 1 to 10, where 1 indicates an activity for which you might possibly use a computer and 10 indicates something you must do that you can accomplish only with a personal computer. If your total score is 10 or more, consider buying a personal computer of your own.

COMPUTING TASK	PRIORITY
Research selected topics	_____
Manage household expenses	_____
Keep accurate records	_____
Complete work assignments	_____
Organize time	_____
Communicate with others	_____
Entertain yourself	_____
Total score	_____

write letters and reports, make presentations, telecommunicate, and organize their time. Many use computers at home to manage household expenses, keep accurate records, communicate with others, and entertain themselves. Table A.1 is a checklist of some common applications. Follow the instructions with the table to develop a rough indication of your real need for your own personal computer system.

Some people buy computers for poor reasons:

- It seems like a good idea to them, but they cannot say what they will really do with their systems.
- They can afford the price, and the market seems to offer some good buys.
- They know people who own computers.
- They think their children will not be able to "keep up" with classmates without a computer.

Almost all computer owners discover new applications for their systems that they did not anticipate when they decided to buy. Still, some idea of the computer's probable role in your life should guide your decision whether to make the purchase.

What Is Your Budget?

If you decide to buy a personal computer, you should set a total budget for the purchase before heading to the store. Of course, hardware accounts for just part of the total system expense. Recall from Chapter 3 that expanding capabilities require new applications software; the prices of these packages account for a large and growing part of the cost of any information system. In addition, a computer owner must buy certain supplies, and desirable peripheral equipment will raise the system's cost as well. Table A.2 lists some categories of expenses that may help you plan how much to spend. Individual expenses add up quickly, so the table may work best if you enter the total that you can afford first and then divide that amount among the system components.

TABLE A.2

Complete Computer System Cost

SYSTEM COMPONENT	COST
System unit (including keyboard and disk drives, possible CD-ROM drive)	_____
Monitor (color/black and white, size)	_____
Printer (laser/ink jet/thermal wax, color/black and white, page size)	_____
Peripheral hardware (modem/fax-modem/voice modem and speed, CD-ROM drive, surge protector, cables, backup storage, etc.)	_____
Operating system software	_____
Applications software (word processing, spreadsheet, database, graphics, Internet access, and other packages)	_____
Supplies (paper and ink cartridges for the printer, blank diskettes, etc.)	_____
Total system cost	_____

Study New Computer Developments and Prices

Now you know what you expect to spend, but you should not buy the first personal computer system you see that fits your budget. Before you start comparing specific systems, take some time to check new developments in PC technology and normal market prices. You can find valuable, up-to-date information in the computer industry magazines listed as resources for literacy in Chapter 1. These magazines publish user reviews of all types of personal computer systems, devices, and software. They also evaluate emerging technologies that will affect system performance. Finally, advertisements by personal computer companies and mail-order vendors provide reliable information about prices.

Another set of magazines covers broader developments in the computer industry. These magazines provide reports on the companies that make and sell computer equipment, software, and services. Also, general business journals cover business applications of computers and information systems.

As you read about dazzling new hardware speeds and exciting software capabilities, keep your own needs firmly in mind. If you will not produce videos with elaborate special effects, you probably do not need an expensive new video editing program. But *do* keep in mind future needs. For example, if your home-based design business expands, you will want some flexibility, not limitations that make buying a new system necessary. Be realistic, but keep future plans in mind.

The Intel Pentium® Pro processor comes in a variety of speeds and prices. (Source: Courtesy of Intel Corporation.)

The background information you gather at this stage will make you an informed shopper and help you to make a good decision. Before you contact a vendor, though, you may want to reconsider the cost information that you entered in Table A.2. Compare your budget with the prices you found in your research to get a clear price range for a computer that will do what you want it to do. After completing this preparation, you are ready to go shopping for a new computer.

BUYING A PERSONAL COMPUTER SYSTEM

Someone new to the personal computer market may feel intimidated by the bewildering range of choices and prices. This section develops a sensible decision process to help you sort through competing claims and information system demands. Your information needs or those of your company should guide your choice of IS components.

Buying Software

Many people start shopping by comparing the prices and capabilities of available hardware packages. Remember, however, that you are buying a personal information system rather than just a computer. Applications programs perform the useful work that an information system requires, so the purchase decision should begin with these packages. You then choose the operating system and hardware configuration that will effectively run your chosen applications.

In Table A.1 you listed the computing jobs that you need to complete and set your priorities. These needs determine the applications you should buy.

Return to the magazines you gathered from the list in Chapter 1 to read user reviews of competing applications packages. Ask other users (especially staff at your school computer lab) which programs they prefer. Also, take time to try out the software yourself before buying. Even a short demonstration while standing in a store aisle or using demonstration programs downloaded from the Internet can give you a feel for a package's capabilities and operating routines.

Of course, your budget will govern your software choices, but consider more than just cost. Evaluate each package's capabilities, speed, ease of use, user support (perhaps including training programs), documentation, and compatibility with other programs. Shareware or freeware may do what you need at extremely low cost, but you may have to figure out how to use these programs on your own without

Take some time to determine your needs before selecting a software package. (Source: Alan Levenson/Tony Stone Images.)

user support or even much documentation. Many publishers of popular applications offer substantial discounts to students; check with your lab assistant or college bookstore.

An integrated package like Microsoft Works, ClarisWorks, Lotus SmartSuite, or Perfect Office can often meet several computing needs at low cost. In fact, hardware packages frequently include these programs. Buying software bundled with hardware can save both money and time, since you would have to spend time installing separately purchased software.

People who need more sophisticated capabilities can gain some of the same benefits by purchasing suites of dedicated applications. For example, Microsoft's Office bundle includes its popular word processing package Word, its spreadsheet Excel, its database program Access, and its presentation program PowerPoint. The suite costs much less than the total of the prices of the separate programs, and all of the applications share both data and operating routines. Other suites offer similar benefits and capabilities.

Sources of Software. You can buy the same application from many vendors. Some software publishers sell their products directly to customers. Computer retailers offer competing packages side by side for easy comparison, and their sales staff can give useful information. In addition, these stores often give advice about problems installing and using the software, and many of them run training classes as well. Mail-order vendors may offer the best prices, but they usually provide little or no after-sale support or service. Check the prices at your college bookstore before buying anywhere else.

Choose an Operating System. Your chosen applications packages run under specific operating systems, so your purchase decisions actually determine your systems software needs as well. Today, most new computers have the system software already loaded, and the systems are usually the most current available. You can find many good programs in each platform for computing needs. Make sure that the operating system will handle your highest-priority application, and compromise, if necessary, in selecting less important packages. Remember that newer operating systems will usually run older applications, but newer applications will generally not run on older operating systems. (This is a consideration if you are buying a used computer.)

Most personal computer users choose one of these two operating system platforms: Windows and the Macintosh operating system (although many high-end workstations work under versions of Unix). Many users match their own systems to those at work or school to ensure that they can manipulate the same document files on different systems. Fortunately, today's applications, perhaps supplemented by utility programs, can often convert and read document files created in other applications and even other platforms. Also, software publishers often sell versions of popular applications with comparable features for both platforms, giving you some flexibility in this choice. (See Figure A.2.)

Still, compatible, well-matched systems can most easily share data. The effectiveness of your information system depends on how well its components—applications, operating system, and hardware—work together to perform the processing that you need. Build your system to make the most of links with other systems.

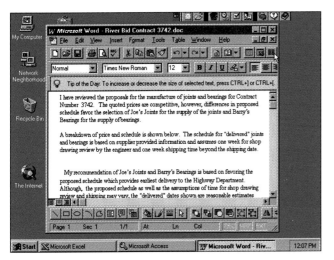
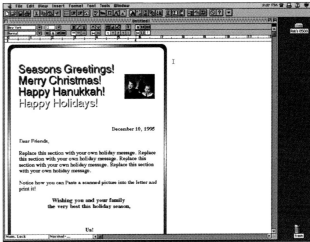

FIGURE A.2

Applications and Operating Systems
Software publishers offer popular applications programs for both PC platforms. Choose the one that does the best job on functions that you need most often.

Finally, the Hardware

To run Windows and its family of applications, you will need an IBM-compatible computer (one with an Intel microprocessor). To run Macintosh applications, you must buy a computer from Apple or one of its clones (e.g., Power Computing). The types of applications you will run determine the power and speed of the CPU you will need, as well as the additional system components.

A system limited to basic report writing might require only 8 MB of RAM, a 200-MB hard disk, and a printer. Your applications will probably require a more elaborate configuration, though. Hardware needs grow quickly if you run more than one program at the same time, especially if you will be running multimedia applications. To take full advantage of applications programs, your computer system will likely need at least 16 MB of RAM and a 1-GB (1,000 MB) or 2-GB hard disk. Form 1 at the end of this appendix is a Software Selection Grid. You can fill this in to compare hardware needs, capabilities, and costs and take it with you as you shop.

Choose your hardware configuration in anticipation of changes in your computing needs. Consider buying more capacity than you currently need; you would probably spend even more later to install additional RAM, hard disk, and processor capacity. Look for a system board that offers empty expansion slots to accommodate circuit boards with new capabilities, including an interface card through which you can connect to a network.

Some information systems require portable computing functions, perhaps to take class notes or provide information to customers during sales calls. If you have needs like these, you must buy a laptop or notebook computer. If not, a desktop computer often provides the same information processing capabilities at lower cost. Along with the criteria for all personal computer systems, several unique criteria affect the choice between portable units:

- Weight
- Battery life and type of AC power supply
- Mouse, trackball, or other pointing device
- Peripheral equipment like small printers and matchbox-sized modems
- Carrying case
- Docking station availability, if larger screen output is a consideration

Resist the temptation to save money by purchasing a poor-quality monitor; a low-resolution display can dramatically increase the physical strain of extended computing sessions. If you plan to create or view complex graphics, you may spend more for a large, high-resolution screen display than you pay for your system unit! A laptop or notebook unit probably includes an LCD display. Recall from Chapter 2 that passive-matrix LCD displays cannot match the clarity and resolution of active-matrix displays.

Many software publishers now distribute the program files for their applications packages on CD-ROM, and you may want to run other CD products on your computer. This storage device has become standard equipment on almost any personal computer system. Also, if you plan to work with multimedia, look for a computer system bundle specifically intended for multimedia applications. Such a package often costs less than you would spend to outfit a generic system with a CD-ROM drive, speakers, TV tuner, and other components.

You may also want a tape backup unit, scanner, joystick, and other miscellaneous hardware for your system. Your instructor, computer lab staff, fellow students, friends, and family may all offer recommendations about which hardware components to include in your system and which brands to buy. Read reviews and other reports in the magazines mentioned in Chapter 1 to determine what criteria experienced users consider when they compare hardware, as well as the performance ratings of specific brands. Spend some time trying out different configurations to see for yourself how quickly each one loads a file and completes a processing operation, how clear the monitor screen looks, how sharp the printer output seems, and so on.

Besides price and computing capabilities, the purchase decision should consider warranty terms, availability of repair service, and the manufacturers' reputations. A multiyear service contract might reduce any uncertainty about the reliability of your new system.

There are several components you can purchase for your computer system; each has a specific function such as a camera for video conferencing. (Source: Courtesy of IBM Corporation.)

WHO'S WHO

Michael P. Krasny/CDW

Michael Krasny is a salesman who founded a phone-order computer company. He's also a computer buff. And he happens to be one of *Forbes* magazine's top 20 technology executives.

As recently as a few years ago, mail-order computer businesses were not considered a viable source for computers. IBM, Apple, Compaq, and other manufacturers didn't want to supply the outfits, which were perceived to be fly-by-night. But that has changed—thanks in part to Michael Krasny's CDW and other companies such as Gateway 2000 Inc. Direct selling is cost-effective for manufacturers and sellers such as CDW; it is convenient for customers. In short, it is a win-win situation.

Krasny first got into the business when he needed some quick cash. He'd left his family business and had nothing else solid lined up. So he decided to sell his own computer and printer by placing a classified ad. The system sold right away. He then began buying new, stripped-down IBM clone computers and packaging them with moderately priced monitors and printers. He advertised those in the classifieds, and they sold right away, too. Next he bought a national ad in *PC World*, and his phone wouldn't stop ringing. "The phone started to ring like crazy," says Krasny. "People started sending certified checks by Federal Express." A couple of years later, Krasny sent out his first catalog (eight pages in two colors). Now, CDW mails a 96-page, four-color catalog to nearly half a million customers. The company, which has offices in Buffalo Grove, Illinois, also has a 105,000-square-foot office and sales associates who generate 90 percent of the company's sales through the phone banks.

Krasny believes that the company's success depends on its telemarketing efforts. He has electronic tote boards posted around CDW's offices so that managers can determine at a glance how many callers are on hold and how many seconds they have been waiting for assistance. Sales staff are expected to field at least 70 calls per day. That sounds like a lot of pressure, but Krasny also pays his employees well. "I made the decision to make my people the best-paid in the business," he notes. He is also available to anyone who needs to talk with him. "You always know that Michael is downstairs," notes a CDW sales rep. "You can always e-mail him with a question."

How do the big computer manufacturers feel about CDW these days? IBM, Apple, and Compaq are now CDW's largest suppliers. Krasny knows he needs his vendors in order to stay in business. He also knows he needs to procure their products at the best price he can get. "[Krasny's] business has been built on negotiating on price," says Chris Schultze, a senior account manager for Ingram Micro Inc., a $1 billion computer wholesaler. She also concedes that "he is one of the major players in the mail-order arena."

So far, Krasny hasn't made a big play for Internet customers. But he may change his mind, if he thinks CDW's presence on the Internet will increase business. In either case, he won't be standing still. "Here's a guy who has made it as big as anybody," observes one colleague, "yet he's running scared." He's also running toward a $1 billion goal by the turn of the century.

Source: Mark Veverka, "Car Lots to Computers," *Crain's Chicago Business*, March 11, 1996, pp. 14–15.

Hardware Vendors. The same retailers and mail-order vendors usually sell both software and hardware. (See "Who's Who: Michael P. Krasny/CDW.") If you will need help installing your system or learning to use it, consider buying your PC from a local dealer that offers these services.

Different types of vendors sell used computers. Newspaper ads, bulletin boards, and on-line newsgroups list offers by private parties to sell used computers. This market resembles that for used cars. Prices can seem attractive, but you may buy nothing more than someone else's problems.

Complete the Hardware Selection Grid (Form 2) at the end of this appendix for each system you will consider as you shop. Later you can compare the hardware configurations and their prices to identify which is best for your needs.

Peripheral Components, Supplies, and Services

Peripheral equipment, software, and supplies can provide important resources for your personal information system. Hardware packages often include printers, or you may choose one in a separate purchase. Be sure to buy all needed cables to connect remote components to your system unit. Every personal computer system should plug into a power strip with surge protection; technically an optional piece of equipment, the surge protector safeguards your expensive hardware against damage due to variations in electrical voltage. It also allows you to turn power on and off to all system devices at once. Do not forget paper, spare ink cartridges, and blank diskettes.

The growing popularity of commercial on-line hookups and Internet access has made these services a critical part of the system purchase for many people. You need both hardware (a modem) and communications software to go on-line; purchase these system components by following the guidelines for hardware and software discussed previously in this section.

Most colleges and universities offer e-mail, access to the Internet, and other telecommunications services to students and staff. Magazines print ads for and reviews of many national on-line services, and your instructor or lab assistant might offer information about local alternatives. Ask users of these services about their own experiences. In particular, ask whether repeated delays or prolonged breakdowns prevent customers from connecting. A service that you want to evaluate may offer a short-term, trial membership to allow you to judge its features for yourself.

Different services give you different capabilities. Your choice depends on whether you want full Internet access or just an e-mail address. Be sure that your modem's speed will allow you to do what you need. Downloading large files (such as the graphics associated with World Wide Web pages) will stretch your patience if your modem does not reach a speed of at least 14.4 kbps. As mentioned in Chapter 4, a fax/modem (together with communications software) adds an attractive capability to your system for a small increase over the price of a standard modem.

Also, an important warning from Chapter 4 bears repetition: Be careful about transmitting your credit card number over the Internet to buy products—even computer products. Someone may intercept your transmission and charge purchases to your card unless you have a safe method to do so.

Finally, remember that relentless change in technology will continue after you buy your system. Software publishers will announce new versions of applications you have just bought, kindly allowing you to upgrade for another $100 or more. The new software will fill more space on a hard disk that seemed to offer such a vast amount of storage when you bought it. Your shiny new computer will almost certainly seem outdated soon after you take it home, but resist the temptation to second-guess your purchase decision. If you wait for the next new development before buying, you will never own a computer. Instead, concentrate on using the computer you buy to do what you need to do.

Once you purchase your system, you can begin using your new personal computer after you install both hardware and software. These steps need not intimidate even a relatively new computer user. Most hardware installation occurs before the computer reaches you; you simply connect components and verify that they work as you expect. Similarly, applications packages for both

Windows and the Macintosh operating system come with simple routines for installing them on your hard disk.

Regardless of the installation routine, it is important to locate your PC on a desk or stand in a clean, cool location away from high-traffic areas and sources of magnetic fields. It should be close to an electrical outlet and near a phone jack if you will be using a modem. Also, to ensure that you have received the correct equipment, it is best to clear your work area and carefully unpack all of the equipment. This will verify that you have everything you need, including equipment, cables, and manuals.

USING A PERSONAL COMPUTER SYSTEM

Once you install your personal computer system, you must use your hardware and software correctly to get the best results. Of course, command routines vary for different applications. This section gives some general hints, suggestions, and recommendations.

Using Hardware

A PC can perform without problems if you treat it with care. Observe some suggestions for proper system use and maintenance:

1. Keep your work area clean. Food and drinks can easily spill and damage your PC.
2. Keep your equipment clean. Periodically wipe off the monitor and vacuum the keyboard. A dust cover can prevent a build-up of dirt.
3. Optimize your hard disk. Delete old programs and unneeded data. Periodically run a defragmentation utility to keep your hard disk running efficiently.
4. Be sure that you have a system disk backup so you can boot or start your computer if your hard disk crashes or fails to work. In such an emergency, insert the system diskette in the first drive and turn on the power. The computer should boot up from the diskette.
5. Take care of your diskettes. Insert them carefully into the disk drive, and protect them from heat, dust, food, magnetic fields, and static electricity. Any of these can damage or destroy the data on a diskette.

screen saver

a utility that helps you avoid continuously displaying the same image on-screen and burning out phosphors

write-protected file

a file that prevents others from inadvertently changing them

6. Take care of your monitor. Use a **screen saver** utility to avoid continuously displaying the same image and burning out phosphors at those locations. Keep your monitor clean and free of dust.
7. Designate important files as **write-protected** to prevent anyone from inadvertently changing them.
8. Check for viruses. Run a virus-checking program each time you boot your computer to protect it from harm. Before you read, copy, or launch a program from a diskette that you did not create, scan it with a virus-checking program. Also check for viruses on any programs you download from the Internet.

Using Software: General Principles

Chapters 5 and 6 presented specific guidelines for using word processing, spreadsheet, database, graphics, and communications applications. Some general suggestions can help you use all application packages to support the needs of your personal or organizational information system.

Carefully Plan Your Use of an Application. Before you begin using your applications, you need to consider which tasks you need to accomplish and which programs can do those most effectively. Formal requirements analysis in business determines exactly what output the user wants from the software (output requirements) and the input he or she must supply (input requirements) to allow the program to produce that output. You can do much the same for your own work so that you can accomplish tasks efficiently.

Thoroughly Learn the Capabilities of Your Software. As you learn about new things that your software can do, you might expand your original goals. You may find that you have enough form letters to do that you can create templates and do mail-merges to speed your tasks, for example.

Keep Your Processing Jobs Simple. Many beginning PC users take on bigger, more complex jobs than they need to complete. Is your task so big that you really need a detailed database? Or would a simple word processing file be more efficient? Do you really need a huge spreadsheet with detailed formulas? A simple rule is: Do not waste time making a program do something just because it can. Do look ahead to future needs, but don't waste time on useless input for dubious purposes.

Make Frequent Backups. Save your document files frequently while working and at the end of each session. You can easily forget to update your file on disk while working and lose the results of your efforts. A flash of lightning may knock out power unexpectedly, leaving you with nothing in RAM and an old version of your file on disk. If you have not saved for two hours, you have two hours of work to repeat. Most application packages have automatic backup features through which you can direct the programs to save your work every few minutes.

Similarly, you may lose files on disk if you delete them accidentally or your drive suffers a mechanical failure. A few minutes backing up hard disk files on diskettes or a tape backup system can save you the effort of re-creating those files.

Revise and Maintain Your IS Skills. Periodically, you may need to revise the formats of databases, spreadsheets, documents, and other information system tools that you create. Be sure to keep your skills up-to-date so that you can take advantage of program capabilities.

Document Your Work. Include notations, instructions, and other documentation to help other users understand the input and output practices you follow. If someone else must access your files, for example, that person will need to know how you have organized your files and the general method you use to name them.

prompts

instructions and explanations of required input and resulting output

Many kinds of applications allow users to include instructions and explanations of required input and resulting output, called **prompts,** to help users understand and operate the information system. These statements may appear along with actual data on input screens or in output reports. A simple column heading in a table, for example, would prompt users to enter the information in the correct place. Without these aids, users might misinterpret formats or data.

external documentation

printed instructions or explanations of program functions separate from those functions

In addition, **external documentation** includes printed instructions or explanations of program functions separate from those functions. These materials explain general functions of your application, just as the manuals that accompany the application package explain its functions.

Using Software: User Interfaces

Today's popular operating systems (Windows and Macintosh) brought a valuable new benefit for users when they defined certain shared features and control routines for all applications. Previous operating systems worked only in the background, and each application presented its own user interface. Users worked hard just to learn the control techniques a particular package required to complete basic activities like saving and printing files. In contrast, all programs that run under Windows perform some common functions in the same ways.

Sharing Data between Applications. Recall from Chapter 3 that Windows and Macintosh operating systems support multitasking—that is, they allow you to run several applications at the same time. This convenient and powerful capability allows you to transfer data from one application to others. For example, you can type a letter in a word processing program and easily incorporate information from a database like names, addresses, and customer preferences. You can also share data from a spreadsheet. This feature saves the time and trouble of retyping information.

Windows and Macintosh OS accomplish this integration of applications with a **clipboard,** a temporary storage location in RAM that holds data cut or copied from one application's document file for insertion into another. (See Figure A.3.)

Dynamic data exchange (DDE) extends this capability by automatically linking data from one application's files to files for another application. Cut-and-paste operations use the clipboard to move specific data between applications; the duplicated or moved data does not change, however, to reflect changes in the original document file. In contrast, DDE links the applications, so a change in one application's document files automatically produces a corresponding change in the other application's files. If a customer moves, the user can update the address, and a linked word processing program will automatically pick up the new address for any later use of the letter file.

---

clipboard

a temporary storage location in RAM that holds data cut or copied from one application's document file for insertion into another

dynamic data exchange (DDE)

computer technology that automatically links data from one application's files to files for another application

---

FIGURE A.3

Sharing Data via the Clipboard
The Windows clipboard allows you to move data between document files created by different applications.

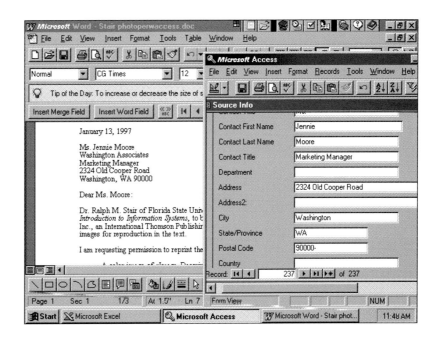

Windows provides some still more advanced integration tools, including Object Linking and Embedding (OLE). This capability implements the principles of object-oriented programming (discussed in Chapter 3) by combining functions of many applications to create customized capabilities. The applications work together to support the user's information needs rather than forcing the user to process information their way.

The tempting possibilities of multitasking require an important warning, though: Do not try to run too many Windows applications at one time. Each application takes up some RAM, so a number of them running simultaneously will slow down the operation of your computer system. Limited RAM may even prevent you from doing what you want to do. If you need to run a large number of programs together, you may need large amounts of RAM.

WHEN SOMETHING GOES WRONG

No matter how much you plan or how carefully you develop your information processing tools, things will go wrong. This section addresses some common problems and steps you can take to recover from them.

General Strategy for Solving Problems

Program functions sometimes do not work exactly as you expect. While the computer or application may malfunction, problems often result from something the user does or fails to do. Follow a nine-step procedure to diagnose a problem:

1. Confirm that all system components are connected and turned on. This simple but often overlooked step can save considerable frustration. If the monitor does not display any image, its power cord may be unplugged or its switch may be turned off. A loose cable may prevent data from reaching a monitor, printer, external modem, or other component.
2. Does the problem affect one application or several? If several applications share the same problem, the cause may be a fault in the hardware or operating system.
3. Give an Undo command and try again. You may have made a simple error like pressing a different key than you thought you pressed.
4. Carefully think about when and how the problem started. If you know when the problem started, you can often figure out what you should have done differently. For example, if your computer system stops printing or prints nonsense characters, you may have accidentally chosen the wrong printer while specifying other details for a printing job.
5. Consult the instruction manual or on-line help function for your program. The index may guide you to the page or screen you need. Also, many printed manuals arrange information and steps for specific commands in alphabetical order for quick reference.
6. Check with a friend, lab administrator, or instructor.
7. If earlier steps do not resolve the problem, consider taking a break before mounting frustration prevents you from seeing any solution at all. Sometimes the most obvious problem is the hardest one to see. Come back after a while and make a fresh attempt to find and correct the problem.
8. Run diagnostic software. Such software (included with your system or installed separately) can often reveal the causes of hardware problems.

9. Get help from the computer manufacturer or software publisher. If you cannot solve a problem after working through the previous steps, you may need to call for user support. Note that some companies charge fees for this service, though many offer free advice for some period immediately after you buy their products.

These steps define a procedure for approaching most computer system problems. In addition, some common problems deserve specific discussion.

The Computer Will Not Boot. If your computer system will not start up when you turn on the power, check the power cords and other cables for all components. If the monitor is not turned on or plugged in, you will not see your user interface screen, even when the computer has booted up normally and awaits your input.

If a DOS or Windows system displays the error message "Non-System Disk or Disk Error," you have tried to boot up with a data diskette in the drive. Remove it and press any key to boot from the hard disk. If the computer still will not boot up, try inserting a diskette with the operating system files and pressing Control–Alt–Delete together.

Not Ready Reading Drive A: Abort, Retry, Fail. This DOS/Windows error message usually appears when you try to read from a diskette without placing one in the drive. The diskette may not be seated fully in the drive, or the drive door may remain open. Once you insert the correct diskette fully into the drive, type *R* for retry. If you want to cancel the operation, press *A*.

File Not Found. This DOS/Windows message means that the computer cannot locate a file you requested or a program you tried to launch. Perhaps you deleted, moved, or renamed the file. If so, give new instructions to find the file, rename it, or copy it back to the appropriate spot on the hard disk. You can use File Manager in Windows 3.1 or My Computer or Explorer in Windows 95 to locate one or more files.

An Application Program Will Not Run. If you encounter this problem the first time you try to run a program, you may not have installed it correctly on your computer system. Error messages may indicate other problems like insufficient memory. You may have to reinstall the software, perhaps in some customized form that requires less RAM. If the program has run in the past but does not run now, you may need technical support from the software manufacturer. (See "Business Bits: Getting Technical Support.")

The Mouse Will Not Work. Usually, the mouse works fine, but the pointer is hidden somewhere on the screen where you don't see it. If a newly installed mouse does not work properly, you may have incorrectly installed the software that translates its movements into commands. If the pointer jumps around or moves strangely on the screen, check the ball under the mouse for dirt or other contamination. Are you moving your mouse across the right surface? Verify that the mouse cable is connected to your computer.

The System Will Not Respond. Wait for a while to be sure that the computer is not simply completing an intense processing task. Pressing the Escape key may return you to a previous point in the command sequence from which you can again control the computer. Try issuing an Undo command. As a last resort, you can reboot your computer by pressing Control–Alt–Delete, but this step will clear

BUSINESS BITS

Getting Technical Support

It's bound to happen sometime: your software doesn't work, and you can't figure out why or how to fix it. Software developers are already way ahead of you; most have some form of technical support via the phone. Until recently, that support has been free of charge. But several years ago, Microsoft changed that practice by announcing that it would charge for certain support services. Lotus, Borland, Corel, and WordPerfect quickly followed suit. Of course, this seems like just another way for software makers to make money, but consider that many of them have already cut costs by trimming staff, and they have reduced their prices as well. These companies are now leaner and meaner than they were only a few years ago.

Still, this leaves the PC user to figure out exactly what type of support is best, and at what price. Most software companies now offer various support programs at various prices. Some offer 900-number phone lines, payment by credit card, annual plans, even customized services (including house calls) for those customers who need them. In addition, independent companies offer fee-based support programs. So how do you choose what's best for you or your business?

First, consider your needs or the needs of your business. Consider also the needs of the other users at your company or in your department. If you are in charge of buying support for a staff that has varying computer skills, don't let them go it alone. "The most expensive support option a company can implement is a sneaker-net [i.e., walking over for a visit] to the PC guru," notes Joe Jacoboni, president of Software Support, and independent support provider. Of course, if your office relies mostly on one product, the best source of support is the software developer itself. If your office uses software from several different publishers, however, third-party support might be the best option (some offer plans for as little as $150 per year). If you are simply considering the level of support you need for home applications, most of that is usually free from the software makers, but it may be somewhat limited. You can go on-line for more free support (also for some business applications), but you may have to wait up to a day for answers to your questions.

How do PC users in general feel about the new kind of support? *PC World* conducted a survey to find out. The survey revealed that most people don't mind paying for support, so long as it is fast and accurate. "The cost is irrelevant if I get the support I need," explains John Cary, owner of a small business in Los Angeles called Cary Printing and Graphics. "The downtime is more expensive than the service. If I get up and running sooner, I'm dollars ahead." On the software makers' side, Sid Saleh of Claris notes, "We expected major complaints from customers [when Claris introduced fee-based support], but we were completely surprised by the lack of them." However, Saleh points out that the support must be of high quality. "You can't charge for something if you're bad at it."

So technical support has changed; it is unlikely that software makers will revert to free support, and independents have discovered a new niche to fill. Now it's up to PC users to decide which support is best.

1. What type of support do you have for your own PC? What would you recommend to a small business? How often do you use it? Are you satisfied with the service? If not, what improvements would you recommend?
2. Access the Internet to search for different types of software support that are on-line. You may be able to find what you need there.

Source: Christina Wood, "The Hidden Cost of Tech Support," *PC World*, May 1995, pp. 143–150. Photo courtesy of Robbie McClaren.

your current document file from RAM. (If you saved your document file recently, you can open it almost as you left it when you rebooted.) If the computer will not accept even a reboot command, you can turn off the power, wait a few moments, and turn it on again. If the system still will not work properly, seek help from a friend, your instructor, a lab administrator, or a repair technician.

UPGRADING AN EXISTING COMPUTER SYSTEM

Eventually, your hardware or software (or both) will no longer meet your information needs. Breakdowns create obvious problems, but they also create occasions when computer users must decide whether to repair, upgrade, or replace information system components. You can also inexpensively upgrade your system by adding new capabilities to existing components.

Hardware units like a disk drive can cost more to repair than to replace. The benefits of a new CD-ROM drive or hard disk can also provide valuable new storage capacity for the price of repairing an old unit. Of course, you lose any files that you cannot retrieve from a damaged hard disk, but a careful backup routine can protect against such a catastrophe.

Rather than replacing an old hard disk, you might consider adding another drive to the existing one(s). Many users also decide to add RAM to their systems by installing single in-line memory modules (SIMMs), if they have expansion slots to do so. (Note that SIMMs in a bank must be matched in speed and size.) New systems and applications software may demand more memory than earlier packages. This simple, inexpensive system upgrade can allow your existing computer to continue to function. It can also increase processing speed by moving data from relatively slow hard disk storage to faster RAM.

A math or video coprocessor may also increase the processing speed of an older computer by relieving the CPU of this work load. These additions to processing capacity benefit only certain kinds of applications, however (complex calculations and elaborate on-screen graphics, respectively). Also, Intel's 80486 and Pentium microprocessors include built-in math coprocessor circuitry.

Keep your existing system as long as it continues to meet your needs. If you do not need to run the latest version of every elaborate new application, your old computer may serve you well for a long time. As new programs come to dominate the systems at work or school, however, outdated capabilities may prevent you from doing the work you want to do.

Upgrading your software to a new version or a different package may provide the functions that you need. Follow the suggestions for buying and using

CAVIAR
AC21000,
AC21200,
AND
AC31600

1.0, 1.2 and 1.6
Gigabyte, 3.5-Inch,
Low Profile,
Enhanced IDE Drives

You can upgrade your computer system with a new hard drive to expand your storage capacity. (Source: Courtesy of Western Digital Corproation.)

software in the first part of this appendix to make this purchase. You may want to wait before buying a brand new software package or version, though. The program may include errors and problems that the software publisher must correct over the first few months on the market. Let someone else discover these problems.

Eventually, probably earlier than you expect, your old computer will no longer run its programs quickly enough to meet your needs, even with elaborate upgrades. In fact, your existing system may not run desirable new software at all. At today's prices, you may find a new, powerful system selling for little more than the cost of upgrading your existing computer. If you face one of these situations, consider buying a new computer.

Follow the suggestions detailed early in the appendix to choose your new hardware:

- Choose applications first, and then buy an operating system/hardware platform that will effectively run them.
- Include plenty of storage, RAM, and processing power in the new system, so it will continue to meet your needs as long as possible.
- Look for a package with a high-resolution monitor, fast modem, and state-of-the-art CD-ROM drive. You can buy new software as part of such a bundle, too. You probably will spend less for a new computer bundled with these luxuries than you would spend to add them later. Also, remember that today's luxuries quickly become tomorrow's necessities.

- As you encounter dazzling new hardware and exciting software capabilities, keep your own information needs firmly in mind.

- Applications programs perform the useful work that an information system requires, so the purchase decision should begin with these packages.

- Relentless change in technology will continue after you buy your system almost as soon as you take it home; resist the temptation to second-guess your purchase decision, and concentrate on using the computer to do what you need to do.

- Often, the cost of repairs or upgrades exceeds the value of the component, and it makes sense to spend more for new equipment with the latest capabilities.

SUMMARY

1. *Prepare before shopping for a personal computer system.* Before you start shopping for features and comparing prices, decide whether you really need a computer system of your own. If you decide that you do, set a preliminary budget for the purchase, study new developments and prices in the computer market, and revise your budget based on this research.

2. *Buy software and then hardware appropriate for your personal information system.* Begin the purchase decision process by choosing applications software packages that perform the information pro-

cessing tasks you need to accomplish. Next, choose an operating system/hardware platform that will effectively run your chosen applications. You can save money and time by buying needed hardware components (and software, when possible) in bundled systems. Peripheral components and services, especially on-line information services with Internet connections, are important parts of a computer owner's purchase decision.

3. *Use hardware and software effectively.* Several principles help to ensure productive use of computer hardware. Keep your work area and equipment

clean, optimize your hard disk, copy operating system files to a diskette, take good care of your diskettes and monitor, and secure your computer system against inadvertent changes and viruses. Similar principles should guide use of all applications software: Carefully plan your use of an application, thoroughly learn the capabilities of your software, keep your processing jobs simple, make frequent backups, revise and maintain your IS skills, and document your work.

4. *Formulate a constructive response when something goes wrong with your system.* A general strategy for solving problems begins with a step to confirm that all system components are connected and turned on. Determine whether the problem affects one application or several. If only one, give an Undo command and repeat the operation. If that does not correct the problem, think about when and how it started, and try to figure out what you should have done differently. Printed and on-line documentation can provide explanations, as can friends, lab administrators, and instructors. Take a break before frustration prevents you from seeing any solution at all, and consider running diagnostic software to identify a hardware fault. If the problem persists, contact the user support function run by a hardware manufacturer or software publisher.

5. *Decide when and how to upgrade a personal computer system to maintain or improve its performance.* Keep your existing system as long as it continues to meet your needs. You can often upgrade your system performance by adding components or enhancing existing ones. A new hard disk can supplement existing storage capacity. Many users find that they can inexpensively improve performance by installing SIMMs to expand RAM if they have expansion slots to do so. Upgrading your software to a new version or a different package may provide the functions that you need without any change in hardware. Eventually—probably earlier than you expect—your old computer will no longer meet your needs, and you will need to replace it.

 **Key Terms**

screen saver 315	prompts 316	clipboard 317
write-protected file 315	external documentation 316	dynamic data exchange (DDE) 317

FORM 1

Software Selection Grid

Fill in this table to help you determine what software to buy and the hardware your system will need to run it. Assign priorities from 1 (low) to 10 (high) to indicate how much you need the software. Set capability ratings from 1 (weak) to 5 (powerful) to indicate the relative functional strength of the packages. Compare the capabilities, hardware requirements, and prices of several software packages before you make your final selection.

SOFTWARE	HARDWARE NEEDS (CPU, RAM, HARD DISK)	CAPABILITY RATING	COST	PRIORITY SCORE
Word processing				____
1. _____	_____	____		
2. _____	_____	____	____	
3. _____	_____	____	____	
Spreadsheet				____
1. _____	_____	____	____	
2. _____	_____	____	____	
3. _____	_____	____	____	
Graphics				____
1. _____	_____	____	____	
2. _____	_____	____	____	
3. _____	_____	____	____	
Database				____
1. _____	_____	____	____	
2. _____	_____	____	____	
3. _____	_____	____	____	
Suites				____
1. _____	_____	____	____	
2. _____	_____	____	____	
3. _____	_____	____	____	
Other software				____
1. _____	_____	____	____	
2. _____	_____	____	____	
3. _____	_____	____	____	
Total cost of selected applications			____	

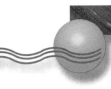

FORM 2

Hardware Selection Grid

Fill in this table to help you determine what hardware configuration to buy. Assign priorities from 1 (low) to 10 (high) to indicate the importance to you of each hardware feature. Set capability ratings from 1 (weak) to 5 (powerful) to indicate the relative functional strengths of the packages for each feature. Compare the capabilities and prices of at least three hardware configurations before you make your final selection.

SYSTEM AND FEATURES	PERFORMANCE (SPEED/ CAPACITY/RESOLUTION)	CAPABILITY RATING	SYSTEM COST	PRIORITY SCORE
1. _____			_____	_____
CPU: _____	_____	_____		
Hard disk	_____	_____		
RAM	_____	_____		
Warranty	_____	_____		
Monitor: _____	_____	_____	_____	
Printer: _____	_____	_____	_____	
Modem: _____	_____	_____	_____	
CD-ROM	_____	_____	_____	
Other: _____	_____	_____	_____	
2. _____			_____	_____
CPU: _____	_____	_____		
Hard disk	_____	_____		
RAM	_____	_____		
Warranty	_____	_____		
Monitor: _____	_____	_____	_____	
Printer: _____	_____	_____	_____	
Modem: _____	_____	_____	_____	
CD-ROM	_____	_____	_____	
Other: _____	_____	_____	_____	
3. _____			_____	_____
CPU: _____	_____	_____		
Hard disk	_____	_____		
RAM	_____	_____		
Warranty	_____	_____		
Monitor: _____	_____	_____	_____	
Printer: _____	_____	_____	_____	
Modem: _____	_____	_____	_____	
CD-ROM	_____	_____	_____	
Other: _____	_____	_____	_____	
Total cost of selected system			_____	

GLOSSARY

activity a limited, independent unit of work that contributes to the completion of a project

align objects a feature that perfectly lines up symbols, drawings, and the like

American Standard Code for Information Interchange (ASCII) the code that defines machine-language representations of letters of the alphabet

analog signal a telecommunications signal represented by continuously varying voltage

application server a server that stores program and document files for a particular application

application virus a virus that infects executable program files for such applications as word processing programs and spreadsheet packages

applications software programs that help users to solve particular computing problems

arithmetic/logic unit (ALU) the CPU element that performs mathematical calculations and makes logical comparisons to execute program instructions

artificial intelligence (AI) systems that combine sophisticated hardware and software with elaborate databases and knowledge-based processing models to demonstrate characteristics of effective human decision making

assembly languages the second generation of programming languages, which replace binary digits with symbols that people can more easily understand

automated teller machines (ATMs) special-purpose input/output terminals used by banks

bandwidth the range of signal frequencies that a given medium can carry at one time

batch processing procedure in which a group (batch) of programs is run on the computer system at one time; ideal for a large number of business transactions that occur regularly and in sequence

batch processing languages languages that support programming for routine processing tasks that handle large sets of data at regular intervals

bitmapped graphics graphics that store data about the color that the monitor should display at each point on the screen

bits pulses of electricity (short for *BInary digiTS*)

bits per second (bps) the number of data bits a medium can transfer in one second

bookmark a word processing tool that helps you reach sections that require more work or contain information you want to review or reread without scrolling through screen after screen of text

booting up the essential step completed by the computer immediately after the power switch is turned on; this step loads the operating system software into RAM

bridge hardware that connects two or more networks that use similar protocols

bus line electronic circuits that connect processing components

bus line width the measurement that determines the number of bits a bus line can transfer at any one time

business a formal collection of people and other resources established to accomplish a set of goals

bytes groups of eight bits

C a high-level, general-purpose language that supports programming for real-time processing in both business and scientific applications

cache memory memory that provides an area for high-speed primary storage from which a processor can access data more rapidly than from RAM

canons of professional conduct principles of conduct that specify ethical standards and disciplinary rules

carpal tunnel syndrome (CTS) a repetitive stress injury that occurs when prolonged, repetitive motion of the hands irritates and inflames the nerve pathway through the wrist

cells the intersections of a spreadsheet's rows and columns

cellular telephone service telephone service that divides an area into cells; a radio receiver accepts signals from mobile phones and other devices within each cell and integrates them into the regular phone system

central processing unit (CPU) electronic circuits that perform essential tasks to handle and manipulate data

choice stage the stage of the decision-making phase during which someone with authority must select a course of action

client/server system a system in which the server does all or most of the processing

clip art such graphics as fancy borders, pictures of famous people, decorative designs and initials, and many small drawings

clipboard a temporary storage location in RAM that holds data cut or copied from one application's document file for insertion into another

clock speed the predetermined rate at which the CPU produces electronic pulses

coaxial cable a type of cable that consists of a dielectric surrounded by a conductive shield

COBOL a high-level language developed as a procedure-oriented, business-focused language to develop batch-processing applications

color graphics adapter (CGA) a color graphics standard of eight colors and resolution of 320 × 320 pixels

command-based user interface an interface that requires users to enter text commands to direct the computer to perform basic activities

communication the transmission of a signal through a medium from a sender to a receiver

communications satellite a microwave station that orbits the earth

compact disk–read-only memory (CD-ROM) a form of optical disk that can hold about 650 MB of data

compiler a language translator that converts a complete program into machine language to produce a program that the computer can process in its entirety

computer an electronic device that can execute instructions or commands to accept data (input) and process them to produce and store useful information (output)

computer literacy a basic knowledge of computer systems and equipment and how they function

computer mistakes human errors, system failures, and other incorrect user actions that reduce the usefulness of IS output or even generate destructive output

computer output microfilm (COM) devices hardware that records computer system data directly onto microfilm for future reference using microfilm readers

computer system a collection of devices, centered on at least one electronic processing mechanism, that work together to input, process, store, and output data and information

computer waste waste that results from inappropriate uses of computer technology and resources

computer-aided software engineering (CASE) automation of most of the detailed activities required for systems development

computer-assisted design (CAD) technology that allows repeated changes to a single product design

computer-assisted instruction (CAI) instruction in which the computer presents self-paced sequences of text, graphics, and sound

computer-assisted manufacturing (CAM) technology that allows central, electronic control of shop-floor activities

computer-based information system (CBIS) hardware, software, databases, telecommunications, people, and procedures to collect and process data to produce and store information

connect time the time spent connected to the provider's computers

content bar a spreadsheet feature that reveals the formula, number, or label stored in the current cell

contents layout determines the information that appears in the report and its organization

continuous improvement a corporate goal of which the idea is to constantly seek ways to improve the business processes or tasks to add increased value to products and services in order to remain competitive and keep a strong customer base

control unit the CPU element that accesses program instructions sequentially and coordinates the flow of instructions and data into and out of the ALU, the registers, primary storage, and even secondary storage and output components

coprocessor an element that speeds processing tasks by executing specific types of instructions while the main CPU circuitry works on other types

copy to duplicate a block of text and place it in the clipboard

criminal hacker a computer-savvy but ethically weak person who attempts to gain unauthorized or illegal access to other computer systems

critical path the sequence of activities with zero slack (i.e., those that will delay the entire project if not completed on time)

cross-tabulation statistical tables that show relationships between two variables

cut to remove a block of text and place it in the clipboard

data raw facts

data communications system a kind of telecommunications system for electronic collection, processing, and distribution of data, typically between computer systems

data compression a process that allows storage of more data on a given disk by completing reliable procedures to substitute sophisticated codes for original data

data havens countries that place few limits on uses of telecommunications and databases

data manipulation language (DML) sets of commands and procedures that allow users to change or manipulate the contents of databases

data projectors output devices that project monitor images onto large screens

data protection a spreadsheet feature that prevents unwanted changes to cell contents

database an organized collection of facts and information

decision support system (DSS) an organized collection of people, procedures, databases, and devices that helps managers to identify and study alternative solutions to specific problems and then choose between them

decision-making phase the three stages of the problem-solving process that include intelligence, design, and choice

default settings formatting choices that do not change until you change them

defragmentation a process that relocates parts of files to create more efficient layouts of disk space

demand reports documents that answer specific questions when requested

design stage the stage of the decision-making phase during which decision makers develop potential solutions to the problem at hand

desktop computers computers that place enough processing speed, memory, and storage capacity for complex business computing tasks on the surface of a desk

detail formatting determines exactly how the report displays each record

digital cameras cameras that record and store images and video in digital form

digital signal a telecommunications signal represented by discrete voltage states

direct-access storage device a storage device that can move directly to the storage location for desired data without reading through other data in sequence

disk cartridges high-capacity hard disk platters within removable cartridges

diskettes magnetic disks that store small amounts of data on circles of Mylar film protected in hard plastic or flexible paper covers

distance learning a method of remote instruction that connects classrooms at different locations via computers and telecommunications

document file where data are stored by the user

document layout the overall appearance of a report

document virus a virus that attaches itself to a document file rather than a system file or an application's program file

documentation written material that describes the program functions to help the user operate the computer system

draw program a graphics program that generates vector graphics

DSS generator a DSS component that controls interactions among the database, model base, and external resources to complete the required processing

dynamic data exchange (DDE) computer technology that automatically links data from one application's files to files for another application

effectiveness a computer benefit that measures how well people or organizations realize their goals

efficiency a computer benefit that measures an amount of work produced (output) for a given amount of resources consumed (input)

electronic data interchange (EDI) technology by which common network resources, standards, and procedures allow one system to pass its output directly to other systems as input

electronic mail (e-mail) mail that is sent and received via computers

embedded computers systems that act entirely within larger mechanical or electrical systems without direct control by operators

encapsulating grouping relevant program steps and data to capture a routine for performing a particular function or task

ergonomics the science that studies the effects of work tool designs to identify and reduce continued stressors like repetitive motion, awkward posture, and eye strain

ethics standards that determine generally accepted and discouraged activities within a company and society

exception reports documents that are produced in response to unusual circumstances or events that require management action

executive support system (ESS) a specialized DSS that combines hardware and software with data about economic conditions and complex planning models to help top managers develop and evaluate major new organizational initiatives

expansion boards add-on circuit boards that plug into the system board to enhance system functions

expansion slots slots on the system board that accept add-on circuit boards

expert system an organized collection of people, procedures, databases, and devices that suggests decisions and acts like a human expert in a certain area or discipline

external documentation printed instructions or explanations of program functions separate from those functions

facsimile (fax) machine device that transmits images of documents via standard telephone lines

fax board a device that uses a circuit board to send document files in electronic format to other personal computers or standard fax machines without first printing hard copy

fax/modem a device that combines faxing capabilities with the telecommunications functions of a modem

feedback output that guides adjustments or changes to an information system's input or processing activities

fiber-optic cable cable that transmits signals as pulses of laser-generated light over extremely thin strands of glass or plastic bound together in a jacket similar to that of a coaxial cable

field this stores one type of element (alphabetic or numeric) about each employee, customer, or other individual subject in the database

fifth-generation languages (5GLs) programming languages that support creation of programs for expert systems and artificial intelligence

file a collection of related records

File Transfer Protocol (FTP) utility software that allows users to transfer files back and forth between Internet sites and their own computers

file server system a system in which the file server transfers the necessary files and programs to a node or an individual PC on the network

files where computers store and manipulate collections of related data

fill by example a spreadsheet feature that can anticipate later entries based on the first one and suggest complete cell contents for a row, column, or other block

fill down/fill right a spreadsheet feature that duplicates data and/or formulas in a specific cell throughout a row, column, or block of rows and columns

filter same as Find command

Find command a command that executes a query by quickly scanning a database to locate and display information that supports a specific processing need while overlooking the rest

first-generation computers electronic computing devices that began with vacuum tube technology in the late 1940s and 1950s

fonts styles of type

formulas spreadsheet equations that perform calculations based on specific data or the contents of one or more cells

fourth-generation languages (4GLs) high-level programming languages with less emphasis on processing procedures and a closer resemblance to English than third-generation languages

fragmentation a process that spreads related data over different locations on the disk surface

freeware same as shareware

front-end processor a device that performs processing tasks related to sending and receiving telecommunications transmissions

full justification justification in which the computer varies spaces between words as needed to align characters at both margins

functions spreadsheet elements that complete certain standard calculations

fuzzy logic a set of rules and techniques that is used in artificial intelligence to represent imprecise, uncertain, or unreliable knowledge

gateway hardware through which networks based on dissimilar protocols can communicate

gigabyte approximately 1,000 MB

global positioning system (GPS) technology that can indicate an individual car's location within 100 feet anywhere on the face of the earth based on data broadcast by satellite

global search a word processing function that allows you to specify a string of characters and then direct the computer to locate them anywhere in your document

global strategic alliance a partnership formed by two or more companies from different countries to cooperate in joint production and distribution of goods and services

grammar checker a word processing feature that detects grammatical mistakes

graphical user interface (GUI) an interface that displays pictures called *icons* on the screen to represent document files and application programs

graphics tablet a specialized input device that translates movements of a stylus across its surface into an image on the screen

group decision support system (GDSS) an integrated collection of hardware, software, people, databases, and procedures that encourages interaction and sharing of data

group facilitator a person who works specifically to help other group members effectively use the resources of the GDSS

group header/footer elements that appear before and after groups of records to document their meanings and significance

groupware applications software that helps to link separate computer systems in a way that helps a team of managers and employees work effectively together to use word processing, databases, spreadsheets, and related software packages

hacker a computer enthusiast who enjoys manipulating the capabilities of computer systems as a personal challenge

handheld personal computers PCs that are smaller and more portable than laptops but are typically not as powerful

hard disks magnetic disks that store large amounts of data on thin, steel platters permanently housed in closed, metal cases

hardware computer equipment or devices that perform input, processing, and output functions

heuristics procedures that allow learning along empirical lines using "rules of thumb"

high-level languages the third generation of programming languages, which use more symbolic code than do assembly languages

home page a document on the World Wide Web that includes pictures of the page authors and describes the authors' personal and professional activities, usually supplemented with links to related Web pages

hypertext links within Web pages that permit easy navigation to new information

implementation stage the stage of the problem-solving process during which a person or the company puts the solution into effect

information a collection of facts organized in a way that gives them additional value beyond the value of the facts themselves

information system a set of related components used to collect, process, store, analyze, and disseminate information for a specific purpose

infrared transmission transmission that sends low-frequency light waves rather than microwaves through the air

input the raw data that the system will manipulate and the activity of gathering that data

integrated packages personal productivity software packages that combine the processing functions of several applications into one software package

Integrated Services Digital Network (ISDN) technology that maximizes the capacity of existing transmission media to simultaneously carry voice, video, and image data in a digital format at high speed

intellectual property creative works of someone's imagination

intelligence stage   the stage of the decision-making phase during which decision makers identify and define potential problems and opportunities

international (global) networks   networks that link systems between countries

Internet   an example of an international network through which computers can gain access to a wealth of information

interpreter   a language translator that translates one program statement at a time, as the program is running

intranet   software packages that use web sites within the company to facilitate the sharing of databases and projects

ISDN switch   a switch that connects digital communications services directly to computer systems

Java   an object-oriented language that automates procedures to incorporate video, audio, and 3-D animation into applications software

joystick   a device through which computer game players enter input to control the movements of on-screen characters

justification   a word processing function that allows you to align text at the left or right margin

key field   a common field shared by tables

key-indicator reports   documents that summarize the previous day's critical activities

keyboard   a standard device for inputting text, numbers, and commands; includes Control, Alt or Option, and sometimes Command keys that alter the functions of certain other keys

kill file   file of addresses from which users do not want to accept e-mail messages

kilobyte   approximately 1,000 bytes

language translators   the interfaces between high-level programming languages and machine languages

laptop computers   PCs that are small and lightweight enough to fit inside a briefcase

learning system   a system that includes software to track the results of the computer system's actions and then varies system functions in similar situations based on this feedback

line-of-sight signal   a signal that requires an unobstructed straight line between the sender and receiver

liquid crystal displays (LCDs)   flat-screen monitors that trap liquid crystal between two polarizers; applications of electricity cause this material to form characters and graphic images on a backlit screen

local-area network (LAN)   a network that connects computer systems and devices within a small geographic area

logic bomb   an application or system virus designed to execute at a specified time and date and do explosive damage to the infected system

low-level language   computer language whose binary symbols (1 and 0) resemble the way the computer works (circuits on and off)

machine language   computer language formed by the binary digits of the CPU

macro   a word processing feature that automates combinations of keystrokes

magnetic disks   secondary storage devices that store data bits by magnetizing small areas on circular storage media coated with iron oxide

magnetic ink character recognition (MICR)   a process by which data are encoded in magnetic ink on the bottom of a check or other form

magnetic tape drives   sequential-access storage devices that store data by magnetizing spots to represent data bits on reels of Mylar film coated with iron oxide

magneto-optical (MO) disk   a hybrid between magnetic disks and optical disks

mail merge   a word processing function that allows you to prepare hundreds or thousands of personalized letters simply by incorporating selections from an address file to be merged with a word processing document file

mainframe computers   large, powerful computers with impressive processing capabilities that meet the needs of medium-sized to large companies and universities

management information system   an organized collection of people, procedures, databases, and devices that provides information about routine business operations to managers and decision makers

massively parallel processing (MPP)   processing that combines a large number of powerful processors to operate together

megabyte   approximately 1,000 KB

megahertz (MHz)   a measurement for clock speed that indicates millions of machine cycles per second

memory management   a function of operating systems that allows software to use the storage capacity in RAM

microprocessor chip   circuits densely etched onto a silicon wafer

Microsoft Disk Operating System (MS-DOS)   the operating system released by Microsoft for IBM-compatible microcomputers

microwave transmission   transmission that sends messages through the air as high-frequency radio signals

middleware   systems software that controls interactions between clients and servers

minicomputers   larger systems that can accommodate several users at one time

MIPS   a measure of speed for computer systems of all sizes (stands for *Millions of Instructions Per Second*)

modem   a device that converts telecommunications messages back and forth between the analog signals of phone lines and the digital signals of computers

monitoring stage   the stage of the problem-solving process during which a person or the company evaluates the implementation of the solution to determine whether it has achieved the anticipated results

monitors   glass screens that display images of text and graphics by contrasting bright and dark areas

motherboard   same as system board

mouse   a standard device that allows the computer user to point to elements on the display screen and select them or issue commands

multiplexer   a device that helps control the cost of transmission by transmitting several telecommunications signals over a single medium at a time

multiprocessing   processing activities completed by more than one central processing unit

multitasking   a capability offered by some operating systems that allows a user to run more than one application at the same time

multithreading   multitasking within a single application, so that several parts of one program can work at once

natural languages   programming languages whose syntax closely approaches human language

network   groups of computer systems linked electronically in a way that allows them to share wider ranges of hardware and software resources

network interface card   a device through which an individual PC usually connects to a LAN

network operating system (NOS)   an operating system for large disk drives, printers, and other hardware connected to a telecommunications network

neural network   a system that simulates the functions of the human brain

nodes   individual computers and other connection points within networks

noise   distortion to a signal caused by unintended fluctuations

numerically controlled (NC) machines   machines that can process materials and complete production tasks in response to instructions from computer systems

object-oriented programming (OOP) languages   programming languages that group program instructions and data into modules called *objects* that perform individual processing tasks

object-oriented systems development   using interchangeable software components (objects) to model concepts, places, and behavior in the real world

off-the-shelf software general-function software that buyers can literally pull off the shelves of retail stores

on-line information service a service that extends a computer system to reach vast collections of outside resources

on-line transaction processing (OLTP) real-time processing, in which data are entered as business transactions are completed

on-the-fly correction a word processing function that monitors your input and automates the process of bringing it in line with quality standards

operating system a set of computer programs that control hardware devices to support users' computing needs

Operating System 2 (OS/2) an operating system released by IBM in 1988 to compete with Windows and to take advantage of the expanded capabilities of more powerful personal computers

optical character recognition (OCR) readers optical data readers that sense reflected light to recognize various characters

optical disk a rigid plastic disk permanently encoded with data

optical mark recognition (OMR) readers optical data readers that automatically score tests and interpret data recorded on other types of forms after people fill in boxes using No. 2 pencils

outlining a word processing feature that helps create and manipulate a logical hierarchy of statements and then ties text selections to this structure

output the useful information—usually in the form of documents, reports, and transaction data—that an information system produces

paint program a graphics program that produces bitmapped graphics

parallel port a port that transmits data in parallel (eight or more bits at a time)

parallel processing a form of multiprocessing that speeds the computer's data handling and manipulation by linking several general-purpose processors to operate at the same time

paste to move the contents of the clipboard from one location to another

peer-to-peer network a network that allows a small business to connect personal computers to share files, printers, and other resources

Personal Computer Disk Operating System (PC-DOS) the operating system developed by Microsoft and released by IBM with its Personal Computer in 1981

personal computers (PCs) relatively small and inexpensive computers (also called microcomputers)

personal productivity tools general-purpose software programs that support a number of processing activities common among individual users

pixels individual points of light on a display screen

plotters hard-copy output devices that draw smooth curves and precise angles without jagged edges

plug and play a standard used by Microsoft in its Windows 95 operating system software that eliminates much of the complexity of reconfiguring a personal computer system

point-of-sale (POS) terminals terminals used by retailers to enhance customer service and data collection at the same time

polling what the front-end processor does to terminals and other devices to identify and accept new messages

ports parts of the system board through which additional hardware components connect

power supply the element that provides electrical power to the entire computer

presentation graphics program software that helps users to develop pie charts, line drawings, bar charts, trend lines, organization charts, and a wide range of other illustrations

primary sort key the first criterion by which the computer arranges records

primary storage the memory that holds program instructions and data for the CPU to process (also called random access memory [RAM])

printers devices that generate most hard copy, operating at different speeds with different features and capabilities

Privacy Act of 1974 the law that serves as a nationwide moral guideline for privacy rights and activities by private organizations that affect those rights

problem-solving process the process by which people identify threats or opportunities and formulate appropriate responses

procedures the strategies, policies, methods, and rules that humans apply to operate a CBIS

processing the action that an information system completes when it converts or transforms data to generate useful information

process reengineering process that involves investigating and changing the tasks and activities performed by the organization and the technology used to support these tasks and activities

program file a collection of instructions given to the computer to execute or run in order to perform some function for the user

programming languages computer languages that assign terms that programmers can recognize and remember for sets of machine-language instructions that direct a computer's CPU to accomplish certain functions

project crashing a function that determines the cheapest investment of additional resources to shorten total project completion time

project management program programs that help users plan, monitor, and control goal-directed sequences of activities

prompts instructions and explanations of required input and resulting output

proprietary software software developed by a company for its own needs

protocol a summary of certain communications standards that allow any computer system or network to communicate effectively with any other system or network

prototyping creating a preliminary model, a major subsystem, or a scaled-down version of an entire system

query something that certain commands do to search for specific values in any table or combination of tables

query languages programming languages that allow users to ask questions in sentences that resemble human language

random access memory (RAM) same as primary storage

range a spreadsheet rectangle that encompasses one cell, a row, a column, or rows and columns of adjoining cells

read-only memory (ROM) memory that provides a nonvolatile storage area for data and instructions that do not need to change

read/write heads heads that can move directly to any spot on the storage media to retrieve or store data

real-time processing languages languages that must support programming to generate immediate output on demand for less predictable processing tasks

record a collection of related fields

reference software software that provides applications tools and database material designed to provide help on a particular topic

regional network telecommunications systems that join resources within specific geographic regions

relational database a collection of files

repetitive stress injury (RSI) injury produced by long-term work with computer keyboards and similar equipment

report footer an element that appears once at the end of a document to state any assumptions, conditions, or other qualifications that may help readers to evaluate the report

report header an element that appears only at the beginning of a document to state the title of the report, the names of the people who developed it, the date, and other information

resolution clarity or sharpness

reusable code the sequence of programming instructions that can be reused within an object for a variety of applications

robotics a field involving mechanical, usually computer-controlled, devices to perform tasks that require extreme precision or tedious or hazardous work by people

scenarios combined spreadsheet versions

scheduled reports documents with standard sets of data about activities for predetermined time intervals delivered on set dates and times

screen saver a utility that helps you avoid continuously displaying the same image on-screen and burning out phosphors

search and replace a word processing function that allows you to specify one string of characters for the computer to find and another to replace them

search tools large electronic indexes that catalog Web pages and information on the Internet

second-generation computers computers that processed data through circuits based on transistors

secondary sort key the second criterion by which the computer arranges records

secondary storage computer memory that offers a nonvolatile and relatively economical way to store large amounts of data

sequential-access storage device a storage device that must review and retrieve data in the same order in which they were stored

serial port a port that transmits data to an external device in series (one bit at a time)

shareware software that can be used without paying anything

signal frequency transmission capacity stated in hertz (Hz) that measures the number of times per second the transmission medium cycles between high and low voltage to carry a signal

slide show a display of images in sequence

Smalltalk an object-oriented language for use on desktop computers

Smartmaster graphics feature that provides entire collections of presentation slides for specific themes

snap on grid a feature that forces all lines or shapes to the nearest point on the grid so that lines, box corners, and so on, meet

software programmed sequences of instructions for the computer

software piracy illegal duplication of program files

software suite a bundle of single applications designed to function together and share data

source data automation a process that collects input through devices that automatically capture data as transactions occur without special data-entry activities by system personnel

speaker note notes that you can incorporate into your graphics to provide information and prompts as guides to the presenter

special effects a word processing feature that alters fonts to condense or expand the letters, outlines characters, and draws simple drop shadows

specialized productivity software software that handles many kinds of limited processing tasks, such as personal information management, legal assistance, and travel assistance

spelling checker a word processing feature that detects spelling mistakes by comparing every word in a document against a huge dictionary file of allowable words

spreadsheet a program that automates numerical calculation tasks by processing user-defined data according to specified formulas

standards performance guidelines approved by accepted industry groups

Structured Query Language (SQL) a popular 4GL that is a standardized system for searching and manipulating databases

style sheet a word processing feature that summarizes a wide range of formatting choices

summary reports documents that filter the highly detailed data stored in databases by transaction processing systems

super video graphics array (SVGA) a display standard that provides color and resolution vastly superior to that of CGA

supercomputers the largest computer systems with the fastest processing speeds

syntax the element of language that dictates how the programmers can combine symbols and terms into program statements that convey meaningful instructions to the CPU

system board a single, complex circuit board within the system unit into which the processor and memory chips normally plug

System 7.5 the current version of the Macintosh operating system

system unit a cabinet in the computer system that houses its processing components

system virus a virus that infects operating system programs or other system files, usually as soon as the user boots up the computer

systems analysis the second stage of the SDLC, which involves developing a general understanding of an IS solution that would respond effectively to the problem or opportunity identified during systems investigation

systems design the third stage of the SDLC, which involves selecting resources and planning a system that fulfills the previously defined requirements for the problem solution

systems development a process of defining information needs, designing a system that satisfies users, and effectively implementing that design

systems development life cycle (SDLC) the five stages of developing information system needs: investigation, analysis, design, implementation, and maintenance and review

systems implementation the fourth stage of the SDLC, which involves creating or acquiring the components specified in systems design, assembling them, and beginning to operate the new or modified system

systems investigation the first stage of the SDLC, which involves identifying operating problems and opportunities that affect the information system and evaluating their causes and scope

systems maintenance and review the fifth stage of the SDLC, which involves reviewing, updating, and modifying the system after implementation to ensure that it continues to perform as designed

systems software the set of programs designed to coordinate the activities and functions of the hardware and various programs throughout the computer system

table lookup a spreadsheet feature that pulls certain standard, unchanging values from separate tables within the spreadsheet

telecommunications components that allow organizations to link computer systems together into networks

Telecommunications Act of 1996 legislation that removed regulatory barriers to competition among traditional telephone, computer, and cable TV companies

telecommunications system collections of resources that support electronic transmissions of communication signals

telecommuting a way of working that involves employees working some or all of the time at home PCs, accessing input from company computers and returning output via modem

teleconferencing technology by which many people using separate phones confer together in a single voice call

template a spreadsheet tool that supplies a matrix of spreadsheet cells with all of the formulas needed to perform a standard set of calculations but no numerical values

terminals devices that connect to computer systems over some distance to support data input functions, and sometimes output, but not processing or storage

thesaurus a word processing feature that lists alternatives to selected words

third-generation computers computers that were devised after the development of microchips and integrated circuits in the 1960s

time-sharing a capability offered by some operating systems that allows access to a computer system by more than one user at a time

title bar a spreadsheet feature that states the name of the document file for the currently displayed spreadsheet

touch-sensitive screen a display screen that allows the user to touch certain parts of it to choose a program command or cause the computer to take an action

trackball a device that does essentially the same things as a mouse; the user rotates a ball to move the cursor on the computer screen

transaction processing system (TPS) an organized collection of people, procedures, databases, and devices that records information about completed business transactions

trigger points parameters in an exception report

Trojan horse apparently useful programs that actually mask destructive programs

tutorial on-screen presentations that incorporate examples to guide new users through actual commands and menu choices to accomplish important program tasks

twisted-pair wire cable a type of cable that moves signals over one or more pairs of twisted, copper wire bundles

Unix an operating system developed by AT&T in the 1970s for minicomputers

user interface an element of operating systems that incorporates the routines that give one or more individuals access to and command of the computer system

utility programs systems software programs that perform useful functions like merging and sorting sets of data and keeping track of computer jobs as they run

value chain an element that links an entire sequence of suppliers and customers to control production and distribution at every stage from raw materials to the final consumer

vector graphics stored sets of instructions and procedures for creating lines, circles, and other color images

version a spreadsheet feature that allows you to carry out calculations with different values for key variables to gauge the impact of different possibilities on the entire spreadsheet

videoconferencing technology that combines voice, video, and data transmissions from several sites and sends them over phone lines to display all participants' input together on a single monitor at each site

virtual memory a capability offered by some operating systems that allocates space on disk to supplement the immediate, functional memory capacity of RAM

virtual office a way of working that involves employees sharing resources but not physical facilities

virtual reality a system that incorporates both input and output hardware to simulate real-world experiences

virus a program that enters a computer system without the user's knowledge disguised within the program files of another application

virus scanning software software that detects and eliminates known viruses in a system

vision system a hardware/software system that permits computers to capture, store, and manipulate visual images

visual programming languages languages that allow a programmer to use a mouse, on-screen icons, and pull-down menus to create programs in traditional languages

voice output devices devices that allow computers to send output-synthesized speech over speakers and phone lines

voice recognition devices devices that allow users to enter data through microphones; in this way, the computer system records and converts the sound of the human voice into digital input

web browsers applications software packages that allow users to navigate and search through resources on the Internet and the Web

what-if analysis a spreadsheet practice in which data in output cells show the effects of specific inputs on an entire set of numerical calculations

wide-area networks (WANs) networks that expand telecommunications links to encompass resources spread over large geographic regions

Windows the GUI released by Microsoft to run with MS-DOS

wizards smart document development tools that work like predefined style sheets

word processing a function that applies the computer's power to the tasks of creating, revising, and distributing written documents

word wrap a word processing feature that starts a new line as the text characters reach the right margin

wordlength a measure of the size of the CPU

work group a word processing feature that helps to integrate the contribution of several people to a document

workstations advanced personal computers with more memory, processing capacity, and graphics capabilities than standard PCs.

World Wide Web (WWW) a huge and rapidly expanding collection of electronic documents that can combine text, still and moving images, sounds, and automatic links to other documents

worm a program that replicates its own files until it destroys other programs or interrupts IS operations

write-once, read-many (WORM) disks optical disks on which special drives control high-powered lasers to record customized data and information

write-protected file a file that prevents others from inadvertently changing them

zoom a word processing function that allows you to magnify parts of your document on-screen to get a closer look without affecting the finished product

NOTES

CHAPTER 1

1. Ani Handjian, "Welcome to the Revolution," *Fortune,* December 13, 1993, p. 66.
2. W. H. Davidson, "Beyond Re-engineering," *IBM Systems Journal,* vol. 32 (1993), p. 65.
3. Don Boroughs, "Paperless Profits," *U.S. News & World Report,* July 17, 1995.
4. C. R. Franz and C. Robey, "Organizational Context, User Involvement, and the Usefulness of Information," *Decision Sciences,* vol. 17 (1986), pp. 329–356. See also C. A. Reilly, "Variation in Decision Makers' Use of Information Sources: The Impact of Quality and Accessibility of Information," *Academy of Management Journal,* vol. 25 (1982), pp. 756–771; D. Robey and D. L. Farrow, "User Involvement in Information Systems Development: A Conflict Model and Empirical Test," *Management Science* (1982), pp. 73–85.
5. Philip Ross, "Software as a Career Threat," *Forbes,* May 22, 1995, pp. 240–246.
6. Louis Gerstner, in an address to State Farm corporate headquarters staff, October 31, 1995.
7. David Churbuck, "Help: My PC Won't Work," *Forbes,* March 13, 1995, p. 101.
8. J. C. Camillus and A. L. Lederer, "Corporate Strategy and the Design of Computerized Information Systems," *Sloan Management Review,* vol. 26 (Spring 1985), pp. 35–42.

CHAPTER 2

1. L. Hooper, "CD Ventures Planned by IBM, Blockbuster," *Wall Street Journal,* May 11, 1993, p. B1.
2. "Speak to Me," *The Economist,* September 17, 1994, p. 15.
3. Naomi Freundlich, "Harnessing the Power of Light to Make Speedier Chips," *Business Week,* November 16, 1992, p. 81.
4. Alan Clements, *Principles of Computer Hardware,* 2nd ed. (Boston: PWS-Kent, 1993), pp. 622–623.
5. "CD-ROM: A Mass Medium at Last," *Business Week,* July 19, 1993.
6. Richard Brandt, "The Coming Firefight over Flash Chips," *Business Week,* February 1, 1993, p. 68.

7. Monua Janah, "NewsTalk at the New York Times," *Forbes ASAP,* December 5, 1994, pp. 86–88.
8. Richard C. Morias, "A Car Pool that Really Works," *Forbes,* December 19, 1994, pp. 108, 110.
9. Ellis Booker, "Retailers Wary of Electronic Commerce," *Computerworld,* October 24, 1994, p. 20.
10. Mary E. Thyfault, "Bigger Role for ATMs," *Information Week,* July 25, 1994, p. 18.
11. Doug Bartholomew, "Ending the Paper Chase," *Information Week,* July 25, 1994, p. 56.
12. Ron White, "Upgrades that Pay," *PC Computing,* November 1994, pp. 200–201.

CHAPTER 3

1. Scott Spandbauer, "Windows NT," *PC World,* June 1993, p. 161.
2. Alice LaPlante, "New Software—Faster Factories," *Forbes ASAP,* August 1994.
3. Doug Bartholomew, "There's No *I* in Team," *Information Week,* July 25, 1994, p. 52.
4. Teresa Reeder, "Software for Sharing," *Nation's Business,* August 1990, p. 13.
5. Steve Bass and Scott Dunn, "Software for Next to Nothing," *PC World,* May 1995, p. 117.
6. "The Rush to Object Speeds Up," *Datamation,* June 10, 1995, p. 47.
7. Doug Bartholomew, "Teaching an Object Lesson," *Information Week,* July 25, 1994, p. 52.
8. Andy Kessler, "Fire Your Software Programmers—Again," *Forbes ASAP,* August 29, 1994, p. 23.
9. Joseph Garber, "Working Faster," *Forbes,* April 12, 1993, p. 110.
10. "Making C++ More Approachable," *Datamation,* January 15, 1993, p. 37.

CHAPTER 4

1. Alan M. Cohen, *A Guide to Networking* (Danvers, Mass.: Boyd & Fraser, 1994).
2. Mary Thyfault, "The Dish at Holiday Inn," *Information Week,* May 11, 1992, p. 25.
3. Luisa Simone, "Data Transfer at the Speed of (Infrared) Light," *PC Magazine,* June 25, 1996, p. 36.

4. Bart Ziegler, "Faster Internet Service Is Feasible If Providers Will Put Up the Cash," *Wall Street Journal,* August 23, 1996, p. B2.
5. Robert Frank, "Technology Openers," *Wall Street Journal,* November 14, 1994, p. R25.
6. Bart Ziegler, "Slow Crawl on the Internet," *Wall Street Journal,* August 23, 1996, p. B1.
7. Rick Tetzeli, "The Internet and Your Business," *Fortune,* March 7, 1994, p. 86.
8. Melanie Berger, "The Other 'Net," *Sales & Marketing Management* online. http://smmag.com/smt3f.htm (September 6, 1996).

CHAPTER 5

1. Silvia Ascarelli, "Success at Home Gives Star Division a Ray of Hope as It Looks Abroad," *Wall Street Journal,* September 9, 1996, p. B5F.

CHAPTER 6

1. David Abrahamson, "Presentation Perfect," *Inc. Technology,* September 17, 1996, no. 3, p. 90.
2. *Inc. Technology,* September 17, 1996, no. 3, p. 91.

CHAPTER 7

1. Steven Jobs, quoted in "Waking Up to the New Economy," *Fortune,* June 27, 1994.
2. *Wall Street Journal,* October 25, 1995, p. B1.
3. *Inc. Technology,* September 17, 1996, no. 3, p. 89.
4. "Groupware Makes Its Move," *Computer* 28(9), September 1995, p. 11.
5. "Workgroup Computing: A Survey," *Datamation,* June 1995, p. 34.
6. Stephanie Losee, "Groupware Goes Boom," *Fortune,* December 27, 1993, p. 99.
7. Frank Derfler Jr., "Corporate Intranet Strategies and You," *PC Magazine,* April 23, 1996, pp. 106–108.
8. "The Intranet Rolls In," *Information Week,* January 29, 1996, pp. 76–78.
9. "Enter the Intranet," *The Economist,* January 13, 1996, pp. 64–65.
10. Laton McCartney, "How ESS Keeps Hertz Managers Out In Front," *Business Week,* July 1989, p. 46.

11. *Investor's Business Daily,* December 27, 1995, p. A6.
12. *Science News,* February 24, 1996, p. 119.
13. *Business Week,* July 17, 1995, p. 68.
14. Carolyn Geer, "For a New Job, Press #!" *Forbes,* August 15, 1994, p. 118.
15. Sri Kumar Rao, "The Hot Zone," *Forbes,* November 18, 1996, p. 252.
16. "New Technologies Help Commercial Operations," *Computer,* 29 (1), January 1996, p. 17.
17. "Bridging the CASE OOP Gap," *Datamation,* March 1, 1992, p. 63.

CHAPTER 8

1. Gregory Spears, "U.S. Mails about $5 million Every Month to the Dead," *Tallahassee Democrat,* April 16, 1991.
2. Mark Silva, "HRS Computer Glitch May Aid Next Year's Budget," *Miami Herald,* reprinted in *Tallahassee Democrat,* March 12, 1993, p. 4B.
3. Leo Mullen, "Glitch Shorts Retirees by $478 million," *USA Today,* November 18, 1994, p. A1.
4. Prodigy Interactive Personal Service, October 11, 1992.
5. *Infosystems,* vol. 1, no. 11 (March 20, 1994).
6. "The Price Is Wrong," *Information Week,* September 14, 1992, pp. 26–30.
7. Andrea Gerlin, "Businesses Tired of Faxed Ads Sue the Senders," *Wall Street Journal,* May 9, 1995, p. B1.
8. Mike Godwin, "Cops on the I-way," *Time,* Spring 1995, pp. 62–63.
9. Andrew Pollack, "Desktop Forgery," *Tallahassee Democrat,* October 14, 1990.
10. Diane Medina, "Users Hit with More Fraud," *Information Week,* March 23, 1992, p. 14.
11. Bart Ziegler, "Savvy Hacker Tangles Web for Net Host," *Wall Street Journal,* September 12, 1996, pp. B1, B12.
12. Jared Sandberg, "Undetected Theft of Credit-Card Data Raises Concern about On-line Security," *Wall Street Journal,* February 17, 1995, p. B6; see also *Tallahassee Democrat,* February 17, 1995, p. 1A.
13. Dan Keating, "New Viruses Hungry for Microsoft's Word for Windows," *Tallahassee Democrat,* September 17, 1995, p. B1.
14. Laurie Hays, "Working It Out," *Wall Street Journal,* November 14, 1994, p. R22.
15. Laurence Barton, *Ethics: The Enemy in the Work Place* (Cincinnati: South-Western, 1995), pp. 240–241.
16. John Greenwald, "Your Chips or Your Life," *Time,* May 2, 1994, p. 43.

17. William Carley "A Chip Comes in from the Cold," *Wall Street Journal,* January 19, 1995, p. A1.
18. Michael Alexander, "Operation Sundevil Nabs First Suspect," *Computerworld,* February 17, 1992.
19. June Daley, "FBI Closes Bulletin Board, Seeking Privacy Evidence," *Computerworld,* June 15, 1992, p. 12.
20. Alice LaPlante, "Networked PCs Become a Crime Fighting Tool in New York," *InfoWorld,* May 25, 1992.
21. William Barret, "We're Basically Insurance," *Forbes,* November 9, 1992, p. 196.
22. James A. Martin, "Spam Isn't Just a Lunch Meat Anymore," *Macworld,* September 1996, pp. 185–187.
23. Jared Sandberg, "America Online Creates Barricades against Cyberspace Junk Mailings," *Wall Street Journal,* September 5, 1996, p. B8; "AOL Ban on Junk E-mail Is Temporarily Blocked," *Wall Street Journal,* September 9, 1996, p. B2.
24. Nikhel Hutheesing, "Big Modem Is Watching," *Forbes,* February 13, 1995, p. 186.
25. Fryer and Furger, "Think Your E-Mail Is Safe from Prying Eyes? Think Again," *PC World,* August 1993, p. 166.
26. David Foster, "Be Careful What You Say: Deleted E-Mail Messages Are Actually Saved," *Tallahassee Democrat,* September 20, 1995, p. D16.
27. Louise Lee, "E-Mail among Officials May Be against the Law," *Wall Street Journal,* February 16, 1995, p. B1.
28. Thomas Maugh, "No Link between Electric Fields and Cancer," *Tallahassee Democrat,* March 16, 1993, p. 10B.
29. David Green, ed., *Operative Hand Surgery,* 3rd ed., vol. 2 (New York: Churchill Livingstone, 1993), p. 1373.
30. Steve Lohr, "Waving Good-bye to Ergonomics," *New York Times,* April 16, 1995, sec. 3, pp. 1A–B, 14C–F.
31. Brian Nadel, "The Green Machine," *PC Magazine,* May 25, 1992, p. 110.
32. John McPartland, "Ethics," *Information Week,* July 13, 1992, p. 30.
33. R. Dejoie, G. Fowler, and D. Paradice, *Ethical Issues in Information Systems* (Boston: Boyd & Fraser, 1991), p. 305.
34. "The Patent Pirates Are Finally Walking the Plank," *Business Week,* February 17, 1992, p. 125.
35. Evan Schwartz, "The Rush to Keep Mum," *Business Week,* June 8, 1992, p. 36.
36. Mitch Betts, "Personal Data More Public than You Think," *Computerworld,* March 9, 1992, p. 1.

CHAPTER 9

1. "The One Book," *Technology Review,* May/June 1996, p. 12.
2. "The Digital Future for the Networked Society," http://www.ti.com/corp/does/digfuture.htm/ (October 25, 1996).
3. Amy Kover, "Techno Sapiens," *Fortune,* July 8, 1996, p. 82.
4. "Computing Comes to the Big Screen," *Investor's Business Daily,* March 22, 1996, p. A19.
5. Howard Baldwin, "Your Mac Is Ringing," *Macworld,* November 1996, pp. 133–137.
6. "JASON Project III: Adapting to a Changing Sea," *Science Activities,* Winter 1996, p. 38.
7. "Telecommuting," *Informationweek,* January 22, 1996, pp. 32–40.
8. Jeff Young, "Going Country," *Forbes ASAP,* 1993, p. 124.
9. Sandra E. O'Connell, "Ten Terms Linked to the Virtual Office," *HR Magazine,* March 1996, p. 57.
10. Chris O'Malley, "Talking Heads," *PC Computing,* December 1994, pp. 222–225.
11. "Worker 54, Where Are You?" *Scientific American,* November 1995, p. 36.
12. "Technology Openers," *Wall Street Journal,* November 14, 1994, p. R222.
13. Michael Hammer and James Champy, *Re-engineering the Corporation* (New York: Harper Business, 1993).
14. "Auto Sound Systems Go through the Roof," *Business Week,* December 4, 1995, p. 116.
15. Bruce Rayner (ed.), "The Global 100: Outstanding Users of Information Technology from around the World," *Computerworld,* September 19, 1994, p. 8.
16. Michael Sullivan-Trainor, "Premier 100: Best of the Breed," *Computerworld,* September 19, 1994, p. 8.
17. Allan Alter, "Toyota: The Global 100," *Computerworld,* May 1, 1995, p. 19.
18. Marc Ferranti, "ABB Asea Brown Boveri: The Global 100," *Computerworld,* May 1, 1995, p. 17.
19. Rich Karlgaard, "ASAP Interview: Percy Barnevik," *Forbes ASAP,* December 5, 1994, pp. 65–68.
20. Joseph Maglitta, "Global Titans: The Global 100," *Computerworld,* May 1, 1995, p. 14.
21. Joseph Maglitta, "United Parcel Service: The Global 100," *Computerworld,* May 1, 1995, p. 15.

INDEX

A boldface page number indicates a key term and the location where its definition can be found.

A

ABB (Asea Brown Boveri), 298–299
ACM code of professional conduct, 271
Activity, **200**
AI (artificial intelligence), **226**
Align objects, **193**
Alphanumeric data, 6
ALU (arithmetic/logic unit), **40**
American Business Information (ABI), 201
American Standard Code for Information Interchange (ASCII), **90**
Analog signal, **110,** 111
Animal House Pet Shop, 143
Antivirus utilities, 83
Apple Computer
    Newton Message Pad, 37, 38, 61
    operating system (Macintosh), 79, 82, 319–320
    and VisiCalc, 161
Application server, **291**
Applications software, 6, **75,** 84–85
Application virus, **252**
Aptiva S Series, 36
Arithmetic/logic unit (ALU), **40**
ARPAnet (Advanced Research Projects Administration Network), 251
Art, computerized, 285–287
Artificial intelligence (AI), **226**–231
ASCII (American Standard Code for Information Interchange), **90**
Asea Brown Boveri (ABB), 300–301
Assembly languages, **91**
Association for Computing Machinery (ACM), 271
Audio data, 6
AUTOEXEC.BAT, 83
Automated teller machines (ATMs), **59**

B

Backsolver, 169
Backups, 318
Bandwidth, **112**
Batch processing, 48, 211–213
    languages, **97**
Beck, Harry, 29
BIOS (Basic Input/Output System), 83
Bitmapped graphics, **193**
Bits, **40**
Bits per second (bps), **112**
Blocking and moving text, 146–147
Bookmark, **152**
Booting up, **82**–83
    problems with, 321
Bricklin, Dan, 161
Bridge, **127**

British Computer Society (BCS), 271
Brooks, Rodney, 281
Burkelo, David, 174
Burns, Charles, 70
Business, **16.** *See also* Business trends
    and CBISs, 16–21
    and finance on-line service, 198
    impact of telecommunications in, 289–293
    organization, model of, 17
Business information systems
    artificial intelligence, 226–231
    decision support systems, 217–226
    management information systems, 213–217
    systems development, 231–236
    transaction processing systems, 210–213
Business trends, 293
    at Asea Brown Boveri (ABB), 298–299
    embedded IS technology, 296–297
    global environment, 297
    process reengineering, 294
    quality, 294–295
    speed, 295–296
    at Toyota, 298
    at United Parcel Service (UPS), 299–300
Bus line, **42**
Bus line width, 41–43, **42**
Buyer's guide
    to hardware, 64–66, 311–313
    to peripherals, 314–315
    to software, 99–101, 309–310
Bytes, **40**

C

C, **91**
C++, 97
    and Java 1.0, 96
Cable Act of 1992, 261
Cables, 112–114
Cache memory, **43,** 44
CAD (computer-assisted design), **295**
CAI (computer-assisted instruction), **279**–280
CAM (computer-assisted manufacturing), **296**
Canons of professional conduct, **271**
Careers, 24–25
Cargill Inc., 216
CARL System, 107
Carpal tunnel syndrome (CTS), **265**
Cars @ Cost, 3

Cary Printing and Graphics, 320
Cascade virus, 253
CASE (computer-aided software engineering), 237
Cash, James I., Jr., 14
CBIS. *See* Computer-based information system
CDnow, 131
CD-R (compact disk-recordable) technology, 53
CD-ROM (compact disk–read-only memory), **52,** 53
CDW, 315
CEBus (Consumer Electronics Bus), 281
Cell, **160**
    formats, 163
Cellular telephone service, **117**
Centralized systems, 39
Central processing unit (CPU), **40**
CGA (color graphics adapter), **61**
Chicago Board of Trade (CBOT), 34–35
Chin, Bob, 218
Choice stage, **9**
Circular reference, 162
CISC (complex instruction set computing), 43
CIX (Commercial Internet Exchange), 129
Cladding, 113
ClarisWorks, 87, 88
Client/server systems, **126,** 291–292
Clip art, **194**
Clipboard, **317**
Clock speed, **41,** 42
CMOS (complimentary metal oxide semiconductor), 70
Coaxial cable, **113**
COBOL, **91,** 92, 97
    visual language translator for, 98
Cocke, John, 43
Code of Ethics (DPMA), 271
Code of Professional Conduct (ACM), 271
Cog, 281
Colorado Alliance of Research Libraries (CARL), 107
Color graphics adapter (CGA), **61**
Command-based user interface, **78**–79
COMMAND.COM, 83
Commercial Internet Exchange (CIX), 129
Common Business-Oriented Language. *See* COBOL
Common Object-Oriented Language (COOL), 97
Communication, **108**

Communications. *See also* Telecommunications
   buyer's guide, 135
   media, 112–118
   processors, 120–121
   protocols, 122–125
   software, 122–125
Communications satellite, **115**–116
Compact disk-read-only memory (CD-ROM), **52**
Compact disk-recordable (CD-R) technology, 53
Compaq (and Internet), 65
Compiler, **98**–99
Complex instruction set computing (CISC), 43
Complimentary metal oxide semiconductor (CMOS), 70
Computer, **4**. *See also* Computer systems
   benefits of, 22–23
   crime, 247–257
   general-purpose, 36–39
   literacy, **24**–26
   mainframe, 38, 45
   mistakes, 242–247
   personal (PC), **36**–38, 306–322
   super-, **38**–39, 45
   types of, 45
   waste, **242**–243, 245–247
Computer Abuse Amendments Act of 1994, 261
Computer-aided software engineering (CASE), 234
Computer-assisted design (CAD), **295**
Computer-assisted instruction (CAI), **279**–280
Computer-assisted manufacturing (CAM), **296**
Computer-based information system (CBIS), **15**
   in business, 16–21
   elements of, 15–16
   evolution of, 16, 17
Computer crime, 247–257
   data alteration and destruction, 249–253
   illegal access and use, 249
   international, 257
   preventing, 255–257
   theft, 254
   viruses, 250–253
Computer Emergency Response Team (CERT), 256
Computer Fraud and Abuse Act, 256
Computer literacy, **24**–26
Computer Matching and Privacy Act of 1988, 261
Computer mistakes, **242**–247
Computer output microfilm (COM) devices, **62**
Computer Professionals for Social Responsibility (CPSR), 271
Computer systems, **34**–35
   centralized, 39
   decentralized, 39

distributed, 39
embedded, 35
general-purpose, 36–39
mainframe, 38
mini-, 38
personal, 36–38, 306–322
platforms, 99
super-, 38–39
upgrading, 321–322
workstations, 38
Computer-telephone integration (CTI), 287
Computer waste, **242**–243, 245–247
Computerworld Global 100, 298
Computerworld Premier 100, 298
CONFIG.SYS, 83
Connect time, **198**
Consumer Electronics Bus (CEBus), 283
Content bar, **161**
Contents layout, **188**
Control unit, **40**
COOL (Common Object-Oriented Language), 97
Cooperative work. *See* Work groups
Coopers & Lybrand, 25
Coprocessor, **44**
Copy, **147**
Corbis Corp., 206–207
Cost, 23
   checklist, 310
   of computers, 45
   of data storage, 48
CPU (central processing unit), **40**
CREST, 15
Crime. *See* Computer crime
Criminal hacker, **249**
Critical path, **200**
Cross-tabulation, **183**
CTI (computer-telephone integration), 287
Curle, Robin, 229
Cut, **147**
CyberCash, 202
Cybershopping, 202
   and security, 239, 250
Cyc, 283
Cycle time, 41

D

Dark Avenger virus, 253
Data, **5**–7
   alteration and destruction, 249–253
   communications system, **109**
   compression, 51, 84
   havens, **129**
   input display, 186
   projectors, **63**
   protection, **168**
   storage, 48
Database, **16**
   building, 185–186
   in DSSs, 219
   elements of, 179–180
   modifying, 186–187
   programs, 178–192
   relational, 180–183
   structure, 183–184

using, 191–192
wizard, 192
Data communications system, **109**
Data compression, **51**
   utilities, 84
Data havens, **129**
Data manipulation language (DML), **181**
Data Processing Management Association (DPMA), 271
Data projectors, **63**
Data protection, **168**
Decentralized systems, 39
Decision-making phase, **8**
Decision support systems (DSSs), **19**, 217–219
   components of, 219–221
   and executive decisions, 225–226
   and group decisions, 222–225
Default settings, **148**
Defragmentation, **50**
Delco, 305
Dell, Michael, 16, 37
Dell Computer, 37
   and Internet, 65
Demand reports, **216**
Demodulation, 118
Demo software, 100, 104–105
Design stage, **9**
Desktop computers, **36**, 45
Desktop organizers, 84
Detail formatting, **188**
Diagnostic utilities, 83
Dialog manager, 219
   and GDSSs, 222
Digital cameras, **58**
Digital signal, **110**–111
Digital video disk (DVD), 54, 284
Direct-access storage device, **47**
Disk cartridges, **50**
Diskettes, **49**
Disk-killer virus, 155
Display screens, **61**
   spreadsheet, 164
Distance learning, **288**–289
Distributed systems, 39
DML (data manipulation language), **181**
Documentation, **74**
Document-centric approach, 144, 157
Document file, **6**
Document layout, **188**
Document virus, 253
Douglas, Ken, 14
DPMA code of ethics, **271**
Draw program, **193**
DSS generator, **219**
Dynamic data exchange (DDE), **319**

E

Eaton, 305
EDI (electronic data interchange), **292**-293
Editing
   cell contents (spreadsheet), 164
   text, 146–147
Education Privacy Act, **261**
Effectiveness, 23

Efficiency, 23
EIS (executive information system), 225–226
Electromagnetic field (EMF), 265
Electronic data interchange (EDI), **292-293**
Electronic Funds Transfer Act of 1979, 261
Electronic mail (e-mail), **129**
    and privacy, 258, 259, 262–263
Electronic publications, 138
Embedded computers, **35**
Embedded IS technology, 296–298
EMM (expanded memory manager), 77
Encapsulating, **93**
Enterprise Systems Architecture/370 (ESA/370), 82
Entertainment, computerized, 283–285
Equation editor, 155–156
Ergonomics, **266**
Ertl Co., 218
ESS (executive support system), **225–226**
Ethics, 267–272
    and codes of conduct, 271–273
    and Internet, 250
    and networking, 133, 134
Evolutionary Technologies International, 229
Exception reports, **216**
Executive information system (EIS), 225–226
Executive support system (ESS), **225–226**
Expanded memory manager (EMM), 77
Expansion boards, **46**
Expansion slots, **46**
Expert systems, **20–21**
    and artificial intelligence, 227–228
Extended graphics array (XGA), 61
External documentation, **318**
Extract Tool Suite, 229

F

Facsimile (fax) machine, **119**
Fairbanks, Frank, 30
Fair Credit Reporting Act of 1970, 261
Fair information use, 263–264
Fax board, **119**
Fax/modem, 119, **120**
    buyer's guide, 135
Federal Express (FedEx), 296
    and streamlining, 15
Feedback, **12**
Ference, John, 305
Fiber-optic cable, **113, 114**
Field, **179**
Fifth-generation languages, **93**
File, **6, 180**
File management
    in spreadsheets, 163
    utilities, 84
    in word processing, 149–150
File server system, **125**
File Transfer Protocol (FTP), **130**
Fill by example, **166**
Fill down/fill right, **165**
Filter, **181**

Find command, **181**
First Albany Corp., 173
First-generation computers, **16**
First Virtual, 202
Flash chip, 54
Flash memory, 54
Floppy disks, 49
Fonts, **147**
Footnotes and endnotes, 155
Formatting documents, 147–148
Formulas, **162**
Fourth-generation languages (4GLs), **91**–93
Fragmentation, **50, 51**
Frank, Malcolm, 14
Franke, David, 95
Frankston, Bob, 161
Freedom of Information Act of 1970, 261
Freeware, **89**
Fro-Do virus, 155
Front-end processor, **120**–121
FTP (File Transfer Protocol), **130**
Fukuda, Bryan, 173
Full justification, **148**
Functions, **162,** 163
Fuzzy logic, **231**

G

Gateway, **127**
GDSS (group decision support system), **222**–225
General Motors, 63, 305
General-purpose computers, 36–39
Gerstner, Louis, 69
Gigabyte, **41**
Ginsparg, Paul, 140
Globalization
    and business environment, 299
    and networks, 128
Global positioning systems (GPSs), 115, **296,** 303
Global search, **147**
Global strategic alliance, **297**
Grammar checker, **149**
Graphical user interface (GUI), **79**
Graphics, 155
    programs, 192–196
    in spreadsheets, 166
Graphics tablet, **285**
Green Caterpillar virus, 253
Griffin, Ethel, 30
Group decision support system (GDSS), **222**–225
Group header/footer, **188**
Groupware, **89**
    and GDSSs, 224
GUI (graphical user interface), **79**

H

Hacker, **249**
Hamaker, Chuck, 140
Hammer, Katherine, 229
Handheld personal computers (HPCs), 37–38
Hard copy, 61

Hard disks, **48**
    fragmentation on, 51
Hardware, **15**
    buyer's guide, 64–66, 311–313
    computer system components, 39–40, 314
    computer types, 35–39
    input and output, 55–63
    processing, 40–46
    secondary storage, 46–55
    selection grid, 327
    upgrades, 63–64, 321
    using, 317
Harford, Douglas, 115
Harnad, Steven, 140
Headers and footers, 155
Health and medical software, 201
Health concerns, 265–267
Healthsource Inc., 218
Hertz, 41
Heuristics, **227**
High-level languages, **91**
Home computers, 280–285
Home improvement software, 204
Home Medical Advisor, 203
Home page, 132, **287**
Hoteling, 291
Hotlinks, 8
Huber, George, 9
Hummel, Fred, 15
Hypertext, **131**
Hypertext Markup Language (HTML), 131, 159

I

IBM
    Aptiva S Series, 36
    and Internet, 65
    and mainframes, 69–70
    and Maytag, 14
    and SNA, 125
    supercomputers, 38–39
Icons, **152**
Illegal access and use, 249. *See also* Computer crime
Image data, 6
Implementation stage, **9**
Index feature (word processing), 155
Inference engine, 21
Information, **6–7**
    on-line, 26, **197–199,** 286–289
Information Age, 17
Information reporting system. *See* Management information system
Information Superhighway. *See* World Wide Web (WWW)
Information system (IS), **4.** *See also* Computer-based information system; Management information system
    functions of, 11–15
    reasons for studying, 22–26
    role of database in, 189–190
Infrared transmission, **117**

Inheritance, 94
Input, **11**
    automating, 56
    hardware, 56–60
    to management information system,
        214–215
Institute of Electrical and Electronics
    Engineers (IEEE), 271
Integrated packages, **87**
Integrated Services Digital Network
    (ISDN), **121–122**
Intellectual property, **254**
Intelligence stage, **9**
Interfaces. *See* User interfaces
Internal calculations, 182–183
Internal programming
    and databases, 183
    and spreadsheets, 169
International (global) network, **128**
Internet, **7**, 129–132. *See also* World Wide
    Web (WWW)
Interpreter, **98**
Intranet, **132**–133
    corporate, **222–223**
IS. *See* Information system
ISDN (Integrated Services Digital
    Network), **121–122**
ISDN switch, **121**
ISO 9000, 295
IS Robotics, 281
Issues and trends
    in business, 289–300
    at home, 280–285
    at school, 279–280
    telecommunications, 286–293

J
JASON Project, 289
Java, **97**
Java 1.0, 96
Jerusalem virus, 253
Jobs, Steven, 210
Journals, 26
    on-line, 138
Joystick, **58**
Justification, **148**

K
Kay, Alan, 79, 97
Keyboard, **56–57**
    port, 47
Key-indicator reports, **216**
Kill file, **258**
Kilobyte, **40**
Klein, Andrew D., 200
Knapp, Ellen, 25
Knowledge base, 20–21
Krasny, Michael P., 313

L
LAN (local-area network), **125–127**
Languages. *See* Programming languages
Language translators, **98–99**
Laptop computers, **37**

Lauing, Edward, 105
Lawn and garden care, 282
Laws, privacy, 259–263
LCDs (liquid crystal displays), **61**
Learning system, **230**
Legal assistance software, 203
Leica, 303
Leisure, computerized, 283–287
Lenat, Douglas, 281
Levi Strauss & Co., 73
Liemandt, Gregory, 95
Liemandt, Joe, 95
Lighting and appliance control, 282
Lincoln Continental, 296–297
Line-of-sight signal, **114**
Line spacing, 148
Liquid crystal displays (LCDs), **61**
Local-area network (LAN), **125–127**
Logic bomb, **253**
London Stock Exchange, 15
Lotus SmartSuite 96, 153
Louisiana State University, 140
Lower CASE tools, 205
Low-level language, **90**
Lufthansa, 56

M
Machine cycle speed, 42
Machine cycle time, 41
Machine language, **90**
Macintosh, 79, 82
    and multitasking, 317
    and printing, 105
    and user interfaces, 317–318
Macros
    and databases, 183
    in spreadsheets, 165
    in word processing, **152**
Magazines, 26
    on-line, 140
Magnetic disks, **48–52**
Magnetic ink character recognition
    (MICR), **60**
Magnetic tape drives, 47–48
Magneto-optical (MO) disk, **53**
Mail merge, **154**
Mainframe computers, **38**, 45
    at IBM, 69–70
    and operating systems, 82
Main memory, 40
Malfunctions, 318–320
Management information system, 18–19,
    213–217
    Phoenix's, 29–30
Maney, Russ, 25
Manual systems, 13, 15
Mapping (spreadsheet), 166
Massively parallel processing (MPP), **44**
Mathematical elements (word
    processing), 155
Matson, Daniel, 143
Maytag, 14
MCC, 281
McConnon, Shaun, 275

McCurdy, Barry, 173
Mead, Gary, 177
Megabyte, **41**
Megahertz (MHz), **41**
Memory, 43
Memory management, **77**
Merging
    in databases, 182
    in word processing, 154
Mi Amore Pizza & Pasta, 177
Michelangelo virus, 253
MICR (magnetic ink character
    recognition), **60**
Microcode, 41
Microcomputers, 36–38. *See also* Personal
    computers (PCs)
Microprocessor chip, **40**
Microsoft Disk Operating System. *See*
    MS-DOS
Microsoft Windows. *See* Windows
    (operating system)
Microsoft Works, 87, 88
Microwave transmission, 113–116
Middleware, **292**
Miller, Jeannie, 30
Minicomputers, **38**, 45
MIPS, **41**
Mobile Assistant, 33
Model base (DSS), 220–221
Modem, **118**–119
    buyer's guide, 135
Modulation, 118
Monitoring stage, **10**
Monitor port, 47
Monitors, **61**
Monkey virus, 253
Motherboard, **46**
Mouse, **57**
    problems with, 321
MPP (massively parallel processing), **44**
MS-DOS (Microsoft Disk Operating
    System), **80**
    and printing, 105
Multicolumn text, 148
Multifunction devices, 63
Multimedia computers, 36
Multiple document editing, 147
Multiple Virtual Storage/Enterprise
    Systems Architecture
    (MVS/ESA), 82
Multiplexer, **120**
Multiprocessing, **44**
Multitasking, **78**, 317
Multithreading, **78**
Musical Instrument Digital Interface
    (MIDI), 6
Myers, Allen, 115

N
National Information Infrastructure
    (NII), 293
National Research and Education Network
    (NREN), 293

Natural languages, **93**
    and artificial intelligence, 229–230
Network, 60, **123**
    configurations, 125–134
    and networking, 133-134, 291–292
    neural, 230–231
    operating system, 123–**124**
    ports, 47
Network interface card, **127**
Network operating system (NOS), 123–**124**
Neural network, 230–**231**
News and features (on-line), 198
Newton Message Pad, 37, 38, 61
NII (National Information
    Infrastructure), 295
Nodes, **125**
Noise, **112**
Notebook computers, 37
NREN (National Research and Education
    Network), 293
Numerically controlled (NC) machines, **296**

O

Object-oriented programming (OOP)
    languages, **93**
Object-oriented systems development, **236**
OCR (optical character recognition)
    readers, **59**
Off-the-shelf software, 85, 86–87
Olim, Jason, 131
Olim, Matthew, 131
Olivetti Research Laboratory, 290–291
OLTP (on-line transaction processing), **211**
OMR (optical mark recognition) readers, **59**
On-line information services, 26, **197**–199
    buying, 135, 314
    impact of, 286–289
On-line shopping, 202
    and security, 239, 250
On-line transaction processing, 211–213
OnStar, 303
On-the-fly correction, **153**
OOP (object-oriented programming)
    languages, **93**
Open database connectivity (ODBC), 182
Open Systems Interconnection (OSI),
    124–125
Operating system, **75**–79
    choosing, 310
    initiating, 82–83
    Macintosh, 79, 82, 317–318
    mainframe, 82
    MS-DOS, 80
    OS/2, 80
    PC-DOS, 80
    Unix, 83
    Windows, 79, 80, 81, 95, 317–318
Operating System 2 (OS/2), **80**
Operation Sundevil, 256
Optical character recognition (OCR)
    readers, **59**
Optical data readers, 60
Optical disk, **52**–54

Optical mark recognition (OMR) readers, **59**
OSI (Open Systems Interconnection),
    124–125
OS/2 (Operating System 2), **80**
OTR Express, 86
Outlining, **155**
Output, **12**
    from databases, 187–189
    hardware, 60–63
    from management information
        system, 215–217

P

Page layout (database), 188
Paging, 77
Paint program, **193**
PalmVue computers, 38
Paper size and margins, 148
Parallel port, **46,** 47
Parallel processing, **44,** 45
Paste, **147**
PC-DOS (Personal Computer Disk
    Operating System), **80**
PCMCIA cards, 54
PCs. *See* Personal computers
Peer-to-peer network, **294**
Pensak, David, 275
Peripheral components, 314–315
Personal Computer Disk Operating System
    (PC-DOS), **80**
Personal Computer Memory Card
    International Association
    (PCMCIA), 64
Personal computers (PCs), **36**–38
    buying, 306–315
    and malfunctions, 318–320
    using, 315–318
Personal productivity software, **201**–204
Personal productivity tools, 87
Peterson, Chris, 259
Phoenix (city), 29–30
Physical cables, 112–114
Ping-Pong virus, 253
Pixels, **61**
PKZIP, 52
Plotters, **62**
Plug and play, **64**
Poe, Buck, 218
PointCast, 198
Point-of-sale (POS) terminals, **58**–59
Polar Heart Rate Monitor, 283
Polese, Kim, 96
Polling, **121**
Ports, **46,** 47
POWERparallel supercomputer, 39
Power supply, **46**
Presentation graphics program, **194**–196
Price Waterhouse, 224
Primary sort key, **182**
Primary storage, **40**
Printer drivers, 150
Printers, **61**–62

Printing
    database results, 189
    documents, 150
Privacy, 257–264, 269
    and networking, 133, 134
Privacy Act of 1974, **259**–260
Problem-solving process, **7**–10
    and computer malfunctions, 318–320
Procedures, **16**
Processing, **12**
    hardware, 40–46
Processors, 120–121
Process reengineering, 294
Professional associations, 271
Program file, **6**
Programming, internal
    and databases, 183
    and spreadsheets, 169
Programming languages, 89–**90**
    and artificial intelligence, 229–230
    classes of, 97
    generations of, 90–93
    and language translators, 98–99
    natural, **93**
    object-oriented, **93**–97
    visual, **97**
Project crashing, **200**
Project management program, **199**–200
Prompts, **318**
Property rights, 269–270
Proprietary software, **85**–86
Protocols, **124**–125
    File Transfer (FTP), **130**
    Secure Encryption Payment
        (SEPP), 239
    Transmission Control/Internet
        (TCP/IP), 125, 224
Prototyping, **235**–236

Q

Quality (and standards), 294–295
Query (database), **181**–182
Query languages, **93**, 182
QWERTY layout, 145

R

RAID (redundant array of inexpensive
    disks), 50
Random access memory (RAM), **40,** 43, 45
    choosing, 311
    upgrading, 321
Range, **162**
Raptor Systems, 275
Read-only memory (ROM), **43**
Read/write heads, **49**
Real-time processing, 211–213
Real-time processing languages, **97**
Record, **180**
Reduced instruction set computing
    (RISC), 43
Redundant array of inexpensive disks
    (RAID), 50
Reed Elsevier, 140
Reference software, **201**

Regional network, **128**
Registers, 40
Register storage, 39
Relational database, **180**–183
Reliability, 23
    and networking, 133
Repetitive stress injury (RSI), **265**
Report footer, **188**
Report header, **188**
Reports, 213, 216
Response time (networking), 134
Reusable code, **95**–96
Right to Financial Privacy Act of 1978, 261
RISC (reduced instruction set
        computing), 43
Ritchie, Dennis, 91
Robotics, **228**
ROM (read-only memory), **43**
Rowan, Doug, 206
Rule base, 21

S
Satellite transmissions, 113–116
Saving, databases, 189
Scanning hardware, 59–60
Scenarios, **168**
Scheduled reports, **216**
Schools, computers in, 279–280
Screens, 61
Screen saver, **315**
SCSI (Small Computer System Interface), 64
SDLC (systems development life cycle),
        232–235
Search and replace, **147**
Search tools, **132**
Secondary sort key, **182**
Secondary storage, 46–55, **47**
Second-generation computers, **16**
Second-generation languages, 91
Secure Electronic Transactions (SET),
        202, 239
Secure Encryption Payment Protocol
        (SEPP), 239
Secure Transaction Technology (STT), 239
Security (home), computerized, 282
Security (networking), 134
Selling Chain, 95
Sequential-access storage device, **47**
Serial port, **46**, 47
Services (on-line). *See* On-line information
        services; Shopping (on-line)
Shareware, **89**
Shopping (on-line), 199, 202, 314
    and security, 239, 250
Shoup, Rich, 218
Siegel, Nick, 281
Signal frequency, **112**
Simon, Herbert, 9
Single in-line memory module (SIMM), 46
Slide show, **195**
Small Computer System Interface (SCSI), 64
Smalltalk, **97**
Smart cars, 303
Smartmaster, **195**

SmartSuite 96, 153
SNA (Systems Network Architecture), 125
Snap on grid, **193**
Software, **15**
    applications, 84–89
    buyer's guide, 99–101, 311–312
    communications, 122–125
    off-the-shelf, 86–87
    overview, 74–75
    programming languages, 89–99
    selection grid, 326
    systems, 75–84
    and TestDrive, 104–105
    theft, 254–256
    upgrading, 323–324
    using, 317–320
    virus scanning, 251–252
    for work groups, 293
    on World Wide Web, 100
Software Arts, 161
Software Garden, 161
Software piracy, **254**
Software Selection Grid, 324
Software suite, **87**
Sorted elements, 155
Sorting (database), 182
Source data automation, **56**
Speaker note, **195**
Special effects, **151**
Special-purpose output devices, 62–63
Speed, 22
    and competitiveness, 295–296
    CPU, 41–43, 45
    of input/output hardware, 55–56
Spelling checker, **148**–149
Sports, computerized, 283–285
Spreadsheets, **160**–163, 173–174
    changing, 164
    dynamic use of, 169–170
    and graphics, 157
    linking, 167–168
    supplemental features of, 165–169
    and word processors, 157
Spring Street Brewing, 200
SQL (Structured Query Language), **93**, 182
Standards, **63**
    ISO 9000, 295
    and quality, 294–295
Statistical functions, 182–183
Stein, Lynn Andre, 281
Steinkrauss, Robert A., 275
Storage capacity, 23
Structured Query Language (SQL), **93**, 182
STT (Secure Transaction Technology), 239
Style sheet, **152**
Subnotebook computers, 37
Summary reports, **213**
Sun Microsystems, 96
Supercomputers, **38**–39, 45
Super video graphics array (SVGA), **61**
Syntax, **99**
System board, **46**

Systems. *See* Business information systems;
        Computer systems; Management
        information system; Operating
        system
Systems analysis, **234**
Systems design, **234**
Systems development, 231–236
Systems development life cycle (SDLC),
        232–235
System 7.5, **82**
Systems implementation, **234**
Systems investigation, **233**–234
Systems maintenance and review, **235**
Systems Network Architecture (SNA), 125
Systems software, 6, **74**, 75–84
System unit, **44**, 46
System virus, **253**

T
Tab and indent, 148
Table lookup, **167**
Table of contents (word processing), 155
Tables
    database, 186
    in word processing, 156
Tax Reform Act of 1976, 261
TCP/IP (Transmission Control
        Protocol/Internet Protocol), 125
    and intranets, 224
Technical support, 320
Telecommunications, **16**
    in business, 289–293
    devices, 118–122
    at home and school, 287–289
    impact of, 286–293
    signals, 110–111
    system, 108–112
Telecommunications Act of 1996, 268, **286**
Telecommunications system, **108**–112
Telecommuting, **289**
Teleconferencing, **290**–291
Telephone Consumer Protection Act of
        1991, 261
Telephone port, 47
Telework centers, 289
Template, **165**
Terminals, **58**–59
Terrestrial microwave, 114–116
TestDrive, 104–105
Texas Instruments, 303
Theft, 254–256. *See also* Computer crime
Thesaurus, **149**
Third-generation computers, **16**
Third-generation languages, 91
Times Direct Marketing, 259
Time-sharing, **78**
Timmerman, Tina, 229
Title bar, **161**
Toolbars, 152
Touch-sensitive screen, **61**
Toyota, 298
Trackball, **58**
Transaction processing systems (TPSs), **18**,
        210–213

Transmission capacity, 112
Transmission Control Protocol/Internet
    Protocol. *See* TCP/IP
Travel assistance
    on-line, 198
    software, 200
Trigger points, **214**
Trilogy Development Group, 95
Trojan horse, **253**
TRW, 305
Tufts Health Plan, 218
Tutorial, **279**
Twisted-pair wire cable, **112**–113

U

Uniform Resource Locators (URLs), 8, 130
United Parcel Service (UPS), 129, 298–300
Unix, **82**
Upgrades
    computer system, 321–322
    hardware, 63–64
Upper-CASE tools, 235
UPSnet, 129
User guide, 315–320
User interfaces, 21, 317–318
    command-based, **78**–79
    graphical (GUI), **79**
    Musical Instrument Digital (MIDI), 6
    Small Computer System (SCSI), 64
U.S. Postal Service, 13
Utility programs, **83**–84

V

Value chain, **297**
Vector graphics, **193**
Version, **168**
Videoconferencing, **290**
Video data, 6
Video Privacy Act of 1988, 261
Virtual memory, **77**

Virtual office, **289**
Virtual reality, **63**
Viruses, **250**–253
Virus scanning software, **251**–252
VisiCalc, 161
Vision system, **228**–229
Visual programming languages, **97**
Voice output devices, **62**
Voice recognition devices, **58**

W

Web. *See* World Wide Web (WWW)
Web browsers, **132**
What-if analysis, **169**
Wide-area network (WAN), **128**
Windows (operating system), **80,** 81, 95
    and document-centric approach, 157
    and multitasking, 317
    and printing, 150
    and upgrading, 64
    and user interfaces, 79, 317–318
Wingfield, Teresa, 218
Wizards, **152,** 195
Wordlength, 41–43, **42**
Word processing, **145**
    basic features of, 145–150
    and graphics, 157
    and integrating with other
        applications, 156–157
    and productivity, 157–160
    and spreadsheets, 157
    supporting features, 150–156
Word wrap, **145**
Work environment, 264–267
Work force composition, 264–265
Work groups, **154**
    software for, 291
    and spreadsheets, 168
    word processing, 154

Workstations, 38, 45
Work stressors, 266
World Wide Web (WWW), **130**–132
    browsers, 132
    and computer crime, 250
    and corporate access, 65
    and customer service, 197
    and ethics, 250
    history of, 8
    and hypertext markup language
        (HTML), 159
    impact of, 286–288
    interest in, 287
    and security, 250
    shopping on, 65, 199, 202
    and software access, 100
    and systems development, 232
Worm, **250**–251
Write-once, read-many (WORM) disks,
    52–53
Write-protected file, **315**
WWW. *See* World Wide Web

X

XGA (extended graphics array), 61
Xybernaut Corporation, 33

Y

Yankee Doodle virus, 253

Z

Zoom, **147**

WEB INDEX

Cars @ Cost
  www.webcom.com/~carscost/
CDnow
  www.cdnow.com
CheckFree Wallet
  http://www.checkfree.com
City of Phoenix
  www.ci.phoenix.az.us
Corbis Corp.
  http://www.corbis.com
CyberCash
  http://www.cybercash.com
Cybertown mall
  http://www.cybertown.com
Delco
  http://www.delco.com
E-trade
  http://www.etrade.com
Evolutionary Technologies International
  http://www.evtech.com
FedEx
  http://www.fedex.com
First Albany Corp.
  http://www.fac.com/
First Virtual
  http://www.firstvirtual.com
Florida State University
  http://www.fsu.edu
General Motors
  http://www.gm.com
IBM
  www.ibm.com
IS Robotics
  http://www.isr.com
Java 1.0
  http://java.sun.com
  http://www.surinam.net/java/jars

Liaison International
  http://www.liaisonintl.com
Lotus
  http://www.lotus.com/
MasterCard
  http://www.mastercard.com
Maytag
  http://www.maytag.com
  http://www.maytagcorp.com
MCC
  http://www.mcc.com
Occidental Petroleum Corp.
  http://www.oxychem.com/
PhotoDisc
  http://www.photodisc.com
Picture Network International
  http://www.publishersdepot.com
Spring Street Brewing
  http://www.witbeer.com
Sprint
  http://www.sprint.com
Telecom Information Resources
  http://www.spp.umich.edu/telecominfo.html
Texas Instruments
  http://www.ti.com
Times Direct Marketing
  http://www.tdmi.com
Toshiba
  http://www.toshiba.com
UNAVCO
  http://www.unavco.ucar.edu
United Parcel Service
  http://www.ups.com
Visa
  http://www.visa.com
White House
  http://www.whitehouse.gov